Labor Relations in Argentina, Brazil, and Chile

ROBERT J. ALEXANDER

Department of Economics
Rutgers University

McGRAW-HILL BOOK COMPANY, INC.   1962

New York   San Francisco   Toronto   London

LABOR RELATIONS IN ARGENTINA, BRAZIL, AND CHILE

DEDICATED TO
SERAFINO ROMUALDI

Foreword

The industrialization process everywhere drastically transforms the pre-existing or traditional society. It not merely introduces new and more efficient methods of production and modern technology, but it creates new relationships: those between managers and industrial workers at the immediate work place and those among management groups, labor organizations, and government in the national community.

The transition toward the industrial society takes place in countries with different natural resources, diverse cultural and political traditions, starting from different levels of economic development, under the leadership of different elites with distinctive strategies and ideologies, and dedicated to proceed toward industrialism at different speeds. This generation is in the midst of keen competition throughout the world among different programs for industrialization. Each newly industrializing country is confronted with a growing assortment of models and experiences to consider in shaping its own destiny.

The comparative method used by Professor Alexander has great advantages in portraying the industrialization process and labor-management-government relations. It illuminates not only the central tendencies in industrialization but also those divergencies which are related to the distinctive features of a country. The choice of Argentina, Brazil, and Chile is a singularly happy one since these countries have a great many features and traditions in common and yet the diversity of their experience is a bar to easy generalization and abstraction. Moreover, these three countries are of pivotal concern in the renewed public interest in the United States in Latin American affairs.

This volume provides a useful account of the development of industrial relations in each of the ABC countries. There is well portrayed the common problem of changing the paternalistic attitudes and relations between agricultural workers and large land holders when workers have moved to an urban and industrial work place; there is the common task of recruiting and training industrial managers and the gradual change in traditional family management; the protest of new industrial workers expressed in the many forms of absenteeism, turnover, job action, and group action are common features of industrializing work forces everywhere; the struggle among employers and political and military leaders to capture or control the organization of workers is dramatically outlined in the experience of Brazil under Vargas and Argentina during Perón; the influence of economic limitations, including the international balance of payments, on an industrial relations system is well illustrated in these countries. But these general themes should not be allowed to obscure the rich detail and variations among the countries, which are carefully portrayed.

This type of study is vital to discussions of private and public policy making in the United States concerned with our relations to Latin America. Far too frequently our labor unions and businesses, and our governmental representatives too, have tried to export "free trade unions" and "private enterprise." These large labels have not sold very well, nor are they likely to be more acceptable in the future. However, there are some features of our labor organizations—such as concern with plant level grievances, the education of labor leaders, and welfare activities—which may be of genuine interest in modified form in a Latin American context. Similarly, there are some aspects of our organization of business—such as the emergence of professional managers, the importance of management education in university programs, the personnel staff, and the limits to bureaucratic government and the significance of the market—which may be adapted to Latin American experience and problems. Professor Alexander's volume should help us to understand that the attempt to transplant wholesale our cherished institutions is futile, but that some of our labor-management-government arrangements may be assimilated and adapted in other countries embarking on the road to industrialism.

Professor Alexander brings to this volume fifteen years of interest and experience in Latin American labor-management-government relations. He has traveled widely and written extensively in this area. This volume reflects not only extensive study of documents and the literature, but a period of intensive interviews for this volume in each of the three countries with local and foreign managers, labor leaders, government representatives, and those in political and academic circles.

This study is part of the Inter-University Study of Labor Problems in Economic Development.[1]

AUGUST, 1961

JOHN T. DUNLOP

---

[1] For a summary, see Clark Kerr, John T. Dunlop, Frederick Harbison, and Charles A. Meyers, *Industrialism and Industrial Man, The Problems of Labor and Management in Economic Growth* (Cambridge, 1960).

Contents

Tables

Author's Preface

For more than a dozen years I have spent much of my time traveling around Latin America, collecting material on, among other things, labor relations in that part of the world. In 1946 and 1947 I spent six months in Chile, working on my Ph.D. thesis on the subject of labor–management relations there. At that time I visited virtually every important industrial and mining enterprise in the republic and talked to most of the leading trade unionists and many government officials. In the present volume I have borrowed heavily from the materials which I collected at that time and which were used in the thesis presented at Columbia University in 1950.

When, in 1955, Dr. John Dunlop of Harvard University suggested the possibility of making a survey of labor relations in the ABC countries of South America, as part of the broader Inter-University Project on Labor Relations in Economic Development, I was very pleased indeed. My wife and I spent seven and a half months in Latin America, principally in the three countries discussed in the present book. Most of the material on Brazil and Argentina was collected during that trip. In Chile I confined myself largely to bringing up to date the information which I had gathered almost a decade before, and visiting certain enterprises and institutions which had not been in existence when I was first there.

The three countries that are discussed in this book are among the most important and interesting nations of Latin America. Throughout most of the nineteenth century they were the leading powers of the South American continent, economically the richest and politically and militarily the most powerful. During the present century they have continued to be leaders. Brazil has grown into the most populous and rapidly industrializing country of the region; Argentina has the highest general standard of living in Latin America; Chile has been a pioneer in social legislation and education.

Labor relations in these three countries have developed differently in each case, as will become clear in the pages which follow. None of them is "typical" of labor-management systems either in underdeveloped countries or in the more limited Latin American area. Perhaps there is no typical pattern for conducting labor relations in such countries. However, I hope that this study will provide some insights into the role which employer-employee relations play in the economic development of underdeveloped countries.

Since the subject of this book is virtually virgin territory for the researcher, most of the material for the present volume has, of necessity, come from the interviews and observations of the author during various visits to Argentina, Brazil, and Chile. Latin American scholars, when they have written about our subject, have tended to be principally concerned with its legal aspects and not with the problems of day-to-day relations between workers and employers.

Since labor relations are much more regulated by law in Latin America than in the United States, the author has perforce relied heavily, in the cases of Brazil and Chile, on the labor codes of those countries—respectively, the Consolidacão das Leis do Trabalho and the Codigo del Trabajo. However, in Argentina no such codified body of labor law exists, and the author has used in place of it Jeronimo Remorino's *La Nueva Legislación Social Argentina,* published in 1953 by the Argentine Ministry of Foreign Affairs.

To supplement the Labor Code in Chile, as well as for certain general ideas concerning labor and social law in Latin America, the author has borrowed heavily from two books by noted Chilean scholars of labor law. These are Alfredo Gaete Berrios' *Derecho del Trabajo* (Santiago, 1943) and Francisco Walker Linares' *Panorama del Derecho Social Chileno* (Santiago, 1947). In the second connection, Alfredo Palacios' *El Nuevo Derecho* (Buenos Aires, 1935) is the classic.

Of course, for the general framework and orientation of the present volume, the author has had frequent reference to two articles which appeared in scholarly journals in 1955. These are "The Labour Problem in Economic Development" by Clark Kerr, John T. Dunlop, Frederick Harbison, and Charles Myers, which appeared in the *International Labour Review* in March 1955; and "The Structuring of the Labor Force in Industrial Society: New Dimensions and New Questions," by Clark Kerr and Abraham Siegel in the *Industrial and Labor Relations Review* of January 1955. Although the author obviously has certain quarrels with the point of view expressed in these articles, they are invaluable for any attempt to place labor relations in Argentina, Brazil, and Chile in the broader world framework.

Numerous other books, pamphlets, and periodicals have been referred to in the present volume. A full compilation of these can be culled from the Notes.

Many debts of gratitude are owed for help in making this book possible. First of all, I owe a great deal to Dr. John T. Dunlop and his associates on the Inter-University Project—Drs. Clark Kerr, Frederick Harbison, and Charles Myers—for making possible my trip to Latin America in 1956. Dr. Dunlop has been particularly helpful in offering criticisms of the manuscript. I also want to thank Mrs. Joan Stifler for typing the book at several stages.

Of course, I am deeply indebted to all those in Latin America who have submitted themselves to my constant interrogation, and have frequently been kind enough to provide me with valuable printed material as well. They include:

I. In Brazil

Kurt Renner, Director of A. J. Renner Cia. Ltda.; Engenheiro Cotrim, Director of Labor Relations, Volta Redonda; Custodio Sobral Martins de Almeida, Administrative Director, Fabrica Nacional de Motores; Luiz Carlos Andrade, Economist of Banco Nacional de Desenvolvimento Economico; Sr. Miranda, Office Manager of Cia. Industrial de Brasil; Adolpho Araripe, Director of Administrative Division, Cia. do Valle do Rio Doce; William Embry, lawyer of Interamericana Investment Co.; Derek C. Fey, Assistant Manager of Cia. Interamericana de Financiamentos e Investimentos S.A.; Leonard Hall, Professor of Economics at Michigan State University, Adviser to School of Business, São Paulo University; Luciano de Carmo, economist of Federacão das Industrias de Minas Gerais; Robert F. E. Suchanek, Director of Mechanical Tests of Instituto de Seleccão e Orientacão of Fundacão Getulio Vargas; João Caetano Faria, President, Sindicato dos Empregados no Commercio de Santos; João Aristoteles de Andrade, President, Sindicato dos Empregados no Commercio de Santos; José Gonçalves, President, Sindicato dos Operarios nos Serviços Portuarios de Santos; Severino Jolzo Javier, ex-President, Sindicato dos Trabalhadores de Alfaiates e Costureiras; Arlindo Martins de Oliveira, Grievance Secretary, Federacão dos Trabalhadores na Industria de Fiacão e Tecelagem do Estado de São Paulo; Olavo Previatti, President, Federacão dos Trabalhadores nas Industrias do Papel, Papelão e Cortiças do Estado de São Paulo; Diocletiano de Hollanda Cavalcanti, President, Confederacão Nacional dos Trabalhadores na Industria; José Nuñez Bras, Assistant to

Director of Productivity of Federacão da Industria do Distrito Federal; Ernesto Street, member of Economics Staff of Confederacão Nacional da Industria; Fernando Sequeira, Secretary of Federacão da Industria do Distrito Federal; Roberto Danneman, Director of Division of Regional Organizations, Serviço Nacional de Aprendizagem Commercial; José Carlos Graça Wagner, lawyer of Sindicato da Industria de Perfumes e Artigos de Toucador do Estado de São Paulo; Agilberto de Lacerda Figueiredo Santos, lawyer for Sindicato da Industria de Condutores Electricos e Treflacão of São Paulo; Silvio Guimarães, Assistant to Executive Secretary of Federacão de Industria de Baia; Benjamin Monteiro, Sub-Chief of Departamento Sindical, Federacão da Industria de São Paulo; Eugenio Lobato, Secretary of Federacão da Industria do Estado do Rio Grande do Sul; Paulo E. de Souza Queiros, official of Federacão do Commercio do Estado de São Paulo; Expedito Fernandez, Vice-President, Federacão da Industria do Estado de Pará; José Mosci Magalhães Brandão, Assistant Secretary of Federacão do Commercio do Estado de Para; Celio Dinaro L. Lacerda, head of Registration Section of Serviço de Organizacão e Registro Sindical of Ministry of Labor; Antonio Luiz Lins de Barros, Regional Labor Delegate; Vinicius Ferraz Torres, Acting Regional Labor Delegate; Henry Madeira de Luz, head of Syndicalization Section of Regional Delegation of Labor; Ary Campista, Vice-President of Confederacão Nacional dos Trabalhadores na Industria, and member of Comisão do Imposto Sindical; Paulo Marzagão, Regional Labor Delegate of São Paulo; Capt. Francisco Vincente Vulcão Vianna, Capitão dos Portos of the State of São Paulo; Nelson Ribeiro, member of Secretariat of Departamento Nacional do Trabalho; Antonio Barreto, Director of Control of Regional Labor Delegation of São Paulo; Julio Amorin Botelho, Regional Labor Delegate; Raimundo Moura, President of Eighth Regional Labor Court; Manoel Passos Tavares, Statistician of Tribunal Superior do Trabalho; Delfim Moreira Junior, President of Tribunal Superior do Trabalho; Pedro de Albuquerque Montenegro, Judge of Regional Labor Tribunal of Recife; Celso de Magalhães, Chief of Analysis Section, Ministry of Labor; Helio Palhãeres, Secretary to President of Instituto de Aposentaduria e Pensões de Transportes e Carga; Octavio de Sousa Leão, President of Conselho Superior de Previdencia Social; Armando Assis, Sub-Director of Staff of the President of Instituto de Aposentaduria e Pensões dos Industriarios; Sr. Suares Emaral, Personnel Director of Instituto de Aposentaduria e Pensões dos Commerciarios; José Cerqueira Rocha, Director of Public Relations, Instituto de Aposentaduria e Pensões dos Servidores do Estado; Paulo Cabral de Mello, Secretary, Sindicato da Industria de Açucar de Pernam-

Alliance for Progress, could emulate this example (of the Communist Party) by setting up their own school, based, say, in Mexico, which has the longest and most successful example of revolution in Latin America, and training men in skills needed to overthrow undesirable régimes . . . the United States must be prepared to foment physical upheaval in order to instal governments with reformist lines. These suggestions, it must be repeated, are made only in a sense of desperation and because all other measures are failing in Latin America' (pp. 418–419). And so they are. While Messrs. Gordon, Radler and Clark were writing, revising and printing their books, seven Latin American governments were overthrown by right-wing military revolts. On the other hand, since the Cuban revolution there has not been a single successful left-wing uprising in the whole continent.

Mr. Radler, who has lived in Latin America since 1958, sincerely and frequently deplores the arrogance with which United States citizens comport themselves in Latin America. Yet he can also write with patronising ease that 'perhaps our southern neighbors need not be on our side, but we certainly cannot *tolerate* having them on the other side' (p. 5, my italics). However, 150 pages later, he endorses with enthusiasm the view that the best interest of the United States 'lies with the growth of authentic states capable of looking after their own affairs . . . such states need not be allied to us, or even be especially friendly . . .' (p. 155).

However, it is dealing with the powder-keg at his feet that Mr. Radler shows most strikingly his interesting blindness. He selects Honduras and Guatemala as two countries where Communism is particularly dangerous and powerful and quotes ex-President Villeda, of Honduras, as saying, 'I confess that we are incapable of overcoming the Castro infiltration into Honduras by ourselves. The democratic countries should abandon their passive attitudes' (p. 94). They did, but not in the way President Villeda had in mind. In Honduras and Guatemala military uprisings toppled the constitutional governments. In Honduras the victim was precisely Sr. Villeda who was apparently so busy protecting the country from the advancing Communist hordes that he did not hear the sabres rattling behind him.

Mr. Radler and Sr. Villeda—now in exile—were not alone in their blindness to the right-wing military menace. Mr. Lincoln Gordon, who is United States Ambassador in Brazil, has published a collection of his speeches delivered in that country to explain and defend the Alliance for Progress. One-tenth of the book is devoted to the Communists but not a word is said about the military danger. This is odd considering that only a few months after Mr. Gordon delivered his speeches the Alliance for Progress is being defeated, not by the wily Reds but by a handful of right-wing generals.

Mr. Gerald Clark uses learning, understanding and an impressive journalistic technique as tools to try to discover the direction of events in Latin America. His conclusion is dramatically contained in the title of his fascinating book. Unfortunately, although this is a splendid piece of reporting, most of the constructive suggestions which Mr. Clark advances are too naïve to be taken seriously. The book also shares with the other two works the interesting characteristic of being so obsessed with the possibility of an extreme left-wing revolution that it overlooks the peril already visible on the extreme right.

CLAUDIO VELIZ.

X   **Labor Relations in Argentina, Brazil, and Chile.** By Robert J. Alexander.
       Foreword by John T. Dunlop. *New York, San Francisco, Toronto,
       London: McGraw-Hill. 1962. 411 pp. Map endpapers. Tables. Index.
       69s. 6d.*

Unionism in Latin America. By Miles E. Galvin. *Ithaca, New York: State
       School of Industrial and Labor Relations at Cornell University. 1962.
       58 pp. Table. Bibliog. (Bulletin 45.) 50 cents.*

The Rise of the Latin American Labor Movement. By Moisés Troncoso and
       Ben G. Burnett. *New Haven, Conn.: College and University Press.
       1960. 179 pp. Bibliog. Index. $1.75.*

PROFESSOR ALEXANDER, who has studied labour questions in Latin America
for many years, observes in the preface to his book, *Labor Relations in
Argentina, Brazil, and Chile,* that the subject is virtually virgin territory for
the researcher, and that most of the material for the present volume ' has,
of necessity, come from interviews and observations of the author '. The
impressive list of representatives of labour, management and governments
who submitted to his questioning testifies to his industry in this respect.

Each country is dealt with separately in a series of chapters that cover
the whole field of labour-management relations, the development of trade
unionism, past and present government policy, the procedure for settling
wage claims and disputes, social security, employers' organisations and
related matters such as recruitment and training. These chapters, lucid and
comprehensive, form a major contribution to the scanty literature on the
subject in English. The efforts of political leaders, especially in Argentina
and Brazil, to mould labour movements for their own purposes are clearly
analysed, and developments in labour relations in recent decades are related
to the broad trend of political events. Occasionally the reader may feel
that a more specific reference to contemporary politics would be illuminating.
For example, the references (pp. 160 and 215) to the Argentine employers'
insistence in 1956 on linking wage increases with productivity might with
advantage have included some mention of the emphasis placed on this very
point, and on the overriding necessity of avoiding another wage-price spiral,
in the Prebisch Plan, then supposed to be the guide for government economic
policy.

The chapters that enclose the author's main material are rather less
satisfactory, the economic sections being illustrated by statistics that are in
some cases curiously out of date. Objection may also be raised to the
marginally relevant discussion, in the penultimate chapter, of inflation and
the resources for financing development. In his general conclusion the
author seeks an explanation for the wide differences in the legal structure
of labour relations, the degree of state control and the nature of contemporary labour movements between three countries that are all undergoing a painful process of social adjustment to industrialisation and
urbanisation. That the explanation lies in politics rather than economics has
already been made clear in the admirable earlier analysis of the lasting
effects of Vargas's *Estado Novo* on labour relations in Brazil and of Perón's
manipulation of the labour movement in Argentina.

To the publisher of this otherwise excellently produced book must no
doubt be attributed the absence of some of the notes for which numbered
references are given in Chapter II, and the truly hideous coloured maps with
which the endpapers are embellished. It is to be hoped that these will not
deter any sensitive reader from acquiring a book whose
central chapters are replete with information on labour
questions in three of the most important republics of
Latin America.

H. A. HOLLEY.

buco; George Latache Pimentel, Secretary of Sindicato da Industria de Fiacão e Tecelagem do Estado de Pernambuco; J. M. Moreira de Moraẽs, Secretary of Sindicato da Industria de Fiacão e Tecelagem em Geral do Estado de São Paulo; Harry Schuetz, Assistant Director of VARIG; Olavo de Silva Virgilius, Chief of Cabinet of National Director of Serviço Social da Industria; Cyro Noronha Pelucio, Assistant Director of Public Relations of Serviço Social da Industria of São Paulo; Luiz Salamão, Manager, SESI Central Warehouse; Roberto Simonsen, Chief of Food Supplies Section, Serviço Social da Industria of São Paulo; Mario Coelho, Manager, Food Post 6 of SESI; Julio Bella, Director of Public Relations, Serviço Social da Industria; Dr. Freire, Chief of Clinic 1 of SESI of São Paulo; José Serra, social worker of SESI Dental Clinic; Sra. María Braz, Chief of Schools Section of SESI of São Paulo; María de Lourdes Ribeiro, Head of SESI Center of Domestic Apprenticeship 13; Hugo Guimarães Maleiros, Chief of Social Orientation Section of SESI of São Paulo; Carlos Bettencourt, Head of Legal Department of SESI of São Paulo; Lucy Mary Gonçalvez da Cunha, Head of Social Research Section of SESI of São Paulo; E. G. Said, Head of Social Orientation Section of SESI of São Paulo; Paulo Freire, Director of SESI in Pernambuco; Mario Goulart Reis, Director of ESI in Rio Grande do Sul; Josephat Macedo, President, Federacão das Associacões Rurais do Estado de Minas; Achim Fuerstenthal, proprietor of personnel consulting company; Francisco Campos, Assistant Director of Instituto de Seleccão e Orientacão Profissional; Carmino Urcioli, Labor Relations Director of S/A Industrias Reunidas F. Matarazzo; Roque Perrone, Superintendent of Petrobras Baia refinery; Professor João Raimundo, member of Faculty of Technical School of Cia. Siderurgica Nacional; Hildebrando da Silva, Chief of Service of Cia. Brasilieira de Telephones; Luiz Xavier, Sub-Director of Training, Cia. de Carris Urbanos, Luz e Força; Paulo Novaes, Acting Director of Serviço Nacional de Apprendizagem Industrial; Jorge Alberto Furtado, Regional Director of SENAI in Rio Grande do Sul; Luiz Marcondes Nitsch, head of public relations of SENAI of São Paulo; Lauro Barreto Fontes, Director of SENAI in Baia; Herman Falcão, Director of Social and Medical Services, SENAI of Pernambuco; Francisco Montejos, Director of Industrial Education of Ministry of Education; Paulo Carvalho, teacher in Escola Tecnica Parobe of Porto Alegre; Americo Pereira Seabra, ex-President, Sindicato dos Trabalhadores na Construcão Civil of Belem; Duceu T. de Carvalho Racaio, Chief Chemist, Usina Tiuma; Geraldo Suerdieck, President, Suerdieck, S.A.; Major Joaquim Gonçalves Moreira, Assistant Superintendent of Social Services, Cia. Siderurgica Nacional; Guillermo and Fred Sauer, Directors of F. Sauer e Filhos; Fernando Graell, Assistant Personnel Manager, Esso Standard Oil Co. of Brazil; Tito L. G. Marinho, lawyer of coal miners' unions of Santa Caterina state; Pedro Chavier de Paiva, President, Sindicato dos Trabalhadores na Industria de Fiacão e Tecelagem of Recife.

II. In Argentina

Juan Estaban Carozo, Manager, Cámara de la Industria del Calzado; Juan Bautista Pena, Buenos Aires stockbroker; Alfredo Fidanza, Secretary of Sindicato Obrero de la Industria del Calzado; Raul Lamuraglia; Cavétano Perez, member of Advisory Board, CGEC; Pascual Gambino, Interventor in Unión Industrial Argentina; Enrique Prunes, Secretary of Federación Argentina de la Industria Textil; Joaquín Goitisola, Assessor Gremial of Asociación de Industrias Metalúrgicas; José Ber Gelbard, ex-President of Confederación General Economica; Adelaida Logrippo, Secretary of Federación de Comercio e Industria de Rosario; Nicolas Babini, architect; Max Bunge, Manager of Asociación de Fabricantes de Cemento Portland; Salvador Bonsangue, Secretario Gremial, Unión Industrial y Comercial de Mendoza; Juan Rondo Acosta, ex-Manager of Unión Industrial y Comercial de Mendoza; Avelino R. Strologo, Agrarian Engineer of Federación Agraria Argentina; Carlos María Gallo, Secretary to President of Instituto Nacional de Prevision Social; Luis Pincolini, Manager of Pablo Pincolini SRL wine firm; Sr. Fernandez, Secretary of Union Cañeros Independientes de Tucumán; Jesús Fernandez, Interventor in La Fraternidad; Luis V. Delfino, General Adviser on Labor Relations of Fabrica Argentina de Alpargatas; José María Paz, Manager and principal owner of Eugenio Concepción; Orlando Podesta, Secretary General of Regional Labor Delegation; Juan J. Doce, Manager, Asociación Fabricantes de Dulces, Conservas y Afines; Joaquín Geitisolo, Asesor Gremial of Asociación de Industrias Metalúrgicas; Horacio Premoli, Secretary of Regional Labor Delegation; Rafael Seguí, ex- member of Executive Committee of Confederación General Economica; Jesús María Rueda, Regional Labor Delegate, Tucumán; Dr. Manual Vincente Segura, Judge of Segunda Cámara del Trabajo; Dr. Sorassi, Chief of Division of Decrees and Regulations of Secretariat of Labor; Francisco Baeza, Personnel Manager, Grafa textile plant; Tito Caserta, Personnel Manager, SIAM di Tella; Rubén Chesa, Manager of Unión Industrial Hotalera of Córdoba; Dr. Edmondo Molles, Librarian of Instituto Nacional de Prevision Social; Sr. López Cirio, official of Dirección General de Servicios Sociales de Bancarios; Aldo Erdmann, Interventor in Seccional Capital, Unión Obrera Metalúrgica; Ricardo Rojo,

Trade Union Secretary of Unión Civica Radical Intransigente for Federal
Capital; José Hellman, President of Federación de Producción Industria y
Comercio of Cordoba; Jorge Macri, ex-Secretary General of National Employ-
ment Service of Argentine Ministry of Labor; Jose A. Villanuera, Interventor
in Unión Gastronomica de la Republica Argentina; K. S. Flood, General
Works Manager, Industria Kaiser Argentina; Morris A. Schefer, Manager,
Harrod's; Sr. Ibararne, Assistant Personnel Manager, SIAM di Tella; Juan
Rosegno, Manager of Federación Argentina del Vidrio y Afines; Osvaldo
Ruben Rosato, Industrial Engineer of Melinos Rio de la Plata; Odino de
Bernardi; Ing. Carlos Burundarena, Director General of Apprenticeship.

III. In Chile

Oscar Cuellar, Assistant Secretary of Anglo-Lautero Nitrate Co.; Santiago
Ortiz, ex-President, Sindicato Profesional de Lavadores de Oro de Andacollo;
Jorge Vial, Acting Plant Manager, Huachipato steel mill; Pierre Letelier,
Editor of *Socialismo Libro;* Lorenzo Montt, General Manager of El Salto
textile factory; Luis Marty, Manager, Vestex clothing firm; Arturo Alessandri, ex-President of Chile; Fernando Onofre, Labor Judge of Copiapó;
Dr. Moises Poblete Froncoso, Professor of Law at University of Chile;
Alejandro Parra, Tucupal Ahumada, and Gustavo de Cerda, members of
the Corte del Trabajo of Santiago; Sra. M. T. de Armstrong, Chief of
Women and Children Section of Directorate General of Labor; Luis Cárcamo, Santiago Provincial Inspector of Labor; Diogenes Quesada, Secretary
of Corporación de la Vivienda; Felix Garay, head of construction department
of Servicio Nacional de Salud; René Ramirez, Chief of Control Department
of Servicio Nacional de Seguro Social; José Antonio Infante, Manager of
Caja de Previsión de Empleados Particulares; René Santandreu, Secretary
General of the Caja de Empleados Periodistas; Humberto Soto, President of
the Federación Industrial Ferroviaria Chilena; Dr. Figueroa Castro, Head
Doctor of Hospital de Niños y Sala Cuna of Viña del Mar; Luis Duran,
Treasurer of Federación Industrial Nacional de la Construcción; Pedro H.
Arattic, Secretary General of Confederación General de Trabajadores and
leader of Federación de la Imprenta; Franklin Martinez, delegado del
personal on *El Sur;* Juan Vargas, ex-Secretary of Sindicato Industrial "María
Elena"; Samuel Vial, Chief of Social Organizations Section of General
Directorate of Labor; Eduardo Delfín, President, Confederación de Tra-
bajadores de Cobre; Juan Briones, President, Sindicato Profesional de la
Empresa Nacional de Transporte Colectivo; Oscar Orellana Ceballos, Presi-

dent, Sindicato Industrial Braden Copper Co., Sección Rancagua; Luis H. Moraga, President of Sindicato Industrial Cia. Refinería de Azucar de Viña del Mar; Eduardo Ellis, President, Sindicato Industrial S.A. Yarur; Daniel Fuenzalida Mayal, Director of Social Service, S.S. Yarur; Fernando Dohe, Assistant Financial Secretary, Confederación Marítima de Chile; Miguel Bustos Salazar, President of Sindicato de Garzones y Ayudantes; Pedro Bascour, Director, Santiago Regional Textile Workers' Federation; Oscar Videla, Assistant Manager of Sociedad de Fomento Fabril; Raul Rodriguez Marino, lawyer of Sociedad Nacional de Minería; Pablo de Tezano Pinto, Secretary of Cámara Central de Comercio de Chile; Rodolfo Loebel and José Marur, head of commercial and experimental farm departments of Sociedad Nacional de Agricultura; Arturo Aldunate Phillips, Secretary of Sociedad de Fomento Fabril; Enrique Edwards, Manager of Asociación de Industriales Metalúrgicos; Juan Truncado, President of Sindicato de Contratistas de Santiago; Alfredo Navarete, Manager of Cámara Marítima y Portuaria; Enrique Barriga, Manager, ICARE; Lachlan McKenzie, head of Servicio de Cooperacíon Técnica Industrial; Isidoro Godoy, President of Bakery Workers' Federation; Victor Fuentealba, Secretary of Unión de Estucadores de Santiago; Luis Villavicencia, President of Sindicato Industrial Cia. Chilena de Navegación Interoceanica; Bernardo Estay Morgado, President of Sindicato Industrial Cia. Sud Americana de Vapores; Ramon Vidal Montalba, Chief of Social Welfare of Chiguayante textile mill; Percy Keighly, Manager of Grace and Co. textile mills in Chile; Mr. Stewart, head of machine shop of Braden Copper Co. at Rancagua; Nicanor Venegas, President of Sindicato Industrial Fabrica Italo-Americana de Paños de Tomé; Mr. Woodhull, Business Manager of Chuquicamata copper mine; John Kane, ex-Production Manager, Welfare Chief of Potrerillos copper mine; Charles Brinckerhoff, Manager of Potrerillos mine; Arturo Pardow, Welfare Chief of Cia. Carbonifera y de Fundición Schwager; Roberto O'Ryan, Chief of Social Welfare of Cia. Carbonifera y Fundición Schwager; Alberto Weber, Technical Manager, Penco refinery of Cia. Refinería de Azucar de Viña del Mar; Francisco Bassignano, Manager Director of Fabrica Italo-Americana de Paños; Francisco Iduyer, head of Social Service Section of Cia. de Acero del Pacifico; Victor Cavada, Acting Director of Personnel of National City Bank of Santiago; Mr. Woodward, Valparaiso plant manager of Cia. Chilena de Tabacos; Osvaldo Rengifo, Social Welfare Chief of Cia. Chilena de Electricidad; Alfredo Gaete Berrios, leading labor lawyer and Professor of Law at University of Chile; Marina Cerda, Social Worker of Cia. Fabrica Nacional de Loza; Carlos Murzell, Chief of Personnel and Welfare of Cia. Chilena de Telefonos; Eduardo Comien, Sub-Administrator of Cia. Carbonifera y de Fundición Schwager; Tulio Herrera Portales, Head of Labor Relations of Cia. de Consumidores de Gas; Lambert Persson, President of Cia. Chilena de Fósforos; Sergio Valenzuela Matte, Director of Personnel of Cia. Manufacturera de Papeles y Cartones; Hernán Vergara, Administrative Director of Corporación de Petroleo de Chile; Federico Leon, head of Industrial Relations, Chilean Exploration Co.; Alejandro Hartwig, head of Employment and Selection Section of Cia. Acero del Pacifico; George Adams, Chief of Welfare, Chuquicamata; Sr. Rojas Gallardo, Inspector of Houses of El Teniente mining camp; José P. Chito, Technical Director of SIAM di Tella; Victor Kunstmann, Jr., Assistant Manager of Kunstmann flour mill and distillery; Julio Hirschman, Vice Regent of Universidad Técnica Santa María; Norberto Toledo, Head of Research Department, Universidad Técnica del Estado; Raul Gaete, Assistant Welfare Chief of Cia. Carbonifera y Industrial de Lota; René Nayam, Assistant Chief of Personnel of Cia. Sud Americana de Vapores; David Kanterovic, Technical and Legal Adviser to Comisión Provincial de Bueldos de Santiago; Fernando Lemus, President, Sindicato Industrial Obrero de Minas, Potrerillos; Juan de Rosa, Executive Vice-President of Caja de Accidentes del Trabajo; Julio Figueroa, head of Safety Section of Caja de Accidentes del Trabajo; Sr. Frick, Chief of Technical Department, Caja de Accidentes del Trabajo.

Finally, I owe a great deal to my wife, Joan Alexander, who accompanied me on the trip in 1956, and was a very acute observer of things we saw and people with whom we talked. She has contributed a great deal of insight into the subjects discussed here, as well as valuable criticism of parts of the manuscript, and has shown enduring patience with my preoccupation in pushing the book to completion.

RUTGERS UNIVERSITY R. J. A.
NEW BRUNSWICK, N.J.
SEPTEMBER, 1961

CHAPTER I

Industrialization and Its Impact

The ABC countries of South America are in the grip of an economic, social, and political revolution. The impact of modern industrialism has destroyed the traditional societies which prevailed during the colonial period and through the first part of their history as independent nations. Each of these countries is evolving in its own way a modern, mixed, agricultural–industrial economy and social institutions appropriate to it. One of the most important areas in which this adjustment is occurring is the field of labor–management relations.

Argentina, Brazil, and Chile first felt the effects of industry as a result of the search by Western Europe and the United States for foodstuffs and raw materials to feed their growing populations and rapidly expanding industries during the latter part of the nineteenth century. During those years Brazil became the world's great source of coffee, Argentina supplied grains and meat to much of Western Europe, and Chile became virtually the world's only producer of natural nitrates.

This growth of the export trade to Europe and North America in raw materials and foodstuffs heightened the tempo of economic activity in these countries. It brought into existence railroads, port facilities, packing houses, and other enterprises needed to serve the overseas traffic. It stimulated the development of numerous small businessmen—some of them incipient industrialists—engaged in some phase of the export of foodstuffs and raw materials. It introduced for the first time a small wage-earning proletariat.

However, two world wars and the Great Depression—with the resulting difficulties of selling their principal export products and purchasing manufactured goods from abroad—convinced the people of these three countries of the dangers of monoproduct economies dependent for their very existence on the sale of a few agricultural or mineral products in world markets. Since the 1930's and particularly since the 1940's Argentina, Brazil, and

Chile have been undergoing a swift change which has fundamentally altered not only their economic life but social conditions and politics as well.

Some idea of the degree of industrialization in these three countries is indicated by Table 1, which shows the distribution of gainfully employed people in each.[1]

Table 1. Gainfully employed people in three countries.
(in thousands)

Part of economy	Argentina (1947)		Brazil (1950)		Chile (1952)	
	Male	Female	Male	Female	Male	Female
Total	5,163	1,283	14,610	2,508	1,616.2	539.1
Agriculture	1,534	88	9,609	761	606.0	42.1
Mining & quarrying	32	0.5	—	—	99.0	2.4
Manufacturing	1,024	403	1,842	387	276.9	131.9
Construction	334	4	—	—	101.1	1.2
Electricity & gas	29	1.4	—	—	19.8	0.7
Commerce	748	107	972	102	166.9	56.0
Transport & commun.	375	12	668	29	89.7	5.6
Services	779	596	1,480	1,218	192.8	286.2
Not classified above	179	22	38	9	64.1	13.2

The share of Argentina, Brazil, and Chile in the total manufacturing output of Latin America is demonstrated in Table 2.[2]

Table 2. Countries' industrial output.
(percentage of value added, 1953)

Industry	Latin America	Argentina	Brazil	Chile
Tobacco	100	21.8	15.1	2.5
Textiles	100	28.0	30.0	4.6
Clothing & footwear	100	30.1	24.9	4.5
Wood products	100	23.9	41.1	3.5
Paper & paper products	100	28.5	32.4	3.0
Printing & publication	100	24.5	27.2	4.4
Leather	100	25.4	24.3	4.0
Rubber products	100	19.8	25.7	2.4
Chemicals	100	22.1	16.0	1.7
Nonmetallic minerals	100	23.6	28.5	3.0
Basic metals	100	15.5	27.8	2.6
Metal products	100	43.1	26.4	3.3
Miscellaneous	100	30.4	34.8	1.7

As a result of the industrialization process, political power, in general, has passed in all three countries from the hands of the rural and commercial aristocracy to a heterogeneous group of urban elements in which the new industrial middle class and the white collar workers and manual laborers play important roles.

In each of these countries industrialization had begun before this transfer of political power. However economic and political processes were interacting, so that the drive toward industrialization received little encouragement from the government until control of the state was in the hands of the people of the cities. Thus, for example, the ruling agricultural and grazing aristocracy of Argentina in the 1930's signed international trade and economic agreements favorable to the country's grain and meat exporters and inimical to the progress of industrialization.

Only with the transfer of political power to the urban middle- and working-class groups was the tempo of industrialization increased by the overt encouragement of the government. In Brazil this change from rural to urban political leadership took place as a result of the Revolution of 1930, which first brought Getulio Vargas to the presidency. In Chile a partial transfer occurred in 1920 and was confirmed with the election of the Popular Front government of Pedro Aguirre Cerda in 1939. In Argentina the Peronista Revolution of 1943 ended once and for all the domination of the country by the wheat and cattle barons of the pampas, and put effective political power in the hands of the middle and laboring groups of Buenos Aires and other cities.

Although in all three countries the control of the nation as a whole is no longer the monopoly of the rural aristocracy, in none has there been a thorough attempt to destroy the economic—and resulting political—power of the landlord class in its own rural bailiwick. Despite some talk of agrarian reform in Brazil and Chile, no positive action has been taken in this direction. During the Perón administration in Argentina, the dictator's policy of squeezing agriculture for the advantage of industry, the workers, the army, and graft, had a detrimental effect on the country's agriculture. Although Peron talked a great deal about agrarian reform, there was no real action in this direction.

As it has wrought profound changes in economic and political life, industrialization has also brought a fundamental alteration in labor–management relations in Argentina, Brazil, and Chile. It is, of course, wrong to say that the problems of the interaction between the workers and employers began with industrialization. However, the coming of large-scale urbanized factory society has profoundly changed the nature of and solutions to these problems.

In all three countries, the pattern of labor–management relations in the preindustrial era was patriarchal. The owner of the large *fazenda, estancia,* or *fundo* (as large landholdings are called in Brazil, Argentina, and Chile, respectively) was much more than the employer of those who worked for him. He was their banker, landlord, confessor, doctor, and, in many ways, their father.

In Brazil, slavery was only abolished in 1888, and much of the pattern of nearly four centuries of master–slave relationships still persists in rural sections, and its traces are even to be found among those agricultural workers who in recent decades have moved to the cities. In Chile the largely Indian *roto* (agricultural worker) of the countryside was not a slave, but he was in a real sense a serf, and still is in many parts of Chile. His landlord provided him with food, clothing, shelter, and a little spending money with which to get drunk on week ends, and his dependence on the landlord was nearly absolute. Even in Argentina, the relationship between the farm laborer and his landlord–employer in the pre-Perón period was a patriarchal one.

Since the Great Depression, hundreds of thousands of workers from rural Argentina, Brazil, and Chile have been moving into the cities to seek work in the new factories, on the railroads, in construction. In Buenos Aires, Santiago, Rio and São Paulo they have found not only a vastly different way of life but have found that their relationships with their employers were very unlike those to which they had been accustomed in the country.

The adaptation of these rural workers coming from a patriarchal semi-slave, semi-serf background to the new life of factory workers in the cities is the story of labor–management relations in Argentina, Brazil, and Chile.

Framework of the Labor Problem

The traditional analysis of the role of labor relations and the labor movement has been criticized because it generalizes for the whole world the experience of Western Europe and the United States. The interpretation of the rise of organized labor as a reaction to capitalism—one held by writers from Marx through Perlman and beyond—is not, it is claimed, universally valid in the nations today going through the transformation from a nonindustrial to an industrial society. Rather, it has been suggested that trade unionism (and more generally "the labor problem") arises with industrialization itself, whether the growth of an industrial society comes about under the institutional framework of capitalism, Soviet Communism, or something in between.[3]

This analysis is certainly valid for the three countries with which we are dealing in the present study. Certainly the examples of Great Britain, Germany, or the United States are of only relative value in understanding the development of labor relations in Argentina, Brazil, and Chile.

All three of these nations are capitalistic in the sense that most of the means of production and distribution are in the hands of private individuals or institutions. But in none of the three nations does there exist the laissez-faire capitalism of eighteenth- and nineteenth-century Great Britain or of the late nineteenth-century and early twentieth-century United States.

One of the things which most impresses an observer is the fundamental lack of concern of most thinking people with the ideological problems of "capitalism" versus "socialism." Other issues are of much greater importance, and that of economic development has one of the highest priorities. The concern is chiefly with getting the job of industrialization done, not with who should do it. If a certain field of development can best be handled by private enterprise, there is little objection to private entrepreneurs handling it. On the other hand, if the intervention of the state is necessary, there is little ideological opposition on grounds of "creeping Socialism" or any other slogan.[4]

The three countries have had strikingly different experiences with regard to the role of the state in general economic affairs. But the basic structure in all three has remained one of private enterprise, with varying degrees of state participation.

Brazil experienced from 1937 to 1945 an attempt to impose a corporate state pattern on the economic, social, and political life of the nation. Though this had a lasting impact on the labor movement and the means of expressing labor's protest, it had little effect on the general conduct of business, and its imprint upon the forms of economic organization did not much outlast the Second World War.

Argentina had its totalitarian experiment *sui generis* under Perón from 1943 to 1955. Perónismo was never successful in submitting business to complete state control, except in the field of labor relations. The controls his government established over other aspects of business tended to disappear with Perón's overthrow, and in the long run the Perón experience will prove to have influenced labor much more than business.

Chile has had a comparatively democratic government since World War I, with no really totalitarian regime in power since the beginning of the Industrial Revolution in that country. Its short experiment with dictatorship from 1927 to 1931 had little impact on the economy or economic institutions, though it did have some influence on the labor movement—particularly upon the political alignments within organized labor.

The "labor problem" in these three South American countries, then, has not been fundamentally caused by capitalism but by industrialism. Some light on this is shed by the assertion of Professors Kerr and Siegel that "industrialization makes one general and universal demand: it requires real capital formation and technical organization."[5]

In Argentina, Brazil, and Chile, in spite of the more or less important contributions to the process of capital accumulation by foreign investors, capital formation has largely depended on the ploughing back of profits by manufacturing firms into more plants and equipment. The possibility of capital expansion in this manner has depended on the accumulation of large profits. In turn, high profits have been assured by keeping the workers' real wages relatively low.

In all three countries there exists a tradition of large profit margins in commerce and agriculture. This has made the process of capital accumulation through high profits more psychologically and politically acceptable to the general public (and even to the workers) than might otherwise have been the case. The inflation which has characterized the Brazilian and Chilean economies since the beginning of their Industrial Revolution has been the most effective way to keep real wages down in spite of trade-union efforts and sporadic government encouragement to wage increases.

The fact is that workers in these three countries have shared relatively little in the rising productivity due to the industrialization of their nations. Generally speaking, it is probably a fact that the industrial worker of Brazil or Chile had a lower real income in 1956 than in 1940. However, it must be noted that during this period large numbers of workers were brought in from the countryside to work in industry: these did enjoy a sizable increase in real wages. (For further discussion see chapters IX, XVI, and XXIII.)

The situation in Argentina is somewhat different. During the first part of the Perón Era, 1943 to 1948, when Argentina was able to sell its grains and meat at exceedingly high prices in the world market, it was possible for Perón to bring about an increase in the real wages of the Argentine urban workers without seriously impairing employers' profit margins. However, during the last decade the situation in Argentina has not been basically different from that in the other two nations. (See chapter XXIV.)

This failure of the worker to share in a manner which he considers adequate in the proceeds of his own increased productivity is a fundamental cause of "the labor problem" in Argentina, Brazil, and Chile. It is complicated by a psychological transformation in the worker himself. He finds his real wages kept down at exactly the time when he first becomes aware of the possibilities of advancing his own economic and social status.

In the countryside the social and economic difference between the landlord and his tenant or agricultural laborer is usually so great that the tenant–laborer seldom if ever aspires to equality with his master. In the city or mining camp the situation is different. There is greater social and economic mobility. There are more rungs on the social and economic ladder, and though the worker may not be able to climb to the top of the ladder, he does for the first time have the chance of moving up at least a step or two.

One of the most difficult problems in labor–management relations in the three countries is that of convincing the worker of the existence of greater mobility in an industrial society than he has been accustomed to in his rural environment. The stories of workers who drink up their wage increases or come to work less frequently really are true. Time and experience are necessary before the worker realizes that he, or at least his children, may be able to move out of their social and economic class.

However, once a worker becomes convinced of this, his desire to improve himself, his family, and his home tends to be very great. As the zeal of a convert is likely to be greater than that of someone born into a faith, so the zeal of the worker who has suddenly realized the possibilities of improving his station may be much greater than that of a worker to whom these possibilities are no novelty. As a result, the new industrial worker is likely to be restless and discontented, and his relations with his employer will reflect this state of mind.

Professors Kerr and Siegel further explore the causes of labor unrest in developing countries when they talk of "the efforts to define via a web of rule some structured role for the labor force in relation to the work process." The "web of rule" in industrial society is likely to be much more finely spun than in the agricultural societies from which the Argentine, Brazilian, or Chilean worker has come.

There are undoubtedly a number of aspects of the "web of rule" in the factory which the new industrial worker of these countries finds hard to understand and harder still to submit to. The discipline of factory life is alien to him. He must stick to his machine while he is on the job, he must produce exactly as the employer demands, he must not smoke where it is forbidden, he must not come to work inebriated. These rules can be galling, even to a worker in a highly developed industrial economy; they are infinitely more so to a South American worker just in from the countryside.

The eight-hour day and the six-day week are also hard to take. Although his dependence on his agricultural employer may have been greater, and his real income was certainly less, the worker was in many ways more his own boss in agriculture. If he were suffering from a hangover, didn't feel quite up to working, or had earned what he considered enough money for a while, he was not forced to come to work on the *fundo* or *fazenda*. However, if he misses work too often in the factory, he is likely to lose his job, or suffer some other penalty.

There is little doubt that the new industrial laborer may find his work monotonous. On the farm he had a variety of occupations, something different every day. In the factory he is likely to be tied pretty much to one job all day long—every day. Psychological steam built up by the resulting monotony may well find its expression in quarrels with the foreman, or in joining a strike against the "oppressive" factory owner.

Of key importance, too, as a source of labor protest is undoubtedly the lack of status of the industrial worker. Dr. Frank Tannenbaum, in his book, *The Philosophy of Labor,* published in 1950, insists that this is the principal cause of the rise of trade unionism in the older industrial countries. It is undoubtedly one of the reasons for its rise and its militancy in the underdeveloped countries.

On the *fundo* or *fazenda* the status of the agricultural worker was undoubtedly far below that of his employer. But he knew what his position was and he was accustomed to it. His status is not so clear in the factory. It takes time for the worker to become accustomed to social relationships in industry, to know just where he stands in relation to other workers, to his foreman, to the owner of the factory. He may never be quite sure. This lack of assured position undoubtedly draws him toward the union, which has a common enemy, and a common objective that he can understand or thinks he can understand. There, he can play a role, if it be only to vote for what the union leader suggests.

All these factors contribute to labor unrest, and have little to do with whether the plant in which the worker is employed belongs to the state or to a private entrepreneur. It is not capitalism against which the worker is protesting. Rather, it is the new industrial system of which he has become a part. He would feel moved to protest no matter who owned the plant.

Channeling the Workers' Protest

There are many groups which can attempt to lead or channel the workers' protest against industrialism and in establishing the "web of rule" which governs industrial society, as Professors Kerr and Siegel point out. They say:

. . . The traditional "labor movement" in whose conception the worker assumes the independent role of prime mover may be an extremely important instrumentality in forging or influencing the rule-making and rule-enforcing relationships which emerge in structuring the labor force. But so may organizational instrumentalities which are imposed by the employer, or designed by the state. The contemporary labor theorist confronted with a variety of patterns of industrialization finds universality not in the "labor movement" response but in labor organization in the sense of the structuring of a web of rules relating the work force to the work process.

Certainly, the channeling of labor protest and the structuring of the labor force are interacting processes. Unless there is provided in the "web of rule" some recognized and reasonably standardized procedure for channeling the discontents of the worker (be it through a union grievance procedure, a labor court, or some other means) the "web" is not itself going to be successfully maintained. Indeed, it is in attempting to deal with the workers' protests that many of the rules of the industrial society come into being. This has certainly been the case in Argentina, Brazil, and Chile.

Four principal groups have attempted to lead the workers' protest in these three countries. These are the trade unions, the state, the employers, and the political parties. The first three have also played a significant role in structuring the labor force, though the political parties, being essentially outside the framework of industry, have had little or no effect in this direction.

The trade unions have been most successful in monopolizing the workers' protest in Chile, and in Argentina during the first part of the Perón regime. They once again sought to assume this role in Argentina after the overthrow of the Perón regime. They have been least successful in Brazil.

In Chile, in Argentina during and after the Perón Era, and in Brazil, when government controls over the unions have been relaxed, the workers' organizations have been notable for their "class-struggle" mentality. The reasons for this are probably several. First of all, although capitalism is not basically the cause of labor protest, many labor leaders have inherited from older trade-union movements of Europe the idea of the inevitability of the class struggle against the capitalist, and of the importance of the unions as a revolutionary force in the struggle against capitalism itself.

This position is reinforced by the influence of the political parties in the trade unions. The stock in trade of the Socialist, Communist, Peronista and other parties has been the alleged irreconcilability of the interests of the workers and the capitalists. Therefore, to the degree that the unions have been under party control—and this is considerable—the party leaders have emphasized the class struggle.

Also very important in determining the unions' attitude have been two other factors: the continuing gap between the levels of living and social status of the workers and the upper classes in society, and the fact that the union leaders do not share to any appreciable degree in major decisions in industry. Although the urban worker can move a little way up the social and economic scale, he still has a very long way to go to get into the middle class, though class differences are somewhat smaller in Argentina than in Chile and Brazil.

Time will undoubtedly change this. As the industrial worker sees his sons and daughters get a better education than he had and move into the white collar positions in the front office, perhaps the social and economic gulf between himself and the middle class will seem less profound. Certainly, when the industrial worker's grandchild is able to get a university education and go into a profession or even into management itself, "class consciousness" should become considerably less acute.

The limited role of the unions has intensified the workers' class consciousness. The labor organizations have remained almost purely organs of protest. There has been relatively little attempt by employers to give the unions even "consultative status" in formulating policies on such matters as the training of workers, housing, medical services, or production and productivity. Furthermore, in cases where this has been tried by employers, the union leaders who were consulted and who tried to work with, rather than automatically against, employers ran the risk of being labeled the Latin American equivalent of "yellow unionists." "Class collaboration" is still a sin in the Latin American trade-union lexicon. It will take time and the establishment of much more confidence between union leaders and rank and file on the one hand, and management on the other, before the unions can assume the "responsible" posture which they generally have in the United States and many Western European countries.

The Unions. In Argentina and Chile, where collective bargaining is general, the unions undoubtedly play a part in "forging or influencing the rule-making and rule-enforcing relationships" of which Kerr and Siegel talk. Argentine collective agreements set forth in some detail the general conditions which are to prevail in the industry covered, and there is a highly developed system of shop stewards who take the initiative in presenting grievances and thus holding the employers to the rules which have been jointly agreed upon. Although under Perón the Ministry of Labor undertook a key role in both collective contract negotiation and grievance procedure, the role of the union was still important to both these fields. Subsequent to the overthrow of the Perón regime, the unions' influence grew and that of the ministry declined.

In Chile collective agreements are by no means as detailed as on the other side of the Andes. However they do establish certain minimum rules to be followed in the firm, and union grievance machinery is of key importance in enforcing the contract, modifying and changing the rules laid down by the employer, and enforcing the laws decreed by the state.

The role of the Brazilian unions in developing the "web of rule" and structuring the labor force is much less important than in either Argentina or Chile. The unions had virtually no part in this process during the Vargas dictatorship from 1937 to 1945 when the role of the state was at its apogee. Since 1945 the unions have been struggling to achieve greater independence and to have more say in determining the conditions of the employment of their members. They have done this by being more active in presenting cases to the labor courts and to a less degree by engaging in direct collective bargaining with the employers.

In all three countries the efforts of the unions to have a part in establishing and administering the "web of rule" have been felt both on the individual plant level and in a wider sphere. In Chile collective agreements are generally negotiated on a plant-by-plant basis, though there are some cases of industry-wide unions or federations which attempt to standardize the terms of local contracts. In Argentina collective agreements are usually on a nation-wide basis, but there is generally close consultation with representatives of local units before, during, and after the negotiations.

In Brazil collective demands usually are presented either to the employers or the labor courts on a regional basis, although in a number of cases only one employer is involved.

In all three countries the unions are active in seeking to apply and interpret the "web of rule" through grievance procedures which originate in the local enterprise, but may, in certain circumstances, become a matter for consideration by industry-wide officials, at least in some industries. In none of the three nations is there a division between the trade unions which negotiate collective agreements on a national level, and "workers' councils" which handle grievances locally, such as exists in West Germany, for instance.

However in all three countries union class consciousness and employer resistance have so far prevented the unions from participating as much in the process of rule-making and rule-enforcing as might otherwise have been the case. The increased concern of the employers with problems of productivity as well as with human relations, however, may alter this in the proximate future. A certain disillusionment with the politicization of the trade unions which is noticeable among the workers of all three countries may operate in the same direction.

The Political Parties. Political parties have also played a leading role in trying to channel the workers' protest. In Chile there are few unions which are not controlled by one party or another. Under Perón, in Argentina, virtually all unions were dominated by the Peronista Party, and after Perón's overthrow many political parties were seeking influence in the labor movement. In Brazil, after the end of the corporate state dictatorship of Getulio Vargas in 1945, the Vargasite Partido Trabalhista Brasileiro and the Communist Party fought for the control of the workers.

In their attempt to gain the backing of labor, the political parties have generally resorted to extensive social and nationalistic demagogy. The parties have tried with considerable success to make the trade unions their tools, and as yet there has been little movement in the other direction by the unions to make the parties serve them.

The reasons for the political parties' interest in the workers and their organizations are not hard to find. Until the last few decades politics in all three countries was a monopoly of the upper classes. However, in recent decades the urban lower middle and working classes have entered into the political arena. The parties and the politicians who lead them are well aware of the potentialities of the city workers. As voters they are the single largest bloc—aside from the agricultural workers, who in Brazil and Chile vote pretty much as their landlords tell them (for the conservative parties) although in Argentina they were won over by Perón.

However the importance of the workers goes beyond merely being potential voters. In critical situations the trade unions can support or oust governments through the medium of the general strike, as was demonstrated in Argentina when Perón was restored to power in October 1945 after being ousted by a group of rival military men. In some exceptional cases the workers' organizations might even be mobilized to give military support to a regime or a revolution.[6]

In the structuring of the labor force, the political parties have no constructive contribution to offer. They are more often stirring up conflicts for political reasons or upsetting attempts to establish rules and regulations within industry.

The state in all three countries has tried to control and channel the workers' protest and has played an important part in structuring the labor force. Labor legislation has a peculiar place in the legal system of the Latin American countries. The rise of sizable bodies of laws to protect the worker, to legalize and regulate his mutual help organizations, and to regulate his relations with his employer and with the state has brought forth a great deal of discussion among those interested in the field as to the exact nature of labor law. Alfredo Palacios, the Argentine scholar, lawyer, teacher, and legislator, has called this new development *El Nuevo Derecho,* or the New Law. He has cited the claims of the great French Socialist leader of the early part of the twentieth century, Jean Jaurès, who professed to see in the heart of the old individualist civil law the seeds of a new socialist system of law. Says Palacios:

Against the liberty-killing freedom of the old, must be proclaimed the necessity for a body of labor legislation, ample in its scope, which will attenuate capitalist exploitation and prevent the degeneration of the workers.

The state cannot, without absolutely denying the claims of society, remain impassive before the sacrifice of the health and the life of the workers who constitute the very lifeblood of the nation itself.

The codes are old. They must be rejuvenated, they must be adapted to life and be directed so as to develop the seed of socialist law which exists within them, in order to realize peaceably the inevitable structural change in society.[7]

Although most writers on the subject do not make such revolutionary pretensions for the New Law, they all realize that it raises novel and fundamental problems. Alfredo Gaete Berrios, one of the leading Chilean authorities in the field, notes that there has been much discussion as to whether labor law is public or private law. Some authorities place it in one and some in the other category, and there is still a third group which maintains that labor law lies somewhere in between. As for himself, Gaete Berrios thinks that "in reality, labor law cannot be classified as either public law or private law; it is a body of law with distinctive characteristics, special peculiarities and which overflows the narrow bounds of the great divisions into which law has been classified." [8]

Dr. Gaete Berrios states that the characteristics of social and labor law are:

a. It is a new form of law;
b. It is autonomous and differs from civil law and other juridical disciplines;
c. It is realistic, adaptable to variable economic conditions;
d. It is not formalistic, being easy and clear, without technicalities or rigidities in its terminology;
e. It is a public nature, one not being able to renounce the rights conferred by its laws;
f. It is a class law, for the protection of the weak;
g. It is universal, being adopted in the statutes of many states in a more or less standard form.[9]

Dr. Francisco Walker Linares, Professor of Labor Law at the University of Chile, agrees with Dr. Gaete Berrios that social law and labor law should be put in a classification all its own.[10] He declares that it is "absurd" to consider labor law as merely a category of one of the older legal disciplines: "It stands apart, and is in reality much more the true common law than that which has hitherto borne that title, because it is the only one which is applied permanently to almost all men, being the law of the masses of the people; other categories of law would be exceptional alongside of it." He notes that social law has made serious modifications in many of the previous categories of legislation. These alterations include the following:

a. It regulates the labor contract which common law had hardly touched previously; and not only does it regulate the individual labor contract, but it creates a new form, the collective contract.
b. It has differed from civil law in giving special protection to women and children.
c. It has in certain cases, such as pensions for labor accidents, done away with the common law's distinctions between legitimacy and illegitimacy.
d. In the case of labor accidents it has changed the concept of guilt in the Civil Code to that of professional risk, putting the full burden on the employer.

e. It has established a new category of associations, the *sindicatos.*

f. Popular housing laws have modified seriously the ideas of real estate property.

Other fields of law have been invaded. Commercial law has been seriously influenced by the statutes for the protection of the white collar workers; the Mining Code has had all things pertaining to labor removed from it and transferred to the Labor Code; the court system has been changed by the establishment of special courts for labor problems.

The antecedents for the labor law or social law which has flourished in Argentina, Brazil, Chile and other Latin American countries in the last few decades are usually traced back to the nineteenth century. Undoubtedly, the doctrines of the Socialists of that period were among the most important precursors of the social law of the twentieth century. Their attacks on the individualist philosophy which was dominant at that time laid the groundwork for a development of a comprehensive body of social legislation. In this connection the Utopian Socialists and other non-Marxians were of equal importance with Marx and his followers. Credit is also given to the State Socialists, the Fabians, and last, but certainly not least, to the Catholic social thinkers, epitomized particularly by Pope Leo XIII, author of the encyclical "Rerum Novarum."

Argentina, Brazil, and Chile all follow the traditions of Roman rather than Anglo-Saxon law. They, therefore, have "codes" covering various aspects of the law. Chile and Brazil have added "labor codes" to the older bodies of legislation, although Argentina has not done so formally.

The State. There have been various methods which the state has used in Argentina, Brazil, and Chile to channel the workers' protests and aid in structuring the labor force. One of these is legislation providing for extensive control over the organization and functioning of unions and the collective bargaining process.

Controls over the trade-union movement have been of various kinds. They start with requirements that a labor organization gain government recognition before it can function in defense of the workers. This has been both a boon and a bane to the unions. On the one hand, it has made strikes for recognition unnecessary in these countries. On the other, it has provided the state with a powerful weapon for crippling unions which do not please it, and an excuse for further intervention.[11]

The law in all three countries establishes provisions concerning the form and jurisdiction of the workers' organizations. It also provides control over union finances and elections. Finally, it establishes greater or less control over collective bargaining—and in the case of Brazil makes such bargaining virtually nonexistent.

There are various reasons for such encouragement and controls over the labor movement. Some politicians have had a genuine concern for the conditions of workers in their countries, and wished to give legal support to their organizations. Another motive has undoubtedly been a desire "to keep up with the international Joneses," a wish to bring the country's labor legislation up to international standards. The International Labor Organization has been very important in engendering this desire.

Finally, the politicians and government officials have undoubtedly been very much aware of the political potential of the organized workers. They have at one and the same time wanted to gain the support of this group and to have legal means to curb it if that became necessary.

Control over the unions has varied a good deal from country to country and from time to time. In the long run it has probably been the least exercised in Chile because of the democratic nature of that country's government, and the leftist orientation of the governments in power between 1939 and 1952. The tendency during the administration of General Carlos Ibañez after 1952 was toward much greater government intervention in the unions' affairs, though in the last months of his government this course was reversed by the action of Congress in repealing much of the legislation which made it possible.

During the Perón administration in Argentina, government control over the unions was very extensive. The upper- and middle-union leadership was completely dependent for its tenure in office upon Perón and those who managed labor affairs for him. In spite of this, the Argentine unions —in contrast to those in Brazil under Vargas—remained intact as powerful institutions. The regime which succeeded Perón proclaimed one of its objectives to be the reestablishment of trade-union independence but this proved very difficult to achieve. The administration of President Arturo Frondizi, who came to power in May 1958, restored much of the union-control legislation of the Perón government which had been abolished by the provisional regime of President Aramburu.

The most complete control over the unions is practiced by the government of Brazil. During the eight-year-long "New State" (*Estado Novo*) dictatorship of Getulio Vargas, the existing labor movement was emasculated. Strikes were forbidden, and there was the strictest control over elections and finances of the unions. No one was permitted to hold office who was not in complete sympathy with the Vargas regime.

The trade-union leaders were tied closely to the Ministry of Labor, upon whose good will they depended to remain in office. At the same time, the unions were deprived of virtually all their original functions. Collective bargaining was superseded by a system of labor courts to which all conflicts between employers and workers were referred.

At the same time, the trade-union movement was made almost completely dependent upon the government for its financial resources. All workers were forced to pay one day's pay each year to the trade-union system. This money was divided between various parts of the trade-union movement and the government. With their share of the wage deduction, the unions were required by the government to establish extensive social services—health protection, schools, libraries, etc. These were, in effect, the only things upon which the unions were allowed to spend their funds.

This system was still largely intact in 1961. Although collective bargaining was making some headway, the vast majority of labor disputes was still being resolved through the government's labor courts. The labor protest was thus largely monopolized by the government, with the trade unions, the political parties, and the employers playing subsidiary roles.

The governments of the three countries have channeled labor protest in other ways in addition to control over the unions and collective bargaining. They have done so through extensive and sometimes exaggerated social legislation which has also served to establish a good deal of the "web of rule" in Brazilian industry. Laws establishing maximum hours and minimum wages, legislation for the shielding of machinery, and a variety of other types of statutes extending protection to the worker are common in all three nations, but other matters are also dealt with. Perhaps the most exaggerated case of such legislation is the Brazilian provision that a worker cannot be dismissed without permission of the labor court if he has been employed for ten years or more. Such laws are bids by the government and the politicians controlling it to gain the favor of the workers and channel the workers' grievances.

Social security also exists in the three nations. In all three cases there is extensive protection for ill, old, and disabled workers. The social security systems of Brazil and Chile can honestly be described as excessive in terms of their cost to the economy, and this same charge might conceivably be leveled against that of Argentina. These laws were certainly passed more to gain political support from the workers than to conform to any strict analysis of the economic possibilities of the three countries.

The Employers. The employers also play a role in trying to channel the workers' protest against unfavorable aspects of industrialization and have a major part in developing industry's "web of rule." This is most evident in Brazil, a bit less so in Chile, and is least important in Argentina.

In Brazil some private employers have extensive social welfare programs for their workers. The services provided by such programs include subsidization of cooperative stores, special medical aid, sports and recreation facilities, and similar projects. However, much more important in the general picture is the Serviço Social da Industria, the famous SESI.

The SESI is a semiofficial program administered under the direction of the Confederacão Nacional da Industria and its regional federations, and financed by a tax on every industrial employer in the country. The administration of the SESI is decentralized, and each state Federacão da Industria provides the appropriate services for the workers of its state. There is a similar but less extensive organization, the Serviço Social de Commercio, the SESCI, in the mercantile field.

In Chile the employers' attempt to channel the workers' protest takes a variety of forms. In the first place, there are what in the United States are called "company unions," unions subject to the influence or control of the employers. These are particularly numerous in the textile industry.

Another method of channeling protest on the part of the employers is an attempt to anticipate the workers' demands. There is extensive employer paternalism in Chile. The employers not only provide low-cost stores, they supply medical care supplementary to that given by the social security system, they give their workers and the workers' children educational assistance. Some employers provide housing.

There is a growing tendency in Chile against paternalism. This is particularly true in the great mining companies where the management is interested, insofar as possible, in substituting wage increases for those paternalistic items which can conveniently be dropped.

In Argentina there is relatively little attempt on the part of the employers to channel the workers' protest. Perón was not anxious to have the employers provide special services for their workers—he wanted the workers to feel that all their blessings flowed from him and from the trade-union movement which he controlled. There has always been a stronger feeling among Argentine employers against paternalism than in the other two countries.

The employers play the most important part of all in establishing and enforcing rules in industry in Argentina, Brazil, and Chile. Upon them rests the principal responsibility for organizing and directing their enterprises. They select their employees, they have to maintain discipline, they organize production, they establish the schedules for their firms.

The employers have the advantage over the government in being on the spot throughout the working day. The state can lay down certain rules which are to be followed, but it is the employer who actually has the responsibility for carrying them out. The employer also has the advantage over the union leader in possessing an over-all view of how the firm is functioning.

Of course, the employers have powerful sanctions at their command to enforce their rules. Although it may be severely limited, they have in the last instance the ability to dismiss the worker, and have within their grasp many lesser sanctions.

At most, the other two factors in the rule-enacting procedure act as checks upon the employer. The final decision in most matters is up to him. Many employers in all three countries have developed to a fine art the process of evading or twisting the law and avoiding commitments involved in collective agreements or labor court decisions.

Generally in Argentina, Brazil, and Chile the employers take what might best be summed up as a "fatherly" attitude toward the workers. Although they deal with the workers' unions, and may upon occasion have considerable respect for individual labor leaders, they have not as yet developed a frame of mind which would permit real cooperation between themselves and the unions.

Employers of the three countries are still very jealous of the "prerogatives of management," and are loath to share these with the workers or the state. They seek to keep under their own control the utmost possible part in the process of rule-making and rule enforcement.

The industrialist class like the workers has had to make great adjustments to adapt to the new industrial society. It is a relatively new group in the society of the three South American countries and it has had a great deal to learn, while having little in its own environment which could help in the learning process.

The industrialists not only have had to adapt to modern engineering and manufacturing techniques, but they have also had to learn how to manage an industrial enterprise. For the most part, they are self-made men with relatively little formal training in management.

The Argentine, Brazilian, and Chilean industrialists have had to face problems which have not existed for many decades in countries like the United States or Great Britain. They have been faced with a lack of services usually provided by the community or by specialized enterprises in the more advanced industrial countries—services such as water supply, electricity, housing for their employees. In many cases the industrialists themselves have had to supply these needs.

They have also had to face a large measure of social disapproval from their "betters." The older rural and commercial aristocracy has tended to look down on the "upstart" new rich of the industrial class. Such attitudes have contributed to the industrialists' difficulties in obtaining credit for their firms.

Most important for our study, the industrialists have been faced with the gigantic problem of transforming a group of raw farm hands into workers in modern industry. They have had to overcome illiteracy, drunkenness, and lack of ambition upon the part of their employees. They have faced the necessity of filling the void in the worker's life left by the disappearance of the agricultural "patron" upon whom the laborer was so dependent.

As a result of all this, the factory owner during the first phase of industrialization has paid little attention to "scientific management," including labor and human relations. He has approached each problem as it presented itself, and although different employers developed different philosophies of management and labor relations, these philosophies were drawn from their own experience and the experiences of other firms with which they had contact rather than being the result of scientific study or formal training.

Industry in Argentina, Brazil, and Chile is just entering the second phase of its development in which the factory owners and managers have a growing interest in costs, prices, efficiency, and human relations. Many industrialists in all three countries have reached the conclusion that they must rationalize their enterprises and develop new forms of relationships with their workers. Continuing inflation, caused in part at least by industrial inefficiency and unnecessarily high prices for manufactured goods, and the growing militancy of organized labor are two of the factors which have impelled them to this conclusion. It is too early to see what the results of this change in emphasis will be, but it is clear that it is of great importance for the future development of labor–management relations in these three nations.

In the pages which follow we shall deal with some of these problems. We shall frequently raise the question of what gives rise to labor protest in the three countries. We shall examine how this protest is expressed or diverted and by whom. We shall note the "web of rule" which exists in industry, and how it is developed. We shall trace the conversion of illiterate agricultural workers into modern industrial workers, and shall find out what is being done to develop skilled workers in the three nations.

We shall also seek to determine how the new industrialist class is recruited, what training it receives, and how the industrialists are meeting the problem of relations with their labor force.

We begin with Brazil because it is the largest country in Latin America —larger even than the continental United States. It is a nation experiencing the full impact of industrialization and seems likely in the near future to pull far ahead of its Spanish-speaking neighbors, and perhaps within a few decades to become one of the great economic and political empires of the world.

PART ONE—BRAZIL

CHAPTER II

Economic and Political Background

Brazil's population was estimated as 61,268,000 people in 1957. Only five years before, the number of Brazilians had been estimated at only 55,772,000, and the population was growing at the rate of 2.4 per cent annually.[1] The economic history of Brazil is the story of a series of spurts of development. Soon after the foundation of the Portuguese colony in the New World, it went through a fifty-year Brazil wood period when this much wanted crop was the main economic excuse for existence. This was succeeded by the sugar-cane cycle which lasted throughout the seventeenth century. From about 1690 to 1770 a third product, gold, dominated the colony's economy, to be succeeded by diamonds during the latter part of the eighteenth century.

For a century after 1830 the most famous phase of Brazilian economic history transpired when its economy was dominated by coffee. During this same period (from 1860 to 1910) the ephemeral rise of the rubber industry took place.[2]

Industry is providing the latest of this long series of economic ground swells. However, until the growth of manufacturing during the last quarter of a century the economy of the nation was largely controlled by coffee. In the 1920's the coffee industry provided approximately 70 per cent of the country's income from exports.[3] A change in the price of the bean or in its volume of sales could mean prosperity or disaster for the nation's economic life, a situation which led to numerous attempts on the part of the Brazilians to stabilize the sales and price of their principal product. Those attempts were mostly unsuccessful, and served principally to pave the way for commercial rivals to Brazil in the coffee business.

The coffee economy was dealt a stunning blow by the Great Depression, and despite a sharp rise in coffee prices during the 1950's which arrested the long-range trend toward decline in the industry, the day of complete domination of the Brazilian economy by coffee was already a thing of the past. The bean remained, however, the nation's chief foreign exchange-earner.

All these earlier phases of economic development brought with them a plantation-type society. Of the coffee area, Wythe notes that "the general pattern of agriculture was like that of cotton and tobacco culture in the American Old South, the planters exhausting their land and moving south-ward and westward to exploit new soil. . . . In Brazil large areas of virgin land await cultivation. . . ." [4]

Manufacturing

The diversification of the nation's agriculture and the development of manufacturing during recent decades have brought about fundamental transformations in the nation's economic life.

The six-year period following the establishment of the republic in 1889 was notable for industrial expansion. However, despite the growing hum of industry during the early decades of this century, the occupational census of 1940 showed that agriculture was still the keystone of the economy.[5]

It was not until the Second World War that manufacturing received a tremendous impetus. The report of the Abbink Commission has the following to say about this:

It is estimated that the gross value of Brazil's industrial production for the year 1947 was three or four times as great as before the war. A substantial part of the increase over 1939 was, of course, due to the rapid rise of prices since that year. There is no question, however, but that Brazilian industrial production did increase materially during the war years, particularly in the manufacture of textiles (which employs 25 per cent of all Brazilian industrial workers), iron and steel, cement, food-processing, coal, leather, glass, paper, pharmaceuticals, chemicals, plastics, shoes, matches, printing and furniture. The most striking development of the period was the marked increase in the production of heavy industrial goods, particularly steel and steel productions. The commencement of operation of the Volta Redonda Plant for the production of steel shapes, plate and sheet, including galvanized sheet and tinplate, marked a major step in the achievement of Brazil's heavy industry.[6]

The principal center of manufacturing industry has been São Paulo. That state is not only the principal industrial area but is now also the largest coffee, sugar, and cotton-growing region of the union. It produces almost half of the national income. It is the largest textile-manufacturing center, is of growing importance in chemicals, and will soon have an iron and steel industry. Other industries of importance in the city of São Paulo and the other cities and towns of the state are clothing, shoemaking, cement, automobiles, metal fabrication, and the processing of agricultural products.

There are other important industrial centers. The principal one is Rio de Janeiro, where the textile industry is of particular importance, as well as pharmaceuticals, metal fabricating, and other lines. Rio is, in addition, the principal port of the nation, although its biggest single economic activity is government.

The state of Minas Gerais is already one of the principal centers of manufacturing, and is likely to be increasingly important in the future. It possessed the first iron and steel industry, the Cia. Belgo-Minera, and is planning for another government-owned steel plant by the early 1960's. Minas Gerais has a vast store of minerals—iron, copper, diamonds, gold, and many of the rarer metals. The residents, perhaps too optimistically, see the state in the not-too-distant future as the principal heavy-industry center of Brazil.

The far-southern state of Rio Grande do Sul is another booming manufacturing center. Being the largest grazing section of the nation, it is also the largest leather-processing region. It has packing houses, an important grain-processing business, and thriving textile, clothing, and shoe industries. The manufacturing activities of the state are becoming increasingly diversified.

Other parts of Brazil are also becoming industrialized. One is the state of Parana, just south of São Paulo, the capital of which, Curitiba, is one of the country's fastest-growing urban areas. Pernambuco, the old center of the sugar industry in the northeastern hump of Brazil, is developing an increasing amount of factory industry, much of it in branch plants of firms from the south. Salvador, halfway between Pernambuco and Rio de Janeiro, capital of the state of Baia which is the center of the cacão industry and one of the republic's principal grazing regions, is also becoming an important manufacturing city—listing the making of textiles, cigars, cigarettes, as well as agricultural-processing industries, among its principal economic activities.

Brazil thus has a number of rapidly growing cities which are the principal centers of the new manufacturing industries. The 1957 edition of the *Anuario Estatistico do Brasil,* published by the Conselho Nacional de Estatistica, lists the following ten largest cities:

Rio de Janeiro	2,303,063
São Paulo	2,017,025
Recife	512,370
Salvador	389,422
Porto Alegre	375,049
Belo Horizonte	338,585
Belem	225,218
Fortaleza	205,052
Santos	198,405
Niteroi	170,868

The census of 1960 will undoubtedly show a significant change in the listing of these cities. In all probability, São Paulo will have passed Rio as the nation's largest urban center and Curitiba will undoubtedly have taken its place on the list. There may also be other cities among the top ten.

The tendency of Brazil's population and economy is to push into the vast interior of the country which has been practically deserted during the four and a half centuries of Brazilian history. The great states of Goyaz and Matto Grosso not only have vast grazing and agricultural lands, but also possess important resources which will assure their industrial growth as their populations increase. The transfer of the national capital to the new city of Brasilia, built in the center of the state of Goyaz, will undoubtedly act as a strong stimulus to the rapid growth of this part of the country.

In 1949 the states of São Paulo, Rio de Janeiro, Minas Gerais, and Rio Grande do Sul and the Federal District—all in the south—produced 85 per cent of the gross value of all industrial products, compared with 76 per cent twenty years earlier. São Paulo had grown from 31 per cent of the total in 1920 to 50 per cent in 1949. The northeastern state of Pernambuco, with 4 per cent of total Brazilian industrial output, was just behind Rio de Janeiro and Minas Gerais (each 5 per cent in value of industrial output).[7]

George Wythe has described some general characteristics of Brazilian industry in the middle 1950's:

1. Production is concentrated primarily in the field of consumer goods. The textile, apparel, and food industries account for 42 per cent of the total value added by manufacture in all industries as compared to 23 per cent for the same groups in the United States. At the same time the relative importance of these groups has declined since 1919, owing chiefly to the growth of metal-working and construction groups. Local plants supply practically the entire consumption

of all consumer goods of general use, and a substantial proportion of other types of goods.

2. In some respects, Brazil is still in the "quantitative stage of industrialization, since the bulk of the output consists of articles of low grades but reasonably satisfactory to consumers having on the average a low per-capita income. As the broadening distribution of wealth has created wider markets for articles of better quality and higher price, and as overproduction of the common grades has developed, manufacture has begun of types of goods (such as cotton cloth) not previously produced. Branches of foreign concerns manufacturing trade-marked goods attempt to maintain the same quality of product as in the United States.

3. A substantial start has been made with heavy industry: integrated iron and steel plants, metal-working, cement, and some industrial chemicals. The range of simpler types of machines made in Brazil is considerable and expanding.

4. Capital goods comprise the major item in Brazil's import trade, while imports of manufactured goods for direct consumer consumption are relatively small. . . .

Growth of Economy

The rate of growth of the Brazilian economy in recent years has been very rapid. According to the Banco Nacional de Desenvolvimento Economico (National Bank of Economic Development), the increase in the national income between 1948 and 1952 was from 190.8 billion cruzeiros to 359.2 billion cruzeiros. When this is deflated for price increases occurring during the same period, it amounts to a 34 per cent rise, or 7.5 per cent per year. When these figures are adjusted for the increase in population, they amount to a 21 per cent increase for the five years, or almost 5 per cent a year.

Investment has been heavy. During the period, 1948 to 1952, for a 62 billion cruzeiro increase in real income, there was invested 125 billion cruzeiros. Of this, 5 billion came directly from abroad, and foreign contributions in terms of trade amounted to 11 billion cruzeiros. Thus, only a small part of Brazil's capital expansion has been coming directly or indirectly from foreign sources.

During the Second World War, 20 per cent of Brazil's total production was for export. In 1948 only 14.4 per cent was for export and in 1952 only 8.5 per cent. However, the internal market increased at the rate of 7.4 per cent a year.

Between 1948 and 1952, agriculture which increased 3.8 per cent a year, fell from 32 per cent to 30 per cent of the national income. Tertiary industry increased at 5.3 per cent a year, staying relatively the same with regard to the total increase in income. Industrial production increased 9.7 per cent a year, and increased from 17 per cent to 20 per cent of the whole national income.

Total agricultural production for internal consumption between 1939 and 1948 increased 3.7 per cent a year, and output of agricultural food products rose 5 per cent a year. Export agriculture declined 18 per cent during this period. Between 1948 and 1952 agriculture for internal con-sumption increased 4.2 per cent a year, and foodstuffs only 3.8 per cent. Export agriculture increased during the first four years of the period by 15 per cent. This all means that foodstuff production per capita increased during both these periods, since population was increasing at the rate of only 2.5 per cent.

Textiles, which in 1920 represented over 77 per cent of total manu-facturing production, in 1940 were 66 per cent and in 1950 were 61 per cent. Metallurgy was 23 per cent in 1950 and had been only 12 per cent in 1920. Other manufacturing rose between the two dates from 11 per cent to 16 per cent of the total.

Road and air transport increased at the rate of 11 per cent during the five years.

Consumers' imports from 1947 through 1948 were 31 per cent of total imports, higher than prewar. But by 1952 they had fallen to only 23 per cent. Fuel imports from 1941 to 1952 were 12 per cent of the total, and gasoline particularly increased. Raw materials imports increased from 23 per cent to 27 per cent and equipment from 34 per cent to 37.5 per cent from 1941 to 1952.[8]

Private Entrepreneurs. Most of the economic development of Brazil is being undertaken by private investors. The great majority of the larger industrial enterprises of Brazil are in the hands of corporate enterprises which are generally controlled by a single family or a small inner group consisting of the original entrepreneurs. The most famous of these is the S. A. Matarazzo Reunidas, of São Paulo. It is a vast, vertical and horizontal combination which turns out not only textiles but fabricated metal products, vegetable oils, canned hams, canned fruits and vegetables, margarine, and a wide range of chemicals.

The Matarazzo firm has grown largely by ploughing back profits. It has had relatively little support from the government but has expanded with the growth of São Paulo and of Brazil. There are other firms of the same kind. One of the soundest is the Renner firm of Porto Alegre. Founded in 1912 by A. J. Renner, a Brazilian whose grandfather had come from

Germany in the middle of the nineteenth century, the firm is the largest producer of ready-made clothing in Brazil, and in addition turns out shoes, textiles, and various other products.

In addition to these older industrial combines, there is a newer group which grew up under the wing of Getulio Vargas. The Revolution of 1930 resulted in the shifting of political power to the urban centers, paving the way for the growth of industry. Many of the new generation of entrepreneurs were greatly helped in their rise to power by being in a position to manipulate the numerous government "controls" established during the Vargas dictatorship (1937 through 1945). Although many of these controls were dismantled after World War II, the most profitable source of "aid" to "deserving" friends of the group in power—exchange controls administered by the Banco de Brasil—has continued to exist.

Undoubtedly some of the funds which have been extracted from the Banco de Brasil and other sources have found their way abroad. However, a sizable portion has been invested by the recipients in the country's booming manufacturing industries. Some of these firms have been purely Brazilian, others have been partnerships between Brazilians and foreign investors.

Thus, much "informal" aid has been given to the development of Brazilian industry from government sources. However, it was not until the early 1940's that the government officially entered the manufacturing field, and it was not until a decade later that an institution was established to give general aid to the development of the national economy.

The Government Role. Since 1930 the Brazilian government has played an important part in the process of economic development. The revolution of that year took power out of the hands of the coffee and cattle oligarchy of the states of São Paulo and Minas Gerais, and installed a government which was in favor of economic diversification, and in particular of the development of manufacturing.

The government, rather than participating itself in the industrialization process *per se* on a large scale, has tried to create conditions under which the diversification of the economy could progress more rapidly. One aspect of this activity has been described by the Brazilian economist João Paulo de Almeida Magalhães:

> The result of this new state of affairs was the rapid flourishing of national industry. Everything occurred as if a customs union had suddenly been newly created and high tariffs raised, so that many articles, until then imported, commenced to be produced internally. . . .
> In truth, industrialization, characterized by manufactures produced essen-

tially for the internal market, required a more intense circulation within the national frontiers. For this purpose the government succeeded in linking the different railroad networks of the country. On the other hand, it undertook to construct a system of roads to serve the needs of the interior market. From all of this resulted more easy and frequent communication among the economic zones of Portuguese America, and therefore the disappearance of institutional obstacles to the circulation of the factors of production. Consequently, the industrialization process produced an effect similar to the disappearance of regional tariff barriers. . . .

During World War II, the government undertook the establishment of two manufacturing projects—the National Steel Factory of Volta Redonda and the National Motors Factory outside of Rio de Janeiro. Financed in part by loans from the Eximbank, Volta Redonda began operation soon after the end of the war with a capacity of 350,000 tons of steel a year[9] and recent plans were on foot to expand it to 1,000,000 tons capacity. The National Motors Factory, planned during the war, was completed a few years afterward. In 1954 a loan from the National Development Bank, accompanied by a change of management and the launching of a truck production program, put this government plant on a firm basis and it began to be successful.

Another field in which the government has directly participated in recent years has been in the development of the country's oil resources. After a bitter fight inside and out of congress, a law was finally passed in 1953 which conferred upon the Petroleos Brasileiros (Petrobras) the exclusive right to search for and develop the country's petroleum resources.

In their desire to make effective the slogan *Petroleo e Nosso* (Petroleum Is Ours), the Brazilian legislators made certain that no foreign firms would be able to participate in the development of the country's oil resources; but, at the same time, they also made certain that the actual development of these resources would come relatively slowly.

The Banco Nacional de Desenvolvimento Economico. The Banco Nacional de Desenvolvimento Economico (National Bank of Economic Development) has a somewhat wider scope than any of the other government enterprises we have mentioned. It is similar to the Puerto Rican Development Corporation, the Corporación de Fomento de Chile, and other such institutions. However, it differs in one fundamental aspect—it cannot directly invest in the industries in which it is interested, or start industries; it can merely make loans.

The Banco Nacional de Desenvolvimento Economico was set up as a result of the work of the Joint United States–Brazilian Economic Commission which functioned from 1950 to 1953. It has as income certain mandatory investments by insurance companies and other institutions, and a levy of 15 per cent of all income taxes on corporations and private individuals, plus an additional surtax on corporations. It has been given the authority by congress to guarantee, in the name of the government, loans granted by international lending institutions such as the Eximbank and the International Bank.

The bank is supposed to concentrate chiefly on certain bottlenecks in the Brazilian economy such as transportation and electric power development, principally hydroelectric power. However, it is also empowered to finance "basic industries," which is subject to wide interpretation. Those in charge of the bank's operations felt in 1956 that by and large it had been successful. It had made several loans to the government railroads, had helped a number of electric power projects, and had made some loans for agriculture.[10]

Aid to Amazon and Northeast. In addition to the establishment of the Banco de Desenvolvimento Economico, the government has undertaken to aid the development of the two most distressed regions of Brazil—the Amazon Valley and the northeast. Special lending institutions have been established, and a provision was written into the constitution of 1946 providing for mandatory budget items for this purpose.

The Amazon Valley has been in great economic distress since the end of the rubber boom just before the First World War. Rubber is still gathered there, though now the supply fails to fill even Brazil's own needs. Other crops such as babassu nuts, brazil nuts, etc., are collected in the area but are not sufficient to keep the vast valley region in any state of prosperity. Only two cities of any size exist in the valley, Belem and Manaõs. The former is the principal port, and the latter, the old rubber capital.

The Banco de Amazonia has been one of the principal supports to the area. However, its operations are largely confined to the rubber industry.

In addition, the government is bound for a period of twenty years according to the constitution of 1946 to spend at least 3 per cent of its annual income on the Amazonia area; and to spend indefinitely at least 3 per cent of the budget on improvement of the northeast.[11] These funds are spent largely on improving transportation, providing local public utilities, and other needs.

The northeast was the early center of the sugar industry and sugar still dominates the region. However, in recent decades successive sieges of drought have turned much of the region into a huge desert and have caused a large migration to the southern states of the republic.

The Banco del Noreste has been the government organization established for the purpose of aiding the recovery and development of this northeastern region. This bank works very closely with the Banco Nacional de Desenvolvimento Economico and they frequently collaborate on projects for the drought-stricken area.

Another government-sponsored aid to this region has been the São Francisco Valley program. A project patterned after the Tennessee Valley Authority of the United States, the São Francisco Valley scheme has as its objective the harnessing of the hydroelectric resources of one of the largest river valleys of the nation, as well as stimulating the agricultural development of an important region which has hitherto lagged behind the rest of Brazil. The vehicle for the fulfillment of this program is the Companhia Hidro-Electrica de São Francisco. The principal project of the company was the building of a dam at Paulo Affonso in the middle part of the São Francisco River Valley. Part of its total cost was borrowed from the International Bank for Reconstruction and Development.

The significance of this project was pointed out by the International Bank in its press release 188 of May 29, 1950. It stated:

Lack of power has been a major obstacle to the economic development of Brazil, particularly in the northeast area. The hinterland behind Recife and Salvador and the area in the vicinity of the Paulo Affonso Falls are relatively undeveloped. On the completion of the project, electric power will be available for the development of this area and may assist in a desirable decentralization of industry in Brazil.

At present, most of the power in Recife and Salvador is provided by thermal plants owned and operated by subsidiaries of the American and Foreign Power Company. The cost of fuel necessary for these and other plants in the area makes power expensive, and importing fuel oil is a drain on Brazil's foreign exchange resources. When the Paulo Affonso project has been completed, hydroelectric power will replace thermal power and so affect a considerable saving of foreign exchange. The São Francisco Hydroelectric Company will then sell power to the American and Foreign Power Company subsidiaries, and to other companies operating in this area, for distribution through their existing facilities. Some of the present thermal plants will be maintain in a standby capacity.

It was already obvious in 1956 that there had been a quickening of economic activity in the region, and that plans for future expansion had been greatly augmented as a result of the advent of relatively cheap and plentiful electric power. However, successive droughts still plagued the region. Furthermore, in the late 1950's the first significant movement of discontented peasants appeared under the leadership of Francisco Julião. In an effort to head off this unrest, and to coordinate the efforts to foster the economic development of the northeast, President Kubitschek, shortly before leaving office, established a new aid and development agency for the northeast, headed by a dynamic organizer and administrator, Celso Furtado. In a visit to the United States in 1961 Furtado received the promise of several hundred million dollars in aid for his work from the United States.

Cia. do Valle do Rio Doce. Another interesting governmental development operation is the Cia. do Valle do Rio Doce in the state of Minas Gerais. This firm began about the turn of the century as the Tirois-Minas Railroad under predominantly Belgian ownership, and until World War II was a poor railroad at best. In 1940 the whole thing was reorganized, as a result of the Allies' need for iron ore, the principal product handled by the road. It then became a three-way enterprise with British, American, and Brazilian interests represented. The American part was contributed by the Eximbank.

By the middle 1950's the Cia. do Valle do Rio Doce was a Brazilian, mixed, public-private company playing an important role in opening up the mineral resources of the rich state of Minas Gerais.[12]

It can thus be seen that official government stimulation to the economy has come largely in the form of trying to widen some of the bottlenecks which are holding up the nation's general development, and to bring special aid to those sections of the nation which have lagged farthest behind the general growth of the economy. However, the development of manufacturing and even of public utilities in many instances has come largely through the efforts of private entrepreneurs.

Political Background

The ghost of Geutlio Vargas still hangs over Brazilian politics as it does over most aspects of life in that country. Although his dictatorship ceased fifteen years ago, and he himself committed suicide in 1954, virtually all political parties are still either Vargasista or anti-Vargasista.

Before the Revolution of 1930 which brought Vargas to power there were no really national political parties. Different political factions fought for control of each individual state, and the government of the nation was decided by bargains made among those who controlled the most powerful constituents of the union. Active participation in politics was confined to a small economic and intellectual elite.

During the first years of the Vargas regime, this situation did not change fundamentally. However, during Vargas' dictatorship from 1937 through 1945, no political parties were allowed to function, and he developed a regime highly centralized in Rio. Vargas appointed all the state governors (who were labeled "interventors" during this epoch); and he attempted to break down state loyalties and supplant them with allegiance to the nation.

With the army's overthrow of the dictatorship in 1945, the drafters of the 1946 constitution felt that it was necessary to prevent the return of state political parties, which lent themselves to the kind of manipulation which had marked pre-1930 Brazil, and to encourage national political organizations. Thus, no party was permitted to be established on a purely state-wide basis.

If this move was intended to limit the number of political parties, it fell far short of its mark. During the decade and a half since the fall of the dictatorship, a plethora of political parties has appeared on the scene. These can be divided roughly into three classes—those which have donned the Vargas mantle to a greater or lesser degree, those which are anti-Vargas, and a few which are neither one nor the other.

The Partido Social Democratico. Among the Vargas heirs there are two principal groups, the Partido Social Democratico (PSD) and the Partido Trabalhista Brasileiro. They may be said to represent the right and left wing, respectively, of the Vargas movement.

The Partido Social Democratico was established as the vehicle through which to secure the election of General Eurico Dutra who was officially the Vargas-supported nominee in the 1945 election. It is a polyglot party but, in general, may be said to be the most conservative group in the country. In part it is a remnant of the pre-Vargas period. In the days before 1930 the system of political bosses was widespread throughout Brazil. The most important landlord of a region would be the political "owner" of that part of a state as well. Groups of these local bosses would constitute one or another of the state-wide parties of that era. They were thus highly personalized parties. Under Vargas many of the local bosses were displaced, but in many instances he encouraged the development of other ones loyal to him. In any case, the boss system reemerged after 1945, particularly in the rural areas of the country, and most of these bosses joined in the forming of the Partido Social Democratico.

However, another important element in the PSD is the presence of the *nouveaux riches* of the Vargas period. Those industrialists, bankers, and businessmen who profited from their connections with the Vargas regime gravitated to the Partido Social Democratico as soon as it was established. So did those officeholders of the dictatorship period who were not particularly connected with the "social" aspects of that regime.

Together these elements constitute the present-day Partido Social Democratico. Naturally, in such a big country as Brazil, there are regional variations in the PSD, as in other parties, but basically it is as we have described it. Its voting power comes mainly from the rural areas where agricultural workers still generally vote as they are told, or paid to do, by their employers or landlords, when they can vote at all.

The Partido Trabalhista Brasileiro. The other major party among the pro-Vargas organizations is the Partido Trabalhista Brasileiro (PTB). It was established in the waning days of the dictatorship by officials of the Ministry of Labor, principal among them the Director General of Labor of the time, José Segadas Vianna. It was frankly organized for the purpose of rallying the workers to Vargas' cause, and was partly designed to prevent them from following Luiz Carlos Prestes, the Communist leader.

In the beginning the principal officials of the PTB consisted of staff members of the Ministry of Labor and officers of the government-controlled trade-union movement. However, with the passage of time the influence of the trade unionists within the leadership of the PTB has waned. At the March 1956 convention of the PTB not one single trade-union leader was elected to a post in the national leadership of the PTB.

Those who have taken over the PTB leadership are professional politicians and medium-sized and small "operators" around the government. It is notorious, and a cause for popular jokes, that the PTB is job-hungry. It is not uncommon to hear a Brazilian comment that the *tiboroes* (sharks) of the Vargas regime found their way into the PSD, and the smaller fish were left in the PTB. The Partido Trabalhista is riven with factions, and particularly since the death of Vargas there has been a merciless struggle for power on all levels within the party. There are a few elements who would like to convert the PTB into a Brazilian version of the British Labor Party, but most of the contenders within the party are interested in little more than power and pelf for themselves and their associates.

However, the significance of the PTB is that it still has the loyalty of the majority of the country's city workers. To them the PTB is still the party of Getulio. To them it is still the party of the small man, and most particularly of the worker. With the passing of Vargas, their hope was that the leadership of the party would go to Jango Goulart, who, they expected, would make the PTB a stronger vehicle of the social reform program (which the majority of workers still believe Vargas upheld).

The Partido Trabalhista Brasileiro has produced innumerable splinter parties. These include such groups as the Partido Nacional Trabalhista, the Partido Social Trabalhista, the Partido Trabalhista Republicano, and several more. These are generally the personal vehicle of some politician who found it impossible to assuage his ambitions for office within the PTB. They are of little real importance except for bargaining purposes—and because they sometimes shelter Communist candidates who are not allowed to run under their own colors.

The Partido Social Progresista. Another party which can generally be classed in the pro-Vargas grouping is the Partido Social Progresista (PSP), the personal property of ex-Governor Adhemar de Barros of the state of São Paulo. Adhemar, as he is popularly called, is one of the most colorful politicians in Brazil. A doctor who has rarely, if ever, practiced medicine, Adhemar got his political start under the tutelage of Vargas. He was made "interventor" of the state of São Paulo and held that post throughout most of the dictatorship.

During his tenure in the post of interventor, Adhemar became immensely wealthy. After the end of the dictatorship, he began to put this wealth to work on his own political behalf. He has never hidden the fact that he would like to be President of the Republic.

As the vehicle for his ambitions, he organized in 1946 the Partido Social Progresista and on its ticket won election as governor of the state of São Paulo for the 1947–1951 term.

In 1950 Adhemar was a sufficient power to be bought off by Getulio Vargas, once again seeking the presidency. Adhemar agreed to back Vargas in return for the post of Vice-President for a member of his party, João Cafe Filho. Although Cafe Filho turned out to be a bitter disappointment both to Vargas and Adhemar, as well as to their friends, the alliance of Getulio–Adhemar continued so long as Vargas lived.

The Partido Social Progresista is not a party of principle but of personalism. It is built around Adhemar and in different states has attracted different people. In one or two of the northeastern states it has the reputation for having in its ranks the regions' most honest politicians; in São Paulo its reputation for probity is something else again. In some areas the local political bosses, who generally have congregated in the PSD, are also to be found in the PSP. In any case, the PSP is a party of some national importance.

The Anti-Vargas Parties. On the anti-Vargas side, the most important force is the União Democratica Nacional, the UDN. This was established originally as a united front for everyone (from Communists to conservative businessmen) opposed to Vargas in the 1944–1945 period. The Communists deserted it in May 1945 when Prestes plumped for support of the continuance of Vargas in office. Subsequently, the UDN became a political party, first supporting General Eduardo Gomes—Dutra's opponent—in the 1945 presidential election.

The UDN is principally a middle-class party. It has a reputation for being very conservative. It is strongest among professional men, among businessmen not closely connected with the Vargas regime, and among some of the workers who feel that a degree of honesty is necessary in governmental affairs. Its program contains the same bows to social and labor legislation possessed by similar documents of other Brazilian political parties. It has within its ranks some of the survivors of the pre-1930 political arena, from whence perhaps comes its reputation for conservatism.

For many the UDN has been a great disappointment. Not only has it not come up with any challenging new ideas to confront the demagoguery of Vargas and those associated with him, but it also compromised from time to time in its opposition to Vargas himself. During part of his 1950–1954 administration, Getulio had members of the UDN in his cabinet. The UDN was the largest party in the coalition behind Janio Quadros in the 1960 election. It gained considerable ground with his victory, but suffered a serious setback in the crisis leading to Janio's resignation in August 1961.

Also part of the anti-Vargas faction of Brazilian politics is a group of small parties which have arisen since the end of the *Estado Novo*. These include the Partido Libertador, a group with its main strength in Vargas' own state of Rio Grande do Sul, with glorious traditions dating to the last century but little influence at the present time; the Partido Democratico Cristiano, patterned after the European Christian Democratic movements; and the Partido Socialista, which has sought to become an orthodox democratic Socialist party, but has never been able to break away from the conflicting pulls of Vargas and Prestes.

Communists and Integralistas. Two parties can be labeled as being neither Vargasista nor anti-Vargasista. These are the Partido de Representacão

Popular (PRP), and the Partido Communista. The former is the one-time Integralistas, the "green-shirt" fascists of the 1930's whose leader, Plinio Salgado, returned from exile in 1945 but has not been able to build up more than a relatively small following in the intervening years. The PRP claims to be the most democratic of the democratic parties now that Fascism is in ill repute.

In 1958 the Partido Communista was probably the strongest party of its kind in Latin America. Starting with a handful of followers early in 1945, the party grew rapidly in membership during the succeeding two years. However, most of its growth at that time came from the personal attractiveness of its principal leader, Luiz Carlos Prestes, famed guerrilla warrior of the 1920's (before he became a Communist) and an almost legendary figure in Brazilian history.

In 1947 the party was outlawed and its national deputies and senators were removed from office. Since that time the party has suffered intermittent persecution which has served to "disillusion" the opportunists who joined its ranks in the period of euphoria, and which has resulted in the forging of a much more disciplined and better organized party.

The Communists gained ground after Vargas' death largely because of lack of effective opposition. So long as Getulio was alive, his personal magnetism served to keep them in check. However, after his death, the Communists increasingly pictured themselves as his successors, the continuers of his work "for the poor" and the defenders of the "national sovereignty." They seriously infiltrated the Partido Trabalhista, and in the congressional elections of 1958 had a national alliance with the PTB, electing several members of congress on the Trabalhista ticket. The 1958 poll indicated that the Communist Party still had a considerable way to go before it became one of the major parties, in vote-getting terms. Some elements in the PTB felt that their party had lost more than it had gained from the alliance with the Partido Communista do Brasil. In 1960 the PCB supported the unsuccessful candidacy of General Lott.

The Communists in Brazil are particularly dangerous because of their connection with the military. Prestes still has a certain prestige in the ranks of the armed forces and the party has been quite successful in lining up military names for various petition campaigns and other "front organization" ventures.

The great tragedy of Brazilian politics since 1945 has been that there has not appeared a reasonably honest party of the democratic left with leaders capable of attracting the workers and lower middle class.

The Aftermath of Vargas' Death

The death of Vargas and the events which succeeded it precipitated a serious political crisis in Brazil. For a year the government was in the hands of João Cafe Filho, Vargas' Vice-President. He attempted to put an end to the Vargas Era, clean up the administration, and bring order into the chaotic economic situation. However, the elements supporting him lost out in the election of October 1955 to Jucelino Kubitschek.

The months between Jucelino's election and his inauguration in January 1956 were a period of tension. In November the Minister of War, General Lott, deposed President João Cafe Filho to forestall, he said, a move to prevent Kubitschek's inauguaration. This split the armed forces wide open for the first time in more than a decade. Since before the end of the Vargas dictatorship, the army had been the stabilizing element in the country's political situation. It had pledged itself to the preservation of constitutionalism, had forced Vargas out in 1945 when he gave evidence of not wanting to fulfill his promise to hold elections. It guaranteed the tenure in office of Dutra from 1946 to 1950 and thwarted attempts to prevent Vargas from taking office again in 1950. Finally, it forced Vargas out again in 1954 when the army leadership felt that his policies threatened the continuance of a constitutional regime.

However, the actions of General Lott in November 1955 divided the army and put the navy and air force in the opposition, politically speaking. Furthermore, the defeat of General Juarez Tavora in the 1955 election convinced many anti-Vargas politicians that the only way out was another revolution.

In spite of these political difficulties, the expansion of the Brazilian economy continued apace under President Jucelino Kubitschek. He carried through the gigantic program for building an entirely new capital city in the Goyaz region of central Brazil, seven hundred miles from the coast. Although this project strained the country's foreign exchange resources to their limits and, in 1959 tripled the rate of inflation which had become "customary" since World War II, the building of Brasilia undoubtedly represented a significant step in the drive to open up the country's vast hinterland.

The election campaign of 1960 centered largely around the issues raised by Kubitschek's economic program, particularly the increased rate of inflation and the corruption which had reportedly surrounded the building of

Brasilia. Pledged to a continuance of the Kubitschek policies was the PSD candidate, Marshall Henrique Teixeira Lott, whose running mate was Partido Trabalhista leader João Goulart. Running as the nominee of the opposition was former São Paulo governor Janio Quadros. The victory of Quadros seemed to promise a definitive end to the Vargas era in Brazilian politics. However, his sudden resignation in August 1961 left the government to Getulio's chosen heir, João Goulart.

In spite of serious inflation and desperate foreign-exchange crises, the nation was still booming in 1961, its potentialities without horizon. If the Brazilians are able to avoid the Scylla and Charybdis of a military dictatorship and a Communist regime, their nation will, within the next generation, become one of the great economic powers of the earth and one of the pillars of democratic society.

CHAPTER III

The Dramatis Personae

Brazil is a nation of individualists. This is apparent in innumerable small ways even to a casual visitor. Take the country's favorite dance, the samba, for instance. Although in North American ballrooms the samba is taught as a definite, coordinated series of steps done in unison, in Brazil the dance is anything but that. Anyone who has watched the performance of the famous *escolas de samba* during a carnival period is well aware that the samba is what each individual dancer wants it to be. There is no standard way of doing the dance; whatever suits the fancy of the individual dancer is the "correct" way to do it.

In Brazil there is no proliferation of voluntary organizations—fraternal societies, brotherhoods, women's clubs, leagues of women voters, missionary societies, businessmen's lunch clubs (although with the growth of Rotary these are becoming more popular)—which are such a characteristic feature of the North American social structure. The Brazilian does not feel the urge to congregate in the same way as does the North American.

There are perhaps two basic reasons for this: first, there has not grown up in Brazil what we in North America would call "community spirit." Second, the needs which are in many cases satisfied by organizations in North America are met in Brazil by a complicated network of personal and family relationships which exist on a purely individualistic basis among most Brazilians.

The lack of community spirit is in part the legacy of the old preindustrial patriarchal, large landholding system which was so characteristic of colonial, imperial, and early republican Brazil. In some measure, it is the legacy of the Roman Catholic Church in Brazil which tended to leave the individual alone so long as he met his formal religious obligations. The moralistic puritan forebears of North America often went to excesses, it is true, but they did leave a feeling that one's neighbor's problem is one's own problem.

It is also the legacy of a political system in which the army can overthrow governments and in which the parties are founded on the personality of leaders and not on principles. In a democracy a majority gains power through legal means. In Brazil, in the past at least, a minority could gain power through having a strong leader and through the support of the emperor (or later, the army) while the vast mass of the people counted very little in the calculations of the politicians.

Finally, this lack of community feeling is the legacy of the dictatorship of Getulio Vargas. By imposing a fixed system of social relations in industry, Vargas freed both sides from active responsibility. He twisted the old patriarchal traditions to make himself patriarch of all Brazil. He encouraged his propagandists to picture him as "father of the poor." Furthermore, by attempting to place everything in the hands of the state or organizations supervised by the state, the Vargas regime seemed to relieve the individual citizen of all responsibility for the welfare of his neighbor—and sometimes even of himself.

The lack of a feeling of responsibility for the fate of one's neighbor is particularly noticeable in the field of employer–employee relations. Under Vargas, the state took unto itself the settlement of all problems between the worker and his employer. At the same time the government social security system, minimum wage, and countless additional legislation seemed to make any interest by the employer or by individual citizens in the welfare of the workers superfluous. Later, this state apparatus was supplemented by the gigantic SESI and SESCI welfare organizations maintained by the employers organized as a group, and the smaller but important social welfare activities of the trade unions. All of these tended to make the individual employer say, "Let SESI do it," or "Let the unions do it," and feel relatively little responsibility himself.

The "Robber Baron" Period

Undoubtedly another factor in this situation is the period of economic development through which Brazil is now passing. The North American observer who knows a little about the history of his own country is frequently struck with the parallel between mid-twentieth-century Brazil and the United States in the 1870's or 1880's.

Great fortunes are being piled up by those who are leading Brazil's industrialization. With the Rockefellers, Morgans, and Carnegies of the United States eighty years ago, Brazil can match the Loides, the Lafers, and the Matarazzos of today. And there is the same lack of scruples among the robber barons of contemporary Brazil as existed among their counterparts in our own past. These gentlemen are eager to make a fast cruzeiro and they are not particular about how they do it.

This corruption is rife in the highest quarters in and out of government and has seeped down through the lower echelons of society. Undoubtedly one of its major causes is scarcity, which is such a general feature of the Brazilian scene. Foreign exchange is scarce; therefore those who control it are in a position to benefit greatly by its apportionment. Capital is scarce, so those who have it can demand a fancy price for transferring it to someone else. Even common everyday commodities are scarce and those who control sizable stocks of them can get a large profit, legal and otherwise.

All these factors have no doubt reinforced the natural tendency of the Brazilian to feel that he is on his own and must watch out first and foremost for his own welfare. If this were all there were to Brazilian society, there would be chaos indeed. However, there is in the background a powerful and complicated web of individual relationships among people of all classes and conditions of society which serves to hold the social structure together.

Personal Relationships in Business

These ties which provide the fiber of the Brazilian social fabric are remnants of the plantation society of Brazil's past. They are strongest in the rural districts, but they also exist in the cities, and even have their reflections in labor–management relations.

A foreman, for instance, has close personal relationships with many of those working under him. If he is liked, they will invite him to weddings, christenings, and funerals. He may also be asked to be the godfather of some of their children, and he is honor-bound to accept such invitations, thus becoming their *compadre*. He, in turn, can freely call upon his *compadres* to help him out. At the same time he is obliged to help them in an hour of need.

This relationship of *compadre* is a key one. The Brazilian does not ask just any important person to be *padrinho* (godfather) to his children. However, if he has some relationship with a person who is important in his own sphere, he will often ask that person to be *madrinha* (godmother) or *padrinho*.

For instance, a middle- or upper-class lady may have as many as thirty godchildren. Perhaps half a dozen or so of these will be relatives, but the others are likely to be sons or daughters of former servants, or even of the plumber who regularly visits the house. The lady in question must remember the birthdays of all these children; and from time to time most of them will come to call upon her, just to keep alive the relationship. If ever any of them, or their parents, should be in trouble they have the right to call on her for help.

Another unique relationship is that between a certain kind of servant and her ex-employers. Many families have the custom of taking young girls of ten or eleven years of age into service and virtually bringing them up. Once these servant girls have grown up, they enjoy a family-like relationship with their ex-employers. These relationships are useful in obtaining all kinds of influence. This system of interrelationships is supplemented by a very complicated series of family connections. One is a "cousin" even though in the United States the connection would seem to be extenuated.

Of course, the impact of urbanization is undermining this system. However, it is still strong enough to provide much of the cohesiveness of Brazilian society.

Racial Composition

The average Brazilian is likely to have ancestors who came from at least two continents. The country is in a true sense a melting pot of races. In 1835, soon after independence, Brazil's population included 51.4 per cent Negroes, 18.2 per cent mulattoes and other mixed bloods, and 24.4 per cent people of more or less pure European descent. A century later those listed as whites accounted for 60 per cent of the total population and people of color only 40 per cent.[1] The figures for the racial distribution of the Brazilian population as of 1950 are shown in table 3.[2]

Table 3. Racial distribution of Brazilian population.

Race	Population	Percentage
White	32,027,661	61.7
Negro	5,692,657	11.0
Mulatto	13,786,742	26.5
Asiatic	329,082	0.6
Unknown	108,255	0.2
Total	51,944,397	100.0

When looking at these figures, one must bear in mind that the Brazilian concept of race is rather different from that in the United States. One is only likely to be classified as a mulatto if one has distinctively Negroid characteristics. Hence, in all probability, the percentage of Brazilians with at least one African ancestor is probably considerably higher than these figures would indicate.

The increased percentage of people of European origin by the middle of the twentieth century is accounted for by the fact that the country received an estimated net immigration between 1872 and 1940 of about 3,300,000 people.

The Race Problem. It is not true to say, as do many Brazilians, that there are no race problems in Brazil. There are. There is undoubtedly social discrimination against people of clearly Negro caste. A white family would cavil at having their daughter marry a decidedly Negro boy. There are few Negroes of high rank in the army, and reportedly none in the navy.

However, the general attitude of Brazilians is favorable to assimilation. One hears much about "whitening the population," by which is meant the intermarriage of Negroes with people of lighter complexion with the ultimate disappearance of the full-blooded African descendant.

The polyglot nature of the Brazilian population did present one handicap for many years. It engendered a feeling of inferiority in the Brazilians. Right after World War II it was common to hear a Brazilian lament that his country would never amount to anything because of the large number of Negroes in the population. This attitude was undoubtedly a holdover from the past, an unconscious acceptance of the old slave society's dictum that the Negro was inferior. It was perhaps also a reflection of the fact that the Brazilian Negro has, to a much greater degree than his North American counterpart, maintained the customs and beliefs of his African ancestors— and other Brazilians felt that this resistance to cultural assimilation would be a handicap in the development of Brazil as a whole.

However, this inferiority complex of the Brazilians is disappearing rapidly. In the decade subsequent to World War II the average urban Brazilian, at least, became conscious for the first time of the potentialities of his nation. He became much more imbued with national pride and with a belief in the destiny of his country; his desire for "progress" was stimulated, and his support for economic development and industrialization was mustered.

The Entrepreneur

Most of the important industrial enterprises of the country are one-man or family firms, or at most are very closely held partnerships. Generally, one finds that the principal owner is the top management person in the enterprise, or at least that a member of the principal owner's family is in a top managerial post.

There are many examples of this kind of family firm. Outstanding are the Matarazzo interests of São Paulo, a multi-purpose firm, and probably the country's largest single industrial and commercial enterprise; the Renner firm in Rio Grande do Sul, which started out making clothing but has branched into a number of other industries; and the Suerdieck tobacco company in Baia.

In recent years many of these family firms have been legally transformed into corporations without, however, ceasing to be closely held. Tax advantages, a desire for legal continuity, and other factors have undoubtedly motivated this legal conversion of private firms into corporations. However, the family firms are often careful to see to it that their stock does not get into the hands of the general public. One thing, however, which has forced many such companies to sell stock to the public in recent years is the fact that the rapid growth of their operations has outstripped their ability to plough back profits or to borrow from the banks. Credit is hard to get and expensive, going as high as 3 per cent a month.

There is still considerable resistance among the general public to investing in stock. For one thing, there is still a hangover from the old agricultural mentality of the Brazilian in his preference for real estate. Another is that stock brokering itself has a bad name in Brazil. There is a long history of stock swindles which makes people suspicious of purchasing shares even in recognized and respectable companies.

There are various types of stock purchasers. One is the businessmen who have their own firms but want to diversify their holdings. Another includes professional people, such as lawyers, doctors, and dentists. A very good market is provided by foreigners resident in Brazil. Stock shares are for the most part made out to the bearer, which makes it very difficult for home countries' income tax collectors to check up on holdings. Furthermore, foreign owners of stock in Brazilian firms can take out their dividends in foreign currency without any restriction—at the free market rate of exchange.

Industrial shares are traded in the stock markets of Rio and São Paulo. However, in Rio such trading goes on only between 2:00 and 2:30 P.M. During the rest of the afternoon the stock brokers buy and sell government bonds—state and federal; in the mornings the market is engaged in the auctioning of foreign exchange. As yet, private stock shares are a relatively small part of the volume of those few markets in which they are handled. Only a few firms, such as the Brahma brewing company, have their stock traded in virtually every day. Some stocks may not be traded in for months.

Management Personnel. There are few companies whose stock is so widely held that the control of the firm is no longer in the hands of the family which founded the enterprise. As yet, there is relatively little room "at the top" for bright young business school graduates—even if there were to be such graduates available to move up the ladder. It will in all likelihood require several generations more before the tightly held Brazilian manufacturing concern has become a "public corporation."

As for the ranks of "middle management," it is probably true that "who" one knows is still considerably more important than "what" one knows, insofar as obtaining a position is concerned. The elaborate management training programs so common in North American businesses are as yet unknown in Brazil. The young manager is still trained largely by experience.

The first School of Business Administration was only recently opened in the University of São Paulo, with the help of a group of United States professors. One of the projects which these North Americans established was an extensive management training program, the first of its kind in the country. Its students are themselves businessmen very eager to learn. But the North Americans in charge had the feeling that their students' knowledge of modern management procedures was as yet extremely rudimentary.

So far the Brazilian businessman has not acquired the idea of selling a large quantity at a low margin of profit. This is perhaps not surprising since individual industrialists have frequently found themselves in a favored, almost monopolistic position. There is so much to be done and there are so many fields in which the budding industrialist can invest his money, time, and effort that he does not in most cases need to be seriously concerned with competition or searching for the consumer.

Furthermore, it is probably true to say that the Brazilian businessmen are highly cartelized. The corporate state setup of the Vargas dictatorship, most of which is still intact, provides a perfect cover for agreements among the businessmen who belong to the government-sponsored *sindicatos,* federations, and confederations. Indeed, the system whereby the Banco do Brasil consults these organizations before it makes foreign exchange available to a businessman who wants to import foreign machinery or raw materials, makes it possible for the existing industrialists to bring influence to bear to prevent "unfair" competition.

On the other hand, the very shortage of foreign exchange which has plagued Brazilian industrialists since the end of World War II makes the industrialist somewhat more cost- and productivity-conscious.

Productivity. So far, most of the interest in productivity problems has been centered in the process of selecting the right worker for the right job (which will be discussed elsewhere in this volume), and related problems. There has been relatively little done to train managerial personnel in better management techniques, although there are some moves in that direction under way. We have already noted the creation of a School of Business Administration at the University of São Paulo.

There has been a good deal of discussion on this problem but few of the state federations of industry have taken concrete steps in improving the qualifications of managerial personnel. The Federacão das Industrias do Distrito Federal, which includes industrialists of Rio de Janeiro and its immediate environs, established a Productivity Center in 1953. It organized a group of productivity experts who visited some twenty factories in Rio to study production methods. These experts talked frankly with the factory owners, showing them ways in which they could be more efficient. However, the federation received discouragingly little response from its efforts.

The Minas Gerais industrial federation has had better success. It has sponsored a program of training within industry, based on North American patterns, which began in February 1955. The courses were given on two levels—in the factory for lower management and in the federation head-quarters for higher management. There was more emphasis on human relations in courses for the higher management personnel, more emphasis on organization of production for the lower management people.

The Federation of Industry of the Federal District has approached productivity from a somewhat different angle. Early in 1956 it announced the formation of the Companhia Brasileira de Productividade. The plans for this new enterprise, as they were announced by the federation, were broad:

Divided in three sectors, it can attend to the interests and aspirations of the technicians, providing them possibilities for expansion within a system of cooperation and free enterprise. It can arouse the interest of the entrepreneurs through facilities and protection of the capital markets and guarantees of profitability of investments, through helping meet the demand for technical assistance, for rationalization of labor, administration, planning, technological innovations, etc. while at the same time taking care of the superior interests of cultural expansion and scientific progress. In an exchange of information it can maintain the highest level of knowledge and ability; and finally, it can expand its financial and economic resources, while at the same time taking care of the interests of the stockholders.[3]

The Institute of Selection and Professional Orientation of the Getulio Vargas Foundation, a semigovernmental enterprise, which is principally concerned with personnel testing of laborers, also offers courses to personnel people in industry and to some government officials interested in the general field. These courses have covered a wide range of subjects, from the history of psychology to the psychology of industrial relations. The institute also publishes a periodical on applied psychology, which carries some material on industrial relations problems.

This does not add up to say that there are not efficient firms in Brazil. There are undoubtedly many entrepreneurs and managers who, without the elaborate training of "organization men" in North American industry, have learned how to run their enterprises with commendable efficiency.

The Case of the Fabrica Nacional de Motores. Perhaps one can cite an instance to indicate the effect of improved managerial techniques upon a single Brazilian firm. The case in point is a government-controlled firm, hence not typical. But improved management has brought about dramatic results in terms of output, labor relations, and profit.

The Fabrica Nacional de Motores, mentioned before in relation to government aid to industry, was notorious until 1954 for the inefficiency of its management by military men. Established originally to build airplane motors, it had since its opening in 1948 been principally producing spare parts for Ford, General Motors, Willys, and other firms, and a small number of trucks of its own make.

Faced with a lack of working capital, the Fabrica Nacional de Motores applied in 1954 to the Banco Nacional de Desenvolvimento Economico for a loan. The bank, which was not very receptive because of the bad reputation of the firm, finally agreed to grant the loan on condition that a member of the bank's staff be placed in charge of the industry.

This was done, and an entirely new managerial policy was laid down. The new director, Custodio Sobral Martins de Almeida, felt that the first need was to explain the aims of the new administration to the workers. He held a number of meetings with them emphasizing the importance of the enterprise to the economy of the country.

Sr. Almeida found that the wage level of the factory was so low that the workers looked on the plant as a training ground, and went on to get jobs in other metallurgical plants. As a result, he decreed a considerable wage increase. Furthermore, he established the policy of trying to deal with workers' complaints before they became serious.

On the production side, the new management decided to concentrate on a single line of heavy-duty trucks. For this purpose an arrangement was made with an Italian motor company to use on license the model produced by that firm. The company also established the policy of building up suppliers of parts for their trucks and by 1956 had some one hundred firms producing parts for the FNM.

The results of this change in management of the Fabrica Nacional de Motores were striking. On the labor side, workers' complaints were dealt with by the firm's labor relations people in strong contrast with the previous situation in which virtually all grievances found their way to the labor court at great expense to the firm. Production results were equally notable. The year before the new administration (and the best year under the old regime) the company produced 373 trucks, and in April 1956, they had attained the rate of 300 per month.

The Immigrant

The immigrant has played a leading role in the development of industry in Brazil. Although so far as we know there are no statistics available on this subject, it seems highly likely that the majority of the larger industrial enterprises were originally set up by immigrants.

This statement is borne out by a study by Emilio Willems, a Brazilian sociologist, in the statistical yearbook of São Paulo. Willems "found that out of 714 industrial enterprises of various sizes, 521 were owned by immigrants or descendants of immigrants." [4] In the northern and northeastern parts of Brazil the successful immigrant industrialist was more likely to have been a Portuguese, though the German-founded tobacco manufacturing firms of Baia are an exception to this. In the south the immigrant was more often an Italian, a German, or an Arab. In recent years a few United States citizens have moved to Brazil and established growing industrial enterprises.

However, in the state of Minas Gerais the local Brazilian entrepreneurs have been more important than any immigrant groups. In the southernmost state of Rio Grande do Sul it has not been so much the actual German or Italian immigrants who have established industries as their sons and grandsons.

From what class do the industrialists come? Here, too, there seem to be regional variations. In the north and northeast the person who goes into industry is usually a merchant who invests a part of his profit in textiles, food processing, or some other enterprise. In the south the majority of the industries seem to have been built up by successful artisans or mechanics who, ploughing back their profits into the business, have within a comparatively short span of years been able to build workshops into small factories, small factories into larger ones and, in many cases, into truly gigantic enterprises.

In the south, too, another group has been important. Since the Revolution of 1930, men who started out as politicians, army officers, or financiers, but who, in any case, had close connections with the government of Getulio Vargas, loomed large in the group of industrial pioneers.

The old landholding class has seldom become interested in industry. Again, the state of Minas Gerais is something of an exception. In that state the local agriculturists and grazers in a considerable number of instances have gone into manufacturing. This is notable in the textile industry. Perhaps another minor exception is found in the sugar-growing state of Pernambuco in the northeast where some sugar plantation owners have gone into sugar refining and from that into other branches of manufacturing. In recent years manufacturing firms in one field of industry have branched out into others.

The Foreign Investor

Of course, foreign investors have played a major role in paving the way for Brazilian industrialization and have taken some part in the actual growth of manufacturing. Most of the original railroads and public utilities were constructed by foreign firms. There has been a notable trend toward Brazilianization, however, since World War II. The Brazilians used blocked sterling accounts to repatriate British-owned railroads and likewise bought out smaller French enterprises. It is probably only a matter of time until the foreign-owned public utility firms will be absorbed by state enterprises.

One finds that General Motors, Ford, United States tire companies and, most recently, North American chemical concerns have established branch firms and plants in Brazil. French companies established pharmaceutical and perfume companies. In recent years the importance of German, Japanese, and Italian firms has been growing in Brazilian industry. The Mannesman Company has established a steel tube plant in Belo Horizonte in the state of Minas Gerais, while Mercedes Benz has a large automobile assembly plant near São Paulo. Japanese interests are contemplating establishment of a large steel plant in São Paulo state. An Italian firm has aided in reorganizing the government's National Motors Factory.

Top management in most of the foreign firms in Brazil still consists of nationals of the country from which the foreign investment comes. However, there is considerable pressure to have these firms use Brazilians in responsible positions.

The German, Italian, and British firms have the peculiar advantage of getting German-Brazilians, Italian-Brazilians, and Anglo-Brazilians for many of their middle–management positions, young men who in time may be able to take over the enterprise. As Japanese interests increase, it will be interesting to see whether they adopt a similar policy. Personnel officers, lawyers, accountants, and other fairly high ranking officials of these foreign-owned firms are generally Brazilian citizens. So one can see that in spite of the role played by foreign and government interests, industrialization is being brought about largely by Brazilian private interests.

The Worker

The Brazilian industrial working class stems from two principal sources—immigrants and their offspring who settled first in the big cities and other urban centers, and recent migrants from the countryside. The early growth of the cities of southern Brazil, where manufacturing first became important and where it is still chiefly located, was due principally to immigration. During the latter years of the nineteenth century and before the First World War, hundreds of thousands of southern Europeans came to Brazil, particularly to São Paulo. That city still has an Italian flavor.

Starting with World War I, European immigration began to slacken off and since that time the work force of the southern cities has been largely recruited from within Brazil itself. These two elements of the industrial work force present different kinds of problems. The earlier European immigrants, though they might not have spoken Portuguese very well, were in many instances literate in their own languages. They had at least the beginnings of a tradition of trade unionism and radical politics. In contrast, the newer migrants from the interior of Brazil were racially different, having a large amount of African blood, and were culturally behind their fellow workers of European origin.

The Brazilian worker is miserably poor. This is particularly the case in the cities north of Rio de Janeiro but it is also true in the south. The *favellas* of Rio de Janeiro are among the most depressing slums to be found anywhere. Hundreds of thousands of people live in the equivalent of American hobo jungles made of packing boxes and corrugated iron. Bad housing conditions and poverty in general are less marked in the more southerly parts of the country. As a result of his poverty the Brazilian worker suffers from under-nourishment. In such towns as Belem in the Amazon Valley and Recife and Salvador along the coast, thousands of workers are literally dying of slow starvation. Along with starvation come almost unbelievable health conditions —yaws, leprosy, and other scourges.

His Docility. The Brazilian worker has benefited relatively little from the increase in his country's industrial productivity in recent years. In spite of the miserable conditions in which he lives, he is a docile person. He has tolerance and a respect for the "patron" inherited from his plantation ances-tors. Although his class consciousness has been on the increase since 1945, he has not become as convinced as his Chilean brethren of the complete divergence of interest between himself and his boss. This is particularly true, of course, of the workers of the north and northeast. Those of São Paulo and other southern cities tend to be more class conscious and less docile.

The meekness of the Negro workers and, to a less degree, the mulattoes probably dates from slave times. It is also the result of religious and super-stitious beliefs and practices which are still strong. These beliefs and cult ceremonies give many Brazilians an outlet for frustrations which might otherwise be expressed through protest and rebellion against the status quo.

The native docility of the Brazilian worker has undoubtedly been rein-forced by the Vargas experience when he was encouraged to turn to the state and to the "father of the poor" for his rights and needs. In keeping with this relatively placid nature, the history of Brazilian labor relations is marked by few, if any, instances of violence which have characterized the histories of organized labor in Argentina and Chile.

His Ambitions. However, the Brazilian worker is not without ambition. This is particularly true of the Paulista (the São Paulo worker). The Paulista worker is always on the lookout for a better job. He shifts from one position to another, is a jack of all trades and master of none. He will go from metal working to construction, to textiles, to something else, if he finds that he can earn a little more money by doing so. This has impeded the growth of a really skilled group of workers. The Paulista worker is also very eager to own his own home. As soon as he is able, he will buy a little piece of land and eventually build a house in the center of his plot. When he has saved a bit more he will build a cement wall around this plot of ground. Then he is safely sealed off from his neighbors and may go for years without saying more than hello to them.

Of course, the number of workers who can do this is limited, even in São Paulo. But the desire for advancement on the part of the Paulista worker does indicate a considerably different attitude and philosophy from that in many other parts of the country.

Since the overthrow of the Vargas dictatorship in 1945 the urban worker has become increasingly interested in politics. However, he approaches this problem with a highly personalistic point of view. By 1946 virtually all Brazilian city workers were divided between the Partido Trabalhista and the Partido Communista. It was not the parties which attracted the workers' attention and loyalty, but rather their respective leaders, Getulio Vargas and Luiz Carlos Prestes. With the death of Vargas many workers turned to other "leaders" who they thought to be their protectors.

Most employers agree that the Brazilian worker was alert, clever, and quick to learn. His chief handicap is lack of education and training. The nature of the Brazilian worker helps to explain in part his exploitation. This same docility and tolerance could easily play into the hands of a totalitarian regime—Communist or otherwise—if it should come to power.

CHAPTER IV

Labor–Management Relations

Brazilian labor–management relations still bear the stamp of the so-called *Estado Novo* (New State). However, the history of organized labor and its dealings with the employers did not begin with Vargas' *Estado Novo*. During the two decades before World War I, the workers in Brazil's fledgling industries, on its docks and railroads, began to establish trade unions. Most of the leaders in this early labor movement were immigrants and they brought with them the ideas which were prevalent in the unions of their Italian, Portuguese, and Spanish homelands.

During this first period of the Brazilian labor movement, most of the unions were led by Anarchists. As early as 1909 these Anarchist unions were brought together in the country's first central labor body, the Confederacão Operaria Brasileira, which was headed by a German immigrant printing trades worker, Edgard Leuenroth. The COB held several congresses during the next twenty years, but found it extremely difficult to maintain continuous liaison among the nation's unions. The great distance separating the northern centers of unionism such as Recife, from the growing southern cities such as Rio de Janeiro, São Paulo, and Porto Alegre, and transportation difficulties militated against the growth of a strong central labor body at that time.

During World War I, the labor movement grew rapidly in Brazil as it did in most Latin American countries. An increase in industrialization and a rising price level both acted as spurs to unionization. There were important strikes on the railroads, in the printing trades, and in the textile industry.

However, this growth of unionism during the war was followed by a period of stagnation and decline during the 1920's. One reason was a bitter struggle for power between different ideological groups in the labor movement. The Russian Revolution had inspired considerable enthusiasm among the Brazilian Anarchist labor leaders, and many of them declared themselves Bolsheviks. Between these and their old Anarchist comrades there developed a bitter split. By the end of the 1920's the Communist forces had gained ascendancy over the Anarchists in the majority of unions.

Another reason for the relative decline of organized labor during the 1920's was the violent assault upon the unions by the governments of the period. The attitude of these administrations was summed up by the statement attributed to a leading politician of the period: "The labor movement is a problem for the police." With fine impartiality, the government treated all organized labor as subversive, and made the life of a union leader a harassed one.

The Revolution of 1930

The year 1930 marks a turning point in the history of organized labor and labor–management relations in Brazil. In October of that year a successful revolution—the first one since 1889—occurred, ousting President Washington Luiz and putting in his place Provisional President Getulio Vargas, former governor of the state of Rio Grande do Sul.

The 1930 Revolution marked the end of an era in Brazilian history. It terminated a period during which control of the government of the nation had been passed back and forth between the coffee planters of São Paulo and the agricultural and grazing barons of the state of Minas Gerais. It paved the way for government participation not only for other states, but for different social and economic groups. The revolution was carried out principally by a group of young military men known as the *Tenentes* (lieutenants) who had revolted unsuccessfully several times during the 1920's.

However, the man whom they put in power was not one of their own number. He was a wily little politician and rancher from the *gaucho* (cowboy) state of Rio Grande do Sul. Getulio Vargas had no intention of letting the *Tenentes* dominate his regime. An exceedingly skillful politician, he succeeded during the next quarter of a century in dividing the *Tenentes* (who never established a solid political party or movement of their own) into mutually antagonistic groups.[1] In a process later made famous by Juan Domingo Perón in Argentina, Vargas succeeded in constructing a regime which rested as much on the workers and on middle-class groups favored by his administration as it did on the armed forces.

One of the first decrees of the Vargas government was the Color Law (named after Getulio's first Minister of Labor, Lindolfo Color), which provided for the legal recognition of trade unions. This law set up a procedure by which trade unions could receive governmental sanction, after which the employers were legally bound to negotiate with them. However, the older labor movement generally fought these legalized trade unions. Neither the Anarchists nor the Communists (who were then in the midst of their so-called "Third Period" of extreme sectarianism and dual unionism) allowed unions under their control to seek legal recognition. They argued that the Vargas measure was a "Fascist" maneuver to undermine the existing labor movement and to weaken the labor organizations. There ensued a bitter struggle between the new unions of the Vargas regime and the older unions under Anarchist and Communist influence.

By 1935, however, the situation had changed. The Communist party had emerged from its Third Period sectarianism and had espoused a "Popular Front" policy. It allowed some of its unions to become "legal" and sought unity for the whole labor movement. In line with this policy, there was organized in 1935 a Confederacão Geral do Trabalho under Communist leadership which included both legal and illegal unions.

On the political plane the Communists also took the lead in establishing the National Liberation Alliance (NLA) composed of all groups opposed to the Vargas administration. The titular president of the NLA was Luiz Carlos Prestes, one of the most famous of the *Tenente* leaders, who, unlike most of his associates, had opposed the Revolution of 1930 and had joined the Communist Party to become its leader in 1935. The NLA included disillusioned *Tenentes,* Socialists, and trade unionists of various shades as well as Communists.

The National Liberation Alliance climaxed its activities with a short-lived military rebellion, principally in the northeastern city of Recife and the capital, Rio de Janeiro, in November 1935. The revolt was easily quelled, but it resulted in a strong campaign by the Vargas government to suppress trade unions under the control of the Communist Party and other dissident political groups.

The "Estado Novo"

Finally, in October 1937 Getulio Vargas cancelled the elections to choose his successor, threw out the democratic constitution of 1934, and proclaimed the *Estado Novo*. This new system of government was quite frankly copied after the Fascist corporate state constitutions of Italy and Portugal. Vargas dissolved the existing congress and proclaimed the reorganization of the state and the economy on the basis of "functional representation." All employers and all workers were to be brought into parallel organizations, and when this process was completed, a new kind of functional legislature would be established in the undetermined future.

The basic unit of the new corporate system was the *sindicato* (best translated as "union" or "trade union") which was to cover all workers or employers in a given trade or industry in each municipality. In a state in which there were five or more *sindicatos* of a specific kind (textile workers, printing trades workers, commercial employees, etc.), these were to be brought together in a state federation. In a field in which there were three or more state federations, these were to be brought together in a confederation. There were to be seven confederations of workers: industrial workers; commercial employees; sea, river, and air transport workers; land transport workers; communications and publicity workers; credit institution employees; and workers in education and cultural institutions. There was no provision for a central labor organization. A similar pyramidal structure was to be constructed by the employers' *sindicatos,* federations, and confederations. Finally, there was to be a National Confederation of the Free Professions (lawyers, doctors, etc.).[2]

To qualify for recognition under the new setup, existing trade unions and employers' organizations were permitted to modify their jurisdictions and titles (the name of each *sindicato* was set forth in the corporate state arrangement and in the Consolidacão das Leis do Trabalho which in 1942 codified the whole system). However, it was up to the Ministry of Labor whether recognition would be granted.

It was specifically provided that the *Estado Novo* framework would not prohibit the formation of workers' and employers' organizations outside the official apparatus. Insofar as the workers' unions were concerned, it was virtually impossible for them to function unless they had government recognition, since they could not use the labor courts and other arrangements for handling labor problems set up under the *Estado Novo*. They could not bargain with employers and were unlikely to have any funds. Hence, unions existing in 1937 either conformed with the *Estado Novo* or went out of existence.

Once recognized by the government, the *sindicato* was under the strict control of the Ministry of Labor. Elections could not be held without the approval of the ministry, which had the authority to pass on the qualifications of all candidates and could veto any candidate or any elected official who was deemed "subversive."

Finances were just as strictly controlled. The unions had to submit their budgets to the ministry for approval. Financial control was, in fact, one of the principal weapons which the government authorities held over the unions. The *Estado Novo* arrangement provided that all workers should contribute one day's pay a year to the *sindicato* setup, whether or not they wanted to "belong" officially to the *sindicato* of their trade or profession. This contribution was the *imposto sindical* (trade-union tax) and it gave the government its justification for interfering in the financial affairs of the unions.

The *sindicatos* established under the *Estado Novo* were not conceived as organizations for collective bargaining with the employers. To take the place of collective bargaining, the *Estado Novo* provided an elaborate system of labor courts, which would handle not only cases involving violations of labor law, but things which, under a collective bargaining system, would be handled through negotiations for a collective agreement and through a grievance procedure.

The function of the *sindicato* in relation to the employer was thus reduced to providing the worker with legal representation before the labor courts. To compensate for its loss of collective bargining functions, the *sindicato* was charged with providing its members extensive social services. In fact, this became the principal office of the *sindicatos* during the *Estado Novo*.

As a final control over the worker, the *carteira profissional,* or workbook, was instituted. Each worker was supposed to have a *carteira profissional* in order to get a job. Each employer hiring a worker had to note in the book when he was hired and for what kind of a job. If the worker should be relieved of his job, the date and reasons for this also had to be entered in the workbook. Employers hiring a worker without a workbook were subject to fines.

The framework provided for in the *Estado Novo* was never completely established in fact. Several thousands of *sindicatos* were organized. However, by the end of the *Estado Novo* in 1945 only a relatively small number of federations of workers' *sindicatos* had been established and no confederations had been set up.

On the employers' side, there was supposed to be a hierarchy of organizations parallel to those of the workers. However, during the *Estado Novo,* the employers showed a marked lack of enthusiasm for joining these official groups. Relatively few employers' *sindicatos* were set up. In those states in which employers' federations were established, they usually violated the framework provided for in the Consolidacão das Leis do Trabalho. Instead of all metallurgical employers or all textile employers or all shoemaking employers in a state, forming state federations, the pattern was for all *sindicatos* of industrial employers to join together to form a Federacão da Industria in a state; and for all *sindicatos* of commercial employers to form a Federacão do Commercio. National confederations of commerce and of industry were also established.

It is notable that government control over the employers' organizations throughout the *Estado Novo* period was more lax than it was over the workers' groups. Nevertheless, most employers wanted to have as little to do with the official setup as possible.

In addition to legislation to regulate relations between workers and employers, the Vargas government during the *Estado Novo* period enacted a good deal of legislation which permitted Vargas to picture himself as *o pae dos pobres* (father of the poor). This included minimum wage legislation, which went into effect for the first time in 1941, and the development of the social security system which, creaking and bureaucratic though it was, brought health protection to workers, and established retirement pensions.

The net result was to intensify an already strong tendency toward paternalism in Brazilian labor–management relations, substituting the government for the "father."

The *Estado Novo* officially came to an end in 1945. During the Second World War the Brazilian people began to believe that the war was a conflict for the preservation of democracy. Getulio Vargas was forced by widespread public pressure to promise presidential elections for the end of 1945.

Also, the Vargas administration late in 1944 began to relax the control which it had exercised over the workers' organizations. It began to permit relatively free elections in many of the *sindicatos,* with the result that opposing factions gained control of a number of them.

In spite of his promises, Vargas was not eager to give up his power. This became evident early in 1945 when officials of the Ministry of Labor and of the *Estado Novo* trade unions organized the Partido Trabalhista Brasileiro (Brazilian Labor Party), the chief objective of which was to solidify the Vargas forces politically and to push for the reelection of *o pae dos pobres.*

In May 1945 Vargas found an unexpected ally in Luiz Carlos Prestes and the Communist Party. The month before, the government had decreed a general amnesty which included freeing Prestes who had been in jail since 1936. In his first speech after release from prison, the Communist leader astounded his friends, and pleased Getulio, by urging Vargas to stay in power, adding that it would be "betrayal" for him not to do so. Instead of an election for President, Prestes urged the election of a constitutional assembly to put an end to the *Estado Novo.*

From May to October 1945 the Communists and the Trabalhistas worked closely together both in the general political arena and in the labor movement. The Communists adopted the tactic of working within the government-established trade unions rather than setting up rival organizations of their own. They were undoubtedly motivated by the great difficulty which they knew would face any parallel independent trade-union movement, and by the fact that if they could capture the government-sponsored trade-union movement they would have the funds of the *imposto sindical* at their disposal.

For about a year the Communists worked toward the establishment of state federations of labor which were not provided for in the *Estado Novo*. A series of trade–union congresses were held in the principal states, and the results of these meetings generally placed the leadership of the state organizations in the hands of the members of the revived Communist Party. The supporters of Vargas participated in these congresses so long as he was in power. On a national level, the Communists worked through the Movimento de Unificacão Trabalhista (MUT) which was completely under their control and which sought the establishment of a national central labor organization.

The MUT finally called a congress to meet in the middle of September 1946 for the purpose of forming the Confederacão dos Trabalhadores do Brasil. However, the Ministry of Labor tried to head off this movement by outlawing the MUT and by calling its own national labor congress a couple of weeks earlier than that called by the Communists. Finally, agreement was reached by the ministry and the officials of the MUT to hold a joint congress.

This national labor congress broke up in confusion. The Communists and some of the supporters of Getulio Vargas established their CTB, and the delegates who were more closely allied with the Ministry of Labor declared their intention of filling out the framework of the *Estado Novo* setup by establishing the national labor confederations—of industrial workers, commercial workers, etc.——provided therein.

Meanwhile the Vargas regime was overthrown in October 1945 when Getulio's actions led the army to believe that he intended to cancel the elections he had promised for December. The election was held in December as scheduled, and General Eurico Dutra was named President, while a constitutional assembly (which was also to be the first congress under the new constitution) was chosen simultaneously. Getulio Vargas was elected senator from his native state of Rio Grande do Sul, and a large number of his supporters were elected as members of the Partido Trabalhista Brasileiro and the new, more conservative Partido Social Democratico. Luiz Carlos Prestes was elected as Communist senator from the Federal District, and fourteen other Communists were also named to the new constituent assembly.

Post "Estado Novo"

After the fall of the *Estado Novo* the situation of the unions changed various times. From 1945 until the outlawing of the Communist Party and the CTB in 1947, there was a considerable development of independence on the part of the trade-union movement. An increasing number of unions entered into collective bargaining negotiations with their employers, bypassing the *Estado Novo* setup. The unions remained divided largely between supporters of Vargas and supporters of Prestes, while the trade-union officialdom was split among Communists, Vargasistas, and those allied with Dutra's Ministry of Labor.

From 1947 to 1950 there was a period of retrogression insofar as the independence of the labor movement was concerned. The Dutra government did not allow any elections in the unions, the persecution of the Communists was more or less intense—although they continued to publish their daily newspapers in Rio and other important cities, and continued to have considerable influence among the workers.

With the reelection of Getulio Vargas as President in 1950, relaxation of government controls over the labor movement was resumed. Elections were held in the unions and the rank-and-file support of the Communists was reflected to a certain degree among the newly elected officials. However, the executives of the federations and confederations continued to be composed largely of Vargas supporters. Most of these officials had supported Vargas in his 1950 election campaign and they continued to support his regime as long as it lasted.

However, during the four years of his second presidency, Getulio lost a great deal of support. He had been elected with the enthusiastic backing of most workers in 1950 because they hoped that he would be able to do something to overcome inflation. But the inflation got worse instead of better under Vargas and the workers began to turn against him.

At the same time, the Communists also lost a good deal of support. This was only due in small measure to the fact that their top leaders were persecuted by the government. In fact, this persecution did not interfere seriously with the functioning of the party. The workers turned against them because of their zigzagging policies and because it was becoming clear that Communist loyalties lay outside of Brazil.

During his one year as Minister of Labor, from 1953 to 1954, João Goulart (popularly known as "Jango"), a young protégé of Vargas from Rio Grande do Sul, attempted to recoup some of Vargas' popularity for his own benefit. He acted with the connivance of Getulio himself. Jango engaged in violent polemics with the high-echelon labor leaders commonly known as *pelegos* who cooperated with the Ministry of Labor no matter who controlled it. In June 1953 he joined with Communists and other dissident elements in a national maritime strike which he finally "settled" with a great flourish. As a result of these activities he made himself Getulio's logical heir in the eyes of the workers, but he was forced to resign in the middle of 1954 by pressure of the army.

Getulio Vargas' career came to a cataclysmic end in August 1954 when, faced with an army ultimatum that he take a "long vacation," he committed suicide. Getulio left behind him two suicide notes which pictured him as champion of the workers and the downtrodden, and the defender of the nation's sovereignty. The notes proclaimed that those elements who forced him out did so because they were opposed to the benefits which he had brought to the workers, and because they resented his defense of Brazil in its foreign economic relations.

For a year after Vargas' suicide, the government was in the hands of his Vice-President, João Cafe Filho, who steered a conservative course, cracking down on Communist and Getulista labor leaders, and acting in general as if the Vargas interlude in Brazilian history were at an end.

The administration of Jucelino Kubitschek, which came to power in January 1956, further relaxed the government's control over the trade-union movement. It refused to exercise the authority given it to veto Communists elected to office in the unions. It also prepared for submission to congress several important changes in the Consolidacão das Leis do Trabalho which would put more emphasis on collective bargaining and less on the use of the government labor courts.

The period subsequent to the overthrow of the *Estado Novo* regime was marked by a change in the attitude of many employers toward the official government labor relations setup. Employers became much more active in establishing *sindicatos,* and in using them in their relations with both the workers and the government.

There are undoubtedly several reasons for this. On the one hand, government intervention in the internal affairs of the employers' *sindicatos* was virtually ended, and the employers were able to run their organizations with very little fear of what the government's attitude might be.

On the other hand, the government became much more insistent on dealing only with those employers' organizations which were part of the official labor–management mechanism. Under the *Estado Novo* the government had been perfectly willing to deal with other employers' groups, but under succeeding regimes it turned more and more to official organizations to seek the point of view of the industrialists and merchants concerning government policies and the relations of those groups with their workers.

Finally, there is no doubt that the growing strength and militancy of the unions forced the employers to belong. Although the unions were still far from being a free labor movement, direct negotiations with the employers were becoming more common and the employers therefore felt the need to counter the workers in this field with organizations of their own.

Although labor–management relations have thus evolved considerably since the end of the *Estado Novo*, they still remained very much under its shadow. The Vargas regime, though it had made the unions financially strong, had made them organizationally weak, subject to the dictates of the Ministry of Labor. The organizational structure of the trade-union movement in the middle 1950's was still that of the *Estado Novo*. The great majority of problems between workers and employers was still being settled through the mechanisms of the labor courts. State paternalism which had been established under the *Estado Novo* was still the most important feature of labor–management relations in Brazil more than a decade after the official end of the Vargas corporate state.

CHAPTER V

Government Control over Class Organizations

The *Estado Novo* provided for the establishment of "class" organizations to represent every conceivable type of employer and employee. Only those organizations recognized by the government were allowed by law to sign collective agreements or obtain *dissidios* from the labor courts. Although Getulio Vargas' corporate state supposedly ended in 1945, most of the workers' and employers' representative organizations still conformed to its pattern more than a dozen years later. Although certain changes, which we shall note, had occurred in both workers' and employers' groups, the fundamental structure of labor–management relations and the laws governing them remained as it had when established.

The only workers' organizations legally empowered to deal with the employers and with the state are the *sindicatos,* federations, and confederations established under the Consolidacão das Leis do Trabalho (Consolidation of Labor Laws), the Labor Code decreed by Getulio Vargas. The activities of the workers' trade unions are quite different from those of the unions in the United States and Western Europe or even from those of Argentina and Chile.

Although a few unions have developed what North Americans would call collective bargaining, the principal job of the workers' unions is to help their members present grievances to the local labor courts. Much more important, however, are the social welfare activities of the workers' oganizations.

In an effort to weaken the unions and make them less concerned with labor–management relations, the Vargas dictatorship required them to use most of their funds for the maintenance of health services, schools, libraries, etc. In fact, the legal recognition of a union largely depended on whether or not it had an ample program in this field. This tradition persists.

Some unions maintain schools which are particularly beneficial since the public school system in most Brazilian cities is inadequate to deal with the large and growing grade school population. This relieves pressure on the government schools while making available educational facilities to children who might not otherwise have them. These good works, however, take up much of the unions' time, energy, and funds.

Workers' Federations

The second level of workers' organizations is the federation, usually composed of all those *sindicatos* of a particular branch of commerce or industry in a given state. Except for maintaining a bureaucracy and collecting the *imposto sindical,* the function of the federation is ill-defined. They also frequently provide legal assistance for workers whose cases come before the regional labor courts in the state capital.

In some cities, however, the federations play an active and important role in the trade-union movement. When local unions are too poor to maintain social services for their members, the social welfare activities are then handled by the federations, as is the case in the Amazon city of Belem.

In 1954 the Textile Workers' Federation of the state of São Paulo was very active in organizing local unions in cities in the interior of the state in which there were no textile workers' organizations and in helping local unions handle situations which arose with employers. When trouble occurs in a São Paulo town in which no textile union exists, the worker or workers involved get in touch with the federation. The grievance secretary of that organization investigates and tries to settle the problem peacefully. Sometimes the organization of a union follows such a case.

Of the nine *sindicatos* affiliated with the Paper Workers' Federation of São Paulo state, four were established due to the organizing activities of the federation. In 1956 three more were in the process of organization as a result of the federation's activity.

This federation is unique since it has taken the lead in establishing a Serviço Social for the paper industry in cooperation with the employers apart from the general SESI. This is the only known instance in which there has been established a "welfare fund" comparable to those in the United States. This fund is discussed more fully in Chapter VI.

Workers' Confederations

The workers' confederations, of which there are three—the Confederacão Nacional dos Trabalhadores na Industria (industrial workers), the Confederacão Nacional dos Trabalhadores no Commercio (commercial employees), and the Confederacão Nacional dos trabalhadores no Transporte Terrestre (land transport workers)—were for many years of doubtful use to the rank-and-file members of the unions. However, in the 1950's they became somewhat more productive.

For one thing, they began to provide legal assistance for those workers whose cases reached the top labor court, Tribunal Superior do Trabalho. In the second place, the confederations began to attempt to use their influence for or against legislation concerning the workers. The National Industrial Workers' Confederation established a National Advisory Council composed of professional people to help in the study and the drafting of legislation.

The leaders of the industrial and commercial workers' confederations became convinced by 1956 that they needed closer contact with the unions and their members since the leaders of the confederations could no longer count on the aid of the Ministry of Labor to keep them in office. The industrial workers' confederation established "delegations" in every state, the purpose of which was to make the unions aware of the activities of the confederation, and to aid the constituent unions as much as possible locally.

Although no general confederation of labor is allowed under Brazilian law, the existing labor confederations have taken a first, informal step toward bringing one into existence de facto. In 1955 they established a council, composed of the top officials of the three confederations.

The confederations are the only organizations allowed by law to have international affiliations. It was not until after the reelection of Vargas in 1950 that the law was modified to permit even this. The three confederations affiliated in 1952 with the International Confederation of Free Trade Unions (ICFTU). It is fair to say, however, that relatively few members of the unions are aware of this membership. The ICFTU and its American regional affiliate, the ORIT, have maintained an office in Rio de Janeiro in the headquarters of the National Confederation of Industrial Workers since 1952. Although this office has issued a monthly news bulletin in Portuguese, its impact on Brazilian labor has been small. Little attempt has been made to popularize the ICFTU while the rival World Federation of Trade Unions has been widely publicized by the Communist trade unionists.

The *sindicatos* in Brazil are prohibited by law from participating in politics. However they are the center of a great deal of "politicking" on the part of those parties vying for power in the Brazilian political arena. In 1961 the great majority of the country's trade-union officials were still officially members of the Partido Trabalhista Brasileiro, though, as we have already noted, they no longer played much of a role in directing the party.

The extent of the relationship between the PTB and the trade unions was amply demonstrated by an incident observed during a May Day demonstration in Porto Alegre in 1956. Most of the speakers on this occasion were leaders of the important *sindicatos* of the city. However, the final orator was the local leader of the PTB, who was greeted with more than ordinary applause. Few people seemed to find it strange that an official of the PTB, who belonged to no union, should be on a trade-union platform.

At its inception, the PTB drew most of its strength from Getulio Vargas. It was regarded by most urban workers as their own party. However, by the middle 1950's the PTB had been converted into a party of middle-class people seeking preferment in the government who depended upon the laboring class for votes. The PTB was in no way an ideological party; it had been built largely on the personality of Vargas and was continuing to a considerable degree on the prestige of his successor, João Goulart. Nor did the PTB carry on any kind of principled and disciplined work in the trade unions. Although it depended on trade unionists or votes of potential trade unionists for its popular support, and although most union officials had at least a token membership, the Partido Trabalhista did virtually nothing to carry on party work in the unions.

The Communists

The lack of ideology on the part of the PTB, and the voracious appetite of many of its leaders made the Partido Trabalhista Brasileiro susceptible to infiltration by better-organized and more determined political groups. By 1956 sizable segments of the PTB were under the influence of the Communists and several of the PTB's members of congress were considered to be fellow travelers. In the 1958 congressional election campaign there was an open political alliance between the PTB and the Communists, and this alliance was renewed in the 1960 presidential election.

The Communists from 1945 onward were the political group carrying on the best-organized and most consistent work within the Brazilian labor movement. From 1945 to 1947, many of the new trade-union leaders who appeared as a result of freer elections were members of the Communist Party. A number of these trade-union leaders became important figures within the party. Probably the majority of the 150,000 members claimed by the Communist Party before its suppression in 1947 were trade unionists, though the Communists never controlled the majority of Brazilian unions. Within the trade unions the Communists organized their forces and built a good core of party members wherever they had the opportunity.

During the years following the outlawing of the Communist Party by the Dutra government, the party lost much of its support within the unions and in the country at large. Its total membership fell to something like 60,000 by 1953. Only a few unions had a full slate of Communist officers. Many Communist union officials were ousted by the Ministry of Labor and in hundreds of unions the ministry named "interventors" to administer the organization. Union elections were not permitted from 1947 to 1950.

When union elections were once again authorized with Vargas' return to power in 1950, the Communists stayed as much in the background as necessary to avoid persecution by the Ministry of Labor which was still authorized to oust Communist union officials. They seldom put forward a completely Communist list of candidates for union office, both because they knew that they had lost ground among the workers, and because they knew that the government would disallow such a list of candidates should it win.

The Communists made full use of what are known in Brazil as *inocentes uteis* or useful innocents. Slates composed predominantly of non-Communists—Socialists, Trabalhistas, or independents—would contain a sprinkling of Communists and would get full Communist support in an election. Thus, throughout the second Vargas administration the Communists held positions in important unions, but in few cases could one say that the union was completely under their control. The same policy has been followed since Vargas' death.

Because of these factors it is hard to assess Communist strength in the labor movement. It is fair to say, however, that they had a great deal of influence in the lower-echelon *sindicatos* during the 1945–1947 period of relative trade-union freedom; that they still continued to hold the loyalty of a sizable number of workers during the succeeding three years though virtually all Communists were removed from official positions in the unions.

Also, during the second Vargas administration (1950 through 1954), the Communists were again able to elect a number of their own members to leadership in the unions though their popular support was probably less than it had been between 1945 and 1947. There existed a vacuum in trade-union politics during the second Vargas administration due to the simultaneous decline in the popularity of the Vargasites and the Communists, but no third group was able to capitalize on this. As a result, the Communist influence in both the unions and the PTB began to grow again after Vargas' death.

There are certain industrial centers where Communist strength has been particularly marked in the unions. One of these is the northeastern city of Recife. There is little doubt that among the maritime and textile workers of this city there has been a great deal of Communist influence. The Communists controlled the most important unions of the city during the 1945–1947 period and ten years later their power was still considerable. Another important center of Communist influence has been the city of Rio de Janeiro. The dock unions there, among the most important in the city, were almost completely under the influence of the Communists from 1945 on. During the period of the Communist Party's legality they also controlled the important public utility workers' unions of The Light (the public utility enterprise covering Rio and São Paulo). However, by the middle 1950's they had lost this foothold. Various industrial workers' unions of the region, notably the Metal Workers' *Sindicato* of the Federal District, were by 1956 very much under Communist influence though the officials of these organizations did not admit to Communist party membership. The Woodworkers' Union of the Federal District was in 1956 perhaps the most openly Communist group of all in Rio, boasting of its association with the Communists' World Federation of Trade Unions and carrying on considerable propaganda inside and out for Communist causes.

Communist influence was very great in the labor movement of São Paulo during the 1945–1947 period. The metal workers, printing trades workers, textile workers, all experienced periods of Communist control. From 1947 to 1955 this influence declined greatly. This was partly a reflection of its general decline throughout Brazil and partly due to the existence of political figures who were competing with both the Communists and Vargas for the loyalty of the workers.

However, by 1955 the Communists had begun to recoup their forces in the São Paulo trade-union movement. They were again fully in control of the Textile Workers' Union of the city of São Paulo and had captured the

Metal Workers' Union of the city (which had escaped their grasp a few years earlier) and had also succeeded in gaining control of the Textile Workers' Federation of the state of São Paulo which they had not controlled for half a decade. They were well on the way to dominating the whole of the labor movement of the city and much of the state.

The Communists have also been strong for more than a decade in the mining areas of the states of Minas Gerais and Santa Catarina. In the former state there are various mines, including iron, copper, and gold, and Communist influence in these unions is virtually absolute. Only in the iron mines of Minas is their influence of secondary importance. In the coal fields of Santa Catarina where the workers suffer great poverty the Communists also built up great influence in the unions right after the end of the *Estado Novo*.

One of the principal centers of Communist influence in the first years after the *Estado Novo* was the port city of Santos in the state of São Paulo. This is the second port of the country, in terms of goods handled, and is the chief exit point for the country's coffee crop. It had been a major center of Communist influence before the establishment of the *Estado Novo* and the Communists resumed their influence among the workers there—particularly the port workers—after the fall of the corporate state system.

However, by the middle of 1956 the Communists had lost most of their backing among the workers of Santos. One reason is that local unionists associated with the PTB conducted a particularly effective fight against the Communists in the workers' organizations. The Communists also met stiff opposition from local port authorities.

More important was the fact that the principal Communist trade-union leaders who had emerged from 1945 to 1946 broke with the party in the early 1950's at the time of a schism led by national committee member and ex-deputy José María Crispim. One of the principal figures in the Crispim group was Leonardo Roitman who had been the principal Communist trade-union leader in Santos and with his exit from the official party the Communists lost most of their grip on the local trade unions.

The causes for considerable Communist influence in the Brazilian labor movement have been several. In the first place, the Communists have been the only political element in the country which has worked in an organized way in the trade unions to form groups of party members in each union, to use the influence of this small but organized minority in determining the results of elections and in influencing the policies of the unions.

Because of well-organized caucuses within many unions, the Communists were able to force many non-Communist and sometimes even anti-Communist labor leaders to work with them out of fear of being ousted in the next election. These trade unionists, consciously or unconsciously, became tools of the Communists.

The Brazilian Communists, like their confreres in other countries, have placed great stress on the training and indoctrination of their members. Not only do they drill them constantly on party doctrine, they also prepare them for work in various outside organizations. Thus, Communist trade-union leaders are taught the niceties of parliamentary procedure and how to run or hinder a trade-union meeting. Their members are always willing and eager to do the "dirty work" in the unions and they are usually capable and devoted when such work is given them to do.

Very few other groups have seriously attempted to train trade-union leaders. Certainly the rival political groups operating in the labor movement have made little effort to do so. The only serious work in this direction which we encountered was being undertaken by the employers' organization, SESI, in the state of São Paulo, by the Confederation of Catholic Workers' Councils in Rio de Janeiro and the Federation of Catholic Workers' Circles in the state of Rio Grande do Sul. However, these efforts were started long after the Communists had already built up a solid core of trade-union leaders. In any case, such isolated efforts have a limited effect on the national trade-union movement as a whole.

The result of the training of Communist trade unionists has been that unions under Communist leadership are frequently the most efficient and most honest labor organizations. Although the Communists mobilize the unions under their control in support of the current Communist line and spend the union's money for this purpose, there has seldom been the kind of private graft and corruption in Communist-led organizations which unfortunately characterizes many of the country's other labor organizations.

Also, the Communists are frequently very effective in their dealings with the employers, preferring to deal directly with them. Many workers support the Communists because they know that, although they may use their organizations for their own political ends, they provide more effective and honest leadership on a purely trade-union level than do most of their rivals.

The Communists have been aided in their work in the trade unions by the general disesteem of the higher ranking leadership in the unions, a leadership inherited from the Vargas period. In fact, one of the Communists' chief elements of strength in the labor movement has been their unceasing attack on the *pelegos,* those high-echelon trade unionists who owe their position more to the support of the Ministry of Labor than to the rank and file or even to the secondary leadership of the trade unions.

When João Goulart as Minister of Labor in 1953 led a concentrated attack on the *pelegos,* these leaders felt themselves isolated and came to realize the need for closer contacts with the rank and file of the labor movement. This new attitude has been particularly noticeable in the National Confederation of Industrial Workers and the National Confederation of Commercial Workers.

After 1953 the ex-*pelegos* were increasingly heard urging the workers to resort to collective bargaining instead of the governmental machinery. They also urged the government to give greater independence to the labor movement as a whole. Undoubtedly one of the reasons for this new line was the fact that they had developed closer relations with the labor movement of the United States and some of them had even been to the United States to study labor–management relations there.

The ex-*pelegos* and many of the secondary non-Communist trade-union leaders seemed inclined by the middle 1950's to try to steer the country's labor movement into economic activities and away from politics. However, it seemed likely that these efforts might have come too late to be effective in the long run. If so, it would only be a matter of time until the Communists would be able to win control of these groups.

Another source of Communist labor strength has been the Communist press and propaganda. For the most part, the non-Communist newspapers in Rio and other cities have paid little attention to the life of the labor movement, except when some strike situation developed. Then these papers have usually been in opposition to the workers' organizations.

The Communist press, on the other hand, faithfully reports the day-to-day activities of the labor organizations. Not only is this true of the party's daily newspapers such as *Imprensa Popular,*[1] it is also true of its national weekly paper *Voz Operaria* which is intended largely for Communist Party members. Finally, the party has published a labor newspaper *Gazeta Sindical* which, though ostensibly non-Communist, has been edited by party members and stresses the party line in trade-union and other matters.

As we have already indicated, the Communists' chief rival for the loyalty of the workers, the PTB, has been an amorphous kind of party lacking an ideology and building its popularity solely on the prestige of Getulio Vargas.

On a national scale the Socialist Party, founded after the *Estado Novo,* made a half-hearted attempt to provide a "third force" rallying point for the country's workers. It conducted a certain amount of organized work in the trade unions but was never able to free itself completely from the opposing magnets of Vargas and Prestes. Instead of taking a forthright position against both, the Socialists wobbled back and forth between the two with catastrophic results for their work in the trade unions. After 1959 the Brazilian Socialists became followers of Fidel Castro.

Thus, the Communists have risen in the unions mainly because of lack of effective opposition. Their activities in the labor movement have also been aided by employers who label any militant trade unionist who tries to fight for his members' rights a "Communist."

One more word must be said about the Communists' activities in the Brazilian labor movement. This concerns their attitude toward the *imposto sindical.* During the 1945–1947 period when the Communists were gaining growing control they were very much in favor of the *imposto sindical* since they were more and more its beneficiaries. They strongly opposed attempts by Socialist Party members of congress to obtain legislation which would recast the whole framework of labor–management relations, giving greater independence to the labor movement and ending the *imposto sindical.*

However, during the 1947–1950 period, when the Communists lost most of their executive positions in the labor movement, they turned strongly against the *imposto sindical,* finding it "oppressive" and "Fascist." With the return once again of Communists to the trade unions after 1950, the party reversed its attitude arguing that the unions would be helpless without this sure source of funds.

Employers' Organizations

The Brazilian employers have a long tradition of organization. For instance, the Federation of Industry of the Federal District (city of Rio de Janeiro) traces its history back to 1830, soon after the achievement of national independence. It went through various name changes before taking its present title, Federacão da Industria do Distrito Federal, and being incorporated into the *Estado Novo* structure in 1941. The Confederacão Nacional da Industria is even older, dating back to 1826, but taking its present title in 1936.

In contrast to the situation among the workers, there still exist among the employers two groups of organizations, those recognized under the

Consolidacão das Leis do Trabalho and those registered merely as civil associations without any connection with the country's labor legislation. Often the latter organization is more powerful than the former.

In some cases the employers in industrial federations recognized under the Consolidacão maintain a parallel organization, known as the Centro Industrial with the same members and officers as the Federacão da Industria. This is done so that if the employers want to speak to the public more frankly than they could as the *federacão,* they have a vehicle to use.

During the *Estado Novo* days, the employers were not enthusiastic about joining the organizations established under the Consolidacão das Leis. They resented the government's extensive control and feared that they could not discuss their affairs freely in them. However, since 1950 there has been a growing tendency by the employers to join the *sindicatos,* federations, and confederations as we have noted.

Employers' Sindicatos. The employers' *sindicatos* negotiate collective agreements with the workers' *sindicatos* or represent the employers in the regional labor courts. Sometimes they participate in the handling of grievances, though this is rare. One such instance is the textile employers' *sindicato* in São Paulo. The secretary of this organization explained that an employer may ask this *sindicato* to help resolve some grievance and that sometimes representatives of the workers' union come in and ask the employers' *sindicato* to intervene.

In addition to labor relations, the employers' *sindicatos* serve their members in a variety of ways. In 1956 the perfume industry *sindicato* in São Paulo was particularly concerned with the tax problems of its members and was pushing legislation to get this tax reduced and to have some of its anomalies cleared up.

The glass industry *sindicato* of São Carlo, according to its office secretary, checks with all its members whenever a new patent is applied for to find out if they produce or have patents on this same product. If such is the case, the *sindicato* enters an objection with the Ministry of Labor.

Many *sindicatos* play a role in granting requests for foreign exchange to firms in their industry. Such requests are sent by a firm to the Banco do Brasil, which then turns the matter over to the *sindicato* without indicating which firm is making the application. The *sindicato* studies the case to find out which markets are the most reasonable and to consider other factors related to the situation. The *sindicato* has forty-eight hours to make its report to the bank.

Employers' Federations. The next step above the *sindicato* in the hierarchy of employers' organizations is usually the federation of industry or the federation of commerce of the state. There are twelve state federations of industry and approximately the same number of federations of commerce. Some of these, in the case of the smaller states, group more than one state under their jurisdiction.

These federations speak to the public and to the government for all of industrialists or merchants in their respective areas. For instance, soon after the inauguration of President Jucelino Kubitschek early in 1956, a delegation representing various federations of industry of the northeastern part of the country paid a visit to the new chief executive to present their program for the relief and economic development of that part of the country.

In some of the bigger states where there are large numbers of employers' *sindicatos,* not all of which are strong, the federation may serve as a central secretariat for many of its smaller affiliates. The outstanding example of this is the Federacão da Industria de São Paulo. Its Departamento Sindical conducts the affairs of some thirty-four employers' *sindicatos* which are not strong enough to have their own headquarters and staff. The Departamento Sindical, which has fifteen employees, organizes meetings of the thirty-four groups under its surveillance. It calls and administers elections in them. It makes up the financial statements which are required by law concerning both the past year's expenditures and income and the budgets for the coming year.

There is a similar arrangement in the state of Rio Grande do Sul. Most of the Federacão da Industria's twenty-eight *sindicatos* have their headquarters in the building of the federation, and their secretarial work is handled by the federation as are their finances. Most of the *sindicatos* hold their meetings in this same building.

Some of the federations offer special services for their members. For instance, the Federacão do Commercio of the state of São Paulo which has associated with it a group of bright young intellectuals, has established an Instituto de Sociologia e Politica. This organization has as its objective the improving of human relations in the state's commercial firms. They started their activities with a special course for labor relations directors. This was followed by other courses on Brazilian labor legislation, on human relations in business and other subjects. Although these courses started out being only for management personnel they were broadened to admit commercial employees as well.

In some of the poorer states the work of the federations is largely confined to supervising the work of the social welfare and vocational training institutions which are associated with them—the SESI (Serviço Social da Industria) and SENAI (Serviço Nacional de Aprendizagem Industrial), in the case of industrial federations and the SESCI (Serviço Social do Commercio) and SENAC (Serviço Nacional de Aprendizagem Commercial), in the case of commercial ones. This is the situation in both the federation of industry and the federation of commerce in the state of Pará, in the Amazon basin.

Employers Confederations. The Confederations of Commerce and Industry are at the top of the employer hierarchy in Brazil. The activities of these two organizations are varied. SENAI and SESI are departments of the Confederacão Nacional da Industria and SENAC and SESCI, departments of the Confederacão Nacional do Commercio. In addition, the CNI has a statistical section, administrative branch, and an economic staff.

The economic staff is one of the principal services rendered by the CNI to its members. Its job is to make special studies of problems of economic interest to industry which are pending at any given time. It also makes surveys of general interest to industrialists or special ones upon request.

The Confederacão Nacional do Commercio maintains a legal staff which handles labor cases appearing before the Tribunal Superior do Trabalho. It was carrying on a campaign in 1956 to build up the tourist industry, under a subdivision, the Conselho Nacional do Turismo. Like its sister organization, it has charge of the federations and *sindicatos* belonging to it.

Government Control

The *Estado Novo* wove a tight net of government control over the workers' and employers' organizations recognized under the Consolidacão das Leis do Trabalho. This control has been more restrictive of the workers' groups than of the employers' because the government felt that the employers' organizations were not as likely to be centers of "subversive" activity as were the workers' groups.

The ultimate goal of the Consolidacão das Leis do Trabalho was for all workers and all employers to be grouped in one section or another of the structure built on the basis of the Consolidacão das Leis. For every legally recognized workers' group there was to be a corresponding employers' organization.

Appended to the Consolidacão was a table showing a breakdown of the Brazilian economy and indicating workers and employers deemed suitable to be grouped in the same organizations. For instance, in the clothing industry the Consolidacão provides that shoemakers, men's shirt makers, men's tailors, umbrella workers, pocketbook makers, button workers, hatters, and women's tailors are each supposed to be organized in a separate union. There is no provision under the law for a garment union to encompass all of these specialized groups.

The basic unit of the *Estado Novo* system is the *sindicato*. The "second-grade" organization is the federation. Generally, the federations were to group together the various workers' or employers' *sindicatos* of a given trade, industry, or profession in a given state. However, there are some exceptions to this. On the workers' side there are a few national industrial federations which cross state lines, notably the Maritime Workers' Federation and the Railroad Workers' Federation.

Above the federations were to be the confederations. No confederation on the workers' side was established during the *Estado Novo*, though as we have noted the employers did have the Confederacão Nacional da Industria and the Confederacão Nacional do Commercio. The confederations were supposed to be national-wide amalgrams of workers' or employers' federations in a wide, economic category—industry, commerce, land transport, and so on.

There was no provision in the Consolidacão das Leis do Trabalho for the establishment of a general confederation of labor comparable to the AFL–CIO in the United States or for the formation of a similar employers' group. Although an attempt was made in 1946 to set up a General Confederation of Labor it was abortive, and the principal structural change in the labor movement since the end of the *Estado Novo* has been the establishment of four large workers' confederations modeled on the Consolidacão—those of industrial workers, commerical workers, land transport workers, and banking employees.

True to the concept of the corporate state, the Consolidacão das Leis do Trabalho was not only supposed to encompass wage workers and employers of labor but the free professions as well. One of the confederations which was provided for in the law was a Confederation of the Free Professions. Although this was never established (and so far as we know no state federation of this type has been set up), there are numerous *sindicatos* among doctors, musicians, lawyers, engineers, and so on. However, they are less influential than the same groups organized outside the Consolidacão das Leis.

On the employers' side, the pattern of the Consolidacão has not been strictly followed since the government has extended legal recognition to general state federations of industry and commerce, although they are not provided for in the law. But a decree-law of 1944 provided for the establishment of *associacoes rurals* on a local scale, *federacoes de associacoes rurals* on a state level, and the Confederacão Agraria Brasileira on a nationwide basis. The unionization of agricultural workers remained illegal.[2]

Recognition. All workers' or employers' groups which wish to engage in collective bargaining legally, appear before the labor courts, or perform other functions within the purview of the Consolidacão das Leis do Trabalho, must first gain recognition from the Ministry of Labor, Industry, and Commerce. The procedure is roughly the same for both employers' and workers' organizations.

Let us take, for example, the case of a workers' *sindicato*. The first step in getting a workers' *sindicato* recognized is the formation of an *associacão profissional*. There can be as many of these as the workers want to establish. This organization has no power to negotiate with the employers or appear before the labor courts, rights reserved for full-fledged *sindicatos*.

Once a group of workers has formed an *associacão profissional,* it must get at least one-third of the workers in the group to sign a petition asking for recognition as a *sindicato.* There are about a dozen different papers which must accompany this request, including a statement of the amount of social assistance the *associacão* has been giving its members, details about the elected directors of the organization and statements of good conduct from the local police for all of them. Until December 1955 it was also necessary to have a statement from each director avowing that he did not profess any ideology foreign to the nation. However, in December 1955 certain amendments to the law omitted this provision, since it was perfectly easy for one who did profess such ideologies to sign a statement to the contrary.

If more than one *associacão profissional* in an area in the same industry or profession applies for recognition as a *sindicato,* the registration section is empowered to decide which application is to be accepted. The custom is to accept the group which has the most property and the greatest program of social services, even though it may have less members than a rival group.

The Consolidacão das Leis do Trabalho sets forth the categories of workers who may join together to form a single *sindicato.* If an *associacão profissional* which is applying for recognition as a *sindicato* has in its membership more than one of these groups (men's *and* women's tailors, for instance), the registration section sends the request for extended jurisdiction to the trade-union category section of the Serviço de Organizacão e Registro Sindical, which gives its opinion as to whether these various groups should be allowed to join a single union. The matter then returns to the registration section for a final decision.

If a *sindicato* already exists which covers more than one of the categories established in the Consolidacão das Leis, and a group of workers from one of these categories forms an *associacão profissional* and applies for recognition as a *sindicato,* it will be recognized by the registration section if it can get together the necessary one-third of the workers. Even if the other two-thirds in that category wish to remain in the *sindicato* of larger jurisdiction they will not be able to do so and will by law come under the control of the narrower-delineated group. Thus, for example, if there is in existence a *sindicato* encompassing the men's and women's tailors of a given town with a third of the men's tailors in the group wanting a separate union, all men's tailors will come under the jurisdiction of the new men's tailors union.

If the more restricted *associacão profissional* is recognized as a *sindicato,* the older *sindicato* loses jurisdiction over that category. The objective of Brazilian labor legislation is to organize workers by professional category and to have the narrowest possible jurisdiction for any given *sindicato.*

The trade-union category section decides upon the nomenclature of new *sindicatos.* It is often necessary for it to make up new titles when a group which has come into existence since the writing of the Consolidacão asks for recognition. The list in the Consolidacão is supposed to be revised every two years but it is not, so the delineation of new categories and the naming of unions in them fall on this section of the Ministry of Labor.

Union Elections. Government control over the unions does not by any means end with the Ministry of Labor's prescription of its jurisdiction and the requirements for recognition. Among the many items prescribed in the Consolidacão das Leis are provisions of what must be voted on by secret ballot in union meetings (Art. 524), qualifications of who may and may not belong to the unions (Art. 549), and a whole group of prohibitions listed in Art. 521 of the Consolidacão:

(a) prohibition of any propaganda of doctrines incompatible with the institutions and the interests of the nation, as well as the candidacies of anyone for elective posts outside of the *sindicato;*
(b) prohibition of the exercise of cumulative elective posts as a paid employee either of a *sindicato* or federation or confederation;
(c) prohibition of payment of those holding elective posts;

(d) prohibition of any activities not included in the purposes mentioned in Article 511, including those of a partisan political nature;

(e) prohibition of the granting gratis or for rent of union headquarters to any organization of a partisan political nature.

The law specifies when union elections should take place (between thirty and sixty days before the end of the term of the incumbent *sindicato* officials), how the various lists of candidates for the election are to be registered, and how the election itself is to be held.

All lists of nominees are to go first to the union president. If he refuses to accept a list he must give his reasons to the Ministry of Labor within three days. Sometimes union elections are held before the Ministry of Labor's registration section makes up its mind whether the president was right or wrong in barring a list, and if the ministry decides that the president was wrong, the election is nullified and an administrator is appointed by the ministry to call new elections within sixty days.

Until December 1955, a protest about a union election automatically held up the inauguration of the new administration—with the old one staying in office in the interim—until the ministry had made up its mind about the election. This process sometimes took the Ministry of Labor three or four months. However, since changes in the law in 1955 no protest about the election can be cause for preventing the newly elected union administration from taking office immediately. Before the changes, a union official could not be reelected. Thereafter, a union official could be renamed as many times as the workers cared to elect him.

The Regional Labor Delegate of the Ministry of Labor must certify the results of union elections. He has no power to intervene in an election, but officials of his office must be present at the time. If there is any irregularity in an election the Regional Labor Delegate can report it to the minister who can annul the results. It is then up to the union officials to administer the second election. If conditions are so disorganized that the union is unable to do so the minister can name an interventor whose job it is to call a new election within sixty days.

Until 1954 it was forbidden for a known Communist to hold office in a union. Congress repealed this law in that year. Some officials still seek to keep out Communists, others make no such attempts.

During the administration of President João Cafe Filho (1954 through 1955) the issue of Communist leadership of the unions was the subject of considerable confusion. The Minister of Labor refused to let Communists take office. However, the labor courts frequently reversed the decision of the minister which made the situation difficult for the Ministry of Labor officials in the field.

If a union election is not held on schedule, the Regional Labor Delegation investigates and notifies the union's officials, giving them a deadline. If this is not met, the union must elect an interim commission which has ninety days in which to hold the election. If it is still not held, the Ministry of Labor intervenes. As a last resort, the ministry can cancel the union's legal recognition. In that case, if the workers want to continue to have a union they have to organize a new one.

Union Finances. Control of union finances is one of the principal methods by which the government holds the workers' organizations under its grip. Article 558 of the Consolidacão sets forth what constitutes the "patrimony" of the union. This includes:

(a) The contributions paid to the unions by those belonging to the economic or professional categories . . . represented by these entities, known as the *imposto sindical.* . . . ;
(b) The dues of members, in the form established in the statutes or by the general assemblies;
(c) The goods and property acquired and the income produced by the same;
(d) Donations and legacies;
(e) Fines and other occasional income.

Article 549 provides that "the property and income of the *sindicatos,* federations, and confederations can only be used in the form provided for in the law and in their statutes." It is followed by an article which specifies that before June 30 of each year the *sindicatos,* federations, and confederations must submit next year's budget for approval to the Ministry of Labor, Industry, and Commerce. In addition, Article 550 says:

(1) The trade unions are obliged to possess, duly sealed and stamped, a day book in which must be registered systematically and in perfect order, the administrative facts of their financial activities. . . .
(2) In the bookkeeping of the trade unions, the financial year will coincide with the civil year, that is, it will end the 31st of March, and the balanced books must bear the seal of the competent authority of the National Labor Department, in the Federal District or in the Regional Delegation. . . .
(3) The certificate of recognition of the unions will be cancelled if there is a deficiency or the financial conditions are not met. . . .

The Regional Labor Delegate has the job of checking the unions' books when they are submitted. If there is something wrong with the records as submitted, the union is notified and advised. If stealing of union funds is suspected, the Regional Labor Delegation investigates very carefully and if the suspicions are justified, the Ministry of Labor intervenes, naming some-one to run the union pending new elections, and criminal charges are lodged against the union leaders involved. In the state of São Paulo criminal prosecutions are said to occur in the case of about 5 per cent of the unions in any given year.

The Imposto Sindical. One of the   principal excuses for government interference in the financial administration and general affairs of workers' and employers' organizations is the fact that all such groups enjoy the benefits of the *imposto sindical* or trade union tax. Sixty per cent of the *imposto sindical* collected from the workers goes to the *sindicato* under whose juris-diction they are. Fifteen per cent is paid to the federation with which this *sindicato* is affiliated, and 5 per cent goes to the confederation to which the federation belongs. If there is no *sindicato,* its share goes to the federation; if there is no federation, its share goes to the confederation; if there is no confederation, the whole of the *imposto sindical* goes into the so-called Fundo Social Sindical.

The Fundo Social Sindical is the most controversial aspect of the *imposto sindical.* The funds are supposed to be spent "for the benefit of the workers" but this is often very broadly interpreted. There are frequent charges heard in Brazil that the money of the Fundo Social Sindical is used for political purposes by the government of the day. The Fundo Social Sindical is admin-istered by the Commissão do Imposto Sindical which consists of eleven members, including two representing labor, chosen by the Minister of Labor from lists submitted by all the federations, and two representing the employers, selected in the same way. One member is delegated to speak for the liberal professions, three others represent medicine and social security. The membership is completed by the Director General of Labor, a represent-ative of the accounting department of the Ministry of Labor, and the Min-ister himself as president.

We were informed that the lineup in the Commissão generally tends to be six to five on most questions, with the two workers' representatives, the two managerial nominees, and the representatives of the liberal professions forming a bloc against the others who are more closely controlled by the Minister of Labor.

The theory behind the Fundo Social Sindical is that it is supposed to be spent on behalf of the nonunion workers. However, it is spent in establishing theaters, special social services, recreation and educational activities which benefit all the workers in an area whether or not they are unionized.

It has frequently been suggested that the *imposto sindical* be abolished as one means of freeing the unions from the strict surveillance of the state. Most of the trade-union leaders are opposed to such a measure since it would virtually abolish the unions' social services and would make it almost impossible to maintain the office staff necessary to carry on union business.

The payment of the *imposto sindical* does not automatically make a worker a member of his union. He must pay a small monthly membership fee in addition.

Exceptions to Consolidacão das Leis do Trabalho. There are five types of worker who do not come under the provisions of the regular Consolidacão das Leis do Trabalho. Four of them are thus listed in Article 7 of the Consolidacão:

The precepts of the present Consolidacão, except when in each case it is expressly provided to the contrary, do not apply:

(a) To domestic employees, to be considered as such those who render service of a noneconomic nature to the person or family in whose residence they live;

(b) To rural workers, to be considered as such those who, exercising functions directly associated with agriculture and fishing, and not being employed in activities which, by the methods of execution of their respective labors or by the purpose of their operations are classified as industrial or commercial;

(c) To public employees of the union, the states, and the municipalities, and to supernumeraries in the service of these entities;

(d) To the employees of semi-state autonomous bodies who, since they are subject to their own system of labor protection, occupy a situation analogous to that of public functionaries.

By 1956 there was considerable discussion of the possibility of permitting the legal organization of agricultural workers' unions, but by 1961 none had as yet been formed.

In spite of the legal prohibition of the unionization of agricultural workers, the Communists were very active in establishing extralegal organizations among these workers. By the middle of 1956 the Communists had well organized groups in four different sections of the key state of São Paulo. It appeared that when and if the legalization of agricultural worker's unions was provided, the Communists would be the principal beneficiaries. In the northeast, Socialist Party leader Francisco Julião had succeeded in organizing a strong peasant movement by 1961.

The fifth group which is not under the regular machinery of the Consolidacão consists of the port and maritime workers who are under the control of the "captain of the port." This official has a dual role. He is in charge of the administration of the port, and as such is responsible to the Ministry of Marine. He is also Maritime Regional Labor Delegate and as such is responsible to the Ministry of Labor. The captain of the port is always a naval officer and in the case of the port of Santos, second largest in the country, he is always a naval captain.

All maritime and port workers have to register with the captain of the port and obtain work permits. Their unions are under the control of the captain of the port, in the same way the Regional Labor Delegate controls land workers' unions. The captain has the right to intervene in a union. In the case of Santos, the captain of the port did so during the longshoremen's strike of 1955 which lasted eight days. The captain closed two longshoremen's unions when they refused to go back to work with a 25 per cent wage increase. The captain broke the strike and the workers returned under the suggested conditions.

The captain of the port also normally handles all grievances among the longshoremen and seamen. Round table discussions are held in his office and only if the situation cannot be settled there, does the case go to the labor courts.

Thus, all those workers' and employers' organizations which are authorized to bargain collectively or make use of the government labor courts are organized under the Consolidacão das Leis do Trabalho, which has only been slightly altered since the days of the *Estado Novo*. The degree of government supervision of these organizations has varied from time to time and place to place, though in general it has been greater over the workers' organizations than over those of the employers.

The freedom of action of both workers' and employers' organizations is seriously impeded. The experience of the corporate state has left the government with a very large degree of control over the contacts between employers and their workers, a control which is exercised through the Ministry of Labor and the labor court system.

CHAPTER VI

Government Direction of
the Workers' Protest

The attempt by Getulio Vargas to direct the workers' protest resulted in the Ministry of Labor's developing into one of the most powerful institutions of the administration. It was given extensive control over the trade-union movement and the employers' organizations established under the Consolidacão das Leis do Trabalho as well as over the process of settling disputes between the workers and employers. It was also given extensive powers over the enforcement of labor laws.

Structure of Ministry of Labor

The ministry involved is a composite group, the Ministry of Labor, Commerce, and Industry. There is considerable dispute over having these three important government activities under one ministerial roof. Since 1956 there has been a bill pending in congress to alter this. The proposal is to leave labor and social security matters in one ministry, and to establish a new Ministry of Economy to handle commerce, industry, and agriculture.

The nerve center of the Ministry of Labor, Commerce, and Industry is its headquarters in Rio de Janeiro. There are two principal sections of the ministry which deal with labor matters. One of these is the Departamento Nacional do Trabalho, which handles workers' and employers' organizations, labor disputes, and enforcement of labor legislation. The other is the Departamento Geral de Previdencia Social which supervises the social security system.

The heart of the ministry is the Departamento Nacional do Trabalho. It supervises the regional delegations of the ministry, collects statistics, handles the recognition of workers' and employers' organizations, and supervises the elections and finances of the duly recognized class organizations.

Regional Labor Delegations. Most of the actual labor inspection and control of the unions is carried out by the regional delegations of labor. There is generally a Regional Labor Delegation in each state although some of the smaller states are grouped together for the purposes of administration.

The labor inspectors who work out of the regional delegations find out if the employer has deducted the *impostos sindical,* if he has given the workers their vacations, if he is paying the minimum wage, and if he is contributing to his workers' social security fund. They likewise note whether the employer has insured his workers against accidents, whether he is obeying the rules concerning the work of women and children, and finally, if he is obeying the special protection laws for workers in dangerous industries.

The inspectors have the right to look at the employers' books. If an employer is found to be in violation of the law he can be fined by the Delegado Regional do Trabalho. These fines can run from fifty cruzeiros to fifty thousand cruzeiros. The employer can appeal to the Director Geral do Trabalho, then to the minister, and finally to the Supreme Court if he wishes.[1]

There are several problems facing the Ministry of Labor in its inspection activities. One of these is the inadequate number of inspectors. There is also the problem of the corruption of inspection officials. In São Paulo, moves were taken to right this situation several years ago. Instead of assigning each inspector to a given territory, as is done in most parts of the country, and giving him free rein to visit when he likes, each inspector is now given his daily assignment in the Regional Labor Delegation. Thus, it is possible to repeat an inspection a day or so after a plant or business has first been submitted to scrutiny. This possibility always hangs over an employer so bribery is not as profitable as it might otherwise be. If the second inspector turns in a report which differs radically from that of the first the situation is looked into. If an inspector is known to have taken a bribe he is forced to resign. This system is reported to have greatly improved the morality of the labor inspection service of São Paulo.

Much of the time of the regional labor delegations is taken up issuing or reissuing workers' *carteiras profissionais.* These are the compulsory workbooks instituted by Vargas in 1933. They are defended by Brazilian government officials as being very useful to the worker. In addition to serving as a general identification, the book is needed when the worker appears before the labor courts, before the social security institute, and so on. He can work without it but the employer is supposed to see to it that he gets his *carteira* within thirty days of being employed. Foreign workers must also have a *carteira profissional*. These workers are admitted to the country to work for a period of two years in a given profession. After the two years they can change their employment, but before doing so they have to get permission signed by the Minister of Justice, which often takes much time.

The regional delegates also have an important role in the control and supervision of the *sindicatos*. They first pass on applications for recognition as *associacoes profissionais* and *sindicatos*. They also supervise elections and check proposed budgets and annual financial statements by the organizations.

They sometimes have an important part in resolving disputes between workers and employers. The "round table discussion" in the Regional Labor Delegate's office, although it is not provided for in the system of labor jurisprudence, is a frequent method of settling disputes outside of the labor court. In all these aspects of labor–management relations in Brazil, the Regional Labor Delegate is a key figure. If he is a man of tact and ability he is often able to do a good deal toward preserving peace between labor and capital in his jurisdiction.

At one point during the Dutra administration in the late 1940's some consideration was given to turning a large part of the work of the Ministry of Labor over to the states. In the case of São Paulo the regional delegation of the ministry was abolished and its place was taken by a State Department of Labor, as the result of an agreement between President Dutra and the governor of the state. However, with the installation of Vargas as President once again in 1950 this arrangement was ended, and since that time labor relations have been the exclusive province of the federal government and not of the states.

The Labor Courts

The labor courts, through which most workers' grievances are handled by the government, are part of the Brazilian judicial system. This system includes the regular criminal and civil courts as well as two specialized jurisdictions, one of which is the labor court system, the other the electoral courts. The judges in the labor courts are career men who start out in the courts of lower jurisdiction and then are promoted by seniority or by merit.

There are three levels of labor courts. At the bottom of the hierarchy are the so-called *juntas de conciliação* (conciliation boards) which are scattered throughout the country. Where towns are too small to justify the establishment of a *junta de conciliacão* its functions are handled by regular local magistrates. The *juntas de conciliação e julgamento,* as they are formally known, are the courts in which most of the workers' grievances are heard. The atmosphere is informal and the parties to a dispute are generally present.

The second level of labor courts are the *tribunais* or regional tribunals. There are nine of these located in some of the principal state capitals. These secondary courts are tribunals of first instance for collective disputes and are courts of appeal for the handling of individual worker's grievances.

The highest labor court is the Tribunal Superior do Trabalho. It is the final level of appeal within the labor courts system and is the court of first instance for national collective disputes. Appeal can be taken to the Tribunal Supremo Nacional, the Supreme Court.

The Tribunal Superior do Trabalho was until 1946 the Conselho Superior do Trabalho, and was a quasi-administrative, quasi-judicial body which had jurisdiction over the social security system as well as over relations between workers and employers. However, in 1946 the social security functions of the group were transferred to the Conselho Superior de Previdencia and the Conselho Superior do Trabalho was rechristened the Tribunal Superior do Trabalho and made an integral part of the country's court system.

As a result of these changes, the labor court system became independent of the Ministry of Labor to which it had hitherto been subordinate. It was given its own financial resources and was empowered to name its own personnel by competitive examination as do other parts of the federal judiciary.

Until the changes of 1946 the labor courts system was subjected to a good deal more political pressure than has been true subsequently. Although political considerations may enter into the original appointment of a judge to the system, it cannot have much effect once he becomes a member of that system since all the labor judges have life tenure.

On all levels of the labor court system there is representation of both workers and employers. In the *juntas de conciliação* there is one representative for each side and the court is presided over by a professional judge. In the regional tribunals there is also one representative for each side in addition to three professional judges. In the Tribunal Superior do Trabalho there are two representatives for each side and five career judges.

The presence of these functional representatives on the labor courts is a matter of considerable dispute. Their supposed purpose is to provide the technical background the regular judges do not have. However, the President of the Third Regional Labor Court in Belo Horizonte explained that the main purpose in having these representatives was a political one. It gives the decisions of the courts more standing in the eyes of both parties if they know that representatives of their group have sat in on the decisions taken. It also makes it much easier to make the decisions of the courts stick. It is generally believed that in the beginning the functional judges tend to be militant in support of their "own" side, but that by the end of the two-year term they have generally learned to take a more judicial attitude, and determine cases on merit rather than on a class basis.

Dissidios Colectivos. Collective disputes begin by a general meeting of a workers' union which draws up a list of demands which it would like to see incorporated in a *dissidio colectivo* (court decision on terms and conditions of work). The Regional Labor Tribunal then summons the employers' *sindicato* and requests their counterproposal. (Under the Consolidação das Leis do Trabalho only employers' *sindicatos* can enter into collective agreements. Individual employers may not do so. However, in 1956 the Ministry of Labor was preparing an amendment to the Consolidação which would permit direct negotiations between individual employers and the *sindicatos* of their employees.) The tribunal then decides what shall be granted. If there is the menace of a strike, the Regional Labor Delegate of the Ministry of Labor can intervene to try to get the two sides to reach an agreement. If he succeeds, he promulgates the agreement and this has the force of law. No further action before a labor court is then needed.

The number of *dissidios colectivos* declared by the regional labor courts is surprisingly small. Before the end of the *Estado Novo,* there were practically no such actions. In 1941, 1942, 1943, and 1944 there were only eight, eighteen, thirty and one *dissidios* respectively emitted by all eight regional courts.

The number of *dissidios* is a fair reflection of the state of labor relations during a given year. The following list indicates the number of *dissidios* between 1945 and 1954:[2]

1945	134
1946	420
1947	295
1948	183
1949	143
1950	134
1951	177
1952	251
1953	376
1954	371

The rise in the number of *dissidios* in 1946 reflects the rising labor discontent during that year and the relative freedom granted the unions by the government; the sharp decline in the following years is the result of the increasingly stern attitude of the government of General Dutra toward the trade unions. Starting in 1951 the more friendly attitude of the second Vargas administration is revealed by the increased number of collective disputes coming before the regional labor courts for decision. This trend culminated in 1953, a year which was highlighted by widespread strike action in São Paulo and other industrial centers. The slight decline in 1954 perhaps represents the crackdown by the government of President João Cafe Filho.

During 1955 the eight regional courts issued 340 *dissidios colectivos.* Thirty-two additional collective disputes were held by the courts to be within their jurisdiction but were not resolved during the year, and 33 others were held to be only partially subject to the courts' jurisdiction. Eight collective disputes were ruled as completely outside of the regional courts' jurisdiction, while 4 others were suspended and 7 filed without being passed upon.[3]

In some instances, agreements between workers and employers are reached by direct negotiations between the workers' and employers' organizations. However, these cases are relatively few. Although the author was informed by some regional labor delegates that most trade-union demands on employers were settled in their states by direct negotiations these cases are certainly exceptions. One explanation for this is given by the Judge of the Regional Labor Tribunal of Recife, who feels that the class-struggle mentality of the leaders of the workers' *sindicatos* makes them uninterested in collective agreements or fixed grievance procedures. He added that workers' *sindicatos* which do adopt these procedures of direct negotiation are often regarded as "yellow" by their confreres.

However, this does not fully explain the dearth of direct collective contract negotiations in Brazil. In the first place, it is exactly those unions with the most class-conscious and political leadership which try to deal independently with the employers rather than go through the labor courts. In the second place, the labor movement in Brazil has still not recovered from its long experience in the strait jacket of Getulio Vargas' *Estado Novo*. During the 1937–1945 period the unions seldom sought *dissidios colectivos* let alone independent collective bargaining agreements. The welfare of the workers during that period was presumed to be almost solely in the hands of the government and the unions confined themselves to helping their members present individual grievances in the labor courts.

Although progress has been made since 1945 in reasserting the role of the unions as representatives of their members in disputes with the employers, they still remain in a subordinate role, vis-á-vis the state.

Strikes. The key role of the state in labor–management relations is shown not only by the very strict control exercised by the Ministry of Labor over the organization and functioning of the trade unions, or by the prevalence of *dissidios colectivos* as opposed to independent labor–management contracts but by the confused status of the strike as a trade-union weapon.

The constitution of the *Estado Novo* forbade strikes as subversive. But while that constitution was still in effect, a decree was issued in March 1946 which provided that strikes were legal in nonbasic industries. That decree, of course, was unconstitutional under the existing constitution. Then the constitution of September 1946 provided that strikes were legal and should be regulated by law. However, by the end of 1961 the law to regulate strikes had still not been passed by congress. As a result, the courts had interpreted the decree of March 1946 as still being in effect. This decree was thus unconstitutional under the *Estado Novo* constitution and is still unconstitutional under the 1946 constitution but in the absence of any other legislation is regarded by the courts as the statute governing strikes.

In spite of the legal limitation on the strike weapon, it has been used with considerable frequency since the end of the *Estado Novo*. During 1945, 1946, and the early months of 1947, there were numerous strikes as a result of the renewed militancy of the labor movement at that time. After the return of Getulio Vargas to the presidency in 1950 strikes grew in numbers culminating in 1953 in a general walkout in the city of São Paulo and a nationwide maritime strike. After 1953 the enthusiasm for the strike weapon declined somewhat.

There are no reliable figures available on the number of strikes in Brazil since 1945. Many strikes are not brought to the attention of the organs involved in collecting labor statistics.

Strikes have not strengthened the unions' position and the number of collective contracts has been extremely limited. Even in cases where collective agreements are signed, they usually concern things which would otherwise be settled by *dissidios colectivos*—that is wages and other monetary fringe benefits. There are few contracts of the sort which have become customary in the United States—documents ranging over the whole field of relations between the workers and the employer. The more important contracts are those of the port workers throughout Brazil, the agreement between the National Steel Company and its employees, and some of the arrangements in public utilities.

Typical of the collective agreements which were in force in Brazil from 1956 to 1957 is that of the Brazilian Telephone Company with its workers' union in São Paulo. The first clause of this document establishes that it covers all workers earning 24,000 cruzeiros a month or less. The second clause sets forth the wage increases which are being granted to different categories of salaried workers. Clause Three provides similar increases for daily and hourly rated workers. Clause Four provides for an annual payment of a bonus in lieu of profit-sharing. Clause Five provides a special increase for minors in the company's employ. The sixth and final clause provides that all the foregoing shall be dependent on the company's receiving an increase in rates which will cover the increase in wage costs accruing from the boosts given in the contract.[4]

One of the most extraordinary agreements negotiated between workers and employers in recent years was that setting up the special Serviço Social da Industria for the paper industry of São Paulo state. This provided for the establishment of an organization to be directed by both workers' and employers' federations which would not only provide medical and dental care for the workers but would also organize clinics in the interior of the state, give the workers legal advice, establish vacation colonies, and consumers' cooperatives. This agreement indicates a special degree of cooperation between the workers' and industrialists' leaders in that field which is rare in Brazil.[5]

This contract, as well as any other which is reached by direct negotiation between workers and employers, must be promulgated by the Ministry of Labor before it has validity. All independently negotiated contracts are apparently submitted to the ministry for approval giving the ministry a chance to interfere, if it desires to do so, even in cases where the employers and workers have reached an agreement independently.

The Grievance Procedure. Dissidios colectivos are only a small part of the work of the Brazilian labor courts and are handled by the special courts, the regional labor tribunals, and the Tribunal Superior do Trabalho. Much more numerous are the *reclamações* or individual grievances of workers against employers which make up the major business of the *juntas de conciliação*. The decisions of the *juntas* in these cases can be appealed to the regional tribunals and in some instances to the Tribunal Superior do Trabalho in Rio de Janeiro.

If there is no grievance procedure within a given plant or enterprise, workers' grievances will be immediately presented to the *juntas de conciliação*. However, there is a growing tendency upon the part of both labor and management to try to handle grievances in the first instance as matters strictly "within the family."

Some of the better-organized trade unions handle virtually all grievances through direct negotiations with the employers. In some cases it is the employers who are taking the initiative to establish a grievance procedure within the firm, rather than have such cases go to the labor courts. Many employers feel that the courts are prejudiced in favor of the worker, and others do not want to waste the time. In most cases, even where grievances are handled principally through direct negotiations rather than through the labor courts there is no standardized method of grievance procedure.

Juntas de Conciliação. The activities of the *juntas de conciliação* in handling grievances can be judged from Table 4 which presents data between 1941 and 1954.[6]

Table 4. Grievances handled by *Juntas de Conciliacão*.

Year	Grievances	
	Received	Solved
1941	16,979	8,086
1942	21,599	22,721
1943	24,084	26,402
1944	36,402	34,688
1945	45,916	39,185
1946	62,110	59,680
1947	60,568	67,263
1948	51,388	51,912
1949	69,646	63,926
1950	66,144	66,065
1951	78,039	78,049
1952	84,499	74,557
1953	124,761	97,386
1954	93,193	80,958
1955	112,985	88,786

The procedure of the *junta* is generally quite informal. The judges usually sit alongside one table, the parties and their lawyers on each side of another table. All this is set off from a row of chairs where the audience and waiting participants sit behind a railing. Anyone is free to come in and observe the proceedings.

One of the principal complaints is the time it takes to get a case on the docket and have it heard, and there is certainly some justice in these complaints. In 1955 it was taking the *juntas* in São Paulo four months between the time a complaint was made and the time it was first heard. In others it was taking ninety days, many took at least a month. However, in 1955 the number of *juntas* was increased throughout Brazil and in 1956 the dockets were being cleared more rapidly.

In those towns and small cities in which there are no *juntas de conciliação* labor cases are heard in the first instance by regular, local, civil magistrates.

Regional Labor Tribunals. When one party or the other is not satisfied by the decision of a *junta de conciliação* or a magistrate's court, he may appeal to the appropriate Regional Labor Tribunal. Thus, the regional courts handle both individual grievances and collective *dissidios colectivos*. In 1941 the eight regional labor courts dealt with 1790 grievances. The number increased steadily, reaching 6796 in 1954.

A session of the Eighth Regional Labor Tribunal in Belem was characteristic of similar courts throughout Brazil. The proceedings were held in a room behind the office of the president of the tribunal. The members of the court consisted of the president, two career judges, and the judges representing the employers and the workers. Everyone spoke quite freely except for the workers' representative who said very little although he voted on each case. At the head of the table, on the right and left of the president, respectively, sat the Procurado do Trabalho (an adviser to the court on points of law) and the secretary of the court.

In front of the judges sat the witnesses. Beyond this table was a group of chairs for visitors to the tribunal's session. In each case one of the judges read a proposed decision, cited the Consolidacão das Leis do Trabalho, the constitution, and other laws. Then there was a considerable amount of discussion after which, a vote was taken on each case. Each case took ten to fifteen minutes.

Tribunal Superior do Trabalho. The third step in the labor courts hierarchy is the Tribunal Superior do Trabalho. Individual grievance cases as well as *dissidios colectivos* can be appealed to this court from the regional labor tribunals. In addition, the court is the tribunal of first instance for *dissidios colectivos* involving national unions.

Each case coming before the Tribunal Superior do Trabalho is assigned to one of the judges who becomes "relator" and reports the case to the court. Another judge is also given the same case and is known as the "revisor." He criticizes and comments on the presentation by the relator.

The judges representing the workers and employers serve as relators and revisors as do the professional judges. After the relator's report, the president of the court calls on the revisor. Then the floor is thrown open for discussion, and a decision is usually taken on the spot. However, it may be decided that more information is needed, or to send the case back to a lower court.

The load of cases coming before the Tribunal Superior do Trabalho grew rapidly during the late 1940's and early 1950's. In 1941 the Tribunal handled only 148 cases but by 1954 the number had grown to 3694.

In 1954 the Tribunal Superior was falling seriously behind in its work, and had a backlog of about four thousand cases. In that year the court adopted the system of *turmas,* whereby the body was divided into three sections, each of which would hear cases independently. Only in cases of conflict between two of the *turmas,* or in certain cases when it feels it must, does the court deal with cases in plenary session. A litigant can appeal from one of the *turmas* to the full membership of the court if he wants to and many times this occurs but in most instances the opinion rendered by the *turma* is accepted as final. All national *dissidios,* in which the Tribunal Superior is the court of first instance, must come before the plenary session of the court. However, these are relatively few.

Of course, the final appeal in labor cases as in all other legal matters, is the Supreme Court of Brazil, the Tribunal Supremo Federal. Very few cases get to the Supreme Court since only problems of interpretation of the law are passed on to the highest tribunal.

The labor courts system thus largely takes the place of both collective contract negotiation and grievance procedure as practiced in the United States. It deals with matters of law and fact, conciliating and arbitrating as well as interpreting and applying the law. It effectively channels most of the complaints of the workers through the government rather than through independent working-class organizations.

The Social Security System

The establishment of the social security system was another aspect of Getulio Vargas' attempt to picture himself as the "father of the poor" and to give the state the major role in handling the worker's adjustment to industrialization. The Brazilian social security system was drawn up in a demagogic spirit, and reasons of political expediency determined its nature more than did considerations of economic viability or the financial soundness of the system. There has been an element of downright dishonesty in the attitude which the governments of Vargas and all his successors have taken toward the financial responsibilities of the state for the various social security institutions.

Although one of the major social security funds, the Instituto de Previdencia e Assistencia dos Servidores do Estado covering federal government employees, was established in 1926[7] before the Revolution of 1930, most of the other organizations which make up the national social security system were set up during the fifteen years of Vargas' first period of power. The system consisted until 1960 of a number of autonomous *institutos* and *caixas* (funds) covering special groups of workers. At one time there were thirty-eight such organizations, and although there has been a tendency toward reducing their number in recent years the country is still a long way from having an over-all, national social security system.

The most important social security institutions are the following:

Instituto de Aposentaduria e Pensoes dos Industriarios, covering industrial workers;

Instituto de Aposentaduria y Pensoes dos Commerciarios, handling mercantile workers;

Instituto de Aposentaduria e Pensoes de Transportes e Carga, covering many of the country's transport workers;

Instituto de Previdencia dos Maritimos, covering maritime and port workers;

Instituto de Previdencia dos Bancarios, handling bank employees; and

Instituto de Previdencia e Aposentaduria dos Servidores do Estado, dealing with employees of the federal government.

In addition, there are a number of smaller social security institutions, generally known as *caixas.* Most of these deal with the employees of state and municipal governments. Others cover special groups such as the railroads, aviation, and public utility workers.

The first five of the institutes noted above have some three million members and protect three times that number of dependents. Several hundred thousand other workers are affiliated with the other units of the social security system.

The industrial workers' social security fund is the largest of the Brazilian social security institutions. It has between 1,500,000 and 1,600,000 workers in its ranks which is almost half of those in the entire social security setup. It includes all workers classified in manufacturing, including self-employed artisans who may join the institute if they so desire. High officials of manufacturing concerns can also become members if they wish.

The institute gives medical service to the workers and a subsidy after the first fifteen days of illness. It also provides a grant to each member upon the birth of a child as well as a funeral grant to his survivors. The institute pays old age pensions, though relatively few workers live to enjoy them, since they are paid after sixty-five years of age.

The institute has *delegacias* (delegations) in every state and in the important towns there are *agencias* (agencies) responsible to the state's *delegacia*. In smaller towns which have industrial workers there are *postos* (posts). They are also responsible to the *delegacias*.

Some of the doctors working for the institute are full-time employees of the organization. The institute also has contracts with doctors to whom it sends workers. In the smaller towns the latter is more general.

Part of the funds of the institute must by law be invested in government bonds. This institute, and all of the others, must also buy shares in certain national economic projects. In voting these shares the institute follows the lead of the government which is the major shareholder.

The institute can also use its funds for low-cost housing. By 1956 it had built about twenty thousand houses and apartments and had made about five thousand loans to members wishing to buy their own homes.

The Instituto de Aposentaduria y Pensoes dos Commerciarios covers all commercial workers, some six hundred thousand in all. It provides retirement benefits for workers over seventy, permanent disability benefits, health care, subsidies, and bonuses equivalent to one month's minimum wage for members when they have a child. The institute has four hospitals —in Rio, São Paulo, São Luiz and in the northern state of Maranhão. The funds of the institute, as we have noted, must first be invested in government bonds. Secondly, they are invested in housing. About 70 per cent of the institute's income was being spent each year in providing benefits for the members.

The IAPTEC, the social security fund covering land transport workers, is said to be the best of the institutes in terms of hospital service. It also has its own firm for making drugs. The Instituto de Previdencia e Aposentaduria dos Servidores do Estado covers some 280,000 federal government employees. It provides the workers with free hospitalization and medical care if his salary is less than 3000 cruzeiros a month. If a worker's income is above that, there is a small charge. The institute also gives loans to government workers and takes a mortgage for the homes which its members buy with its loans. It also builds houses for IPASE members to buy, as an investment of IPASE funds.

There are several serious weaknesses in the Brazilian social security system. The Abbink Mission took cognizance of one of the most important of these when it made its recommendations for changes in the system. It stated:

In light of the evident overlapping and duplication of services rendered and the excessive cost of administration, the following recommendations would seem to be justified: (1) The social security institutes and funds should be integrated to provide more uniform coverage, to provide adequate but not duplicate social services and to reduce overhead cost. (2) Governmental and quasi-government organizations operating in the field of social assistance and welfare should be studied for the purpose of early integration and consolidation to eliminate duplication, to reduce overhead and operating costs, and to provide for over-all planning in the welfare field. (3) The possibility of merging all or part of the other social assistance and welfare organizations into the suggested Social Security System should be given careful consideration.[8]

Certainly, the mission was on solid ground in its criticism of the multiplicity of social security and social assistance agencies (including the "quasi-government" SESI and SESCI organizations). However, the vested interests in the various government institutes and *caixas* are strong enough to prevent any action on this recommendation for eleven years after it was made in 1949. Only in August 1960 was a general social security law passed which placed the six institutes under a common national social security department in the Ministry of Labor, and instructed the department to standardize the payments to and benefits from the various institutes.

One of the most serious weaknesses of the system is the fact that the social security funds come from tripartite contributions by the workers, the employers, and the government, but the *institutos* and *caixas* seldom receive all these contributions. The government, in particular, is delinquent in paying its share. This is due to several factors. In the first place, the revenues originally allocated by the government to the social security system were insufficient but the government did nothing to make up the difference. There was a widespread belief that the institutes were affluent organizations. This derived from the fact that in the beginning the social security institutions followed the policy of building up reserves so that in the first years there was an astronomical difference between their income and benefits paid out. However, the cost of payments in recent years has been rising and, as a result, the social security system is now very much in need of the government's contributions. The government does pay something sporadically whenever there is a crisis.

The state is not the only delinquent. Several of the social security officials complained that employers frequently deduct the workers' contributions but do not pass them on. Needless to say, many of these same employers do not make their own contributions.

There is no doubt that social security is exceedingly expensive in Brazil. It can amount to as much as 50 per cent of the basic wage bill of the employer. It adds to the cost of production, and perhaps contributes to the inflation which has been such a problem for the last quarter of a century.

Many of the workers who belong to the social security institutes complain about the red tape necessary to get the benefits to which they are entitled. Finally, there are complaints that politics interfere in the administration of the social security funds. Whenever there is a change in the Minister of Labor, there is usually a change in administration of the social security funds.

The Conselho de Previdencia Social. There is a system for handling complaints by workers against the social security institutions. A worker who has a grievance against his *instituto* or *caixa* sends it first to the organization to which he is affiliated. If he gets no satisfaction there he can take his complaint to the Conselho Superior de Previdencia Social, the highest tribunal of appeal in the social security system.

The Conselho is not considered part of the regular judiciary. It consists of nine members, including a president, who has only a casting vote. One member represents the workers, one the employers, and the others are supposedly people with special technical training in social security matters. One does not have to be a lawyer to be on the court.

A wide range of cases comes before the Conselho. The author attended a meeting where several different cases were dealt with. The session was attended by five of the nine members and met in a room in the Ministry of Labor building in Rio de Janeiro. Each case was presented to the Conselho by one of its members who had been deputed to study it and report to the body. None of the people whose cases were discussed appeared in the Conselho room though presumably they could have done so.

For all its weaknesses, and possible corruption, the social security system of Brazil does bring positive benefits to the workers. It provides health aid for them which they probably could not obtain otherwise. It helps with the housing problem if only on a small scale. There is little doubt that the social security system was one of the principal factors which rallied the support of the Brazilian workers to Getulio Vargas.

During the *Estado Novo* period all possible protests and grievances were channeled through organs of the state. Not only was the social security system established as a means of reducing or ending some of the worst grievances of the workers, but the trade unions were also converted largely into organizations which provided the same kind of benefits as the social security institutions. Furthermore, all grievances arising in the course of relations between workers and their employers were taken out of their hands and placed in those of the labor court system. Finally, the over-all direction of this system of government control was centralized in the Ministry of Labor.

This system established between 1937 and 1945 has not been fundamentally changed. The state still plays the lead in channeling the workers' protest. Through *dissidios* and the grievance procedures of the labor courts the state has a great deal to say about the framework under which Brazilian industry functions.

CHAPTER VII

Employer Direction of the Workers' Protest

The Brazilian employers have not been unaware of the need for turning the workers' resentments against industrial society away from themselves. Many individual employers have sought to bind their workers more closely to them and resolve the worker's problems through social welfare and paternalism under their own control and supervision.

However, in Brazil there are two unique institutions in the field of employer paternalism which do not have their equal in any country with which the author is acquainted. These are the Serviço Social da Industria and its sister group, the Serviço Social do Commercio. These are gigantic organizations financed by all the country's industrial and commercial employers, which carry out extensive and varied programs of paternalism on a national scale.

The employers in their paternalistic efforts have had at least two objectives in mind. One was to blunt the sharpness of the workers' protest, the other to make it easier for the unskilled, ignorant worker to adapt himself to his new environment.

Employer Paternalism

Paternalistic activities on the part of individual employers are not as common in Brazil as they are in Chile, though they are probably more widespread than in Argentina. It is probably fair to say that the great majority of industrial employers in Brazil have only the most rudimentary social service program for their workers.

As we have observed, the origin of the paternalism of some of the firms is directly traceable to the patriarchal traditions of Brazilian plantation society, particularly in the northeastern part of the nation. For instance, the sugar refineries of the state of Pernambuco, most of which were established by plantation owners, provide schooling for the workers' children and take care of the medical needs of their employees. In 1956 the industry was building a big sugar workers' hospital in Recife, financed by a special tax on each bag of sugar. The sugar refineries usually provide houses for their workers as well.

Another example is the Industrias do Norte textile mill in Salvador, capital of the state of Baia. The biggest mill in the city with three to four thousand workers, it was established about a hundred years ago at which time the workers were provided with housing. Subsequently, a school, a hospital, and a church were all constructed adjacent to the textile plant.

One of the outstanding examples of the more modern variety is that practiced by A. J. Renner Cia. Ltda. of Porto Alegre. This company keeps three doctors and a dentist on the premises during most of the day to treat workers and their families. The firm provides life insurance and has a creche, large enough to take care of fifty babies, for their working mothers. It also provides an allowance of three hundred cruzeiros a month per child for each worker with three children or more if the mother stays home and takes care of the children.

The firm has also helped its workers set up a rather remarkable cooperative store completely run by the workers. Any Renner worker is able to join by purchasing a minimum of 100 cruzeiros worth of stock. The store employees and all other expenses except rent are paid by the cooperative.

Renner also has an education program for its workers. It runs a restaurant where in 1956 a regular meal was provided for ten cruzeiros. Finally, there is a pharmacy, run with the aid of SESI, which sells drugs at cost. This is a considerable saving for the workers because the cost of drugs in Brazil is very high.

A final example of paternalism is the VARIG aviation company. This firm, established in 1927, is one of the fastest growing airlines in the country. Until 1945 it was owned partly by the state of Rio Grande do Sul and partly by private stockholders. In that year the firm was reorganized. A foundation was established, the Fundacão dos Funcionarios de Varig, and 50 per cent of the stock of the firm was handed over to this new institution. The income of the stock belonging to the foundation is used for the benefit of the workers of the firm.

The Fundacão has a diversity of services for its members. It has a loan fund from which workers can borrow money, interest-free, to buy homes. It runs big, low-priced stores in the airports of Porto Alegre, São Paulo, and Rio for VARIG employees. It has low-priced restaurants in the same three cities. The Fundacão has a vacation spot at Ponta Grossa on the river not far from Porto Alegre. There is also a resort in the state of Baia for those workers who take their vacations in the winter. VARIG transports the workers and their families gratis to these resorts.

The foundation pays pensions to superannuated workers and retirement benefits. It also gives pensions to workers' survivors. These pensions and benefits supplement the payments which the worker receives from his social security *caixa* so that he gets his full pay upon retirement. These payments are increased to meet the rise in the cost of living. The foundation provides complete medical aid for the workers and their families.

This is how certain employers have provided many of the things which the new industrial worker needs most—housing, medical care, and education. However, of much greater importance are the paternalistic services rendered by SESI (Serviço Social da Industria) and SESCI (Serviço Social de Commercio).

SESI and SESCI

SESI and SESCI reflect fully and frankly the employers' desire to divert the workers' discontent into channels which are not dangerous to the captains (and subalterns) of industry and commerce. They were organized right after World War II to meet a particular situation which was facing the employers at that time.

As we have noted, the end of the Vargas dictatorship resulted in a sudden blossoming of trade unionism among the workers and in a tremendous growth in the influence of the Communist Party in the ranks of the workers. The leaders of the employers' organizations felt the need for institutions which, though still under the employers' control, could offer benefits to the workers which might make them a little less receptive to both militant trade unionism and the Communist Party.

These institutions are financed by compulsory contributions from all employers of an amount equivalent to 2 per cent of their payrolls. The laws establishing the SESI and SESCI allow these organizations to work out agreements with individual employers with extensive social service programs of their own, exempting them from this impost. However, the officials of SESI and SESCI are loath to make such agreements and the number excused is very small. There have been cases in which employers have refused to pay the tax, claiming that they are spending much more than 2 per cent of their payrolls on their own social welfare programs.

The avowed purpose of SESI and SESCI is to bring "social peace" to Brazil. However, three different philosophies have developed among the employers concerning the means of reaching this objective. The first of these might be called the "preventive charity" approach. Those who hold with this feel that the efforts of the two organizations should be devoted to developing charitable institutions which will make the employers look like "good fellows," thus counteracting the black picture of them propagated by the Communists and other antagonistic elements.

A second group of employers feel that they should treat SESI and SESCI as a *negocio* (a deal) for the political advancement of the industrialist class and sometimes of certain individuals in that class.

The third philosophy is that SESI and SESCI should help individuals, groups, and the community to help themselves. These different points of view are reflected in the administration of SESI and SESCI in different states.

There is a wide degree of decentralization in both SESI and SESCI so that all three philosophies have found expression in one region or another. The administration of SESI and SESCI in any given state is directly under the control of the Federacão da Industria and the Federacão do Commercio respectively. In the case of the Serviço Social da Industria, 75 per cent of the money collected from the employers of a state stays within its borders. The remaining 25 per cent is sent to the national headquarters of SESI where it is apportioned by the national council (composed of the state directors of the organization) to the poorer regions which do not have the resources to carry out an adequate program.

The idea that the SESI and SESCI should be a vast charitable enterprise for the workers is the most widespread of the three philosophies. An example of this point of view is found in Belem in the northern state of Pará where SESI confines its activities largely to extending medical aid to the city's industrial workers, maintaining a low-priced grocery store, and organizing clubs for the workers. In Salvador, capital of the state of Baia, the program of SESI is more extensive, but drawn up along the same lines.

In São Paulo. Undoubtedly the most elaborate SESI state setup on the "charitable" basis is that of São Paulo. Unlike the situation in most states, SESI in São Paulo works not only in the capital city but also in the interior towns. It has local "delegations" in twenty-five towns in the interior of the state which cover not only the towns themselves but the regions around them. The São Paulo SESI has four main operating divisions:

food supplies, social welfare, education and recreation, and social orientation.

The food supplies section maintains a network of 130 stores throughout the state. In these stores some 120 products of prime necessity are carried. Any industrial worker may register with one of these stores by presenting his *carteira profissional* which indicates where he is employed. The rise of these stores dealt a death blow to one form of Communist propaganda in the state. The Communist Party had established a network of neighborhood stores at which it sold goods at reduced prices. When the SESI stores began to operate they succeeded in undercutting them and driving most of them out of business.

The social welfare section of SESI in São Paulo includes a system of factory kitchens where workers can get cheap meals, and an extensive medical and dental service. The workers pay for the services which they receive in the clinics so that they do not feel that they are receiving charity, though they pay at a rate of about 10 per cent the normal cost. If a worker cannot pay, his case is investigated by a social worker and he can pay later.

The education and recreation section of SESI in São Paulo had some eighteen hundred schools in operation in over ninety municipalities throughout the state, with some forty thousand students early in 1956. The schools functioned in whatever buildings they could obtain—including SESI social centers, union headquarters, factories, and Catholic Workers' Circles.

Courses are varied with much emphasis on teaching illiterates to read and write. SESI has developed its own textbooks for this purpose. Courses in cultural as well as homemaking subjects are also given. Still another aspect of the education program of SESI in São Paulo is a circulating library available through the factories.

The social orientation section of São Paulo's SESI maintained a corps of some eighty social workers in 1956 who kept in contact with the industrial workers through SESI medical and dental clinics, SESI social centers, and who were available on special request. All kinds of personal problems are dealt with by these social workers.

In the social centers of SESI maintained by the education and recreation section, the social workers are mainly concerned with group activities. As we have discussed, the Brazilian worker is not a joiner and the social workers devote much of their time in trying to establish a group feeling.

The social orientation section also maintains a corps of lawyers who operate in the SESI social centers. The most common problem with which they deal is the relation of the workers with the social security institutes.

They also help workers acquire or bring up to date their numerous and necessary documents. They handle family legal problems and give advice to workers on labor relations matters, though naturally they cannot represent the workers in court.

Perhaps the most important activity of the social orientation section of São Paulo's SESI is its attempt to develop trade-union leaders. The officials of SESI deny that they are desirous of developing trade-union officials who will be subservient to the wishes of the employers but, rather, that they seek to counteract the trade-union work of the Communist Party in São Paulo.

To this end, the social orientation section of SESI organizes numerous courses in industrial relations. It has courses for foremen in human relations and similar courses for rank-and-file workers. There are courses designed for union leaders such as social legislation, public speaking, the conduct of trade-union meetings, and so on.

Officials of the social orientation section also act as advisers to trade-union leaders who need help in combatting Communists within their organizations. This section also maintains an intelligence service to keep SESI and Federacão da Industria officials informed concerning trends of thought and action among the organized workers.

SESCI in São Paulo is organized on much the same lines as its sister institution. Although it does not have the funds which SESI possesses it does much the same kind of work, except that the only kind of medical help which it offers is dentistry since the SESCI authorities seem to regard the medical services of the social security institute as adequate.

In Rio de Janeiro. The second approach to SESI and SESCI, of regarding it as a *negocio* to be exploited, would naturally be denied by those SESI or SESCI officials involved in it. Fortunately this attitude is not very common, and the chief culprit seems to be the Serviço Social da Industria in the Federal District. Perhaps it is not surprising that it should be in Rio de Janeiro, a city which lives and breathes politics.

In Pernambuco. A quite different philosophy is represented by SESI in the states of Pernambuco and Rio Grande do Sul. These two organizations do not believe in the "charity" approach since they do not feel that their resources are sufficient to cover all needs, and they think that the "charity" attitude has serious evils and lends itself to abuses. They follow the policy of helping individuals, groups, and the community at large to help themselves.

Pernambuco is famous historically for the patriarchal nature of its plantation society which is described so well by Gilberto Freyre in *Casa Grande e Senzala*. Industrialization changed all this. In the cities the factory owner generally lived in his world, the worker in his. In the beginning SESI attempted to bridge this gap by substituting charity, but too many times it heard, "I don't want the *patrão's* money, I want to be called by my first name."

The problem seemed to be that with the destruction of the old patriarchal relationship, nothing had been put in its place. Although the workers were officially self-reliant citizens, they had no feelings of community participation and responsibility. It was toward this problem that the SESI in Pernambuco began to address itself at the beginning of 1955.

SESI in Pernambuco at that time had sixteen centers, seven of them in the working-class wards in Recife. With the alteration of the program, seven of these changed their orientation so as to appeal not only to the industrial workers, but to all the people in the local community. The emphasis was placed on education for democracy.

SESI began its work with a school in each SESI center. Around the schools parents' clubs were organized with monthly meetings where the problems of the students were discussed by the teachers and parents. The parents were thus drawn into the process of education and were given a feeling of participation.

In addition to the parents' clubs, separate adults' clubs were established. In these clubs, which run their own affairs, the workers are given a taste of democracy at the grass roots level. The basic activity of the clubs has been education in the form of group discussions (usually advised by an SESI official with some specialized knowledge of the subject). From neighborhood problems the clubs often branch out to discuss larger questions and sometimes have round table discussions on such issues as the industrialization of Brazil.

Sports and recreation activities are also organized around these clubs. Each center has health and dental facilities, but the emphasis is on helping the residents of working-class neighborhoods learn the lesson of civic responsibility and participation. The Pernambuco officials of SESI feel that by substituting a certain degree of self-reliance for the former absolute dependence upon the *patrão* they are contributing toward the building of a responsible and capable industrial labor force.

In Rio Grande do Sul. In Brazil's southernmost state, Rio Grande do Sul, the same spirit of trying to develop self-reliance and community responsibility has been followed by SESI officials, though on a considerably different basis. Instead of building homes to rent to workers the institution began to sell the workers their homes on a long-term mortgage basis. This provided a kind of revolving fund which could be used for construction of more homes.

The workers in some of the interior cities were faced with the problem of very bad transportation systems, so SESI met the problem by financing the sale of bicycles on terms which they could afford. SESI also runs classes in homemaking, labor law, and other subjects, which is all part of the local program of helping the individual to help himself.

The second objective sought by the SESI of Rio Grande do Sul has been to help organizations to help themselves. Where new facilities were needed, SESI approached unions, Catholic Workers' Circles, and other such institutions, and suggested cooperation between them and SESI. In no case does SESI try to compete with existing services. Instead, it tries to complement and augment services already being given by unions or workers' circles. Also as part of this program the Rio Grande do Sul SESI has given extensive aid to cooperatives which are particularly numerous in the state.

Finally, SESI has sought to help the community to help itself. Where, for instance, existing private or public institutions have been giving medical help to members of the community on a part-time basis, SESI has proposed cooperation. It will frequently rent a room in the establishment or rent all of its facilities during a period when they are not being used. In some cases the rent is paid not in money, but in services, in the extension of SESI facilities to the organization's members during certain periods when SESI's own clientele is not using them.

The Rio Grande do Sul SESI sought to rationalize its services. It has not invested money in fine buildings but has spent most of its budget in actual services. Second, it has sought to reach the largest number of people possible. In the medical field, it first went into preventive medicine, next into general clinics, third into the provision of specialists' services, and only as a final stage does it intend to provide hospital service.

The Rio Grande SESI has given aid to those workers who need it most. Thus, it has helped the fishermen who were the forgotten men of the state. Finally, it has held that all social assistance must be accompanied by education. In line with this, the local SESI has published a considerable number of booklets on a wide range of subjects in simple language. These pamphlets are available wherever SESI has its services. They are placed where workers wait to see the doctor or dentist, or wait for a class to begin.

One innovation in the SESI program in Rio Grande do Sul is its close cooperation with local unions. The regional director of SESI meets regularly with a group of union leaders who advise him on all aspects of the program. Some union leaders thought that the new program, begun in 1950, meant that SESI was willing to give them large amounts of money. However, the director explained that if SESI were to give money it would cast doubt on the union leaders and would end up by bringing about more ills than cures. However, he did agree to lend some organizations a certain amount of money on the signature of a contract. The union leaders in question agreed to this and paid back the loans faithfully. As a result of this understanding, the unions cooperate with SESI in setting up various service programs.

Serviço Social Rural

The SESI idea was extended in September 1955 to rural Brazil when congress passed a law establishing the Serviço Social Rural. The law provided that all industries connected with agriculture, including sugar refining, meat packing, milling, milk processing, yerba mate processing, and cotton ginning would cease paying contributions to SESI and would pay the equivalent of 3 per cent of their wage bill to the new service instead.

The Serviço Social Rural, like its older sisters, is operated on a decentralized basis under the control of the state federations of rural associations. In the state of Minas Gerais the plan was to develop the program initially as medical aid to rural folk. A second proposed step was the establishment of rural schools by the service and campaigns to improve living conditions.

The Effects of SESI and SECI

The effects of the SESI and SESCI programs in Brazil are undoubtedly mixed. There is no doubt that these programs help many individual workers to confront the degrading poverty which is all too often their lot. However, the fact remains that too little is done and there is serious doubt that this is the method of doing it. It is true that the establishment of SESI and SESCI has discouraged individual employers from carrying out programs of paternalism on their own. But in many parts of the country, SESI intensifies the centuries-old feeling of dependence by the worker without mitigating a growing class hatred.

There is little doubt that of all the ways of conducting the SESI program, the "helping others to help themselves" approach is the most worth while. It involves less expenditure on bureaucracy, creates less of an aura of ulterior-motivated charity, and brings about closer cooperation between the organized employers and the organized workers.

Thus, in recent years the employers as individuals and through their organizations have sought to mitigate and orient the discontents of the industrial worker. Their concern with the problem of the workers' resentment has grown rapidly since 1945. The Brazilian employers are less inclined toward individual paternalistic activities than the employers of some other Latin American nations. However, they have evolved institutions in the form of SESI and SESCI for conducting paternalistic activities on a grand scale.

CHAPTER VIII

Recruitment and
Commitment of the Workers

The average Brazilian urban worker is likely to be somewhat darker in complexion than his economic and social "betters"; if he is lucky he possesses a primary school education but is more often semiliterate or entirely illiterate; he has very likely moved to the city fairly recently and probably from a far-distant part of the country. He is, as we have noted, a jack of all trades and a master of none.

He has been attracted to the city by the lure of higher wages, by the excitement and diversions of the Big Town and by the hope of obtaining greater freedom in the anonymity of the city. He has become discontented with the relationship with his rural *patrão* and desires to seek the independence which he feels life in the city will give him. Yet, he has not by any means completely shaken off the psychological dependence which characterized his status in the country.

There are, of course, increasing numbers of Brazilian industrial workers who are natives of the city, sons of European immigrants who have a higher degree of education than their confreres of lengthier Brazilian heritage. There is also a growing number of Brazilian workers who are semiskilled as well as a small group highly trained either by experience or the school system.

The average Brazilian industrial worker obtains his job by applying at the personnel department of the firm or through some relative or other personal source. Employment agencies exist but they play a relatively small role in the general employment picture. Some workers obtain their jobs from want ads in the newspapers.

Although there is a constant stream of new recruits in the industrial centers, unemployment is not a problem. On the other hand, although there is no scarcity of work, there is a dearth of skilled and competent workers. In recent years employers have become more careful in the selection of their employees.

Selection

Of late, a number of testing firms have appeared in Rio and São Paulo which test the workers, either before they are employed or after they are on the job. Some of the larger enterprises also do some of their own testing for skill and adaptability. This is true of "The Light," the public utility enterprise covering Rio and São Paulo. However, the number of firms equipped to do this work on their own is very limited since the personnel departments are rudimentary.

One of the independent testing firms in Rio does this work for a number of the principal foreign industrial enterprises in the capital and São Paulo. When a company requests a specific kind of employee, the testing firm places advertisements in the newspapers, interviews the applicants, gives them a two-and-a-half-hour test and finally a follow-up interview. Those considered eligible are sent on to the company.

This outfit is more concerned with psychotechnical testing then with determining the workers' technical skills. However, they do demand a complete work record. Usually the last two places of employment are contacted and the nature and quality of the work done by the applicant is inquired into. In the case of those applying for particularly skilled jobs, the firm arranges for a test.

An institution which does perhaps more of this employment testing work than any other is the Instituto de Seleccão e Orientacão Profissional of the Fundacão Getulio Vargas. It selects personnel on request for a fee. The jobs filled by the institute range from truck drivers to managers of factories. From time to time they have open competition when they invite anyone who wishes to do so to take their tests for certain jobs, after which the employment agency of the institute helps to place those it deems qualified.

Finally, SESI and SENAI do some of this testing, as does the Catholic University of São Paulo. However, the proportion of workers hired after such examinations is still very small. Most employers continue to take their workers from those who come in off the street, and recruit their skilled workers from among the more talented and experienced workers already in their employ.

Training

One of the most difficult aspects of the problem of committing the Brazilian work force to industry is developing skilled workers. Although the government and Brazilian employers have in recent years become increasingly aware of the importance of this training problem, an adequate solution has not yet been found.

Since the stepping up of Brazilian industrialization in the 1930's coincided with the closing down of mass immigration, the problem of training workers became more difficult than it might otherwise have been. During the earlier handicraft phase of Brazil's economy, many of the artisans were recruited from the ranks of Portuguese, Italian, Spanish, and German immigrants. These people were not only more aggressive and better educated than the average Brazilian worker, but in many cases also had some training in the skills needed in their adopted country. A large proportion of the new industries was established by immigrant artisans.

However, since the 1930's most of the workers have come from the interior of Brazil or from its native urban population. Few of these migrants from the country have any training in the skills required in the factories. The result of all of this has been that the great majority of skilled and semiskilled workers have been trained on the job. For the most part, such training has been carried on with little or no formal arrangements by Brazilian industrialists. A new worker has been placed alongside a more experienced comrade, and has been expected to pick up from him the necessary knowledge.

Some of the larger firms have developed training programs of their own. The VARIG aviation concern not only trains mechanics, pilots, and other operating personnel, but also trains people in the sales force. The mechanics and pilots get a three-year period of education. Pilot–candidates are then commissioned as copilots, and after two years more in this capacity they are made pilots of the company's C-47 aircraft.

When the Petrobras oil firm was preparing to establish a refinery, four engineers were sent to the United States for training, and when they returned they set up a six months' training program for the skilled workers who were going to be employed in the enterprise. There was further training on the job. Workers subsequently went from the Baia refinery to train workers in new plants in other states.

One of the most extensive training programs of any Brazilian industry is that of the government-owned steel plant at Volta Redonda. The Cia.

Siderurgica Nacional maintains a school with a five-year course. The first three years comprehend the basic course, developed by the SENAI (Serviço Nacional de Aprendizagem Industrial), and thereafter, if qualified, the students take an advanced course. They work one day in the plant, go one day to school, except during the first term when they are full-time students. The firm pays the boys the minimum wage in the state of Rio de Janeiro in which the plant is located. The company employs all those who graduate from the school.

One public utility, the Cia. de Carris Urbanos, Luz e Força, the Rio de Janeiro affiliate of "The Light," has an extensive program of education and training. On the lowest level, they have literacy courses for their workers. On a secondary level, they have an apprenticeship training course. This consists of two programs, one for office personnel and one for workshop people. All office boys must take the course which lasts for two years and qualifies them as junior clerks. There are also courses for typists and stenographers. The workshop course lasts for three years. Most of the graduates stay with the company as skilled craftsmen.[1]

SENAI and SENAC

During the Second World War, moves were made by the organized employers' groups in cooperation with the government of Brazil to come to grips with the problem of training skilled workers. The Confederacão Nacional da Industria and the Confederacão Nacional do Commercio both established organizations for the training of workers—industrial laborers, in the one case, and white collar workers in the other. The government itself established a system of schools for this same purpose.

The industrial and commercial training systems were established as a result of a May Day speech made by President Getulio Vargas in the early 1940's when he promised the workers that all factories would have restaurants and schools. Once the speech was made, Vargas turned the idea over to the Minister of Labor. The suggestion for installing restaurants in all factories was ultimately dropped as impractical but the Serviço Nacional de Aprendizagem Industrial (SENAI) and the Serviço Nacional de Aprendizagem Commercial (SENAC) were established to fulfill the other part of the President–dictator's promise.

The industrial employers, through the Confederacão Nacional da Industria, approached the President and told him that they were anxious to do something about the problem of technical education, but suggested that if they were going to pay for it, they wished to control the program. As a result, the power to act in this field was delegated to the Confederacão, under a provision of the 1937 constitution which provided that the President could delegate some governmental powers to private organizations.

The Serviço Nacional de Aprendizagem Industrial was set up in 1941. The law establishing it provided that all employers must contribute an amount equivalent to 1 per cent of their wage bill to the SENAI and that its operations should be controlled by the Confederacão Nacional da Industria. SENAC was established in 1946 and all commercial employers were directed to pay a sum equal to 1 per cent of their wage bill to it each month. SENAC was put under the control of the Confederacão Nacional do Commercio.

The operation of SENAI is decentralized, and the method in which it operates differs a good deal from one state to the other. In each state it is controlled by the local Federacão da Industria. In case there is no such federation several states are sometimes joined together. Thus, the SENAI of São Paulo also controls the states of Goyaz and Matto Grosso and the federal territory of Ampure. The state of Sergipe is under the control of a "delegation" named by the Confederacão Nacional da Industria head-quarters in Rio de Janeiro.[2]

The SENAI. One of the best state organizations of SENAI is that of the southernmost federal unit, Rio Grande do Sul. SENAI of Rio Grande do Sul has eight schools of its own, plus three others which are run by individual employers under the supervision of SESI, and a twelfth which SESI and SENAI run together. All of the schools have three basic courses—metal working, carpentry, and electricity. Beyond these, some of the schools specialize in other things as well. In Novo Hamburgo, for instance, the SENAI school concentrates on shoe and leather work, since that town is one of the principal centers of the leather industry. In Porto Alegre the SENAI school emphasizes textiles.

It is the policy of SENAI in Rio Grande do Sul to keep its functionaries active in the life of the area and in the activities of the business community. Therefore, almost all of them belong to local Rotary Clubs. In Caxias where the population is strongly Catholic, SENAI named a man who is a good Catholic and who takes an active part in church affairs.

In the beginning Rio Grande do Sul SENAI worked on the basis of half the week in school and half the week in the factory. However, they found that this did not work very well and in 1946 they experimented in the Porto Alegre school by having the boys go to school full time for a period of two years. This worked, so they received permission from Rio to have the whole state use that system. Subsequently, the national SENAI adopted the policy of allowing all states to do this.

SENAI in Rio Grande tries not to duplicate the work done by other institutions. However, they do have a system whereby boys go away from home to attend SENAI schools and live with approved families in the vicinity. Fifty-seven per cent of the students in the Rio Grande do Sul SENAI schools are youngsters who have asked for SENAI training, and for whom SENAI has secured jobs. Of the other 43 per cent, a considerable number are boys who have indicated their desire to go to the school to their employers. After the boy has been two years in a Rio Grande do Sul SENAI school he spends one year in industry before he is given his certificate as a skilled worker. In 1956 the SENAI authorities were planning to establish a system of tests, to be given by representatives of the employers' organizations, the workers' unions, and SENAI as a further qualification for its certificate.

SENAI officials have found that the attitude of the employers toward the SENAI graduates has been improving in recent years. The principal problems have come from the foremen and group leaders, and from older skilled workers, who were suspicious of the young SENAI-trained workers. However, an increasing number of SENAI graduates themselves are becoming foremen, and they are tending to give preference to the graduates of SENAI.[3]

We visited SENAI organizations in Belem, Recife, Baia, São Paulo, and Porto Alegre as well as its national headquarters in Rio. In some states SENAI maintains residential schools. The principal work of the SENAI organizations is with youngsters between the ages of fourteen and seventeen. The law expects employers to hire a certain percentage of workers in this age group, some of whom are to be sent to SENAI schools. Those attending the schools are rated as "apprentices" and need only be paid one-half the wage generally given workers of their category. Many employers have abused this provision by paying all their teen-age workers at the lower pay scale, whether or not they are receiving training. SENAI officials try to combat such abuses when they discover them. SENAI state organizations also run courses for adult workers.

Most of the state SENAI organizations have experimented with different systems of school attendance. In Baia, for instance, the students study steadily for five months, then work for five months. This resulted in extending the course from two years to three.

The law permits SENAI to make contracts with companies which have their own training programs, excusing them from paying the payroll tax of 1 per cent. However, in 1956 there were only about twenty such arrangements in the country.

The SENAC. The Serviço Nacional de Aprendizagem Commercial provides a system of training for commercial workers. SENAC has two divisions. One of these deals with minors, the other with adults. The courses for minors are divided into three types. The first, which is a course of only one year, is known as the course of elementary apprenticeship. For this, the youngsters must be fourteen years of age with at least three years of primary school. A student who completes it can go on to one of the other courses.

The second level of courses for adolescents is the course of commercial practitioners and is of two years' duration. Students must have at least four years of primary school before being admitted. The final course is called functional preparation. It is for students who have finished five years of primary school and offers a rounded program in the elements of commerce as well as material in Portuguese, arithmetic, and "civil and moral fundamentals."

All minors who take these courses do so during their working hours. In some states they go to school only two hours a day, in others the SENAC has been able to free them for three hours a day.

SENAC also has courses for adult workers. These are more specialized and technical. They are for workers over eighteen years of age and are given in the evenings.

Although they are large organizations, in 1956 SENAI could only handle 30,000 students and SENAC, 35,000.[4] The officials of SENAI hoped that by concentrating on on-the-job training they would ultimately be able to deal with some 3,000,000 workers, or a hundred times more than those in SENAI schools in 1956.

Various criticisms have been leveled at the SENAI school system. Many individual employers criticize SENAI because the boys whom it trains are under military age, and many do not resume work with the employers who sent them to SENAI when they come back from military service. Some employers are enthusiastic about the SENAI alumni, others insist that the training is inadequate. It seems likely that in those states where SENAI works most closely with local industrial employers it does the best job of training workers needed by the local industries.

Government Industrial Schools

Supplementing the work of SENAI and SENAC the Ministry of Education had in 1956 some sixteen thousand students in its eighty-six industrial training schools. Of these, only twenty-five schools are actually administered by the federal government, thirty-three others are administered by state governments, and twenty-eight are private, but under government supervision.

The government industrial schools differ from those of the SENAI in that the students go full time. Three or four hours a day are spent on general cultural subjects, and three or four hours in workshops. There are various specialties in each school, such as metal working, wood working, and so on. There are metallurgy schools in Ouro Preto and Volta Redonda, near the country's two principal iron and steel plants. The ministry offers about three hundred scholarships in industrial schools for needy students with good marks.

The Tenure Law

We have already noted the tendency of the Brazilian worker to move from job to job as opportunity beckons. This is intensified by the unfortunate "tenure" law incorporated in the Consolidacão das Leis do Trabalho. Article 492 of that document states that "the employee who has more than ten years of service in the same firm cannot be dismissed except for grave misbehavior or *force majeure,* which must be adequately proven."

Although this provision of the Consolidacão was undoubtedly intended to give the workers greater stability in employment, its effect in many instances has been exactly the opposite. Employers who wish to dismiss workers who have *estabilidade* (tenure) find that it is exceedingly difficult to get the necessary permission from the labor courts to do so, and that the only way in which they can get rid of an unwanted employee is to buy him off. Such indemnity—which must in any case be approved by the worker's *sindicato* if one exists—may cost the employer as much as 1,000,000 cruzeiros. The result of such a situation, of course, is that many employers refuse to allow their workers to acquire ten years' seniority. For some time it was customary for employers to dismiss workers after nine years, but the labor courts held that this amounted to an attempt to circumvent the tenure law, and so they came to regard workers of nine years' standing as having tenure. As a result, it is now not uncommon for employers to fire workers after seven and a half to eight years, regardless of ability.

Although there are many firms which do not follow such a policy, virtually all companies scrutinize their workers' records very carefully when they have worked for seven and a half to eight years. If the company concludes that there is any doubt that the worker will continue to be a good employee once he has achieved tenure, he is dismissed. Even so, the author has heard many complaints from employers about workers who, when they reach ten years' seniority, sit back and coast, knowing full well that there is little the employer can do about it. The policies of employers concerning tenure vary a great deal. Some employers feel that if a worker has been a good employee he is likely to continue to be good; and that if his weaknesses haven't been discovered by the critical time, the employer deserves to be stuck with a laggard. This law is undoubtedly an example of the demagogic nature of much of the country's labor legislation. It is uneconomic and tends to hurt the very ones whom it was intended to help. However, it would be politically impossible for any government to suggest that it be removed from the Consolidacão. It is more likely that the period until tenure will be reduced.

The Brazilian industrial worker is for the most part relatively new to this kind of employment and is likely to move from job to job and even from industry to industry, a tendency provoked by the tenure law.

Only in recent years have the Brazilian employers and the government become concerned enough with the question of the quality of their employees to seek to improve the methods by which workers are committed and trained to be members of the industrial labor force.

CHAPTER IX

Working and Living Conditions of the Workers

There is little doubt that the life of the average Brazilian agricultural worker who moves to the city undergoes considerable modification. There is also little doubt that it is a change for the better. How is the situation of the urban worker an improvement over that of the agricultural laborer? Aside from such considerations as greater freedom of action and less reliance on the *patrão,* which in the eyes of some may be considered a mixed blessing, the difference can be stated in purely material terms.

For one thing, the urban worker has medical facilities which were not available to him in the country. Through the social security system, and charity, most workers and their families have access to these facilities. His children can go to school—most primary and secondary schools and all universities are located in the bigger cities. It is rare that an agricultural worker's offspring has the chance to attend school, but the majority of the urban workers' children have a chance to get at least a few years of schooling.

The urban worker probably eats better than his rural comrade, at least in the part of the country from Rio de Janeiro south. And an increasing number of factory and school lunch programs assure the worker and his children of at least one square meal a day—which is not true in the country.

The housing situation in the urban centers is poor, but at that it is an improvement over housing in the rural sections of Brazil.

Finally, there are both opportunity and excitement in the city which are lacking in the rural areas. The urban worker, if he has the ambition and the aptitude, can acquire a certain degree of skill which brings with it an increase in economic and social standing. Perhaps more important, his offspring have chances for advancement which do not exist for rural children.

All these factors are compensations for what is lost by the worker when he leaves his rural home. They make up in part for his loss of environmental stability, for his homesickness, for his feeling of engulfment in the impersonal Big City. With all, the situation of the average worker in urban Brazil remains a miserable one compared with that of workers in more advanced industrial economies, or even with that of the average member of the Argentine laboring class.

Wages and Wage Differentials

The wages of the Brazilian worker would be considered very low in the industrial countries of Western Europe and the United States. Even when compared with the income received by the workers of neighboring Argentina and Uruguay, they are low.

One of the most significant characteristics of Brazilian wages is the wide variations in different parts of the country. Table 5 shows the results

Table 5. Regional wage differentials, in Brazil.
(in cruzeiros)

State	Textiles		Metallurgy	
	Men	Women	Men	Women
Amazonas	Cr $ 785	Cr $ 351	Cr $ 568	Cr $ —
Pará	459	252	619	393
Maranhão	544	335	543	—
Piaui	402	327	376	—
Ceará	448	293	553	263
Rio Grande do Norte	478	236	549	300
Paraiba	461	379	400	270
Pernambuco	579	392	646	763
Alagoas	496	337	428	—
Sergipe	505	378	477	450
Baia	615	372	499	252
Minas Gerais	632	423	657	436
Espirito Santo	520	304	546	700
Rio de Janeiro	756	491	1226	1040
Federal District	1016	665	1106	795
São Paulo	889	604	1148	745
Parana	892	503	892	475
Santa Caterina	911	536	832	555
Rio Grande do Sul	1015	605	1018	568

of a wage survey of textile and metallurgical workers made by the Brazilian economic magazine *Conjuntura Economica* in 1950.[1]

These wage differentials among the various sections of Brazil reflect general differences in per capita income in these areas. A study of the Fundacão Getulio Vargas in 1954 showed that income per capita varied from 13,600 cruzeiros a year in the Federal District (city of Rio de Janeiro) and 7500 cruzeiros in the state of São Paulo in the south to 1250 cruzeiros and 1210 cruzeiros in the Amazonian states of Maranhão and Piaui. Commenting on these figures, João Paulo de Almeida Magalhães has said that "the conditions prevalent in the different regions of the country are as great as those existing between different countries." [2]

Minimum Wage Legislation. One of the elements of the Vargas *Estado Novo* was the establishment of a system of minimum wages first decreed in 1941, and revised several times since. The minimum wage is defined thus by Article 76 of the Consolidacão das Leis do Trabalho:

The minimum wage is the minimum amount which the employer must pay directly to every worker, including rural workers, without distinction of sex, for the normal day of service, and must be capable of satisfying at a given time and in a given part of the country, the worker's normal needs for food, shelter, clothing, health and transport.

Minimum wages are readjusted from time to time when the political pressure for such a change cannot be resisted. The President appoints minimum wage boards for each state, which make their reports on the cost-of-living changes since the fixing of the current scale of wages, and then the President determines the new levels. In 1953 President Vargas' decree of a new minimum was challenged in the courts but it was sustained.

Sometimes the increases in the minimum wage levels are largely illusory. Several months pass between the naming of minimum wage boards and the decreeing of new wage levels, and during this time the businessmen boost prices even more rapidly than the normal increase. As a result it is frequently the case that anticipatory price increases have more than offset the rise in the workers' minimum wages when the latter are finally ordered.

The minimum wage varies from one part of the country to the other. Presumably these differences are determined by the cost of living in the respective parts of the country. In 1956, the minima ranged from 2400 cruzeiros per month in the cities of Rio de Janeiro and São Paulo, to 1300 cruzeiros a month in the cities of the Amazon Valley area. In neither case was the minimum sufficient to "satisfy . . . the worker's normal needs for food, shelter, clothing, health and transport" as prescribed by the Consolidacão. However, this fact was of much greater import to the workers of Belem, in the Amazon Valley, than it was to the worker in Rio and São Paulo, for reasons which we shall discuss.

The range of minimum wages is shown in Table 6, which presents the rates established both in 1953 and in 1956.[3]

Table 6. Range of minimum wages in Brazil.

	Capital		Interior	
State	1956	1953	1956	1953
Amazonas	2900	1300	2500	—
Pará	2800	1300	2300	1000
Maranhão	2000	1200	1600	960
Piaui	1500	1000	1250	810
Ceará	2250	1120	1800	786
Rio Grande do Norte	1800	1000	1250	750
Paraiba	2200	1200	1800	800
Parnambuco	2700	1600	2000	1200
Alagoas	2200	1000	2000	800
Sergipe	2200	1080	2000	960
Baia	2700	1550	2000	1050
Espirito Santo	2800	1800	2500	1600
Rio de Janeiro	3500	2100	3200	1850
São Paulo	3700	2300	3200	1800
Parana	2700	1500	2300	1220
Santa Caterina	2400	1300	2000	1050
Rio Grande do Sul	3100	1800	2900	1600
Minas Gerais	3300	2200	2850	1800
Goias	2400	1300	1800	1050
Mato Grosso	2300	1200	1700	840
Federal District	3800	2400	—	—
Acre	2900	1500	—	—

In the North and Northeast. In Belem, 1300 cruzeiros a month meant virtually a starvation diet for the average worker. After he had paid for his food, there was little left for him to spend on anything else. Furthermore, it was our observation that in Belem, and to a lesser degree in other cities of the north and the northeast, the minimum wage tends to become the average wage. Hence, the level of living of the average Brazilian worker in these, the poorest sections of the country is miserable beyond belief.

The situation of the average construction worker in Belem was described to us by an ex-president of the construction workers union of that city. At a time when the daily minimum was thirty-three cruzeiros, the cost of a kilo of fish was over thirty cruzeiros, a kilo of fresh meat was about thirty cruzeiros, a kilo of coffee was fifty cruzeiros. As a result, most workers lived on one meal a day, consisting of grain and water made into a kind of soup, and coffee, with once in a while a bit of meat. This might be supplemented from time to time by local fruits.

Thus, the minimum wage in Belem reflected the exceedingly low standards of living of the workers in the area rather than the true cost of living in the region. The city must import most of its food supply from more southerly regions of the country, and the cost of food is therefore a good deal higher than in some areas where the minimum wage is more liberal.

Even more important than inequities in establishing the minimum wage is the fact that the minimum wage itself is a great deal more important in the north and northeast than it is in Rio, São Paulo, and the south in general. In the southerly cities an employer could not hold a good worker if he paid him only the minimum wage.

In Belem virtually every employer and trade-union leader with whom we talked indicated that most of the employees in their enterprises or most of their union members received the legal minimum wage. Coming down to the Pernambuco region just south of the hump of Brazil, it was reported that the unskilled workers in the Tiuma sugar refinery, near Recife, received the minimum wage, though a few skilled workers got as much as 4000 cruzeiros a month, three times the legal minimum.

Coming a bit farther south, to Baia, one finds that the basic wage in the tobacco industry—largely cigar making—is the legal minimum wage. Many of the workers work on piece rates, but even when they are good, they gain only about 20 per cent more than the basic wage.

Throughout this northern part of Brazil, the dock workers are among the highest paid manual employees. They are covered by national agreements which provide for payments which are sometimes three and four times the legal minimum and in some cases even more. White collar workers, such as bank clerks, also receive considerably more than the minimum. However, from Baia north, the legal minimum wage tends to be the income the manual workers receive.

This has presented serious problems both to employers and to workers. The problems of the latter are obvious, but in some cases the difficulties of the employer are also considerable. The increases in the legal minimum wage during the 1950's were not accompanied generally in the north (in contrast to the south) by proportionate boosts in the wages of skilled workers. Of course, this is the employer's own fault but this fact has not kept many employers from complaining about the situation. As a result the wage differential between the skilled and the unskilled worker has narrowed until there is little incentive for the laborer to attempt to acquire a skill, thus intensifying a problem which was already very great in this part of the country.

In the South. From Rio on south the legal minimum wage is by no means the average wage received by the worker. For instance, in the Fabrica Nacional de Motores, outside of Rio de Janeiro, very few workers received the minimum wage of 2100 cruzeiros a month in 1956. Skilled workers got from 15 to 26 cruzeiros an hour, and the median average was 22 cruzeiros, which works out to a median average of 5208 cruzeiros a month for the skilled workers of this plant. Most workers in the plant had some degree of skill. In the Volta Redonda steel plant the minimum wage was 3500 cruzeiros a month compared with the legal minimum of 2100, and many workers got considerably more than this in 1956.

Even in a small metallurgical workshop in Rio, with only one hundred and fifty employees, only one worker received the legal minimum wage, and he was an apprentice. The average daily wage in this plant was 176 cruzeiros a day, though the legal minimum for Rio was only 80.

The Esso Standard Oil Company of Brazil, with its headquarters in Rio, brought down a representative of the National Industrial Conference Board of the United States to make a careful cost-of-living survey in the early 1950's. The company has since kept up this survey, and has the policy of making regular wage readjustments in accordance with the changes in the cost of living indicated by its survey.

Farther south the same tendency to pay considerably more than the legal minimum wage is noticeable in such firms as Matarazzo in the city of São Paulo, and the Renner plant in Porto Alegre.

An exception to this general wage pattern in the southern parts of Brazil is generally found in the mining areas. We were informed that beryl miners in the state of Minas Gerais were earning only about 22 cruzeiros a day—or 660 a month—in 1956, and this in one of the higher paying mines of its kind. Conditions are also reported to be particularly poor among the coal miners of the states of Santa Caterina and Rio Grande do Sul.

Thus, the great variation in wage levels throughout Brazil is reflected in the legal minima for various parts of the country, but is even more obvious in the actual amounts paid workers. Those in the more southerly states are much more likely than their fellows farther north to receive an income which permits them to live on a healthy, decent level. Most Brazilian workers get paid either by the hour, the day, or the month, and relatively few are on any kind of incentive pay. In a few skilled occupations, piecework has been the rule for a long time, but recently other employers concerned over productivity, have also started to introduce piecework. One finds that there is a good deal of incentive pay among the Baia tobacco workers; and in the south, the Matarazzo company of São Paulo and the Renner textile and clothing plant in Porto Alegre have been introducing piecework, in the face of some opposition from their workers.

In those concerns and industries in which there are relatively strong and active unions, wages are generally increased as a result of annual *dissidios* in the labor courts, or in rare instances by means of collective contracts. These cases are much more frequent in the south than in the north, and this helps to explain why the minimum wage is more often the average wage from Baia to the north than it is from Rio to the south.

Insofar as individual wage increases are concerned, the worker who seems most likely to be able to fill a job is given a vacated post and with the increase in rank goes an increase in pay. A few firms, usually foreign-owned, have introduced a system of merit raises. The number of firms with such systems is small, and the success of those who do have them has been mixed.

Inflation. The frequent changes which the government has felt constrained to make in legal minimum wages during the 1940's and 1950's reveal a rapid increase in the cost of living during those years. Brazil has suffered inflation since the middle of the nineteenth century, made obvious by the fact that the nineteenth-century unit of currency and account, the "reis" was by the early years of this century so inadequate that calculations were generally made in "milreis" or a thousand of the original unit. In the 1940's the regime of Getulio Vargas substituted the "cruzeiro" for the milreis, but by the late 1950's this new unit was itself threatening to become obsolete.

The inflationary spiral has been particularly acute since the end of World War II. Table 7 gives some indication of this situation. It shows the rises in the cost of living in selected Brazilian cities on the basis of the general Brazilian price level of 1948 as 100.

Hours. The eight-hour day and six-day week is general in most industrial enterprises in Brazil. Concerning this, the Consolidacão das Leis do Trabalho says the following in its Articles 58 and 59:

Art. 58. The normal duration of work for employees in whatever type of private employment shall not exceed eight per day, unless there is some other limit which is expressly fixed.

Art. 59. The normal duration of labor may be increased by not more than two hours by means of an agreement signed between the employer and the worker, or by means of a collective contract.

1. In such an agreement or collective contract it must be provided that such extra hours of work will be remunerated at a rate at least 20 per cent in excess of the normal wage.

2. This wage increase can be omitted by agreement between workers and employer or by collective contract if the extra hours worked on one day are compensated for by a corresponding diminution on another day, so that the number of hours worked per week does not exceed the norm established above, and providing the total number of hours worked in a single day does not exceed ten.

Table 7. Brazilian cost-of-living increases.
(1948 Brazilian average—100)

City	1948	1949	1950	1951	1952	1953	1954
Rio de Janeiro	122	132	145	175	213	240	286
São Paulo	136	138	143	161	197	233	274
Porto Alegre	101	106	114	116	128	139	175
Belo Horizonte	118	125	127	137	163	210	259
Recife	115	135	141	166	188	204	239

It is our observation that most industrial plants are geared to the eight-hour day and six-day week, although this may not be as true in the north as in the south. There are exceptions, particularly in seasonal industries closely connected with agriculture, where speed in processing is of the essence. For instance, the sugar mills of the Recife area generally work on two twelve-hour shifts during the grinding season, though they stick to the eight-hour day in off-season periods. As we have already indicated, the mines are, in many cases, another exception to this rule.

There are special provisions in the Consolidacão das Leis do Trabalho concerning the labor of women and children. Women are not allowed to work between the hours of eleven in the evening and five in the morning, though exceptions to this rule are made for telephone operators, nurses, entertainers, and women who are in administrative posts. Women are forbidden to work underground in mines or in quarries, or in jobs officially proclaimed dangerous or unhealthy. Women also cannot be forced by employers to lift weights heavier than 20 kilos, or in special cases, 25 kilos.

Employers are forbidden to refuse employment to women because they are married or pregnant. All pregnant women are to have six weeks off before and after the birth of their child. If a woman worker has a miscarriage, she is to have two weeks off.[4]

A number of employers prefer male workers to females because it is claimed that women tend to be absent from work a great deal more than men. However, women are heavily employed in the textile industry, in tobacco and cigar making, and naturally, in offices. The employment of the last group has increased a great deal during the last two or three decades, and has brought about a considerable change of custom. Until not too long ago it was not considered "correct" for a young unmarried middle- or upper-class woman to go out of her parental home without an escort, and upon occasion chaperones are still customary for social occasions. However, the increasing employment of women of the upper and middle classes in white collar jobs has gone far to break down these traditions.

Minors under fourteen are forbidden to work by the Consolidacão das Leis do Trabalho, while those under eighteen receive special protection of the law. Children under eighteen are not to be employed in places where their health or morals would be endangered. In the latter category the law includes theaters, movies, casinos, cabarets, circuses, places printing or selling publications which are considered by "competent authorities" to be morally damaging, and places which dispense alcoholic beverages. However, judges of juvenile courts can give special permission for children to work in such employment if it has educational value and is not considered morally damaging, or if such employment is deemed to be absolutely necessary to the maintenace of the minor or his family.

Minors must have at least eleven hours off between work periods, and their normal working period cannot be extended except under unusual circumstances which are set forth in the law itself. They must also obtain special *carteiras profissionais* which, unlike the *carteira* of the adult, remains in the possession of the employer and must be shown upon request to the labor inspectors.

Special provisions are made for minors who are apprentices. Although the employer is only bound to pay them half the minimum wage, he is obliged to give them time off to pursue their vocational training. The apprentices for their part are obliged to attend the classes for which they are registered.

Many employers pay any worker under eighteen only half the minimum wage. In Recife many textile employers as well as those in other industries hire large numbers of juveniles; pay them apprentice wages, then dismiss them when they come of age, and fill their places with other young workers.

In addition to the children employed in industry, Brazil seems to have more than its share of juvenile newsboys, shoeshine boys, and lottery ticket sellers. Until two fundamental conditions are met—sufficient income for adult workers and an adequate school system—it is unlikely that much real headway will be made toward eliminating child labor in Brazil. The provisions of the Consolidacão have helped to reduce the number of children in industry, but they are by no means adequate for dealing with the general problem.

Housing

The problem of housing is certainly one of the gravest concerns of the Brazilian workers. For all the demagoguery of the Vargas period, and in spite of the fact that housing programs have become one of the most popular kinds of social legislation in other Latin American countries, the Brazilian government has done relatively little in this area.

As we have noted in talking about employer paternalism, some employers have sought to provide at least some housing for their employees, but this is a drop in the bucket compared with what is needed. Part of the housing problem is solved by middle-, upper middle-, or upper-class groups moving into a new development and abandoning a poorer house in some other part of the city which tends to be occupied by people of a lower economic and social level.

In 1956 the Auxiliary Archbishop of Rio was engaged in a campaign to arouse the city to wipe out the *favellas* and replace them with decent housing for the workers of the capital city. He was attempting to raise money for the purpose and hoped to be able to wipe out a considerable part of the city's slums within a few years. There were actually some expressions of indignation at the Archbishop's concern with this problem, and some declared themselves fearful that failure to achieve what he was proposing would add fuel to the fire of the Communists who were already active and popular in the *favellas*. Many Brazilians fail to realize that the housing problem is a volcano upon which their country is sitting.

Brazil, the Latin American industrial giant of the future, is experiencing growing pains. Although its industries are growing by leaps and bounds, its cities are rising spectacularly in population, and the national income is increasing at a commendable speed, the economy is beset by bottlenecks.

The transportation system is inadequate. The railroads are antiquated and badly equipped. The roads are insufficient, difficult to maintain, and few are paved. Its airlines have blossomed during the years since World War II making up for many of the gaps in the transport system, but at high cost. Transport is certainly one of the fields on which attention should be focused if the recent rate of growth of the Brazilian economy is to be continued. It is the key, too, to the opening up of the great interior of the country where many Brazilians rightly feel the future of the nation lies.

The power situation also is embarrassing. Not possessing any first-rate sources of coal, Brazil must depend on poor grade native coal, on imported coal, on petroleum, and on hydroelectric resources for overcoming this deficiency. In periods of bad weather which reduce the flow of hydroelectric current, the major industrial cities are often subject to severe rationing of electricity and a consequent slowing down of industrial activity and inconvenience for householders.

The Brazilians have made a bad situation worse by the assertion of a rather absurd economic nationalism in the case of the oil industry. Whatever the dangers in allowing foreign companies to develop their oil industry, the risk of using up an increasing part of their precious foreign exchange in the importation of petroleum and other sources of fuel and power is a greater danger. This expense has already made it difficult to import badly needed machinery for the growing industries, has slowed down the process of improving the transport system, and has crippled the development of other power resources. However, it would seem that the policy of *Petroleo e Nosso* is likely to continue even if the nation's oil reserves remain untapped for another generation.

The nation's period of economic development, as we have indicated, is strikingly similar to that of the United States in the generation after our Civil War. This is the period of vaulting ambitions, of dramatic economic achievements, of huge profits, and of unscrupulous "robber barons." Like their opposite numbers in the United States, many of the great speculators and promoters, the buyers of public officials and of legislatures, are also building up the nation's economy. One of the reasons why this is an era of corruption in Brazil is that it is a period in which everything is being done at once, when there is a shortage of everything, and even the simplest commodities or privileges can be sold to the highest bidder.

But there is one fundamental difference between the robber baron period in Brazil and the same period in the United States, and that is the timing. Brazil is coming into its industrial adolescence in a period when trade unions are commonplace, when labor laws are general, when the social conscience is awakened, and in which there is an international Communist movement. The Rockefellers, Morgans, and Carnegies ran no risk that their activities would stimulate the growth in their country of a reaction led by clever members of an international political and social movement directed by a foreign power. The Brazilians of the same ilk do run that risk.

Great discontents are boiling up in Brazil. The Brazilian workers are to a very large degree paying for their country's industrialization; their real wages are kept down to provide the large profits characteristic of the Brazilian economy, most of which are to a large degree ploughed back into its further development. This is the source of some of the workers' complaints.

Another powerful source of discontent is the readjustment which the Brazilian worker himself has to make when he enters the industrial economy. The thousands of workers who stream back to their northeastern homes, in spite of their miserable existence there, is witness to this.

The Brazilian worker is a more docile person than his counterpart in Argentina and Chile. He is tolerant and he is used to living on nothing. He has the consolation of his *macumba* (the Afro-Brazilian religious cults) and his family and kinship relationships. But in the cities all of this is attenuated, is coming to have less pull on the worker, and he is changing. The Brazilian worker has become a great deal more class-conscious, he has become much more nationalistic, he has become much more ambitious. He has become aware of the fact that his nation is changing, that it is developing, and he has become eager to share more fully in the benefits of that change.

These changes are perhaps inevitable as a nation is transformed from a patriarchal agrarian pattern to an industrial urban one. However, Getulio Vargas both stimulated the change and tried to chain it to his own personal ambition. By picturing himself as father of the poor, and as protector of the worker, he sought to put himself in the role of the landowner *patrão* with whom the worker was familiar. At the same time he aroused the worker to be suspicious of his employer. He kindled the worker's nationalistic instincts by posing as the "defender of the national sovereignty," and he provided the worker with tools to express his discontent—the trade-union structure, and working-class political parties.

While he was alive, Getulio attempted to tie both of these closely to himself. It was he who imposed the *Estado Novo* with its unions tightly controlled by the government. It was he who substituted the labor court for the collective bargaining table. It was he who destroyed the older trade-union movement. Thus, the peculiar characteristics of Brazilian labor–management relations are to be explained in terms of Getulio Vargas' political career and ambitions, and not in terms of anything special in the way Brazilian industrialization has developed or even in its tempo of growth.

However, the danger now is that with the passing of Getulio the whole framework which he developed will fall into the hands of the Communist Party. This danger is a pressing one both in the trade unions and in Vargas' party, the Partido Trabalhista Brasileiro. There is an increasing desire on the part of the workers and those leaders who are most closely in touch with the rank and file, for greater independence for the labor movement, and for a truer expression of the workers' desires and ambitions in the political field. But there seems to be no one present to take the leadership in this movement except the Communists.

Getulio contributed to this situation mightily by his extreme personalism. All good things flowed from him personally. He cared little about the corruption and rot around him so long as those involved would play his game and would cooperate with him. He left behind him no movement with a clear objective, no ideology, no set of principles.

This is a situation which plays directly into the hands of the Communists. The workers are naturally seeking some other leader to take Vargas' place. The Communists are wisely continuing their work at the grass roots and gaining increasing influence in the unions. They are taking over the mantle of Vargas and being more Getulista than Getulio himself. If the workers become disillusioned in the search for a new Messiah, they may well turn to the Communists—who, incidentally have a Messiah of their own, Luiz Carlos Prestes.

The upper classes, in the meantime, seem oblivious to the whole problem. Too often employers accuse a class-conscious, labor leader, who firmly defends his union members, of being a Communist whether he is or not. They are too frequently unable to distinguish between the trade unionist trying to make it impossible for the Communists to take his union away from him, from the man who really is a Communist.

At the same time the corrupt elements continue to grow fat from their rich government connections. They seem not to care that continued dishonesty in high places is eating into the very vitals of the system of which they have been the greatest beneficiaries. Corruption, patronage, and demagoguery remain the order of the day so far as many leading politicians, and the economically powerful, are concerned.

Perhaps one can become too much of a Jonah in viewing the Brazilian situation. The country has been in a more or less permanent state of crisis since the overthrow of the *Estado Novo* in 1945, each highpoint in the crisis seems as if it would be the last, but the country continues to go on without fundamental alteration in its methods of behavior except for the seven months of the Quadros administration. In spite of the decay at the top, the body of the Brazilian economy is increasingly healthy, and the country continues taking rapid strides toward becoming a major industrial nation.

Perhaps this situation will continue. Certainly if Brazil can go on for another generation without a military dictatorship and without falling under the control of the Communists, the New World will wake up to discover that it has two giants, not one.

PART TWO—ARGENTINA

CHAPTER X

Economic, Political, and Social Background

Argentina, occupying most of the southern third of the South American continent, has long thought of herself as the leader of the Spanish-speaking part of the hemisphere. She has for several generations been the richest of the South American countries, her people enjoy the highest standard of living of any country in the region, and the Argentines have been sure of their "manifest destiny" in their own part of the world.

The population of Argentina is second only to Brazil in South America, and ranks behind the United States, Brazil, and Mexico in the whole hemisphere. In 1960 it was estimated that there were a little over 20,000,000 Argentines, and that the nation's population was increasing at the rate of 1.9 per cent per annum.[1]

Economic Background

Although industrialization has progressed rapidly in Argentina during the last quarter of a century, the nation remains primarily an agricultural and grazing country. Argentina had become one of the world's great grain and cattle producers during the second half of the nineteenth century, and wheat and meat are still its most important products. During the colonial period and the first years of independence (which was proclaimed in 1816), the city of Buenos Aires was largely a commercial center for the towns along the great rivers and in the hinterland of the southern part of the South American continent. Much of the interior remained in the hands of the Indians who fought a losing battle with the *gauchos,* wild, half-breed pioneers who lived on huge cattle ranges which spread over the northern part of the great Argentine pampas.

It was the regime of dictator Juan Manuel Rosas, who ruled for nearly two decades before his fall in 1852, that drove the Indians to the south and laid the groundwork for the development of the country into one of the world's great sources of grains and meat. Most of the land of the rich central part of the country was divided among a relatively small number of large landholders, who formed an agricultural oligarchy which was to dominate the economic, social, and political life of the nation for almost a century after the fall of Rosas. This oligarchy proved to be progressive in an economic sense, eager to adopt new methods in order to increase the output and profitability of their land.

The landlord-dominated governments of the last half of the nineteenth century cooperated in the task of increasing Argentine agricultural and grazing output. The keystone of their economic policy was to encourage grain growing and cattle raising for export. To this end, they encouraged the migration of many hundreds of thousands of Europeans to provide labor.

With the invention of barbed wire, it became possible to fence off the plains which meant that it was possible to refine the wild native cattle. Blooded bulls from Britain and other parts of Europe were brought in by the ranchers to improve the pedigree of Argentine cattle.

The improvement of the quality of Argentine cattle was stimulated by an increase in demand for Argentina's products in Europe, particularly in Great Britain. In 1846 the United Kingdom abolished the Corn Laws which had provided protection for home-grown agricultural produce and its markets were thrown open to imported grains, meat, and other products. Great Britain first turned to the United States but as Argentine output increased, the United Kingdom bought increasingly from the South American country.

With the growth in shipments of meat and grains to Europe, there came the development of the Argentine railroad system which still remains the best and most extensive in Latin America. The genesis of this system as a means of getting the country's grazing and agricultural products to overseas markets determined the kind of a railroad network that would be established.

On the one hand, the emphasis on exports determined the direction in which the railroad lines were built. It explains the fact that all the country's roads had as their terminus either Buenos Aires or the river port of Rosario, and the fact that it is still impossible to get from one interior city to another by rail without going several hundred miles out of one's way.

The importance of the railroads in trade with Britain also explains the interest of British investors in helping to construct the rail network. Most of the Argentine railroads were bought by the Perón government from 1948 through 1949 in return for a year's supply of meat. Argentina now has a unified national railroad system. However, due to the depression, World War II, the threat of nationalization during the first years of the Perón administration, and the failure of the Perón regime to reequip the roads, the Argentine rail system was severely run down by the late 1950's.

The Growth of Industry

Although Argentine cattle were first shipped to Europe on the hoof or salted, by the turn of the century improved packing processes made it possible to ship the product in more compact and economic form. This also gave rise to the packing houses which became the country's principal manufacturing industry. The packing plants were located chiefly near Buenos Aires and Rosario.

The First World War gave a new impetus to industrialization. It deprived Argentina of manufactured goods from Europe forcing local craftsmen and merchants to produce many of these things themselves.

In the years that followed, with the return of European goods to Argentine markets, the rate of industrial development slowed down. However, the World Depression acted as a further impetus to manufacturing. Shrinkage of the customary markets for grains and meat left Argentina with insufficient foreign exchange to purchase desired manufactured products. Thus, in spite of the fact that the governments of the 1930's were negative toward industry, the facts of the depression gave protection and stimulus to the development of manufacturing.

The Second World War had the same effect as the Great Depression, and after 1943 there was positive encouragement of industrialization by the Argentine government. Hence, since 1930 the country has experienced an unbroken development of manufacturing.

The Perón regime was particularly encouraging to industry. The first Five-Year Plan, launched in 1947, tried to lay the groundwork for extensive manufacturing. A. H. Tandy has described the scope of this plan:

The first Five-Year Plan (1947–51) contained projects for public health, housing, land, air and sea transport, sanitation, petroleum, gas, coal and hydro-electric development, roads, tourism, a new geological survey and the entrance of 250,000 immigrants. Its cost, to be met by borrowing and by the creation of profit-making Government agencies rather than by charges on the budget, worked out ultimately to an official figure of 18,000 million pesos, nearly three times the original estimates.[2]

After two years following the completion of the first Five-Year Plan, the Perón government started a second Five-Year Plan. Tandy describes it thus:

A second Five-Year Plan (1953–57) got under way in 1954. . . . Targets were set for agriculture, colonization, farming and livestock, conservation of national resources, fuel and power, mining, iron and steel, metallurgical and chemical industries, transportation, roads, sanitation, hydro-electric projects, ports and waterways, communications, forestry, technical research, manufacturing industries, fisheries, public health and safety, social welfare and planning, housing, education, tourism, and the construction of public buildings.

Briefly summarized, the main objectives of the second Five-Year Plan were to increase exportable surpluses while maintaining control and selection of imports, and, as far as possible, to improve terms of trade; to develop the steel and basic chemical industries; to expand petroleum production in order to save exchange on imports; and to intensify agricultural mechanization and productivity.

The Perón regime was overthrown before this plan had run even two years of the five-year course. The succeeding governments did not continue the plan as such, though many of the individual projects which the Perón government had started were carried forward.

Through its newly established Industrial Bank, the Perón government extended liberal credit to those wishing to establish or expand manufacturing enterprises. A policy of high protection for manufacturing firms was adopted by the Perón regime in contrast to previous administrations' opposition to protection. The construction of gas pipelines from the oil fields of the southern part of the country to Buenos Aires provided the new manufacturing enterprises with an important source of fuel.

Among the industries which grew during the Perón regime were cotton textiles, metallurgy, the chemical industry, the motor industry, and the shoe industry. Among the more important projects sponsored by the regime were the nation's first basic iron and steel plant in the Buenos Aires town of San Nicolás, the FIAT agricultural machinery plant, and the Kaiser Automobile factory near Córdoba.

The Perón government paid for its program of economic development with proceeds from agriculture and grazing. The institution used for this purpose, established a few months before Perón took office, was the Instituto Argentino por Producción e Intercamio, or IAPI. In March 1946 it was granted a monopoly on the purchase of Argentine grain production, and some years later meat products were also added to those handled by IAPI.

Throughout most of the Perón administration the prices paid to agriculturalists were held at levels far below world prices. At the same time,

Argentina's agricultural output was sold abroad at what the market would bear. A considerable portion of the profits from these operations went to finance the importation of needed capital equipment for growing Argentine industry.

Another portion of the profits of IAPI went to repatriate most of the foreign investments in Argentina. Part went to expand the country's merchant marine to the point of making Argentina one of the world's larger maritime powers.

The result of this exploitation of the agricultural segment of the economy was a considerable decrease in the area cultivated and in the output of Argentine agriculture. Many agriculturalists, caught between the low prices paid by the IAPI and the additions to labor costs fomented by the Perón government's program for agricultural workers, found that they could not make ends meet. They were not able to import agricultural machinery to take the place of workers who drifted to the cities in search of higher paying jobs in industry because the Perón government would not make foreign exchange available for this purpose. The result was that many agriculturalists gave up farming and moved to the cities, while others drastically cut down the area of land under cultivation or in grazing.

This trend was intensified in the early 1950's by two years of drought which caused a major economic crisis in 1952. It was impossible in that year for Argentina to honor its commitments to ship meat and grain to customers abroad and there were severe shortages of these products in Argentina itself.

In spite of the development of industry during the last quarter of a century, Argentina's economy is still based principally on grazing and agriculture. The nation depends upon income from these exports for a large part of needed manufactured goods. This is particularly true as far as agricultural equipment and machinery for industry is concerned.

Industrialization is still a policy much debated in Argentina. The governments after Perón reversed his policy of encouraging industry to the detriment of agriculture, and voices argued that Argentina should not go any farther along the road to manufacturing, though the Frondize administration renewed the drive toward industrialization.

An argument used by those opposed to industrialization is that although the country has an abundance of agricultural materials, it is lacking essential minerals. George Wythe sums up this situation this:

Various raw materials needed in industry must be imported, among them jute, rubber, and chocolate. The most serious of Argentine deficiencies are, however, those in minerals. Argentina has no commercial production of coal and is short of metals. Yet, though mining is less important there than in most other Latin American countries, it is today developing apace. Lead is now produced in fairly important quantities. Some other metals (silver, zinc, tin, tungsten, manganese and beryllium) are also produced. Unfortunately, iron ore deposits are scarce and of poor quality. Attempts to develop the copper deposits have thus far been unsuccessful and imports of electrolytic copper for use in local industries amount to about 5000 tons a year.[3]

One of the principal deficiencies of Argentina from the point of view of industrialization is its lack of adequate fuel resources. Not only does it have insufficient, poor-quality coal, its potential hydro-electric resources are all in the western part of the country, and the process of developing them and extending power lines to bring electricity to the main markets along the coast is very expensive.

The country is thought to possess sizable petroleum resources. However, until recently these have not been developed very extensively. Between 1929 and 1958 the chief role in the industry was played by the government's Yacimientos Petroliferos Fiscales (YPF), which by 1956 was only producing about 40 per cent of the nation's needs. But in 1958 the Frondizi regime began signing contracts with several foreign oil firms, to aid YPF develop the nation's oil industry. In 1959 Argentine oil output rose 30 per cent and by the end of 1961 the country was self-sufficient in petroleum.

Another factor of importance is the industrial potential of Argentina's neighbors. Brazil has virtually all the natural resources needed to become one of the world's great industrial powers. Chile has most of the raw materials necessary for heavy industry, though its small population does not provide sufficient market for a major industry of this sort, and would seem to point up the practicability of a degree of cooperation in economic development between Chile and Argentina.

One important feature of the Argentine situation which is favorable to industrialization is the fact that the rate of literacy and education is higher in Argentina than in most of the other countries of Latin America. Although there is much need for technical training and specialization among the Argentine workers most of them have the rudiments of basic education, particularly in the cities.

Another factor favoring economic development is the fact that Argentina is not faced with the racial conflicts which plague some of its neighbors. The great majority of the Argentine population is of European descent, and class distinctions are not generally reenforced by racial differences.

Heavy Industry. The establishment of the San Nicolás steel plant is one of the most controversial aspects of Argentine industrialization. The country lacks virtually all the raw materials for heavy industry, and many have argued that the San Nicolás plant will be uneconomical. Those who take this view argue that Argentina would be better advised to develop the iron and steel industry of Chile, which has most of the necessary raw materials and already has a successful steel plant.

However, the advocates of the San Nicolás project have several counter-arguments. On the one hand, they point out, Argentina consumes something like a million tons of iron and steel products a year, an amount which could not possibly be supplied by the Chilean industry in the foreseeable future. In the second place, they argue that it is cheaper for Argentina to import raw materials—particularly iron and coal—and manufacture products rather than import the finished goods. Finally, they use the nationalistic argument that Argentina must have a heavy industry for reasons of defense. It is never clear in these arguments just whom Argentina must defend herself against, though frequently the implication is that it is her northern neighbor, Brazil. In any case, this last argument is a persuasive one for many Argentines.

The Rate of Investment. Savings and investment in Argentina during recent decades have been described by the Economic Commission for Latin America (ECLA) as "satisfactory," insofar as volume is concerned. The ECLA commented that "the rate of saving is relatively satisfactory in Argentina and should not need to be appreciably augmented." With regard to investment, the ECLA reported that "the level of investment which the country has maintained during the last decade is acceptable, in relation to other countries, and has undergone only a minor decrease in the most recent years."

However, there was some concern expressed concerning the direction in which investment has gone. The ECLA compared the investments in basic capital equipment shown in the census of government investment made in 1948 with the investments of the government between 1945 and 1951. The figures are shown in Table 8.[4]

This table includes only those elements in the government capital equipment which have changed most drastically percentage-wise during the period under analysis. They indicate a very grave imbalance in the military capital expenditures, an imbalance which the country can ill afford.

The Geographical Distribution of Industry. One important result of industrialization has been the rapid growth of urban centers, particularly Greater Buenos Aires. A sizable majority of Argentine industries are located in or around the capital city. Even before industrialization it was already the largest population center and thus provided a sizable market; the port of Buenos Aires was the largest in the country and the packing-house industry had early been established there so that meat could be shipped directly to Europe. Industries in the Buenos Aires area were efficiently located for the importation of raw materials.

The population of the capital city and its suburban areas is estimated at approximately five million people, or something more than one-fourth of the total population of the country. Another half million or more live in and around the city of Rosario, a couple of hundred miles up the river from Buenos Aires. Rosario is a city of packing houses, grain mills, railroad workshops, metallurgical plants, and textile factories. It declined somewhat during the Perón regime.

Table 8. Argentine government investments.
(in per cent)

Activity	Basic capital (*1948 census*)	Investments (*1948–1951*)
Highways	18.4	9.4
Railroads	11.9	6.3
Combustibles	14.9	4.3
Industries	3.7	1.6
National defense	2.1	29.3
Sewage works	12.6	4.0

However, there are other industrial centers of importance. Undoubtedly the town of San Nicolás, in the northern part of the province of Buenos Aires, where the new national steel plant is being constructed, will become a hub for other metallurgical plants and perhaps chemical industries as well.

The city of Córdoba, 250 miles northwest of Buenos Aires, is already an important center of the metallurgical industry. It is there that the National Airplane Engine Plant of the air force, the FIAT agricultural equipment factory, and Kaiser automobile plant have been built. It is also a center of the textile industry. Still farther to the north, the city of Tucumán is the center of the sugar-refining business, and also has important ceramics works and railroad workshops. In the west is the city of Mendoza, which is the principal center of the wine industry and also has textiles, small metallurgy, and other industries.

In the south is the city of Bahia Blanca which is an important packing-house center with some textile plants and diversified manufacturing. Still farther south the city of Comodoro Rivadavia has grown up as the principal focus of the oil industry. There are also important naval repair facilities and workshops there and as the region develops it will probably produce other articles for regional consumption.

The city of La Plata, only fifty miles from Buenos Aires is one of the main packing-house centers. It also has an important textile industry and is developing a range of manufacturing enterprises. Throughout the province of Buenos Aires, of which La Plata is the capital, there are many small cities and towns which possess at least one important manufacturing firm.

Thus, Argentina is developing a wide range of industries. Many Argentines picture their nation as the future industrial hub of South America. At the present time, Argentina has neither the raw materials nor the population to compete with Brazil. She will undoubtedly become a nation of a mixed agricultural-grazing-industrial economy. But it is unlikely that she will ever develop into the major industrial nation of the continent.

Socio-Political Background

From a sociological point of view perhaps the most important fact about Argentina is that most of the present inhabitants are either immigrants or children of immigrants. With the fencing in of the pampas paving the way for the growth of grazing and grain growing soon after the middle of the nineteenth century, the stage was set for the arrival of hundreds of thousands of workers from Italy, Spain, and other European countries.

Many of these immigrant workers came only for the harvest season and returned each year after this period. These were the famous "swallows" about whom countless legends have been woven. Others, however, settled on the great *estancias*—the wheat and meat growing farms. Still others filled the growing cities of Buenos Aires, Rosario, Mendoza, La Plata, etc.

The immigrant Italian, Spanish, and Central European workers formed the bulk of the urban working class. They brought with them the radicalism which was becoming popular in their homelands. They also contributed to an existing rivalry between the countryside and the capital city of Buenos Aires.

This competition between the *porteños,* as the people of Buenos Aires are generally known in Argentina, and the people of the interior was noted by Domingo Fausto Sarmiento, the powerful writer of 125 years ago, opponent of the Rosas dictatorship, and subsequently President of the Republic. It was the theme of his most famous book, *Facundo.*

Sarmiento summed up the difference and rivalry between the city residents and residents of the country as follows:

The city man dresses in European clothes, lives a civilized existence similar to that found elsewhere; in the city there are laws, ideas of progressive education, some municipal organization, regular government, etc. When one leaves the city everything changes: the countryman wears what I shall call American clothes since they are common in all neighboring peoples; his habits are different; his needs are peculiar and limited. These appear to be two different societies, two peoples strange to one another. Furthermore, the countryman, far from aspiring to be like him of the city, rejects with disdain the luxury and courteous customs and the clothing of the city man. . . . Everything civilized in the city is rejected in the countryside. . . .[5]

Although the cultural differences between the city and the country have been greatly modified, the struggle between Buenos Aires and the hinterland continues. Originally, this was a struggle between the relatively sophisticated, cosmopolitan, Europeanized populace of the capital and the native, more uncouth American masses of the countryside. The struggle still persists. It has been since the beginning of the republic, one of the principal currents in Argentine politics. The infamous dictator, Juan Manuel Rosas, was the archetype of the *gaucho* who fought for the dominance of rural Argentina over the metropolis.

Subsequent to his everthrow, the political center of the nation shifted to the anti-gaucho faction. The statesmen and politicians who ruled the nation for the rest of the century attempted to Europeanize Argentina.

These men organized the Conservative Party, which ruled the nation until the fateful election of 1916. Although their regime was not a democracy, they were benevolent despots and the country prospered and grew under their direction.

The Radicals. However, the growing middle class, which had found its political expression in the Unión Cívica Radical (Radical Party), was pressing for a larger part in the nation's affairs by the turn of the century. Twelve years later Conservative President Roque Saenz Peña paved the way to Radical victory by pushing a law through congress providing for secret balloting. The *Ley Saenz Peña* also provided that the majority party in each province should name two-thirds of that province's members of the Chamber of Deputies, while the party with the second largest number of votes would receive the other third.

With the election of 1916, the "Europeanizers" were defeated by the Radicals who represented the other—the "American"—tradition in the nation's affairs. Under Radical President Hipólito Irigoyen, Argentina had its first middle-class government. It was succeeded by another Radical regime under an aristocratic landowner, Marcelo T. de Alvear, and then Irigoyen returned to the presidency in 1928.

The second Irigoyen administration was overthrown by a military *coup d'etat* supported by the Conservatives. For the next thirteen years the Conservatives dominated the government, controlling it through force, fraud, and corruption. Successive Conservative-based governments made a travesty of democracy everywhere outside of Buenos Aires. When a provincial government hostile to the national administration was elected, the federal administration "intervened" in the province, ousting the elected officials, and appointing an "intervenor" to administer the province *ad interim* and to see that new elections came out right.

The "Europeanizers" and "Americanizers." The Conservatives had abondoned their role as principal advocates of "Europeanization." The Conservative Party became the vehicle of the large landowners who were determined to maintain their hold on the nation's economy and politics at any cost.

The role as the main "European" party had been preempted by the Socialist Party. It was organized in 1896 by a group of Spanish, Italian, German, and French immigrants and a few young Argentines in Buenos Aires. The party attracted a number of bright young Argentines from the middle classes who became its outstanding spokesmen.

The Socialists were, until the coming of Perón, Argentina's principal working-class party. However, their appeal was strongest among the European masses of Buenos Aires and its vicinity, and it is no coincidence that of all the Socialist parties which have made their appearance in Latin America during the last six decades or more, the Argentine party was the one closest to the European mold.

The Socialist Party was always actively concerned with the trade-union movement and from the 1920's on was the principal political force in the unions. However, following its European model, it never carried on "fraction" work within the unions and when the Peronista movement arose the Socialist loyalty of most of the important trade-union leaders and of the trade-union masses was swept aside.

During the first part of the twentieth century, the Unión Cívica Radical was the principal political representative of the small merchant in the rural towns of the interior. It was the spokesman for the small independent agriculturalist, in his fight against the Conservative large landholder. It also became the spokesman for the industrialists, big and small, during the the 1920's and 1930's.

The Radical Party's form of organization was typical of the interior. The party has never been known, unlike the Socialists, for the intellectual quality of its leadership. Its typical leader, particularly in the interior, has been the local political *caudillo* (the boss) who may be a storekeeper, a rancher, a professional politician. Whoever he is, the local Radical boss usually has a charismatic quality traditional of the leaders of the interior since before the days of Juan Manuel Rosas.

"Caudillismo" and Juan Domingo Perón. Europe vs. America is not the only political conflict in Argentina. Another key factor has been the tradition of *caudillismo,* of the political boss and spellbinder whose hold over his followers is more paternal than partisan. This was an essential reason for the rise of leaders such as Rosas, Facundo Quiroga, and others in the early nineteenth century. The tradition still lived a century later and was part of the appeal of Hipólito Irigoyen, Amadeo Sabattini, and other Radical Party leaders—and of Juan Domingo Perón.

Perón appealed to many facets of the Argentine national character. He appealed to the countryman who had recently come into the city. In this sense he was a spokesman for the country against the city—though like his predecessor, Rosas, he centralized virtually all political and economic power in Buenos Aires.

Perón appealed in terms of the old-time *caudillo.* A man of undoubted personal charm, he was able to harangue the people in their own idiom. Furthermore, he was a man of tremendous vitality and appeared to be *muy macho* (very much a man), a characteristic which has counted heavily among the rural masses since colonial times.

But Perón also appealed to other factors in the complex character of the average Argentine. He appealed to the second generation which tended to reject the Anarchism, Socialism, even the Communism of their parents as part of the old folks' "foreignness," but were ready for a kind of radicalism with an Argentine flavor. This Perón offered them.

Perón also appealed on a more materialistic level. He gave the workers higher wages, a social security system, labor legislation which previous regimes had failed to provide.

There is no doubt that, in making his appeal principally to the workers, and basing his power in considerable part on the organized labor movement, Perón was attempting to arouse the workers' protest against industrialism, and to channel it through himself and the government which he controlled as completely as possible. Although he used the preexisting trade-union movement as a stepping stone, he attempted to destroy the independence of the movement completely once he was in control. He first put himself in the unions' place as Secretary of Labor, and then after he became President he put the Ministry of Labor under the eagle-eyed supervision of his wife as the vehicle through which to present grievances and make demands upon employers.

Finally, Perón waved the flag of Argentine nationalism. Over a century ago Sarmiento recognized the nationalism of his fellow countrymen. In *Facundo,* he says:

. . . The Argentines of whatever class they may be, civilized or ignorant, have a high degree of consciousness of their value as a nation. All the other American peoples taunt them with this vanity and are offended by their presumptuousness and arrogance. I do not think that these taunts are entirely unjustified and they do not annoy me. . . .

Whatever the cause of Perón's success in appealing to the people of his country, he did have such success. Although his was a dictatorship bordering on the totalitarian, it need not have been so. He really had the support of a majority of his fellow countrymen, particularly after his first election. And he continued to have the support of large elements of the population even after he was overthrown.

The Post-Perón Situation. The single biggest political problem facing the nation after the fall of Perón was the fact that public opinion was very closely divided between Peronistas and anti-Peronistas. The military regimes which succeeded Perón did not permit the Peronistas to function openly, but most of the political parties legalized after the "Liberating Revolution" bent their energies to appealing to the large portion of the working class still Peronista in its sympathies.

In fact, the workers were left rudderless with the fall of Perón. Most of them had become accustomed to taking their problems to the Ministry of Labor for solution. However, after December 1955 the Ministry of Labor was in the process of being purged, had indecisive leadership, and was dealing with a group which was fundamentally hostile to the government.

The trade unions to which the workers might have turned were also hamstrung. After December 1955 they were under the control of military officers who in no real sense represented the workers. (See Chapter XVI.)

In the meantime, the employers did relatively little to ameliorate the situation. Although during the Perón regime they had been forced to deal with the unions, one has the impression that with the fall of the regime they hoped to "put the workers in their place."

After Perón, the political parties sought support from the discontented workers, most of whom were still loyal to the fallen dictator. Most of the parties split on the issue of how to deal with the Peronista masses.

By the time of the constituent assembly elections in July 1957, there were over forty registered political parties. However, only a few of these are worthy of comment. The pre-Perón parties revived, and several new ones were founded. However, there was great dissension in the ranks of the old parties, several of which split into rival groups.

The Radical Party was the most badly divided. The national leadership had passed before the fall of Perón into the hands of a group headed by Dr. Arturo Frondizi, a wiry, greying intellectual. Frondizi and his associates felt that their party and the other traditional political organizations had failed to provide the political support and labor and social legislation for the working class which was now the largest single political bloc in the country. As a result, maintained Frondizi, Perón had capitalized on this fact for his own benefit.

Frondizi and his friends therefore developed a program of social development and economic nationalism even before the fall of Perón. Subsequently, they continued this program, and as a result were accused of "out-Perónizing Perón." Large elements of the party membership and leadership refused to go along with the program, or with Frondizi's leadership.

At least three other Radical factions appeared. Two of these were, like the Frondizi faction, political descendants of the early Radical *caudillo,* Hipólito Irigoyen. These factions were led by Ricardo Balbin who had been the united party's candidate for President against Perón in 1951, and Amadeo Sabattini, the chief of the Radical Party in the province of Córdoba, and a redoubtable figure in his own right. The last group, the Unionistas were the most conservative Radical group, descended from the opponents of Irigoyen in the 1920's. These three factions joined before the July 1957 elections to form the Unión Cívica Radical del Pueblo in opposition to the Frondizi faction organized as the Unión Cívica Radical Intransigente.

The Conservative Party, though much reduced by a split between those who felt that it was important to appeal to the Peronista-inclined workers and those who refused to engage in what they called "demagoguery." The much smaller Progressive Democratic Party, with its principal center of influence in the Province of Santa Fé, suffered a similar division.

A split also occurred in the ranks of the Socialist Party. The pre-Perón leadership, headed by Américo Ghioldi and Nicolas Repetto, felt that no compromise should be made with the Peronistas, whether they were workers or not. The opposing faction, headed by Alicia Moreau de Justo, party secretary Ramón Muñiz, and José Luis Romero, felt that if the Socialists were to rebuild as a national organization, it would have to assume leadership of the working class, and could only do so with a distinctly radical program, appealing especially to the workers.

Finally, the Communists were also split. They had been divided during the Perón regime, one faction supporting the government, another opposing it.

New parties also appeared, at least three of which should be mentioned. The Catholic opponents of Perón had begun to organize a Christian Democratic Party more than a year before the fall of Perón. With the fall of the dictator, the Christian Democrats came out into the open, and were the country's fourth largest party.

Another Catholic party to appear was the Unión Federal, composed of right-wing elements which had joined in the overthrow of Perón in 1955. This group included a number of disillusioned followers of Perón from the fringe of the Fascist Alianza Libertadora Nacional. The Unión Federal was strongly opposed to the regime of General Pedro Aramburu, and eager to present itself as a successor to Perón.

Finally, the Partido Laborista was revived. This organization was first established during the 1946 election campaign to back Perón, and had in its leadership at that time most of the pro-Perón trade-union leaders. However, Perón ordered it to merge with his other followers in the Partido Peronista, and a small group, led by packing-house union leader Cipriano Reyes, refused to go along with this merger. Reyes became a violent anti-Peronista, and in 1948 was put in jail, where he stayed until Perón's overthrow. After the downfall of Perón, Reyes revived the Partido Laborista with only moderate success.

Thus, the political picture of Argentina changed considerably after the Perón Era. Thereafter the country remained divided between Peronistas and anti-Peronistas. The old parties were basically split and new factions which appeared inside and outside the old parties felt that until this heritage of the Peronista period was overcome, "normality" could not return to Argentine political life.

The post-Perón provisional government came to an end on May 1, 1958 with Arturo Frondizi's inauguration as constitutional President. His principal opponent had been Ricardo Balbin, candidate of the Unión Cívica Radical del Pueblo. Frondizi had a majority of two million votes.

The Workers

Most workers of Argentina are of European origin. The majority of the original Indian inhabitants of the Argentine pampas were a migratory, relatively savage people not amenable to the rule of their Spanish conquerors. During the nineteenth century, they were pushed back farther and farther to the south and the north, to make way for European settlement of the pampas. There are now few Indians left who live in their ancient ways. However, a sizable number was absorbed into the white population, and the farther north one goes in Argentina, the more Indian features one sees in the populace.

At the time of independence, there was a sizable Negro population in Buenos Aires and other cities. Many thousands of Negro men were impressed into the armies of General San Martín which liberated the southern part of the continent from Spanish rule, and these never returned. The rest have been largely absorbed into the white population and have been lost as a separate group.

Both Indians and Negroes were overwhelmed by the Europeans who came to the country during the last half of the nineteenth century and the early years of the present one. One of the largest groups of immigrants was the Italians, and there is still a distinctly Italian air about Buenos Aires. The characteristic accent of the Spanish spoken by the *porteño* is Italian; his diet puts much emphasis on spaghetti and other *pasta*.

The Argentine worker has always lived better than most of his Latin American brothers. That this is true at the present time is indicated by the following list which shows the per capita income of most of the Latin American countries (as well as that of the United States, for purposes of comparison).[6] The amounts are in United States dollars, and the average is the 1952–1954 period.

Argentina	460
Bolivia	—
Brazil	230
Chile	360
Colombia	250

Costa Rica	—
Cuba	310
Dominican Republic	160
Ecuador	150
El Salvador	—
Guatemala	160
Haiti	—
Honduras	150
Mexico	220
Nicaragua	—
Panama	250
Paraguay	140
Peru	120
Uruguay	—
Venezuela	540
United States	1870

Although Venezuela has a higher per capita income than Argentina, mere figures present a false impression. The very high level of Venezuela is explained by the income from oil which is very unevenly distributed throughout the country's population. The living level of the typical Argentine worker is considerably above that of his Venezuelan counterpart.

The relatively high level of living of the Argentine worker is reflected in various elements in his daily life. Being among the world's great producers of meat and grains, the Argentines have seldom been lacking in these two staple items of diet.

In terms of clothing, too, the Argentine worker has been better off than the workers of most of Latin America. For example, in Argentina the availability of cotton is 5.8 kilograms per capita contrasted with 3.6 in Brazil, and 2.3 in Chile. With wool, it's 1.8 in Argentina, 0.2 in Brazil, and 0.7 in Chile.[7]

Shoes are also more widely available to the Argentine worker than to his counterpart in most Latin American countries. Argentina is one of four Latin American countries which produce more than one pair of shoes per capita.

Housing of the Argentine worker is also better than that in most neighboring countries. Although Buenos Aires and other Argentine cities have their slums they are not like the *favellas* of Rio de Janeiro and other Brazilian cities.

Long before the advent of Perón, the Argentine labor movement had tackled the housing program in earnest. A housing cooperative, known as *El Hogar Obrero* (The Worker's Home), started building cooperative apartment buildings even before the First World War. A number of individual unions, notably the railroad workers, had established housing developments on the outskirts of Buenos Aires and other cities, where unionists could buy adequate homes for modest sums.

Although the rapid growth of the cities in the last two decades has pressed hard on the housing resources of urban Argentina, the situation is still much better than in most Latin American countries. The Perón government had a considerable housing program, although the efforts of cooperatives and labor unions in the housing field were restricted.

The Argentine worker is also better educated than his confreres of Brazil, Chile, and the rest of Latin America. The literacy rate of Argentina is probably the highest in Latin America.

The Argentine urban working class has received new recruits in recent decades from the nation's countryside. These workers have a different psychology from that of the older *porteños,* a psychology molded in the *estancias* of the pampas where there has existed a patriarchal relationship between the Argentine rural peon and his landholding *patrón* similar to, though not as long standing as its Brazilian counterpart.

The relation between the rural worker and his landlord has traditionally been personal in nature. In the days before the fencing in of the range and the establishment of grazing and grain growing in the pampas, the *patrón* was not only the employer, but the leader of his farm hands. He was the best rider, the best roper, the all-round best cattle-handler on the *estancia.* He led his men not only in their work, but also in the frequent civil wars which marked the first quarter of a century of Argentine independence.

Although the colorful *gaucho* disappeared after the middle of the nineteenth century and his place was taken by the more civilized *vaquero* in the cattle areas and the farmhand on the grain *estancias,* the tradition of personal attachment to employer survived this change. The worker was largely dependent upon his employer who provided housing, maintained a store, supported the local church, and sometimes even provided some schooling for the children of the *estancia.* The *patrón* was frequently godfather to his employee's children, and the worker turned to him whenever there was a crisis.

The worker felt a deep loyalty for his *patrón,* a loyalty which in many instances even survived the impact of Perón. There are cases in which rural workers who were themselves Peronistas guided fleeing opponents of Perón across their employers' *estancias* to the neighboring international frontier, because they were asked to do so by their landlords.

This loyalty of the rural Argentine peon extended to politics until the advent of Perón. If the employer were a Conservative—as most of them were—his workers would vote Conservative. If the employer were a Radical, his workers' votes were Radical as well. One of the most significant changes wrought by the Perón regime was the destruction of political domination of rural peons by the landholders.

Another major change brought by Perón was the stimulation of the class consciousness of both rural and urban workers. His demagogic appeal served to arouse once again the feeling of solidarity of the urban workers and to arouse it for the first time among the agricultural workers.

One result of this new class consciousness of the workers was a decline in labor productivity. Figures indicated that productivity per man-hour had dropped decisively during the Perón regime.

One of the most crucial problems after the fall of Perón was that of increasing productivity. And it was something with which management, labor, and the government would have to be concerned for some years to come.

The Employers

Like the working class in Argentina, the employing class sprang from the immigrants. Most of the important firms bear the names of foreign founders—SIAM di Tella metallurgical firm, Massone chemical company; Bunge and Borne, a huge firm with subsidiaries in a great variety of industries including grain milling, chemicals, textiles, vegetable oil processing, and several others.

It would seem that most of the industrial firms of importance in the country were originally founded as artisans' workshops growing to industries of major importance through the ploughing back of profits.

Another group of entrepreneurs who went into manufacturing were owners of commercial enterprises. The great firm of Bunge and Borne is perhaps the most outstanding example of this. Originally a commercial enterprise engaged in shipping wheat abroad, it went into milling and subsequently expanded into a wide range of other activities, and is now probably the largest industrial enterprise in the nation.

Very few industrial firms in Argentina were founded by the preindustrial landowners. Their own business of growing wheat, corn, and cattle was too profitable for them to be interested in other lines of endeavor. Furthermore, in Argentina as in other Latin American countries, great social and political prestige has been associated with land ownership, and this fact acted as a restraining influence on the investment of funds in urban enterprises.

The Corporations. Most Argentine industrial enterprises are closely held by families or small groups of entrepreneurs. There are a few firms controlled by minority stockholders, such as the famous Alpargatas Argentinas (a textile and shoemaking firm), the controlling stockholder of which owns only 20 per cent of the shares. The 80 per cent in the hands of the public is very widely held, making it possible for the holder of the 20 per cent to have control. There was probably no company which had its stock so widely held that a small group could not control it.

There were several circumstances which forced companies to go to the stock market during the 1950's in search of additional capital. One of these was the continuing inflation. Although firms which got their buildings and machinery before World War II seemed to be making very large profits on these investments ten or fifteen years later, the replacement cost of these capital goods had increased to six or seven times the original value of the installations. Hence, those firms had to go to other sources of capital than their earnings to raise funds, notably the banks and the stock exchange.

During the Perón period, it was customary for companies to finance their operations largely on the basis of bank credit. The result of all of this was that there was a real decapitalization. If one looked at the books of most of the important companies of Argentina, one would find that their debts to the banks were so large as to offset a very large part of their assets.

After the fall of Perón the government did not tell the banks to refuse to renew loans, but it did tell them not to expand this system of credit. The net result was that industrial firms turned more and more to the stock exchange to replenish their capital. All during the Perón regime, the movement of the stock market was in an upward direction, except for 1952 when the nation's agricultural crisis was reflected in a crisis in the stock market. After 1952 the stock market again went up steadily.

Another factor which in recent years has encouraged the transformation of private firms—including agricultural ones—into corporations was the inheritance tax. Estates in the form of stocks have not had to pay inheritance tax—each company paying a special tax of 1 per cent on its profits and free reserves in lieu of inheritance tax. Furthermore, stocks in Argentina are always made out to the bearer, and there is thus no way of checking on who owns what stock. Hence, landowners of advancing years often convert their private holdings into corporations, issue stock, and then pass it on to their heirs without paying any tax. If they had kept their fortunes merely as private property, they would have had to pay up to 33⅓ per cent inheritance tax. It is worth noting that the provisional government of President Aramburu ended the "to the bearer" method of registering stock in 1956. One of the first acts of the Frondizi government in 1958 was to restore this method of issuing shares.

With the expansion of the stock market, of course, there had to be new buyers. The market increased steadily in the late 1940's and early 1950's. Stock purchases became increasingly popular with people of moderate means who might in the past have invested in rural real estate or have built an apartment house.

The Government as Entrepreneur. Some of the firms which have participated in Argentine economic development have been government-owned. The merchant marine is in this category as is the aviation industry. The Perón government took over the Dodero Navigation Company, the country's principal river transport firm, and a new State Shipping Line was organized for overseas maritime transport. All the nation's internal commercial aviation was consolidated in the government's Aerolineas Argentinas and in a smaller firm administered by the Ministry of Defense.

The petroleum industry was largely in the hands of the state even before Perón, most exploitation of the country's oil resources being in the hands of the official Yacimientos Petroliferos Fiscales. Although Perón tried to change this—in view of the pressing need of the country for petroleum— by granting a concession to the Standard Oil Company of California, the agreement with California Standard was never ratified by the Perón administration and was allowed to lapse by its successor. It was not until the inauguration of the constitutional regime under Arturo Frondizi in 1958 that the government oil monopoly policy was modified, and contracts were made by YPF with a number of foreign petroleum firms.

The Perón government established the National Steel Corporation and started work on its first large plant in San Nicolás in Buenos Aires province. This is being constructed largely with government funds.

The Perón administration also established the government-owned National Motors Firm outside of Córdoba. As it was first conceived, this firm was to produce airplane motors, automobiles, and agricultural machinery.

However, during the last two years of his administration, Perón split it into three sections. The airplane motor section of the firm was the only part to remain under government control.

The Foreigner As Entrepreneur. Managers of foreign firms are a significant part of the entrepreneurial class in Argentina. The packing houses are still principally American-owned and managed. The British also own a big plant and there are some smaller Argentine packing houses. Other lines in which foreign firms are found include public utilities, chemicals, textiles, and food and drink products and since 1958, oil. A few foreign-owned firms, including the Kaiser Company, have sold shares in the Buenos Aires Stock Exchange. However, generally the foreign firms do not float securities in the Argentine market.

There is not any appreciable indication that the foreign entreprises in Argentina have decisive influence on the country's labor–management relations.

The Argentine As Entrepreneur. Insofar as the native Argentine firms are concerned, there have not as yet developed very many "statesmen" of capital. Many employers seemed to want to "get back" at the workers for advantages conceded during the Perón regime. Of course, this was not true of all employers. We met many who not only accepted trade unionism among their employees, but welcomed it as insurance of more stable relations with their workers.

That many employers fought the rise of trade unionism bitterly is shown by an incident which occurred during Perón's rise to power. Colonel Perón was forced to resign his positions as Vice-President, Minister of War, and Secretary of Labor as the result of an army *coup* on October 9, 1945. Th next day, it was reported in the *New York Times* that many employers had posted notices that October 12, which Perón had proclaimed a paid holiday, would "in view of recent events" not be celebrated as such, and the workers would be expected to be on their jobs as usual on *el dia de la raza* (the Spanish American name for Columbus Day).

The adamant attitude of many employers toward their workers was indicated in the collective bargaining negotiations during 1956. Most employers refused to grant any wage increases unless they were tied to increases in labor productivity. These employers absolutely refused to compromise with their workers' demands for increases to keep up with rises in the cost of living.

The author was left with the feeling that many employers had not yet learned the lesson of the Perón incident in their nation's history—that failure to meet the workers halfway only paves the way for a demagogic politician to exploit the workers' discontent. The future of labor–management relations as well as the political history of the country seemed likely to depend to a considerable degree on whether the employers would be able to learn quickly enough that the unions in Argentina are there to stay and must be dealt with on a basis of equality and mutual respect.

CHAPTER XI

Labor–Management Relations
before Perón

The history of trade unionism in Argentina goes back more than a century.[1] The first trade union was the Buenos Aires Typographical Union, established in 1853. For many years it was the nation's principal labor organization, establishing a pattern of negotiation with employers and calling the first strikes in the 1860's.

It was not until the decade of the 1880's, however, that trade unionism began to spread among the craftsmen and other workers of the nation's growing cities. Immigration from Italy, Spain, and other countries was increasing rapidly, and many of the workers coming from Southern Europe brought political and social ideas from their native lands. Many had been members of the trade unions which were beginning to spring up in Italy and Spain and they sought to establish similar organizations in their new homeland. Many of the oldest unions in Argentina date from the 1880's.

Organization of the immigrant workers was aided considerably by visits of leading figures in the labor and radical movements of Europe. Most notable were the famous Italian Anarchists Enrico Malatesta and Pietro Gori, both of whom made several proselytizing visits to Argentina during this period. Gori ultimately settled there.

An entirely different kind of union was La Fraternidad (The Brotherhood) founded in 1886 among the engineers, firemen, and waterers on the railroads. La Fraternidad was patterned in general lines after the United States railroad brotherhoods.

From its inception, La Fraternidad laid emphasis both on social security and on negotiating with the employers. Although La Fraternidad was several times forced to resort to strikes, it became the most stable and most moderate of the country's labor organizations.

The FORA and Its Rivals

Starting in 1890, attempts were made to establish a national central labor body. However, it was not until 1901 that the Federación Obrera de la Republica Argentina was finally established as a permanent organization. It was torn asunder two years later by a struggle between the Socialists and Anarchists. The Socialists who had first controlled the organization were defeated and withdrew to form the Unión General de Trabajadoes (UGT), while the Anarchists renamed their organization the Federación Obrera Regional Argentina (FORA).

Until World War I the labor movement remained divided between the Anarchist FORA and its rivals. At its fifth congress, the FORA announced that the organization's ultimate aim was the achievement of "Anarchist-Communism."

The period of Anarchist domination of the Argentine labor movement was a turbulent one. Walkouts, including general strikes, were frequent. There was a good deal of violence on the part of both trade unionists and employers, and the government adopted a decidedly hostile attitude toward workers' organizations. The FORA was strongly opposed to collective bargaining agreements, which it regarded as "class collaboration." It relied on direct action to achieve its objectives. It was strongest among dock workers, ship builders, hotel and restaurant workers, and numerous craft groups.

Meanwhile, several attempts were made to unify the labor movement. At the second congress between representatives of the FORA and the UGT in 1909 the delegates were able to agree upon the establishment of a new united labor movement, known as the Confederación Obrera Regional Argentina (CORA). However, this accord was soon repudiated by the FORA and warfare continued between the FORA and CORA, with the Anarchist group remaining the dominant element in Argentine organized labor. Syndicalist elements, who patterned their organization after the French Confederation Général du Travail, had largely displaced the Socialists as leaders of the non-Anarchist branch of the labor movement. The non-Anarchist element was strongest among the printers, railroaders, shoemakers.

This period in Argentine labor history came to a violent end during May 1910. That month marked the first centenary of Argentine independence, and the government prepared an extensive program of festivities to celebrate the event. The FORA, in keeping with its Anarchist philosophy, was opposed to patriotism and announced that it intended to call a general strike during the celebration.

However, the Anarchists' plans were disrupted by an outbreak of violence which swept Buenos Aires and some provincial cities. This was the first of three such violent upsurges which were to play a significant role in Argentine labor history. Anti-Anarchist mobs swept through the capital attacking and burning union headquarters, the publishing plant of the Anarchist daily newspaper, *La Protesta,* and other centers of Anarchist and trade-union activities. Although they had announced their opposition to the FORA's general strike plans, the Socialists and Syndicalists were not spared by the mobs, and the Socialist newspaper, *La Vanguardia,* was one of the victims of their fury. The government did nothing to check the violence of the crowds.

These "May Days," as they are known in Argentine history, marked the end of the dominance of the Anarchists over the country's trade-union movement. For about two years the FORA was forced to operate underground, and meanwhile the CORA, which was not persecuted by the government after the first mob attacks, was able to seize the leadership of the labor movement.

An attempt to unify the trade unions was again made in 1914. This time the leaders of the CORA, although their organization was by then considerably stronger than the FORA, agreed to have their unions affiliate with the FORA, thus liquidating the CORA.

The following year, 1915, saw the Ninth Congress of the FORA where the majority of the delegates voted to erase the part of the constitution which pledged it to "Anarchist-Communism." This resulted in a new split in the organization, and thereafter there were two FORA's, the Anarchist side going by the name FORA of the Fifth Congress or FORA V, the Syndicalist–Socialist group being known as FORA of the Ninth Congress, or FORA IX.

Both organizations grew rapidly during the First World War. The increased tempo of economic activity stimulated the organization and militancy of the workers. There were several notable walkouts during this period, outstanding of which was the strike of railroad workers. La Fraternidad had helped groups of railroaders who were not eligible for membership in the engineers' and firemen's union to establish their own Federación Ferroviaria, and both these organizations participated in the 1917 walkout.

The FORA IX led by its Secretary General, Sebastian Marotta, grew more rapidly than its rival. By 1919 it claimed some 160,000 members and

it had within its ranks the railroaders as well as shoe workers, textile workers, and it had even extended its organization activities to the packing houses
which had hitherto resisted all attempts to unionize their workers. However,
after a brief strike, the packing-house workers' union was destroyed.

The high point of this period of unionization was the famous *Semana
Tragica* (Tragic Week) in January 1919. Spurred by the action of police
and soldiers in firing on pickets at the Vasena Iron Works in Buenos Aires,
crowds of trade unionists rioted throughout the city. For the second time
in a decade the streets of Buenos Aires were in the hands of roving mobs,
this time trade unionists.

Order was restored after President Irigoyen declared martial law in
Buenos Aires. However, the *Semana Tragica* marked the beginning of a
steady decline in the trade-union movement which continued for more
than a decade. During this period the workers' attention turned from trade
unionism to politics with the result that the Socialist Party, which had
previously been able to elect only a handful of deputies from Buenos Aires,
grew rapidly and in 1924 placed nearly two dozen members in congress.

The FORA IX went out of existence in 1922 when a new unity congress
resulted in the establishment of the Unión Sindical Argentina (USA).
However, the FORA V again repudiated the unity move, and so the Unión
Sindical Argentina remained little more than the Syndicalist faction of
the labor movement. It was weaker than its predecessor, the FORA IX,
because the two railroad workers' organizations refused to join the USA.

A significant change had taken place among the railroaders. In 1922
the Federación Ferroviaria was transformed into the Unión Ferroviaria
which was organized on the pattern of the older La Fraternidad. Like the
older organization, the Unión Ferroviaria eschewed "revolutionary" activity
and concentrated its attention on collective bargaining and on social
security and welfare service for its members. From its establishment, the
Unión Ferroviaria was the strongest union in Argentina. It maintained close
relations with La Fraternidad.

In 1926 the two railroad unions took the initiative to form still another
central labor organization. The new Confederación Obrera Argentina
(COA) was under Socialist influence—as were the two railroad unions—
and it affiliated with the International Federation of Trade Unions, the
Socialist-controlled world labor group.

A fourth central labor body was established by the Communists in 1929.
They had previously worked within the Unión Sindical Argentina, but when
the Comintern's "Third Period" line demanded the formation of Com-

munist-controlled trade-union centers in each nation, they established the Comité de Unidad Clasista (Committee of Class Unity).

The CGT

In spite of this fractionalization of Argentine organized labor the idea of unity did not die. Starting in the late 1920's negotiations were conducted among the USA, the FORA, and the COA, toward the establishment of a single central labor organization. These negotiations culminated early in September 1930 in an agreement by the leaders of the USA, the COA, and a number of independent unions to establish the Confederación General del Trabajo (CGT).

Although the CGT was thus set up by agreement among the leaders of several existing organizations, it was prevented from holding a national congress by the unsettled state of political affairs at the moment of its foundation. On September 6, 1930, a *coup d'etat* was executed by the Argentine army, in conjunction with the right-wing Conservative Party, which ousted the President of the Republic, Radical Party chief Hipólito Irigoyen, and substituted a military dictatorship under General Uriburu.

For the next thirteen years there remained in power a Conservative regime which in the beginning maintained itself by army support, and after the election of General Agustín P. Justo as President of the Republic in 1932 kept power through a combination of fraud and force. Almost the only place in which free elections were permitted during this period was the capital city where control shifted back and forth between Socialists and Radicals.

In the meantime, factionalism within the CGT was rife. The first officers of the organization were old members of the Syndicalist USA. Non-Syndicalist elements in the organization felt that the CGT officials were procrastinating too long in calling the Confederación's first national congress. After several bitter controversies in the Confederal Council of the CGT, leaders of the opposition group in 1935 declared themselves to be the "real" CGT and established a separate headquarters. After considerable controversy, the original leaders of the CGT reorganized their group as the revived Unión Sindical Argentina.

The CGT and USA thus continued in existence until the advent of the Perón Era in 1943. The CGT included the majority of the country's organized workers such as the railroaders, metallurgical workers, commercial employees, municipal workers, and textile and building trades workers. It was strengthened in 1936 by the Communists' liquidation of their Comité de Unidad Clasista whose unions joined the CGT.

The two railroad workers' unions constituted the largest element in the CGT. In 1942 the Unión Ferroviaria and La Fraternidad together had almost half the total membership of the confederation. Their influence was even greater than their proportion of the CGT's membership. After 1935 the general secretary of the confederation was always chosen from Unión Ferroviaria. The preponderant role of the railroad workers' organizations was widely resented by leaders of some other unions belonging to the CGT, and contributed to the split in the confederation late in 1942.

The Unión Sindical Argentina had its strength principally among the telephone and maritime workers. Its leadership was largely Syndicalist, which meant that few of the USA leaders were active in any political party. However, unlike the Anarchist unions, those in the USA generally signed collective agreements with the employers' organizations in their respective industries.

The FORA continued to have some strength among shipbuilding workers, port workers, and scattered craft groups, such as the plumbers and taxicab drivers of Buenos Aires. The unions of the FORA continued to believe in "direct action" and were averse to signing collective agreements, preferring to lay down the terms on which their members would agree to work and going on strike until they were accepted.

Changes in the Labor Movement

During the 1930's and early 1940's, several significant changes occurred among the workers and in the trade-union movement, particularly the CGT. In 1930 immigration practically came to a halt. The urban working class, therefore, came to consist of second-generation Argentines and migrants from the countryside.

The second-generation workers were receptive to a native Argentine radicalism. The migrants from the countryside were politically illiterate. For them democracy had been a farce and so they were not impressed when someone who seemed to be helping them was accused of being a "Fascist." They, too, were good tinder for the fire which Perón was soon going to light.

At the same time, there was a growing tendency toward the bureaucratization of the labor movement. Trade-union leadership had become a career in many of the larger unions. The labor organizations had begun to accumulate considerable property, not only headquarters buildings, but hospitals, summer camps, and other institutions built to provide social security and social service for their members.

Because unions had grown strong in such key industries as the railroads, it had become necessary for them to maintain at least an armed truce with the government. The romantic—and irresponsible—ideas of the old Anarchists, who used the unions as a weapon against the state, were not applicable to the new bread-and-butter unions which grew up in the two decades before 1943.

Furthermore, there is considerable evidence that there was a growing gap between the leadership and membership of many of the unions. Attendance at union meetings fell off steadily during the 1930's, as did voting in union elections. Trade-union membership became a duty rather than a privilege.[2]

This gap was first exploited by the Communists whose influence grew in the late 1930's and early 1940's. The Communist-controlled Construction Workers' Union was the second largest organization in the CGT by 1943, and Communist influence was growing in a number of other organizations.

Finally, a large part of the working class remained outside the unions entirely. The packing-house workers, most of the metal workers, the workers on the "factory farms" of the sugar industry, and many other groups were unorganized. The trade-union movement was heavily concentrated in Buenos Aires and its vicinity. Although there were some unions in the interior cities, nowhere was there the relative strength of the labor movement in the capital and its environs.

During the decades before the 1943 Revolution the important Argentine unions had established a pattern for labor–management relations which was adapted for his own purposes by Perón. Its two basic elements were collective bargaining and trade-union social insurance.

Collective contracts varied considerably in their geographical scope. In the railroad, textile, and shoemaking industries, there were nation-wide collective agreements; in the printing trades, the hotel and restaurant industry, retail trade contracts were on a regional basis.

By 1943 some of the collective agreements had become fairly complicated. They dealt not only with wages, but also in many cases with the classification of workers, hours, vacations, and other fringe benefits. In some instances the contracts established social welfare funds financed by employer contributions and administered by the unions.

Negotiation of these contracts was conducted directly between the workers' and employers' organizations. The government played little or no part in the process and the Departmento Nacional del Trabajo was little more than a statistics-gathering agency. Settlement of disputes rising within the collective agreements was also handled directly through union-management grievance procedure. The unions were organized to present those problems which needed solution in the day-to-day relations of workers with employers.

The other emphasis of the union before the Perón period was the establishment of social security and social welfare projects. The most notable examples of these activities were the health and hospital programs of the two railroad workers' unions. These were administered by representatives of the unions, though they were financed by the employers with some help from the government. They provided complete medical care for most of the country's railroaders and their families.

The railroad unions also aided their members in housing. Other unions had different social welfare programs. The Municipal Workers' Union of Buenos Aires, for instance, had a summer colony open to all members of the organization and their families.

The organizational structure of the pre-Perón unions varied a great deal. The railroad unions set a pattern of centralization. The local organizations of La Fraternidad and Unión Ferroviaria were merely sections of the national organization, with relatively little autonomy. The national unions had the right to remove officers of local units, and financial control was centralized in the Buenos Aires headquarters of the two organizations.

On the other hand, there were a number of important unions organized on a federal basis. These included commercial employees, hotel and restaurant workers, and printing trades workers. The center of power in political and financial affairs was in the local units of these unions. Collective bargaining was also done on a local or regional basis, and collective agreements were signed between local affiliates of these unions and their corresponding local employers' organizations.

In all the important unions, day-to-day business was carried on by full-time, paid union officials. Only in the Anarchist unions of the FORA did the old-fashioned prejudice against professional trade-union leaders exist.

At the time of the Revolution of 1943 there were four central labor organizations functioning. The old FORA still had a few scattered unions affiliated with it in Buenos Aires and a few provincial cities. The Unión Sindical Argentina was somewhat larger and was still nominally Syndicalist in its orientation. Its most important affiliates were the Telephone Workers' Federation and the Maritime Workers' Union.

The CGT had split into two rival factions. This division arose from a struggle over the secretary generalship of the organization in its national congress in December 1942. One faction, based mainly on the two rail-road unions, sought the reelection of outgoing Secretary General José Domenech. Most of the leaders of this group were Socialists.

The other faction sought the election of Francisco Pérez Leirós, also a Socialist and head of the Municipal Workers' Union. It was also led by Angel Borlenghi, Secretary General of the Commercial Employees' Confederation and a member of the Socialist Party. However, this group received its main backing from Communist-led unions such as those of the construction workers, metallurgical workers, and textile workers.

When the two factions disagreed over who had won a very close election, they split into two different organizations, each of which called itself the Confederación General del Trabajo. They were generally referred to as CGT 1 (that of Domenech), and CGT 2 (that of Pérez Leirós).

The Employers' Organizations

The employers also had their organizations for collective bargaining and other purposes. Employers of a given industry in a locality were united in a group variously called a *cámara,* a *centro,* or a *unión.* In those industries in which collective bargaining was on a local or regional basis, these groups would negotiate for their employer members. However, their activities were usually not confined to collective bargaining. The *centros* and *cámaras* usually also spoke for their members in dealing with the government on taxes, legal affairs, and similar problems. Typical of these groups was the Unión de Hoteles de Córdoba, which was the spokesman for the hotels of the resort region of the Province of Córdoba.

Generally, in each city or town there was a grouping together of some or all the employers' organizations. This might be the local *bolsa de comercio* (commercial exchange), or it might be a federation of commerce and industry. Some of these local central employer organizations dated from the nineteenth century, and had originally been established as marketing organizations in some of the towns of the interior. Few if any of these regional groups engaged directly in collective bargaining, although they frequently consulted with their member organizations during negotiations.

On a national basis, also, there were important employers' organizations. The Unión Industrial Argentina, which represented in particular the industrialists of the Greater Buenos Aires region, frequently spoke for all of the nation's manufacturers. There also existed various national *cámaras* covering individual trades or industries. Thus, the Cámara Nacional de la Industria del Calzado negotiated collective agreements on behalf of the employers of the shoemaking industry from 1917 onward. In the textile industry there was a series of national *cámaras* representing various parts of the textile trade.

Like the trade unions of pre-Perón Argentina, the employers' organizations suffered little or no interference from the government. Their attitudes toward collective bargaining differed considerably from one organization to another. However, many of the employers' groups had long experience with the process of collective negotiation with the trade unions of their workers.

The agriculturalists of the pampas region, which included the principal wheat- and meat-producing sections of the country, were organized in *sociedades rurales* (rural societies). In other regions, such as the sugar-growing province of Tucumán in the north, there were still other employers' groups. The small farmers and tenants were grouped in the Federación Agraria, which was very active in cooperative affairs until the advent of Perón. Few of the agricultural employers' groups had any experience with collective bargaining since there were few agricultural workers' unions before Perón.

Thus, there had developed in Argentina before the coming of Perón a pattern of collective bargaining. Both the employers and the workers adhering to this pattern had had considerable experience in making it work. Its weakness was that it covered only a small percentage of the country's urban working force, and virtually none of the workers of the countryside. The organized workers constituted a species of "aristocracy of labor" before 1943, and when the organizing fever swept over the hitherto unorganized workers after 1943, the old organizations were vastly altered.

One can draw a parallel between labor–management relations in Argentina in 1943 and labor–management relations in the United States a decade before. In both cases the situation changed suddenly. In the United States, the catalyst bringing about this change was Franklin D. Roosevelt; in Argentina, it was Colonel Juan Domingo Perón.

CHAPTER XII

Government Direction of
Labor Protest under Perón

The Revolution of 1943 brought about fundamental changes in labor–management relations in Argentina. Colonel Juan Domingo Perón, who emerged as the leading figure in this revolution, sought to bring under his control the whole process of negotiation between workers and employers. Ultimately, he largely substituted the government's fiat for collective bargaining.

In order to achieve this complete government direction of the grievances of the Argentine workers and of the establishment of the "web of rule" in Argentine labor–management relations, Perón had to destroy first the independence of both the workers' organizations and those of the employers. By persuasion and force he brought the labor movement almost completely under his control. He was somewhat less successful in converting the employers and in quelling their opposition to him. Nonetheless, by the end of his regime, nearly all official organizations representing the employing class were under the domination of the Perón government.

Perón

Colonel Perón used the labor organization existing in 1943 as a lever to boost him into power. At the same time he tied those organizations to his own destiny, and completely subordinated them. It is interesting to note the difference between Perón's attitude toward the labor movement and that of Vargas in Brazil. Vargas destroyed most existing labor organizations and established new state-controlled groups in their place. Perón, on the contrary, bent the existing trade unions to his will. Perhaps this was why he was never as successful as his Brazilian contemporary in completely destroying the independence of the labor movement.

Although Perón was successful in gaining control of the top leadership of the labor movement, he could never completely destroy the opposition in the rank and file, and there were numerous instances during his tenure in office when the lower-echelon leadership of the unions defied the President. The result of the Perón experience was the acceptance of the fact that the labor movement had become one of the great centers of power in the country's social, economic, and political structure.

The revolution which gave Perón his chance was motivated more by the army's fear of a pro-Allied government coming to power in the middle of World War II, than by any concern with social or economic affairs. The army, which had been trained by German instructors, had for long been strongly pro-German, and in World War II was "neutral" in favor of the Axis.[1] The prospect that the election scheduled for the end of 1943 might bring to power the pro-British landowner Patrón Costas undoubtedly was at the root of the rebellion, June 4, 1943.

The military government which took office under the leadership of the new President, General Pedro Ramirez, dissolved congress, which under the control of the Radical and Socialist parties had been the center of democratic and pro-Allied agitation for a number of years, and suspended freedom of the press.

Most important of all, as things turned out, the military regime suppressed CGT 2 on the grounds that it was "Communist-dominated," and ousted the leaders of some of the country's principal labor organizations, namely La Fraternidad, Unión Ferroviaria, and the Unión de Obreros Municipales, placing military officers in charge.

By September 1943 there were widespread demonstrations. This discontent was shared by an impressive number of retired generals and admirals who issued a statement calling for a restoration of constitutional government. Some of the younger members of the dominant military group saw that the regime was either going to become a violent dictatorship, in which case its tenure would probably be short, or it was going to have to seek support from civilian elements.

The first move was an attempt to win over the industrial middle class. This group had been discontented with the landowner-dominated governments and might have been expected to be friendly to a regime which had overthrown the last of these governments.

However, the industrialists had traditionally supported the Unión Cívica Radical, and they felt that ultimately this party would come to power when constitutional government was restored. They saw no point in mortgaging the future Radical government's position by making what they considered an unnecessary alliance.

The next move was to turn to the industrial working class. This group had also been unfriendly toward the landed oligarchy and had not received sympathetic treatment from any government since the first administration of President Hipólito Irigoyen (1916 through 1922).

Furthermore, a number of the military men already had contact with the labor movement. Colonel Juan Domingo Perón, the leader of this group, had been named Director of the Department of Labor soon after the June 4 revolution and had set about expanding its power and activities. Other officers closely associated with him had been placed in control of the unions taken over by the government. This group of military men conferred at length with leading trade-union officials, in an effort to find out what it was the latter wanted and whether or not an alliance could be formed between military and trade-union officialdom. These inquiries met with limited success.

The result of this change in direction of the June 4 revolutionary regime was the move in November 1943 to convert the old Department of Labor into a new Secretariat of Labor and Social Welfare, with cabinet status for its chief. The first Secretary of Labor was Colonel Perón.

Perón as Secretary of Labor. During the next two years, Perón rose rapidly, becoming Minister of War and Vice-President, as well as Secretary of Labor early in 1944. He also set about to win over the workers. In doing so, he sought to convince them that only through his office could they get vindication for their grievances.

In his assault upon the labor movement, Perón used both the carrot and the stick. For those trade-union leaders who resisted his blandishments he reserved prisons, concentration camps, and exile, and made it increasingly difficult for their unions to function. Meanwhile, many labor leaders who might have wished to resist Perón found that more and more of the rank and file were being won over by his promises and performance.

During the 1943–1945 period, Perón threw his efforts into helping the labor movement expand. There had been perhaps 300,000 to 350,000 organized workers in Argentina when he took office. Within a couple of years this number was increased several fold. Perón forced employers to recognize their workers' unions and to negotiate with them. He personally led campaigns among packing-house workers, sugar plantation peons, and various other labor groups in the interior of the republic. Where dual unions existed, he encouraged rival groups to forget their differences and to launch intensive organizing campaigns with the government's support.

On the other hand, Secretary of Labor Perón intruded his department into the field of collective bargaining negotiations. He first encouraged and then insisted that collective conflicts be brought to the secretariat for conciliation and decision. Many times, after collective negotiations conducted at the secretariat had been concluded, he presided over the formal signing of the new contracts. The workers soon came to the conclusion—which was frequently correct—that Colonel Perón had been more responsible for their wage increases and other benefits than had their own union leaders.

Finally, the Secretariat of Labor began an extensive job of enacting labor and social security legislation. In this field Argentina was considerably behind most of its neighbors in 1943.

This legislative work—by decree—extended into various fields. A more effective system of factory inspection was instigated. Social security legislation was enacted which brought under its scope the great majority of the country's wage- and salary-earning population. During the 1945 election campaign, Perón's successor as Secretary of Labor decreed that all employers must pay an extra month's pay to their workers at Christmas time. A number of legal paid holidays were established.

His Control of the Labor Movement. The result was that by the middle of 1945 Perón had converted the trade-union movement into a powerful personal political machine. He had conquered the Confederación General del Trabajo in the middle of 1944 when he had won its support for a government-sponsored Independence Day (May 25) celebration, the real purpose of which was to indicate political support for the regime then in power. Although certain unions remained hostile to Perón, their number was comparatively small by the end of 1945. The Unión Sindical Argentina was almost liquidated when most of its more important unions joined the Perón-backed CGT.

The degree of support which Colonel Perón enjoyed among the workers was demonstrated in the events of October 1945. On the ninth of that month a military coup by hostile elements of the army resulted in his forced resignation and temporary imprisonment. However, the new military group was unable to rally the support of the civilian politicians and for over a week the country got along without any cabinet.

In the meantime, Perón's labor supporters began to mobilize. A major role in this action was played by Cipriano Reyes, the leader of the packing-house workers in the areas near Buenos Aires. These and other workers began to descend on the capital by train, truck, auto, and even by foot. Civilian opponents of Perón were forced to go into hiding, while the military group in charge of the government did not dare to order their troops to halt the mobs.

As a result, on October 16, Colonel Perón was brought back from prison and the next day appeared on the balcony of the Casa Rosada, arm in arm with President Farrell, to address the cheering crowd of supporters. Although Perón did not return to any of his offices, he was from that time on in full control of the government.

A few days after Perón's restoration to power, a campaign to choose a constitutional President of the Republic was launched. Perón announced his candidacy, although he had no political party supporting him. To fill this gap, he organized three new political groups. The largest of these—which won a majority in both houses of congress on February 24, 1946—was the Partido Laborista, organized by most of the principal trade-union officials of the republic. A dissident group of Radical Party leaders who had thrown in their lot with Perón organized the "Renovated Radical Party," while a third group composed of miscellaneous elements announced their support for him on a so-called Independent ticket.

The opposition to Perón formed the Unión Democratica Nacional which consisted formally of the Radical, Socialist, Progressive Democratic, and Communist parties, and also had the backing of the Conservative Party. They nominated two old-line Radical politicians, José P. Tamborini and Enrique Mosca for the posts of President and Vice-President, respectively.

The campaign was hectic. Both candidates were shot at several times. Although the opposition was allowed little use of the government-regimented radio, it controlled most of the country's newspapers. The opposition felt that they would win if the polling on election day were calm and honest. Although these were the conditions on election day, Perón won.

Organized Labor under Perón. On June 4, 1946, Perón was inaugurated constitutional President of the nation. During the succeeding years, he and his wife set about destroying the independence of the trade-union movement.

María Eva Duarte de Perón was the principal figure in bringing this about. She set up her headquarters in the Secretariat of Labor building and from there molded the trade-union movement to her and her huband's will. Through repeated purges of the unions she removed those leaders who had thought that they were using Perón instead of the other way around. Ceaselessly active, Evita for six years kept constantly on the alert to oust any unionist of independent inclinations, while at the same time seeking to convince the workers that all blessings flowed from the Peróns.

The Ley de Asociaciones Profesionales. One of the most important measures used by the Perón regime to destroy the independence of the labor movement was the Ley de Asociaciones Profesionales. The significance of this measure was twofold. First of all, it officially put the power of the state behind recognized trade unions and implicitly obliged the employers to deal with them. In the second place, and equally important, the law for the first time made it essential for a union to acquire legal recognition before it could function effectively. Before 1945, unions wanting some kind of legal status registered as mere civil associations—on a par with a Rotary Club or charitable society. Many unions sought no kind of legal recognition whatever.

This law started off by defining a *"sindicato* or professional association" as a group "formed by manual or intellectual workers of the same profession or industry, or in similar or connected professions or industries, constituted for the defense of their professional interests." The decree then went on to say that these associations "can be freely established without necessity of previous authorization, always provided their objectives are not contrary to the morality, laws, and fundamental institutions of the nation."

After this proclamation about the complete freedom of the workers for the protection of their interests, the rest of the statute is taken up with limiting this freedom. One paragraph provides that "those organizations which do not possess *personería gremial* (trade-union personality), granted by the government, cannot act as professional associations of the workers."

Four types of workers' organizations are noted in the law. The first is the union having *personería gremial.* The second type is a union with *personería jurídica,* or mere registration as a civil association, a category reserved largely for unions which have for one reason or another lost their *personería gremial.*

Third, there are "professional associations inscribed but without *personería gremial.*" These organizations are registered in special files in the Ministry of Labor and "can act freely and can carry out . . . all those functions which are not expressly reserved to *sindicatos* with *personería gremial.*" In some instances, where no *sindicatos* with *personería gremial* exist in the area of their jurisdiction, these groups can function as if they had such a status.

Finally, there are the workers' organizations which have no kind of government recognition whatsoever. These, as we have already noted, cannot function as normal trade unions. They cannot bargain with the employers, they cannot represent the workers in negotiations with the governmental authorities, and they cannot conduct any of the activities usually associated with a trade union.

The unions which possess the prized *personería gremial* are, under law, the only organizations which enjoy the following rights:

1. To defend and represent the interest of the workers in dealings with the employers and the state;

2. To defend and represent the workers before the social security authorities, the courts and all other governmental bodies;

3. To have representation in governmental organizations regulating labor relations;

4. To participate in collective bargaining, negotiating and modifying collective agreements, contributing to the enforcement of labor legislation;

5. To collaborate with the state as technical consultative bodies in the study and the solution of problems of their profession;

6. To participate in political activities, in conformity with election laws;

7. To conduct their meetings and assemblies in closed halls without previous permission (though they must receive permission to hold open-air meetings);

8. To have exclusive use of their names, all others being prohibited from using titles which might lead to confusion;

9. To determine the suspension and renewal of work;

10. To establish sanctions in case of violation of their statutes and trade-union decisions;

11. To require employers, with previous authorization from the ministry, to install the checkoff;

12. To be exempt from all taxes;

13. To have preference in employment insofar as the state and all firms having contracts with or concessions from the state are concerned.

The law provides certain minimum requirements for a union to gain *personería gremial*. These include having a minimum number of members and having statutes which provide adequate means for protection of the organization's property and collecting dues, and which set forth the officers, name, headquarters, objective, frequency of meetings and financial reports, as well as sanctions on members and means of modification of the statutes and dissolution of the organization.

Presumably the organization which represented the majority of the workers in a given trade or industry was to receive recognition and be granted *personería gremial*. In fact, the Peronista government used this decree on various occasions to destroy an existing union politically hostile to the regime in favor of a new group which was Peronista.

One of the most notorious instances of this was the case of the shoemakers' union. The Sindicato Obrero de la Industria del Calzado had been the dominant union in the industry since its establishment in 1917, and for many years previous to the Revolution of 1943, had negotiated contracts with the employers' organization in the trade. However, when the union applied for *personería jurídica* it was unable to get action from the Secretaría de Trabajo y Previsión, and soon afterward a rival organization was founded, the Unión de Obreros de Calzado, headed by elements expelled from the *sindicato*. This new group was immediately given *personería gremial,* though it had practically no members at the time.

When the Sindicato Obrero de la Industria del Calzado in March 1946 issued a proposal for a new collective agreement, it was notified by the Secretaría that since it did not have *personería gremial* it was not qualified to conduct these negotiations. The employers were forced to deal instead with the new Peronista union. Although the older organization kept going for some time, it was ultimately driven underground and its leaders into exile.

The law sets forth conditions under which a union can lose its *personería gremial* and be succeeded by a rival group, although needless to say, these conditions were not observed in the case of anti-Peronista unions. According to the law it is possible for a rival union to be granted *personería gremial* "when the number of dues-paying members of the rival union during a continuous period of at least six months immediately previous to the request for recognition is superior to that of the recognized union; the latter then losing its recognition if it ceases to be sufficiently representative, although the authorities must also take into consideration the previously recognized union's contribution to the defense of its members' interests in deciding whether to strip it of recognition." Furthermore, in order for recognition to be transferred from one union to another such action must have the approval of the union losing *personería gremial,* "even if its membership is smaller" than that of its rival.

Many unions were squeezed out of existence by use of the Ley de Associaciones Profesionales. Included were organizations of textile workers, shoe workers, hotel and restaurant workers, printers, clothing workers, shipbuilders, and maritime workers.

The Purge of the Unions. Evita went even further than this. She sought to destroy labor leaders who, even though they were supporters of Perón, had been union officials before the Perón regime. Between 1946 and 1951, there was a thorough purge of nearly all those leaders who helped put Perón in power during the 1943–1946 period.

Cipriano Reyes, leader of the packing-house workers, was one of the first victims. He was vice-president of the Partido Laborista and was elected deputy in the February 1946 elections. When Perón announced the merger of the three groups which had backed him into a single government party (first named the Partido Unico de la Revolución Nacional and later changed to Partido Perónista) Reyes opposed this maneuver. He fought the President for two years, then after his term in congress had expired, Reyes was put in jail where he remained until the overthrow of Perón more than seven years later.

Virtually all the old-time labor leaders were ousted in less spectacular ways and were replaced by individuals who owed their posts to Perón rather than to union members. The purge was completed in the middle of 1951 when the leadership of La Fraternidad was forced at gun point to resign by a group of self-appointed union officials.

An important part of Evita's work was assuring the workers that all their grievances would be channeled through and resolved by the Perón government. This was her "philanthropic" activity. One or two days a week Evita held court in the Secretariat of Labor building and received anyone with a problem. The President's wife became a combination marriage counselor, pediatrician, public defender, and Tammany Hall ward leader on those days. Ministers and other officials were in attendance, and would frequently be dispatched to set right some complaint. Few of those who visited Evita went away without the gift of a few hundred pesos.

The Eva Perón Foundation, which was a monopoly of all charity in the republic, carried out a similar function on a grander scale. In addition to building hospitals, children's homes, and similar institutions, it gave handouts to needy people and those stricken by some disaster. The foundation, though it received large "gifts" from unions, employers, and visiting foreign dignitaries, and large appropriations from congress, never had to present any accounting of its funds. There is little doubt that much of the "charity" was given to the leading figures in the Perón regime most closely associated with Evita.

The result of all of this was that by the time of Perón's overthrow, most of the labor movement was a tool of the dictator. The top leadership consisted of unquestioning servants of the regime and their selection was made in the Ministry of Labor or in the Casa Rosada (presidential palace) not in the congresses of the unions which merely rubber-stamped the government's choices. There was no democracy in the middle and upper levels of the trade-union movement—in the CGT, its provincial and city "delegations," or in the national and regional leadership of the industrial unions.

The only level on which a modicum of democracy was preserved was in the election of shop stewards and factory or workshop committees. Here the government allowed the workers in many unions to choose their representatives. However, in cases where these officials showed too much activity which the government interpreted as endangering its welfare, the CGT or the national leadership of an individual union would oust the offending unionists.

This degree of union democracy undoubtedly served two purposes as far as the Perón regime was concerned. In the first place, it kept it aware of discontent among its followers. In the second place, it served as an escape valve for the workers themselves, giving them some feeling of having a say in their organizations.

Occasionally, the unions escaped from the government's control. There were strikes from time to time which either occurred without the government's sanction or got out of hand even if they had been started with government approval. La Fraternidad, Unión Ferroviaria, the printing trades workers of Buenos Aires, the Tucumán sugar workers, the maritime unions, the metal trades unions, and the tobacco workers were among those which at one time or another had this kind of a strike.

The Change in Labor Movement Structure

Submission of the unions to government control resulted in a change in their structure. Those unions which had had a federalized type of organization were forced to alter it to conform to the more centralized system characteristic of the railroad workers' unions. Thus, in most unions the constitutions were changed to provide that all dues be paid directly to the national organizations which then gave back a small percentage of these funds to the regional and local affiliates. In some cases, no money was returned to the subordinate organizations.

At the same time, the structure of the Confederación General del Trabajo was also changed. In 1946 the CGT assumed the right to "intervene" in the affairs of its affiliated unions, that is, to oust elected officials and put its own agents in charge. In the cases of the Packing House Workers' Federation in 1950 and the maritime unions in 1951 the CGT even intervened in unions which did not belong to it. At the same time, the CGT established regional "delegations" in every province, which assumed the same right in local unions. All this was done de facto in the early years of Perón's control of the CGT and was only written into the constitution of that organization some years later.

The labor movement became the key of the Peronista political machine. This was demonstrated by the fact that nearly all the unions accepted as the preamble of their individual constitutions that of the CGT which read as follows:

The General Confederation of Labor, considering

That the Argentine working class has fought for decades through its trade unions to achieve its advancement, by means of conquest of the rights which assure a superior order of material and spiritual existence, which abolish the social privileges that are the cause of exploitation and misery and the source of conflicts, of hate and of insecurity;

That the work designed to procure these transcendental objectives was oriented by alien ideas, extraneous to our tradition and environment, because they lacked an essentially national doctrine, born of our own experiences and elaborated in conformance with our own needs, lacking clear norms and a concrete program which would condense in a homogeneous, practical way the desires for improvement of the laboring masses of the nation in accordance with it social reality;

That the Peronista Doctrine, widely propounded by its creator, General Juan Péron, defines and synthesizes the fundamental aspirations of the Argentine workers and indicates to them the true doctrine, of national origin and spirit, the full and loyal application of which will produce a just, free and sovereign Fatherland;

That the National Constitution promulgated March 16, 1949 and inspired in the wise principles of the Peronista Doctrine, consecrates the fundamental rights which were always the profound desire of the proletariat, such as THE RIGHTS OF THE WORKER: the right to work, to a fair retribution, to training, to dignified working conditions, to the preservation of health, to welfare, to social security, to the protection of the family, to economic improvement, to the defense of their professional interests; and THE RIGHTS OF OLD AGE, proclaimed at the inspiration of Señora Eva Perón: the right to assistance, to housing, to food, to clothing, to the care of physical health, to the protection of moral health, to labor, to tranquility, to respect; as well as also affirming the social function of capital in providing that "The organization of riches and their exploitation must have for its purpose the welfare of the people in an economic order which conforms to the principles of Social Justice";

That the process of advancing gradually to the socialization of the means of production and exchange imposes on the proletariat the duty of participating through its trade unions in solidifying the conquests of the Perónista Revolution, consolidating them in the present and expanding them in the future;

THE GENERAL CONFEDERATION OF LABOR DECLARES:

Its unchangeable decision to constitute itself a zealous defender and loyal executor of the high postulates which orient the Peronista Doctrine, and a loyal custodian of the Perón Constitution, which makes concrete in its spirit and its words the eternal aspirations of the working class, and constitutes the unimprovable rules for the orientation of the Argentine workers in the fulfillment of their irrevocable determination to establish a Fatherland which is socially just, politically sovereign, and economically free. . . .

The importance of the unions to Perón's political organization was shown by the considerable number of trade unionists who were given positions as Peronista members of the national congress and provincial legislatures. Two trade unionists also served as ministers—Angel Borlenghi as Minister of the Interior until less than three months before the fall of Perón; and Minister of Labor Freire, who was in office until shortly after the death of Evita in 1952.

The trade-union members of the federal congress and the provincial legislatures did not in any way act as a "labor bloc." They were almost without exception obedient servants of the dictator. In those few cases in which Peronista deputies or senators got out of line, they were soon ousted from the party and from their legislative posts.

The labor movement played a particularly important part in preparing for the 1951 reelection of Perón. More than a year before this, when Perón had not yet officially "made up his mind" on the issue, unions began passing resolutions "demanding" that he run again. Most of these resolutions also "insisted" that Evita should be the nominee for Vice-President. Only La Fraternidad of the major unions refused to pass such a resolution, with the result that its leadership was soon ousted by force.

These preparations came to a climax when the CGT called a huge meeting in the Plaza de Mayo to express the "demands" of the whole labor movement for the Perón–Perón ticket. That same evening the principals announced their acceptance.

The Perón government frequently used the labor movement as a weapon. When Perón felt himself menaced he summoned the workers to demonstrate in the Plaza de Mayo. Such a gathering was called, for instance, after the failure of the revolutionary attempt of September 28, 1951.

The administration also organized strong-arm squads from among the workers to assure the effectiveness of the few strikes authorized by the regime —those which were against the government's foes or in support of some measure backed by the administration.

One of the most notorious cases in which the government mobilized the trade-union movement for its political purposes occurred at the time of Evita's death. This event was used as a nation-wide political demonstration.

All this underlined the fact that the Perón regime rested fundamentally on two institutions—the army and the labor movement. After the events of

October 17, 1945, Perón was able to threaten the armed forces with a repetition. On the other hand, the military was always a menace to the labor movement's strength and security.

These twin foundations of the Perón government stayed intact until the unsuccessful revolt of the Argentine navy on June 16, 1955. At that time, the army stayed loyal, but in doing so it took full control of the government, subsequently forcing Perón to dismiss Minister of Interior Borlenghi, and refusing to allow him to mobilize his labor supporters on behalf on the regime.

On the afternoon of August 31, Perón seemed to have succeeded in reestablishing the unions as a support for his regime. A huge meeting was called by the CGT in the Plaza de Mayo, and during this gathering Perón urged his assembled followers to shoot personally any of the regime's enemies who might get in their way. In saying this, he is reported to have looked at the group of army officers standing next to him.

This Plaza de Mayo meeting undoubtedly had much to do with the move by the navy, and army units in the interior of the country, to revolt against Perón a little more than two weeks later. The military men were at least as conscious as he was of the nature of the Perón regime before June 16, 1955, and had no intention of letting him reestablish it on that basis. This time they revolted successfully, forcing Perón out four days after the uprising began.

Corruption in the Unions. The conditions under which unions existed and carried on their business during the Perón regime encouraged the growth of irresponsibility and corruption on the part of trade-union leaders. Since the trade-union officials were not subject to any real control from their rank and file, they could do pretty much what they wished with the money coming into the union's coffers. Furthermore, corruption ran so completely through the Perón regime, from the President and his wife on down, that it is not surprising that the labor organizations should be tainted by it.

Petty graft undoubtedly ran riot in the lower echelons of the union movement. Equally serious was the corruption in its upper strata. In the case of the Packing House Workers' Federation, for instance, in the annual contract of 1952 there was a secret clause which apparently provided large amounts of under-the-table funds for the union leaders. Although the workers in 1952 were told that they were being given an increase of 1.50 pesos per hour, the contract in fact called, in a secret clause, for the increase to be 1.86 per hour, the other 36 centavos being paid to the federation. According to Diego Martínez, former member of the executive committee of the federation, this money was apparently pocketed by the Peronista leaders. Martínez estimated that the union officials thus stole about 115 million pesos.

Probably the most outrageous case of corruption of trade-union leadership was that of the Confederación General de Empleados de Comercio, headed by Perón's Minister of the Interior, Angel Borlenghi. Some of the corruption in that union was disclosed by an investigating committee after the fall of Perón. It indicated that during the 1948–1955 period the union spent 3,200,000 pesos for stationery, in itself an excessive figure. Moreover, bills for other purchases frequently showed discrepancies.

In the union records there appeared a mysterious Caja 2, which is not otherwise identified. Large sums, amounting to a million and a half pesos were paid into this *caja*. This money was drawn out by union officials in small amounts over a considerable period of time, individual I.O.U.'s being put in place of the funds. Minister Borlenghi was the recipient of many personal "gifts" and "loans" as were his relations and other pets of the regime. This is only one case of the kind of exploitation engaged in by officials of the top Peronista trade-union organizations, and it is by no means the complete story in the case of this single confederation. It is certain that many scores of millions of pesos were extracted from the unions for the personal benefit of their top leaders during the Perón administration.

Employer Opposition to Perón. Generally, employing interests were opposed to Perón before he became President, and for some time thereafter. For one thing, they were generally supporters of the Radical Party, and felt that this party was likely to come to power as a result of the victory of the Allies in the war and subsequent events in Argentina itself. They thus felt bitter about the Peronista group, which was frustrating the possibilities of the party which most industrialists looked upon as a defender of their interests.

The employers had other reasons for opposing Perón. They had been forced by him, when he was Secretary of Labor, to grant sizable wage increases, to pay new Social Security taxes, to grant paid holidays and to pay a year-end bonus of one month's pay. Many employers were compelled to make "contributions" to the Eva Perón Foundation.

Some of the employers' organizations openly supported Perón's opponents in the 1946 election. Principal among these was the Unión Industrial Argentina. It gathered a good deal of money from the industrialists to pay the expenses of the anti-Peronista Unión Democratica. This money was sent to the Unión Democratica in the form of checks. Several of the checks found their way to Perón, and he made much of this as a campaign issue.

Reprisals Against Employers. Even before Perón formally took office, the government began to take reprisals against the resisting employers. When elections were held in the Unión Industrial Argentina in March 1946 a group of Peronistas, headed by Miguel Miranda (who was later to be Perón-appointed head of the Banco Central) was defeated two to one; thereupon the government "intervened" the UIA. It was never again, during the Peron regime, allowed to elect its own officers.

The leaders of the UIA were persecuted. The textile firm of its president, Raúl Lamuraglia, suffered damages of thirty million pesos and Lamuraglia was jailed. Pascual Gambino, Lamuraglia's successor to the UIA, was forced to quit his job with the Cantabrica metal firm. Many other individual employers were despoiled, jailed, or exiled—or all three. The Massone chemical firm was expropriated; so was the Bemberg firm, which owned large landholdings and many industrial enterprises; and so were the large properties of Patrón Costas, candidate for the presidency in the elections not held in 1943 because of the army's revolt.

Perhaps the most notorious case of reprisals is that of *La Prensa*. This newspaper, owned by Alberto Gainza Paz, had steadfastly opposed Perón before and after he became President. It was subjected for years to all manner of persecution. The climax came early in 1951, Perón using his control over the labor movement to administer the death blow to the newspaper. Since he could not incite *La Prensa*'s own employees against the newspaper because they were loyal to its owner, he used the Peronista-dominated newsboys' union of Buenos Aires. This group presented a series of impossible demands on the paper. When *La Prensa* refused to comply, the union declared a boycott.

For several weeks *La Prensa* closed down, and when it attempted to publish once again, one of its employees was murdered by a gang of Peronistas. Soon afterward, Perón's pet congress passed a bill expropriating the paper; and the government suddenly "discovered" that the publishers of *La Prensa* owed millions of pesos in back taxes—enough to cancel the compensation called for in the expropriation law.

Subsequently, *La Prensa* was turned over to Perón's Confederación General del Trabajo. The CGT continued to use the same format for the paper, though it became a loyal echo of its master's voice.

Employer Support for Perón. While the Peronista government remained in power, added numbers of employers, particularly industrialists, gave at least passive support to the regime. This was due in part to Perón's favorable attitude toward industrialization. It was due, too, to the fact that employers found they could make up wage increases in higher consumer prices. Finally, in view of the rising strength of the labor movement, many employers feared what would happen when Perón's control over the trade unions should be removed.

However, many industrialists remained opposed to Perón though they did not dare do anything overt. The industrialists who had contracts with the government were the administration's Trojan horses in the industrialists' organizations.

Employers still opposed to Perón were forced to help the regime when the occasion demanded. The occasion most often arose during the lifetime of the President's wife. Evita at various times forced employers to make "voluntary" contributions to the foundation. It was impossible for them to refuse because there were elements within each group of employers who would expose the others. Unwilling employers were fearful of expropriation of their enterprises.

Employers' Organizations Under Perón. Various organizations were formed among the employers during the Perón regime. Some of these were actively sponsored by the Perón government, while more successful groups were established with only the tolerance of the administration.

These new employers' organizations were set up along several lines. On the one hand, federations of employers were established in a number of industries, to supplement the small number of existing national and regional *cámaras* in those trades. In the case of textiles, the country's largest industry, the new Federación Argentina de Industrias Textiles brought together thirteen different *cámaras* representing various sections of the industry. The Federación Argentina de la Industria Metalúrgica had only two affiliated *cámaras,* the Asociación de Industrias Metalúrgicas, covering the iron and steel industry and the Federation of Light Metals. In some industries such as shoemaking in which all employers already belonged to a single group, no new organization was established.

A second group of new employers' organizations was established on a provincial basis. All provincial associations of industrial, commercial, and agricultural employers were brought together in provincial "economic" federations.

The third level of organization was the establishment of a national institution to cover all employers in the three lines of economic activity. In 1948 the Perón government sponsored the formation of an Asociación de Producción, Industria y Comercio for this purpose. (The word *producción,* which would normally be translatable as "production," is used in Argentina to signify agriculture.) However, it was established before any sizable group of employers had gone over to support the government. As a result, it failed.

In May 1950, a group of employers from the interior met in the city of Catamarca at the Second Economic Congress of the North. There they drew up the Accord of Catamarca calling for the establishment of a nation-wide organization of employers in the fields of agriculture, commerce, and industry.

Before establishing such an organization, the prime movers in the effort had a meeting with President Perón, who expressed his support. Finally the Confederación Argentina de la Producción, la Industria y el Comercio (CAPIC) was established in a congress held in the city of Mendoza.[2] In the CAPIC, employer elements of the interior were much more fully represented than those of Buenos Aires and its vicinity.

The Confederación General Económica. The CAPIC was the predecessor of the more inclusive Confederación General Económica (CGE). This organization included industialists and merchants of the Buenos Aires region, as well as entrepreneurs of the interior who made up the CAPIC. Among those groups "affiliated" with it was the intervened Unión Industrial Argentina.

The original structure proposed by the CGE at its founding congress called for the establishment of three constituent organizations—a Confederación de la Industria, a Confederación del Comercio, and a Confederación de la Producción to bring together on a national basis all industrial, mercantile, and agricultural entrepreneurs, respectively. These organizations were never successfully established largely because of opposition from entrepreneurs from the interior of the country.

Provincial federations including nearly all the employers' organizations in each province became the basic affiliates of the CGE. Already existing *bolsas de comercio* (commercial exchange), *sociedades rurales* (rural societies), and organizations of industrial employers were affiliated *en masse* with the new federations.

These over-all organizations of employers did not usually engage in direct collective bargaining with the workers' unions, though in some cases they did give aid and assistance to their affiliates in such negotiations. The role of the CAPIC and subsequently of the CGE and its regional affiliates was one of defending the economic and political interests of the employers. They were largely lobbying and public relations groups.

The CGE and its regional affiliates had the open support of the Perón administration. This was demonstrated shortly before the overthrow of the Perón regime by the passage of a Ley de Asociaciones Profesionales del Empresario (Professional Entrepreneurs' Associations Law). This provided, among other things, that every employer had to pay an annual contribution to the CGE and its constituent groups.

However, the leaders of the CGE claimed after the fall of Perón that they had not been pro-Peronista. José Ber Gelbard, who had been president of the organization throughout the Perón period, said that the CGE had had a peculiar position. It had been considered by the Peronistas to be anti-Peronista; and by the anti-Peronistas to be Peronista. Gelbard claimed that there were only two avowed Peronistas on the excutive board of twenty-five members.

The Objectives of Perón's Policy. There is no doubt that Perón sought to use the CAPIC and then the CGE for his own purposes. Many observers felt that he was moving in the direction of a corporate state based on the trade unions, the CGE, the Confederación General de Profesionales (CGP), which was established for the liberal professions, and the Confederación General de Estudiantes which was set up to cover primary, secondary, and university students.

Whatever his objectives, at the time of his overthrow President Perón had not succeeded in making all these organizations effective. This was particularly the case with the Confederación General de Profesionales. The CGP sought to bring into its ranks already existing organizations of lawyers, doctors, dentists, engineers, architects, etc. However, in several cases the professional organizations refused to join the CGP and in most cases their affiliation was largely nominal.

Whether or not the corporate state was Perón's ultimate objective in the establishment of all these organizations, his reasons were undoubtedly political. They frequently provided political platforms. They often expressed their loyalty to him, and attempted to rally the groups under their surveillance to the support of the government.

The Activities of the CGE. The CGE conducted various activities. Two of the most important were congresses which it sponsored during the Perón period. The first was a conference on human relations. Out of it came the Instituto de Relaciones Humanas which sent a group of industrialists to the United States to study university organizations with labor–management institutes.

The second conference sponsored by the CGE was the Congress of Productivity held in Buenos Aires early in 1955.

Many opponents of Perón saw in this congress a further step toward the establishment of a corporate state. They felt that the symbolism of holding this meeting in congress foreshadowed a day when the politically elected legislature would be superseded by a legislature chosen on a functional basis.

The leaders of the CGE later claimed that the idea for this congress had originated with their organization, though they used the Confederación General del Trabajo to issue the call for the conference since they feared that, coming from the employers' group, it would have been turned down without further investigation.

Both the CGE and CGT participated in this meeting, which had Perón's blessing, and was perhaps suggested by the President himself. By 1955 Perón had become concerned with the declining productivity of workers in Argentine industry, as well as the nearly catastrophic decline in agricultural production. He welcomed any move which would seek to reverse this trend.

The conference lasted several days and, if nothing else, provided an opportunity for the labor leaders and industrialists to become better acquainted with one another in an atmosphere not quite so loaded with group interests and politics as regular collective bargaining negotiations. The conference came forth with a number of resolutions urging greater productivity, none of which had been put into effect by the time the Perón government fell a few months later.

Thus, President Perón, during the twelve years in which he was the principal actor on the Argentine scene, sought to subordinate both the workers' and employers' organizations to his and his government's control. However, this story of his emasculation of the class organizations of Argentina is only complete when it is supplemented by a study of how he converted collective bargaining from a process of free negotiation by representatives of the two parties into a method by which the government dictated terms to both sides.

CHAPTER XIII

Rise and Decline of Collective Bargaining

There is no doubt that Perón tried to substitute government dictation for collective bargaining. However, this took time, and there was an evolution of relations between the workers and employers which led in the last two or three years of the regime nearer and nearer the objective.

Collective bargaining—the signing of agreements between workers' and employers' organizations, and the resolution of conflicts arising under these agreements—was already the pattern of labor relations before Perón. He began aggrandizing the role of government in this process by modifying the basis of collective negotiation.

Concomitant with the centralization of the trade-union movement and the grouping of most employers into national organizations, the Perón regime substituted national collective bargaining for local or regional negotiations. Furthermore, since there was a tendency toward consolidation of unions under Perón, some national unions came to sign more than one contract. The National Miners' Union, for instance, negotiated separate contracts for coal, talc, cement, and other branches of industry covered by it.

Only local trades continued to be under regional collective agreements by the end of the Perón regime. For instance, in 1956 there were still twenty-three regional collective agreements in force in the province of Mendoza.

There was often objection from the provinces from both employers' and workers' representatives to the "nationalization" of collective agreements. There is still a good deal of feeling between Buenos Aires and the provinces and many provincials felt that in such national collective negotiations Buenos Aires called the tune. It was even alleged by some provincial employers that workers' and employers' representatives from the capital would sometimes help the workers of the provinces at the expense of the employers, in order to weaken provincial industry to the benefit of Buenos Aires.

Collective Bargaining in Agriculture

Collective agreements in agriculture were innovations of the Perón administration. Although scattered groups of rural workers had been successful in establishing unions before the advent of Perón, these were few in number.

The method of collective contract negotiation in agriculture varied with different crops. In the grain-growing region, which represents the bulk of Argentine agriculture, there was a different system for the two types of workers employed there. Resident agricultural workers were covered by Perón's Statute of the Peon which established a Comisión Nacional de Trabajo Rural composed of representatives of the employers' and of the workers' Federación Argentina de Seccionales Agrarias, an affiliate of the Confederación General del Trabajo. The purpose of this commission was to decide annually what wages should be established for this category of workers. Although the last word, under law, rested with the Minister of Labor, the minister more often than not adopted the recommendations of the joint employer–union commission.

The Statute of the Peon contained other innovations. It provided that agricultural workers should receive paid holidays, should work an eight-hour day, and should enjoy other benefits customary among urban workers.[1]

Itinerant workers were not covered by the provisions of the Statute of the Peon. They were hired just for harvest and were dealt with by the Law of the Agricultural Worker, also enacted by the Perón regime. This produced regional joint commissions in nineteen different sections of the country. In most cases the Federación Agraria Argentina acted for the employers, and the Federación Argentina de Seccionales Agrarias for the workers. The commissions set wages by regions and by crops for the current harvest season. These wages changed every year. The decisions of the joint commissions were promulgated by the Minister of Labor to give them the force of law.

In the grape-growing regions of western Argentina, the system was somewhat different. There are two kinds of agricultural workers in the grape industry, wage earners and *contratistas* or sharecroppers. The wage earners were organized by Perón into local groups of the Federación Argentina de Seccionales Agrarias. The Federación negotiated a collective agreement annually with the employers' representatives. The *contratistas* were brought together in the Sindicato de Trabajadores Contratistas de Viñas, which negotiated a collective agreement with the landlords setting forth the terms of the individual contracts to be signed between each *contratista* and his landlord. Finally, the industrial workers in the wineries were organized into the Federación de Obreros y Empleados Vitivinicolas as their collective bargaining agent.

In the sugar province of Tucumán the Federación Obrera Tucumána de la Industria Azucarera, established with Perón's help when he was still Secretary of Labor, contracted with the Unión Cañeros Independientes de Tucumán, the organization representing the twenty thousand cane growers in the province (not owners of sugar mills), and with the organization of the sugar mill owners. During the Perón period, it was customary for the collective agreement to provide a wage increase, whereupon the independent growers would raise the price of cane to the mill owners who, in turn, would be allowed to raise the price of refined sugar.

Government Intervention in Collective Bargaining

From Perón's days as Secretary of Labor he had insisted that the government participate in the negotiation of collective agreements, and collective bargaining conferences were held more and more often in the Secretariat of Labor or its provincial "delegations." By the late 1940's the regular procedure was for such negotiations to be conducted in the Labor Ministry where the government could keep a sharp eye on what was going on.

The Perón regime did not allow collective bargaining to proceed without its approval. Until 1952 the process of collective bargaining and the signing of collective agreements continued and the two parties were allowed to negotiate more or less by themselves. However, government officials stepped in quickly if there were a deadlock. Usually, the Ministry of Labor officials took the workers' side in such instances. One important employer representative insisted that the Ministry of Labor officials frequently urged the workers' representatives to make impossible demands, then intervened and obtained a "tip" for settling the matter by a "compromise" which went further than the employers would otherwise have been willing to go.

Perón frequently used government intervention in collective contract negotiation. From 1943 until about 1948 he used government influence to force employers to grant wage increases. Subsequently, as prices rose, Perón tried to discourage the workers from pressing for wage increases though government influence was usually behind union demands for changes in working conditions.

Fairly consistently the pressure of the unions and the government was toward narrowing the differential between skilled and unskilled workers. This occurred between different unions and within the same union. Thus, before Perón the railroad workers were among the country's most highly paid, but after the first spurt of wage increases which Perón forced on the railways during his period as Secretary of Labor he discouraged further increases for this group. As a result, the relative position of the railroad workers declined seriously during the latter part of the Perón period.

Within a given industry, the government and unions often brought pressure to reduce wage differentials. The tendency was almost always to force up the bottom wages more rapidly than the higher ones. Employers complained that as a result there came to be very little incentive for a worker to acquire a skill.

During her lifetime, Evita Perón supervised all trade-union matters, including the negotiation of collective agreements. Evita and her husband intervened even more actively in collective bargaining situations when a strike was involved.

In the case of the sugar workers of Tucumán the union leaders called a strike in 1949 which lasted forty days until Perón decided to break it. He ordered the arrest of the strike leaders, as well as one of the leaders of the sugar producers. Once this was accomplished, Perón got on the radio and announced that he was giving the workers more than the requested wage increase and that the union which had called the strike was being "intervened." It remained under intervention throughout the remaining six and a half years of the Perón administration.

The Nature of Collective Contracts

Even before Perón, collective contracts in Argentina had become a good deal more complicated than is characteristic of most Latin American countries.

A typical collective agreement is that negotiated in the glass industry between the Federación Argentina de la Industria del Vidrio y Afines and the workers' Sindicato Obrero de la Industria del Vidrio y Afines during the Perón regime. This is a fifty-one page document signed in the Ministry of Labor. The first two articles which take up over thirty-six pages deal with wages, and relate in detail the wage to be received by every type of worker, by occupational classification, in the industry.

Other parts of the agreement deal with seniority, payments for days when workers are prevented from working, special clothing for workers whose jobs require it, the limit for loads carried by workers, expense money for truck drivers, a payment of two pesos a month to the union for social service work done by it. There is also provision for workers who are called up for military service, provision for workers taking extraordinary leave, and for family allowances.

There is an article dealing with classification of manual workers, and special provisions in case of accidents. The checkoff is written into the contract and all workers are covered by it. Finally, the terms of the contract are made retroactive to the expiration of the previous one, and there is a provision that the first month's wage increase will be divided among the Eva Perón Foundation, the CGT, and the glass workers' union.[2]

After collective agreements were negotiated and signed by the two parties, they had to be promulgated by the Ministry of Labor. This was a step introduced during the Perón administration to give it the force of law.[3] Perón went a good deal further than merely forcing employers and workers to negotiate in the Ministry of Labor, centralizing virtually all contract negotiations in Buenos Aires, and intervening personally or through his wife or the Ministry of Labor in drawing up collective agreements. He also saw to it that in 1952 all the country's collective contracts expired on the same day, March 1st.

The Grievance Procedure

Even before the advent of Perón a fairly standardized system of grievance procedure had developed in the unionized industries. This was completely in the hands of the unions and management. However, under Perón, grievances too were brought to the Ministry of Labor and special labor courts were established to handle certain grievance problems. This system has continued largely intact since the fall of Perón.

Before Perón, nearly every union in Argentina had a system of shop stewards who handled the first step in the grievance procedure. Their role during the Perón period varied from plant to plant. In some cases they were the first ones to take up a worker's grievance with the foreman. In other cases the employers refused to allow the foremen to treat directly with the shop stewards and the steward's job was to report to the plant grievance committee (*comisión del reclamos*) of the union.

During the Perón regime, the shop steward was given legal protection. He could not be fired without cause, and that, to be decided by the Ministry of Labor in Buenos Aires. If a union shop steward was dismissed he had to be paid three times the normal dismissal pay.

The degree to which it was possible to settle matters on this plant level varied a good deal from time to time and from plant to plant. If the local plant leadership of the union was fairly militant or was strongly Peronista, matters usually did not stop there unless the union leadership got full satisfaction from the employer. Under Perón the union leaders preferred to carry matters to the Ministry of Labor.

In some industries the next step in the grievance machinery was an appeal to the local union organization in the region which took up the problem with the employer before going to the Ministry of Labor. This was the situation in the candy and conserve industry. In the iron- and steel-fabricating industry there existed an informal gentlemen's agreement between the employers' Asociación de Industrias Metalúrgicas and the workers' Unión Obrera Metalúrgica whereby the union brought an unsettled grievance to the Asociación, which attempted to iron it out before appealing to the government. However, this was exceptional; most employers' *cámaras* did not intervene directly.

Every local union branch had one or more *asesores gremiales* or grievance secretaries, whose job it was to handle problems which came to the Ministry of Labor or to one of its provincial delegations. In Buenos Aires these people were full-time paid officials of the union who spent most of their time in the ministry. Most employers' organizations had similar officials.

If the local branch of the *sindicato* did not first try to deal with the individual employer or the employers' *cámara* it took the grievance directly to the Ministry of Labor. The first step there was for a member of the ministry's Secretaría de Conciliación to summon the two parties and attempt to get them to agree to a solution. He had only powers of conciliation, not of arbitration.

As the second step in the Ministry of Labor, contracts during the Perón period and since have provided for a *comisión paritaria,* made up of representatives of the union and of the employers with an official of the Ministry of Labor's Secretaría de Conciliación as chairman. A few contracts also provided for regional *comisiónes paritarias*. When the Ministry of Labor's

Secretaría de Conciliación cannot resolve a problem, it goes on to the *comisión paritaria*.

If the *comisión paritaria's* decision is unanimous, it immediately has the force of law. However, if such is not the case the matter is submitted to arbitration of the Ministry of Labor officials, and in very important cases to the minister himself. If it involves a problem of possible violation of the law, a grievance is referred to the labor court. The workers at any time during this process are free to transfer their appeal to the labor court.

The Labor Courts. The labor court system was another innovation in labor relations introduced by the Perón regime. The first such court was established in the Federal District (city of Buenos Aires) in 1945. Subsequently, similar judicial bodies were set up in nearly all the provinces. In most provinces there are two jurisdictions, *juzgado* (magistrate) and a Cámara de Apelación (Appeals Chamber), although in the province of Mendoza there is only one level of labor judiciary.

There are generally two hearings before the court of original jurisdiction. If one of the parties does not appear before the conciliation session, conciliation is dispensed with. However, if one of the parties fails to appear before the second session where the evidence is to be heard, the decision is rendered on the basis of evidence presented. The courts issue subpeonas. The procedures of the labor courts are designed to get rapid decisions. However, in most provinces there are insufficient tribunals, so that in the case of the Mendoza court it usually takes six or seven months before a case can be heard.

There are three career judges on each tribunal. Labor court judges do not undergo any special training, but are chosen among professional civil judges. There is no representation of the workers or the employers on the court as in Brazil, except in very special cases set forth in the procedural law of the respective provincial labor courts.

The labor courts are a part of the provincial judiciary although they deal with labor legislation which, during the Perón period, came to be largely federal in nature. The appeal from the labor court system is to the Supreme Court of the province. Such appeal can only be taken on errors of procedure or law, not on matters of fact. The labor courts apply the law and collective agreements which have the force of law. Though they were established under Perón, they have remained an integral part of Argentine labor-management relations. They have not fundamentally changed their procedures.

The Right to Strike

The Perón regime introduced legal restrictions on the right to strike. The Ministry of Labor and its regional delegates were empowered to declare a strike "legal" or "illegal." Generally, a strike was supposed to be legal if the official conciliation procedure had been gone through, a decision reached, and the employer had not abided by the decision. If this were not the case, a walkout was illegal. These same bases of decision remained in force after the downfall of Perón.

The declaration that a strike is illegal can cost the workers involved a good deal of money. If a walkout is legal, the employer must pay the workers throughout the strike; if it is illegal he has no such obligation. It is also possible for the government to cancel the legal recognition of a union which calls an illegal walkout.

During the Perón regime, almost any economic strike became illegal unless it in some way served the regime. Among the walkouts declared illegal during this period were the 1949 printing trades strike in Buenos Aires, the 1949 strike of the Tucumán sugar workers, the national maritime walkout, and railroad strikes of 1951. These were all stoppages resulting from the breakdown of labor–management relations.

Perón often declared a strike illegal as a means of breaking a union which he had been unable to control. He did so in the case of a walkout of the Anarchist-controlled taxi drivers' union of Buenos Aires in 1946. The same thing occurred at the time of the 1951 national maritime walkout, with the existing unions of maritime workers destroyed and the Perónista-controlled Asociación Marítima Argentina established in their place, and the previously autonomous craft unions reduced to "departments" of the AMA.

Usually when a union struck against the wishes of Perón, it was "intervened" by the CGT, its elected officers removed and an "interventor" put in its place until the government felt it was "safe" to hold new elections. Thus, the printing trades union of Buenos Aires was kept under intervention for several years after its 1949 walkout; and the Tucumán sugar workers' union FOTIA was never returned by the Perónistas.

Any walkout not called for political purposes was regarded by the Peróns as a defiance. Perón was presenting himself to the workers as their great protector, and was trying to break down all independence in the trade-union movement, and any self-reliance of the workers for settling their problems. He wanted them to look to the government automatically, and finally, to him. Independent trade-union action, and particularly a strike, was an admission that the Perón regime had not resolved a given problem to the workers' satisfaction and hence was "subversive."

On the other hand, Perón used the strike weapon for his own political purpose as we saw in the case of *La Prensa*.

During the Perón regime collective bargaining was successively undermined. The negotiation of nearly all contracts was centralized in the Ministry of Labor in Buenos Aires where officials of the ministry together with Sra. Perón actively intervened and often settled matters in dispute; the expiration dates of all contracts were made to coincide. Srikes were virtually forbidden, unless called for Peronista political purposes. Grievances came to be handled more and more through the Ministry of Labor, and special labor courts were established to handle cases involving violations of the law.

All of this added up to an attempt to channel all workers' grievances through the government. Furthermore, the workers were taught to believe that help was not to be sought in their own organizations (which in any case were not independent), but rather through the system set up by their one and only benefactor, Perón. So that the employers would not attempt to resolve too many complaints and grievances, their organizations, too, were closely controlled by the government, and all agreements between them and the workers had to have government imprimatur.

CHAPTER XIV

Legislative Attempts to
Forestall Workers' Grievances

Submitting the workers' and employers' organizations to his control and gradually substituting the fiat of the state for collective bargaining was not the end of Peron's attempt to monopolize the workers' protest. He also sought to forestall many of the grievances of the laboring man through labor legislation and social security.

There is no doubt that the Peronista government, both before and after Perón officially became President of the nation, enacted a considerable body of labor and social legislation to benefit the workers of Argentina. Perón was in the perfect position to do so. First of all, Argentina had fallen far behind in matters of social and labor legislation by 1943, and there was therefore a great deal to be done in this field. Second, during the first years of the Perón Era, Argentina was in a favorable economic condition because of pressing world demand for its exports. This made it possible to put a great deal of labor legislation on the books and establish a social security system without a great shock to the economy.

Such legislation served at least two purposes for Perón. It gained for him the approbation and political support of the workers. It also reduced the range of problems to be dealt with directly by workers and employers through collective bargaining and increased the area in which rules established by the state prevailed.

The Perónista Constitution

The most spectacular exhibition of government policy in this field was the 1949 Peronista Constitution. The followers of the President wrote into the basic document of the nation several chapters stating the aspirations of the workers, the aged, and the family.

By incorporating these features in the new constitution the Peronistas were imitating the Mexican Constitution of 1917 as have most subsequent constitutions in Latin America.[1]

The Peronista Constitution included ten "rights of the worker," as follows:

1. The right to work.
2. The right to just compensation.
3. The right to training.
4. The right to decent labor conditions.
5. The right to the preservation of health.
6. The right to well being.
7. The right to social security.
8. The right to protection of the family.
9. The right to economic improvement.
10. The right to the defense of his professional interests.

Each of these rights was elaborated upon with one paragraph in the constitution. Congress was supposed to assure that the workers received the rights set forth in the basic document. In fact, the Peronista government had already enacted a considerable body of decrees and statutes in the field.

Labor Protective Legislation. An early decree, issued in 1945, provided that an employer could not dismiss a worker "without clear proof of the existence of legal cause" (among which causes are listed "an injury to the security, honor or interests of the employer or his family") without paying the worker an indemnity. This payment must consist of one month's pay for each year of employment, except in cases in which the dismissal is due to lack of available work, in which case the employer is only obliged to pay half as much. In cases in which the worker is fired without receiving "previous notice," the employer has to pay an extra two months' wage to workers with less than five years' seniority and an extra four months' pay to workers with more than five years on the job.[2]

In the case of certain workers in industries in which "professional statutes" were enacted during the Perón administration, there are additional restrictions on the dismissal of workers. There is also special protection for union officials. They cannot be dismissed without cause in any case, and workers who are elected to union positions which take them out of their regular employment temporarily must always be given their jobs back when they cease to hold these union positions.

Some employers complained that these provisions for dismissal pay brought into existence a "dismissal industry." There were some employees who would work for three months in a plant, do something to bring about their dismissal, then seek employment elsewhere and repeat the performance. Since there was virtually no unemployment, this was a comparatively easy way of earning four months' pay for three months' work.

A good deal more serious was the problem presented by the provision that a worker could not be transferred from one part of a plant or from one occupation to another in a plant without his own consent. This very much handicapped the efficient operation of many plants. This was one of the complaints about the Perón administration's labor policies most frequently heard from employers.

The forty-eight-hour week and eight-hour day were fairly generally established before the Perón Era although there were considerable numbers of workers to whom it did not apply. The Peronista administration was very much inclined to refuse to permit longer periods of work but to allow certain groups of workers to have shorter hours. Remorino sums up the Peronista policy when he says, "The Secretaría del Trabajo y Prevision reacted against the easy tendency of establishing exceptions to the legal work day, and reduced the hours of the same."

Among those whose work day was fixed at eight hours by the Peronista administration were night watchmen in factories and warehouses and on ships. Numerous other groups of workers had their hours reduced by the government on the plea that they were engaged in "unhealthy" occupations. These included workers in packing houses; subway office and shop workers laboring below the surface of the ground; most workers in tanning and dyeing of leather; and those working underground with the telephone system.

Work of women and children was also limited in many cases to less than eight hours. Minors between the ages of fourteen and sixteen were only allowed by the government to work four hours a day and twenty-four per week. Minors between sixteen and eighteen years of age could only work six hours a day and thirty-six per week.

Vacations and Holidays. Paid vacations constituted another benefit which the Peronista regime extended to nearly all workers whereas only a few categories had enjoyed it before Perón. As early as 1934 paid holidays had been mandatory for commercial employees. This law provided for ten days' holiday for workers with less than five years' seniority; fifteen days for workers with five to ten years; twenty days for those with ten to twenty years; and thirty days for those with more than twenty years on the job.[3]

The general right to paid vacations was first established by a decree of Secretary of Labor Perón in 1945. Not only did workers receive the right to a paid vacation during the Perón administration, but the unions developed an extensive system of tourist hotels for the accommodation of their members. In the mountain resort region of Córdoba the great majority of the first-class hotels were bought by the unions for this purpose.

In some cases the hotels owned by the unions were used for other purposes. This was notoriously true in the case of the Confederación General de Empleados de Comercio, led by Perón's Minister of the Interior, Angel Borlenghi. According to Juan March, who became one of the principal leaders of this union in the post-Perón period, from 70 per cent to 90 per cent of the guests during the Perón Era were not members of the union. They were government officials and friends of Borlenghi.

Wages. Undoubtedly one of the factors which won Perón the support of the workers during the 1943–1945 period was his action as Secretary of Labor in forcing employers to grant sizable wage increases. From 1943 to 1948 there was certainly an increase in the real wage of the Argentine workers[4] though this rise did not continue much after that time, and in the last few years of the Perón regime there was at least a stagnation of the real wage, if not an actual decline.

One of the most spectacular moves made by the government in the field of wages was the decree issued during the 1945–1946 election campaign providing that each worker receive an additional month's pay as a year-end bonus. This bonus was made a regular part of the wage structure after the reestablishment of constitutional government. The Instituto Nacional de Remuneraciones was established under the original decree, to administer the law and help in determining what should be the basis of calculation of this extra month's pay.[5]

During most of Perón's administration, wage increases came principally through collective contract negotiations. After 1948 the government slowed down the rate of money wage increases, and in 1952 the government took the establishment of wage terms into its own hands, at the same time proroguing the collective agreements then in existence. According to this 1952 wage decree, all monthly wages and salaries which in 1949 were below eight-hundred pesos were increased by 60 to 80 per cent; all wages and salaries more than one thousand pesos in 1949 were raised 40 per cent.

All increases given between 1949–1952 were deducted from these raises. In February 1954 Perón decreed a further increase in all wages.

Although the government generally decreed that the employer was not to make deductions from the workers' pay, there were numerous exceptions to this established by the Perón regime. Income tax for those workers earning enough to pay such an impost was to be deducted. In the case of minors and agricultural workers, a certain amount was to be deducted and deposited in a bank for the worker as savings. Pay for May 1 and October 12 was withheld by the employer and turned over to the Banco de la Nación Argentina to the account of the Fundación Eva Perón.

Furthermore, various collective agreements provided that the first month's wage increase should be turned over to the union, not the individual worker. This held for the commercial employees, the metal trades workers, and others. In several instances a certain part of the wage increase provided for in new collective agreements—sometimes amounting to as much as 50 per cent of the first month's increase—was turned over to the Fundación Eva Perón.

The Enforcement of Labor Laws

Since labor problems became principally a field of federal rather than provincial jurisdiction under Perón, the Ministry of Labor took over the regional labor departments' work of policing labor laws and conditions. "Delegations" of the ministry were established in every provincial capital, and were empowered to see to the enforcement of both federal and provincial labor legislation.

Each delegation contained a section of "labor police" whose job it was to enforce labor laws. The inspectors of the Policía del Trabajo investigated complaints from workers concerning violations of labor laws and collective contracts. If there were not enough complaints to keep them busy, the inspectors went out on regular spot checks on firms within their jurisdiction. If violations of laws or contracts were discovered, the Regional Labor Delegate was empowered to levy fines on the offending employers, though these could always be appealed to the regional labor court. Under Perón the regional delegations of the ministry would not handle complaints presented by individual workers, but would only handle cases which came to them through unions in good standing with the ministry. However, in the post-Perón period, services were established to receive and handle complaints coming from individual workers whether or not they were union members.

Although there already existed a reasonably adequate workmen's compensation law before the advent of the Peronista regime it underwent several changes during that period. Maximum wage limits were removed for calculation of compensation which a worker could receive, while facilities were established for a more rapid processing of workmen's compensation cases. Special rules were adopted in the case of various groups of workers, generally providing for a liberalization of benefits.

In the case of certain trades the Perón regime established special labor codes. These included provisions concerning wage payments, labor conditions, holidays, and other matters. One of the most outstanding of these codes was the Peon's Statute, regulating the conditions of permanent agricultural workers. There was comparable legislation for commercial employees, bank clerks, traveling salesmen, and several other groups.

The Extension of Social Security

Most of the social security legislation on the books in Argentina at the time of Perón's overthrow was the work of his administration. The only social security funds existing at the time of the 1943 Revolution were those of the government employees established as early as 1904, and for the railroad workers and journalists set up during the interwar period.

Perón began expanding the social security system when he was Secretary of Labor. This expansion was continued during his administration as President, and the entire system had been rounded out, in legislation at least, shortly before his overthrow.

As of 1956 there existed the following social security institutions:

Caja de Trabajadores del Estado (government employees)
Caja de Ferroviarios (railroad workers)
Caja de Periodistas (journalists)
Caja de Navegación (sea and river transport workers)
Caja de Trabajadores de la Industria (manufacturing workers)
Caja de Comerciarios (commercial employees)
Caja de Profesionales (members of liberal professions)
Caja de Empresarios (managerial personnel)
Caja de Trabajadores Rurales (agricultural workers)
Caja de Trabajadores Independientes (self-employed workers)

These social security funds provided only for retirement pensions, and with some exceptions noted below, the Argentine social security system does not provide health insurance. In this regard it differs fundamentally from the majority of social security systems established in Latin America during the last twenty-five to thirty years.

Although there is some variation in the amount of contribution and in the benefits provided under the various *cajas,* in general a worker in Argentina can retire at his full wage at the age of fifty-five with thirty years of service. In addition, a number of *cajas* provide for voluntary retirement at an earlier age and before the prescribed number of years of service, though the retiring worker under these circumstances receives a reduced proportion of the retirement pay.

The early retirement provision of the Argentine social security system has been the subject of considerable abuse, particularly during the Perón period. It was not unusual for a worker to retire early, and then seek another job.

After the overthrow of the Perón regime, the Aramburu government specified that a worker receiving a retirement pension could not be employed in any other job. However, there is little doubt that habits formed under Perón still continued to be exercised under his successors.

The workers generally contribute 10 per cent of their wages to the social security fund to which they are affiliated; the employers pay the equivalent of 15 per cent of their wage bill. The government does not contribute at all, except in the case of the government employees' *caja* where its contribution is that of the employer.

The Instituto Nacional de Previsión Social. For the general orientation and guidance of the whole social security system, the Perón administration established the Instituto Nacional de Previsión Social. Its job was to co-ordinate all the social security funds. This job had not been entirely completed at the time of the fall of the Perón regime.

The institute also provided certain services to all the *cajas.* Loans made to members are all handled through the institute. It also has a medical service which gives physical examinations to all workers applying for invalid pensions to determine the degree of invalidism of these applicants. Finally, the institute conducts general surveys of the social security system and draws up plans for its amplification.

The institute is run by a directorate of thirteen members, three of whom are nominated by the workers' organizations, three by the employers' groups, and six by the President of the Republic. The president of the institute is also nominated by the chief executive of the nation, with the advice and consent of the senate.

In addition to this direct representation in the directorate, the workers and employers have representatives in the Cámara Gremial of the institute, which studies and recommends changes in the structure and benefits of the *cajas*. There also exists a *Consejo Técnico* (Technical Council), made up of professional people employed by the institute which has a function similar to that of the Cámara Gremial.

The Instituto Nacional de Previsión Social has a regional delegation in each province. The delegations do not authorize a retirement or disability pension, but merely aid the applicants in filling out the necessary forms, and forward these to the national headquarters of the institute in Buenos Aires where the applications are passed on to the appropriate *caja*.

The regional delegations also have the job of enforcing the social security laws. They receive complaints from workers who suspect that their employers are not making the legally required contributions to the social security funds. The delegations also make spot-check investigations of firms in their areas. In the province of Tuumán it was estimated that 60 per cent of the employers in the province did not pay the taxes which the law required.

Like almost all other aspects of economic and social affairs, the social security system took on political overtones under the Perón administration. The government in 1953 decreed that henceforward all applications for social security benefits should be made through the trade unions. The official explanation for this was that it would make it more convenient for the worker. It was also argued that this would speed up the obtaining of retirement benefits, since the processing of applications would be handled on a widely decentralized basis.

Opponents of the Perón regime felt, however, that the real purpose of turning the processing of social security benefit applications over to the unions was to make it easier to use the social security system as a political check upon the workers. The local union officials would be acquainted with those antagonistic toward the regime and would be in a position to refuse applications for social security benefits if they did not change their political attitudes.

Health Insurance

Health insurance is not generally provided by the Argentine government social security system as we have noted. However, there are certain groups of workers covered by health insurance administered under government control and supervision. All the government ministries except that of foreign affairs have such plans, and there are also government-administered health insurance arrangements for railroad workers, bank employees, and metal workers.

Previous to the rise of Perón, the railroad workers' unions had legally established an extensive system of health protection for railroaders and their families. Although the money for most of this came from the employers, the Railroad Workers' Health and Welfare Fund was administered by the representatives of the two unions in the railroad field, Unión Ferroviaria and La Fraternidad.

In his attempt to tie the workers more closely to the government, Perón took over this system and put it under government control, establishing the Dirección General de Servicios Sociales de Ferroviarios for the purpose.

The Perón administration set up similar services for bank employees, the Dirección General de Servicios Sociales de Bancarios. All services are free to the workers except drugs which are provided at 30 per cent below market prices. The service covers not only the bank clerk, but his dependents as well.

The Dirección General also pays a subsidy to a sick worker in some cases. The banks are obliged to continue a worker's salary for a certain period—in the case of the government banks, two years—after which the bank worker can obtain a subsidy from the Dirección General. The service also pays bonuses of five hundred pesos for the birth of each child, and when a bank clerk gets married. It pays fifteen hundred pesos upon the death of a bank worker.

The service also has a vacation program. All this is financed by a discount of 2 per cent from the bank worker's wage, a contribution of an equivalent of 2 per cent of the wage bill from the employer, and a 4 per cent profit tax on the banks. This gives the Dirección General sufficient funds to run a generous program.

Under Perón this system was subject to political abuses. There was said to be favoritism in the distribution of benefits, with good Peronistas having preference.

In many trades and industries which do not have government-controlled and supervised health insurance schemes, the trade unions conduct them independently. Most of these trade-union programs were established during the Perón period.

A good example of a union health program is that of the Unión Obrera Metalúrgica. This organization provides full medical service for all its members and families. This union also provides another service to its members in the form of cut-rate stores.

Thus, Perón sought to supplement his increasing control over the labor movement and the employers' organizations by enacting an extensive body of labor and social legislation to the advantage of the workers, emphasizing the lesson he was trying to teach them: that Juan Perón was their only protector. Of course, the actual legislation passed by the Perón regime in this field does not contain any startling innovations—it was only new for Argentina, not for Latin America or the world at large.

CHAPTER XV

Effect of "Revolución Libertadora"

It is perhaps too early to make a definitive assessment of the effects of the Perón experience on labor–management relations in Argentina. However, certain general results are obvious.

First of all, it can't be denied that Perón greatly expanded the scope of organized labor and brought collective bargaining into fields where it had never been before. Whether one accepts Perón's claim that there were six million workers in the CGT, or the post-Perón Ministry of Labor's estimate of something over two million, it is obvious that the labor movement had increased in number many times over during the twelve years of Perónismo. Collective bargaining had been brought into the packing house, the cotton textile industry, cement production, manufacturing in general, and agriculture.

Second, there is little doubt that Perón succeeded in arousing class consciousness among the workers. The workers became very conscious of their existence as a separate group and of their power or potential power in the Argentine scene. The old patriarchal relationships were gone forever. In many ways the feeling of human dignity and self-esteem which Perón aroused in many workers was more important than any material benefits he may have given them and is a surer reason for their support.

Third, there is no doubt that the Peronista experience brought about a lowering of labor productivity among the workers of Argentina. Perón had convinced vast numbers of Argentine workers that they could get a higher income with less work, without instilling in them a sense of individual and collective responsibility necessary before this fine state of affairs comes to pass.

Fourth, Perón had bent a going pattern of labor–management relations to his own uses. He kept the procedures of collective bargaining but had added a complicated network of government intervention which succeeding administrations found very difficult to dispense with. He tamed the labor movement and taught it to look to the government rather than to its own efforts for success while establishing a mechanism through which this government control over labor-management relations was to be exercised.

Fifth, Perón politicized the labor movement. He made it a major force in the nation's political life and if he taught the opposing politicians anything it was that there were votes to be found among the organized workers. The twelve years of the Perón Revolution thus had a profound effect on Argentine labor–management relations.

The forces which supported the "Liberating Revolution" against Perón were heterogeneous. They included radicals and reactionaries, democrats and totalitarians, military men and civilians, Catholics and anti-clericals. In the labor–management field they included most employers, as well as workers who had never backed Perón or who had been disillusioned in him.

The military regimes which came after Perón were subject to constant tugging and pulling from the groups supporting them, as well as attempts from the Peronista camp to overthrow them. It is therefore not surprising that these governments did not evolve a consistent policy toward the knottiest problem of post-Perón Argentina—labor–management relations. Though the post-Perón regimes certainly were not as demagogic in their appeal to the workers as Perón had been, they were torn between alternate desires to keep in check the powerful political instrument which the dictator had created in the labor movement, to appease the workers who were still largely pro-Perón, and to increase productivity while proving to the workers that the new regime was not their enemy.

Lonardi

The first post-Perón regime of General Eduardo Lonardi was faced with a ticklish problem in the labor movement. The CGT and its constituent unions were still intact and were still under the leadership of the Peronistas. They were a potential menace to the new regime, particularly in the face of divergences which soon became evident among the supporters of the *Revolución Libertadora*.

General Lonardi chose as his Minister of Labor and Social Welfare, Luis Cerutti Costa, who had for a time been a supporter of the Perón regime and had served as lawyer for a number of unions during the Perón period. For the two months he was in office Cerutti Costa followed a conciliatory policy toward the labor movement.

The Lonardi government did not believe in intervening any more than absolutely necessary in the internal affairs of the unions. Lonardi and Cerutti Costa felt that it was better to allow the workers to get rid of the Peronistas by themselves.

Although the Lonardi administration did force Hugo de Petri, CGT secretary general at the time of Perón's downfall, to resign, they allowed two other Peronista leaders to take charge of the organization. There was no government "intervention" in either the CGT or its constituent unions.

On the other hand, the Lonardi government decreed that new elections should be called in all the country's unions with the hope that the Peronistas would be ousted from many of the more important unions.

The Lonardi regime quarreled with some of its own supporters over the Cerutti Costa labor policy. The Socialists and Syndicalists seized a considerable number of union headquarters during the first few days of the revolution. The Lonardi administration turned them back to the Peronista union leaders, an action which brought strong condemnation from the Socialist Party. In the meantime, another group of Socialist and Syndicalist unionists seized the headquarters of the Buenos Aires provincial organization of the CGT in the city of La Plata and proclaimed it a "genuine" Confederación General del Trabajo. They solicited backing from the trade unions in the interior of the country, and received messages of support from several hundred unions.

The labor problem and other issues brought about a split in the forces supporting the Lonardi government and a military *coup d'etat,* backed by most anti-Peronista civilians, ousted Lonardi and put General Pedro Aramburu in his place. Admiral Isaac Rojas remained as Vice-President.

Aramburu

The overthrow of Lonardi brought a quick reaction from the labor movement. The Peronista leaders of the CGT called a nation-wide general strike against the new government. Faced with this situation, the Aramburu regime adopted an entirely different labor policy from that of its predecessor.

Aramburu's first move was to outlaw the general strike. His second move was to "intervene" the CGT, placing a navy captain, Alberto Patrón Laplacette in charge. In the following days the new Minister of Labor, Raul Migone, and Captain Laplacette appointed interventors in nearly all unions. Most of these were military men, though a few civilians were also named.

Two important unions were left in control of anti-Peronista unionists—La Fraternidad, and the Unión de Obreros Municipales.

Advisory committees, known as *juntas asesoras,* were established in every union to guide the interventors in their work. These were chosen by the interventors and were composed of members of the intervened union. The nature of the interventions varied a good deal from union to union. Some of the military men who took over this task could not shake their barracks habits. In other cases, the military interventors were more understanding. One army captain in charge of a union threatened to call a strike when the employers dealing with his organization proved obdurate.

One of the principal weaknesses of the government's program of intervention was the fact that Aramburu's first Minister of Labor, Dr. Raul Migone, was loath to have dealings with pre-Perón union leaders. His argument was that these individuals were "too political" and were interested in bending the unions to the purposes of Socialist and Syndicalist political groups.

The fact was that the trade-union movement of Argentina was likely to be political for some time to come and the real issue was what political color the labor unions were going to have. And the pre-Perón labor leaders or others who had broken with Perón during his administration were the only people with sufficient experience in the labor movement to put up a really effective opposition to the Peronistas and Communists in the unions.

The Aramburu regime faced a serious crisis in the labor movement three months after coming into power. Because Perón had arranged for all collective bargaining contracts to expire on the same date, the government was faced with the termination of these agreements on March 1, 1956. The regime resolved this problem temporarily by Decree-Law 2739 which provided an immediate 10 per cent wage increase across the board.

New Labor Legislation. Decree-Law 2739 introduced two innovations in Argentine labor law. The first of these was equal pay for equal work regardless of the worker's sex. The decree provided that all women doing the same jobs as men but receiving up to 10 per cent less should henceforward receive the same pay as men. In the case of women whose wages differed from men's in more than 10 per cent, the decree provided that they should receive an increase of 50 per cent of the difference. These increases in women's wages were to be made before the regular 10 per cent across-the-board increase to all workers was calculated.

The second innovation was the system of minimum wages. For Buenos

Aires and its immediate vicinity this wage was set at 1120 pesos a month, or 5.60 pesos an hour, depending on how the worker was paid. The Ministry of Labor was directed to establish the minima for the various provinces, in conformity with differences in cost of living between the capital and the province in question.

Although this decree thus contained several measures favorable to the workers, it also contained items which did not please the union members. For one thing, it cancelled the clause in collective agreements making it impossible for employers to change workers from one place to the other or one job to another—although it protected the worker's seniority and pay in such transfers. It also authorized the establishment of incentive pay, a move looked upon with dark skepticism by most trade unionists.[1]

Another Decree-Law 2446 altered and somewhat extended the list of paid holidays. It also established a category of "nonwork days" mandatory in public employment, banks, insurance companies, and allied activities, but voluntary in other establishments.

Another important piece of labor legislation of the post-Perón revolutionary regime was Decree-Law 326/56 which was the first law providing general regulations for domestic employees. This law also established an identification book from the Ministry of Labor in which would be noted the wages, days off, and vacation time agreed upon between the worker and his employer. This decree-law also provided that the ministry would establish a minimum wage for domestic workers and that domestic servants were to be included in the country's social security system.

The purpose of this decree legislation was to impress the workers with the fact that the Aramburu regime not only did not intend to undermine the gains made by the labor movement during the Perón regime, but intended to improve upon them. However, the government was not successful. In part this was due to the fact that the workers generally felt defenseless because of the intervention which prevented the unions from functioning normally. It was also partly due to the government's difficulty in enforcing its new labor legislation. The Ministry of Labor was badly disorganized as a result of the purge of many of its regular officials and the demoralization of those still remaining.

The Restoration of Union Autonomy. On May Day 1956 President Aramburu announced that within one hundred and eighty days two sets of elections would be held within the unions—first, for negotiating committees to bargain with the employers, and second, for regular officers. A decree provided that in case it was impossible to reach agreement between the workers and employers, contract terms would be submitted to arbitration tribunals to be established within the Ministry of Labor.

During the next two months, unions selected their bargaining committees. In most cases these were elected by the direct vote of union members. In the Commercial Employees' confederation, the Federation of Power and Light Workers, and some other unions, national conventions were called to draw up the lists of demands upon the employers and to elect committees to negotiate with management.

The weeks and months that followed were marked by bargaining sessions between workers' and employers' representatives. Only a small number of collective contracts were signed as a result of these negotiations. Generally, the employers refused any wage increases not tied to increases in productivity, whereas the unions insisted that they should get increases to compensate for price increases. Thus, negotiations were generally deadlocked. In the end, the government had to decree the conditions to be included in most new collective agreements. In some instances more than a year passed before the government decision was finally reached.

The controversy over new collective agreements brought about a number of strikes during the Aramburu administration. Late in 1956 there was a general strike of metal workers around Buenos Aires. About the same time the threat of a railroad workers' walkout brought the mobilization of all railroaders under army orders.

A special case was presented by the long, drawn-out strike of the Federation of Shipbuilding Workers. This union, of Anarcho-Syndicalist persuasion, refused to apply for government recognition but insisted that the employers negotiate a collective agreement nonetheless. The government backed up the employers' refusal to do so. The Ministry of Labor's action in granting recognition to a small rival group brought condemnation from papers usually friendly to the regime, such as *La Vanguardia,* the Socialist weekly.

There was a great deal of discontent among the workers during the Aramburu government. There was a widespread feeling that the regime was supporting the employers and was excessively influenced by them. One of the principal reasons for this suspicion was the fact that the government staffed the Ministry of Labor largely with bright young men from the legal and personnel departments of some of the country's major industries. Another contributing factor was the long drawn-out intervention in the CGT and its affiliated unions.

The results of the elections were certainly not generally to the government's liking. Although a few unions, such as La Fraternidad, the Commercial Employees' Confederation, the Bank Workers' Association, and the Clothing Workers' Federation elected administrations distinctly anti-Peronista and not basically unfriendly to the government, many of the large unions elected officials among whom the influence of the Peronistas and the Communists was by no means lacking.

Late in April 1957 Captain Alberto Patrón Laplacette, the interventor in the CGT, announced the calling of a congress of the Confederación General del Trabajo for the purpose of restoring the organization's autonomy. Some time previous to this, a number of unions which were more Peronista-inclined had established the Comisión Intersindical to function as a *de facto* central labor organization.[2] Although the Comisión Intersindical was strongly denounced by the anti-Peronista unions, the two events may not have been unconnected. Two one-day general strikes called by the Comisión Intersindical late in July and October 1957 were a failure.

The congress of the CGT which met in August 1957 broke up in a dispute over the credentials of the delegates. The unions then divided into two groups known popularly as the "Sixty-two" and the "Thirty-two," the former being largely Peronista-dominated, the latter anti-Peronista. The "Sixty-two" included such organizations as the Packing House Workers' Federation, the Metal Workers' Union, the Trolley Car and Bus Drivers' Union, the Light and Power Workers' Federation. The "Thirty-two" included the two railroad workers' groups, the Commercial Employees' Federation, the Clothing Workers' Federation, the Bank Clerks' Federation, and other unions. The two groups were about equal in strength, although in a number of cases the rank and file of the "Thirty-two" unions was pro-Peronista, though the leadership sided with the anti-Peronista group.

All attempts to bring the rival groups together failed during the Aramburu administration. A few days before Aramburu left office, the government abolished the intervention in the CGT, and turned the organization over to an administrative committee drawn largely from anti-Peronista leadership.

The Law of Professional Associations. In at least one sense, the provisional government of General Aramburu sought to modify the existing pattern of labor–management relations. This was in their alteration of the Law of Professional Associations. A new decree-law on the subject was issued by President Aramburu and Minister of Labor Raul Migone. Among the smaller changes in the law was one to rename the act of government recognition of unions from *personería grenial* to *personería jurídica,* implying that though the trade unions had a special character they were fundamentally no different from any civil association formed by residents of the nation.

Much more controversial, and indeed the core of the new decree-law, was the allowing of more than one union to function with legal recognition in the same field. The law provided that in industries in which there was only one union it should be the recognized bargaining agent for the workers, and in industries in which more than one union existed, negotiation on behalf of the workers should be undertaken by an "interunion commission." The regulations for any such commission "must recognize the rights of minorities." [3]

This provision was strongly attacked by groups inside and outside the labor movement, and particularly by pro-Perón labor elements and the Frondizi wing of the Radical Party. Those opposed to the measure argued that it would undermine trade-union unity. They argued that this would encourage, rather than discourage, the tendency toward a politicized trade-union movement, since each political group would in all probability seek to establish "its" labor movement, with rival unions in many trades and industries as well as rival central labor organizations.

Those supporting the new decree-law did so on three grounds. Minister of Labor Raul Migone argued, first, that for those who really believed in trade-union liberty it was wrong to force all workers to belong to the same union in a given trade or industry. A second argument was that before Perón no government recognition at all had been required for a trade union to conduct collective bargaining, and that the exclusive form of representation established by Perón had been instituted to give the government a weapon with which to crush those unions unwilling to support Perón politically. Finally, it was pointed out that the Peronistas would still, in all probability, constitute the majority in a number of key unions, and that if the anti-Peronistas were to have any chance to combat them in these industries, they must have a chance to organize their own trade-union groups and to participate in collective bargaining negotiations.

Minister Migone explained that in any case the collective agreements of 1956 were to be negotiated by the unions which possessed official government recognition at the time of the issuance of the new decree. The policy of permitting dual unions was to be instituted after these negotiations.

Employers' Organizations. In addition to its actions toward the trade-union movement, the Aramburu government also sought to dismantle partly the pyramid of employers' organizations built up under the Perón regime.

The new government acted on the grounds that the Confederación General Económica (CGE) was a political instrument of the Perón administration.

The Lonardi government had been content merely to "intervene" the CGE. It placed Elpidio Lasarte, a lawyer and industrialist, in charge of the organization and ordered him to reorganize it. However, when President Aramburu took over, he decreed the dissolution of the Confederación General Económica and forbade anyone who had held office in the CGE to hold office in any employers' organizations. Somewhat illogically, this applied to those, such as Lasarte, involved in the Lonardi regime's "intervention" in the CGE as well as to officials who had held office in the organization during the Perón regime.

The provincial federations of employers, organized under the CGE, were not dissolved with a few exceptions, nor did the revolutionary government generally intervene these provincial groups. However, most of the officials of the Peronista period were ousted. The CGE was reconstituted during the Frondizi administration.

In the case of some employers' organizations persecuted by the Peronista government, the revolutionary regime reversed the Peronista policies. This was notably true in the case of the Unión Industrial Argentina (UIA). The last elected president of the UIA, Pascual Gambino who had been forced out in 1946, was appointed by the revolutionary government to be interventor in the Unión Industrial Argentina. In 1956 he was also named chief employers' delegate to the annual International Labor Conference in Geneva. Gambino's job was to arrange for new elections and the restoration of the autonomy of the UIA. In 1957 these elections were called and Gambino was chosen president of the Unión Industrial Argentina.

There was a good deal of difference of opinion among businessmen concerning the dissolution of the Confederación General Económica. In Rosario, where there is strong resentment against Buenos Aires, there was satisfaction with the dissolution of the CGE. In Córdoba we encountered a good deal of sentiment in favor of the CGE, and feeling was expressed that the Confederación was not *per se* totalitarian, though some of its leaders during the Perón period may have been.

Labor–Management Relations Under Provisional Governments

For more than two and a half years after the fall of Perón, the succeeding revolutionary governments groped their way toward a policy in the field of labor–management relations. They sought to reverse the Peronista policy of centralizing the workers' protest with the government and to return to the representative organizations of workers and employers. They were only partly successful.

The revolutionary governments were faced with a situation in which a large part of the working class was still loyal to the deposed President. They felt, therefore, that they had to move cautiously.

The Aramburu regime was anxious to dismantle the totalitarian structure built by the Perón regime. Where the Lonardi administration hesitated, the Aramburu government moved swiftly to disarm the Confederación General del Trabajo as a Peronista political weapon. Through intervention, the control of the CGT and all its affiliates was placed principally in the hands of military men. At the same time, former Peronista officials of the labor movement were forbidden to hold office for some time to come. Only with considerable hesitation did the government move toward restoration of the autonomy of the labor movement.

At the same time, the revolutionary regime attempted to break up the Confederación General Económica, the top of the employers' pyramid constructed by Perón. It moved more cautiously, however, in handling the lower echelons of the employer structure, while moving to restore autonomy to employers' organizations such as the Unión Undustrial Argentina which had been disabled by the Perón regime.

The revolutionary governments attempted to reverse the Peronista tendency toward complete centralization of labor–management relations in the Ministry of Labor in Buenos Aires. Perhaps somewhat precipitately, it sought to return collective bargaining contracts to the employers' and workers' organizations. Although these negotiations were not entirely successful and presented the regime with a number of serious strikes and other crises, a beginning was made toward reestablishing genuine collective bargaining as the basis of labor–management relations.

Meanwhile, the government took a number of steps in the legislative field. It issued several decrees generally advantageous to the workers, including a minimum wage law, a provision for equal pay for equal work, and a statute for domestic employees.

However, the government at the same time sought to modify fundamentally the collective bargaining pattern by its new Decree-Law of Professional Associations which made possible the establishment of dual unionism. This was perhaps the most controversial legislation of the provisional government in the labor–management field.

On balance, the government did not succeed in getting the confidence of the workers. This was partly due to the failure of the Ministry of Labor to play the role of protector of the workers which it had played under Pérón. More important, however, was the fact that the long period of intervention in the labor organizations deprived the workers of effective defense by the trade-union movement, in a period when many employers wanted to get back at the workers for excesses which they felt had been committed under the Perón regime.

Another factor which undermined the workers' confidence in the Aramburu regime was undoubtedly the government's handling of individual labor disputes. Although it was understandable that the government should crack down hard on political strikes the stringent measures were less understandable when used to check economic walkouts. Its mobilization of the railroad workers into the army, and its refusal to allow the Anarchist-controlled Shipbuilding Workers' Federation to negotiate for workers the federation undoubtedly represented, were particularly resented.

Frondizi

With the inauguration of President Arturo Frondizi on May 1, 1958, government labor policy changed once again. Frondizi had opposed many of the actions in the trade-union field during the Aramburu regime. Furthermore, in the election of February 1958, Frondizi had had the support of the Peronistas inside and outside the labor movement. His policies as President reflected this at first.

One of his first moves was to enact a general amnesty for those guilty of "political" crimes. This meant that union officeholders of the Perón regime again became eligible to hold office in the labor organizations.[4] Almost simultaneously, the government decreed a general wage increase.[5]

Perhaps more fundamental than either of these moves was the Frondizi government's action in dissolving the administrative committee of the CGT, which had been named by Aramburu, and in putting the confederation once again in the hands of an "interventor." He was directed to prepare the way for a congress of the CGT which would finally restore complete autonomy to the organization.[6]

In general, the new CGT interventor followed a policy favorable to the Peronista elements in the confederation's constituent unions in the early months of the Frondizi regime. Thus, he refused to approve a negotiating committee named by a special congress of the Confederation of Commercial Employees for the purpose of working out a new contract with the employers.[7] When a split occurred during a convention of the Unión Ferroviaria late in September 1958, he recognized the Peronista faction as the legitimate representative of the railroad workers. However, President Frondizi overruled this move when it provoked a general strike among the railroaders, and finally recognized the rival anti-Peronista executive committee.[8]

In July 1958 the Frondizi government sent a bill to congress to change the Ley de Asociaciones Profesionales once again. This bill restored most of the features of the Peronista law which had been altered by the Aramburu regime. It provided for government recognition of only one union in each field, and for only one central labor organization. It also provided for the compulsory checkoff of union dues for legally recognized unions. Although this law aroused violent opposition from anti-Peronista elements in the labor movement, it was approved by congress, which was overwhelmingly controlled by Frondizi's Unión Cívica Radical Intransigente.[9]

In effect, these measures turned the majority of the labor movement over once again to Peronista elements. The Frondizi government was accused of paying off its political debts to Perón and his followers. However, it should also be noted that the resumption of control over the labor movement by the Peronistas was a reflection of the fact that the Peronistas still made up the majority group within the rank and file of the trade unions.

This early favoritism of Frondizi toward the Peronistas in the labor movement did not prevent a break between the new regime and the labor supporters of the ex-dictator, when it became clear that they were still dedicated to restoring Perón to power, by violent means if necessary. Such a break occurred in October 1958. From then on the Frondizi regime tended to play one political group in the labor movement off against another.

Late in 1958 a new political group appeared in the labor movement when several unions broke from the "Sixty-two" to form the Movimiento de Unidad y Coordinacion Sindical which came to be known popularly as the "Nineteen." The unions in this group were under Communist and left-wing Socialist influence. Meanwhile, a sizable group of unions withdrew completely from all the contending factions. These included the two railroad unions, the printers, and various other important labor groups.

The Frondizi government's Stabilization Program, launched in December 1958, which provided for establishing a single foreign exchange rate for the peso, ending price controls, reducing the government's budget deficits and attempting to limit wage rises aroused wide labor unrest. The first effect of the program was to reduce real wages still further. The normalization of Argentine labor–management relations seemed still to be out of reach. However, one important step was taken early in 1961 when the government finally turned the CGT over to a group of representatives of twenty of its largest affiliates, ten of which were Peronistas, ten, anti-Peronistas. The Communists were left out completely.

By the end of 1961, labor–management relations remained unstable. Although the structure instituted by Perón remained largely intact, popular discontent against the Frondizi economic policies and bitter rivalry among political factions in organized labor remained disturbing factors.

CHAPTER XVI

Recruitment and Commitment of Workers

The industrialization of Argentina since the Great Depression has required a growing number of workers in the new factories and offices. Since many of the new workers have come from the country where conditions are considerably different from the city, this has meant a process of acclimatization and adaptation as we discussed earlier.

However, the changes which the Argentine rural worker has had to make have not been as great as those of his Brazilian counterpart. There is not as sharp a contrast between the city and the country in Argentina as in its northern neighbor.

There is not the racial difference between country and city which is found in Brazil. Although there is probably more Indian blood in the rural Argentine than in his city contemporary, there are few Argentine workers who are purely Indian or come out of an Indian cultural environment.

Many Argentine rural workers are at least partly literate in contrast to Brazil. Argentine agriculture is comparatively highly mechanized and many workers who learned how to tinker with agricultural machinery would not find the machines in factories completely alien.

Finally, many agricultural workers have at one time or another been to the nearest "big city," and even the smaller big cities are less provincial and isolated than many of the Brazilian state capitals.

Nevertheless, the new arrival is attracted by the same things as his Brazilian counterpart, the higher wages and the brightness and activity of the city. He probably welcomes the greater individual freedom though at times he may regret leaving the comparative security of familiar surroundings and acquaintances.

Recruitment

Most Argentine industrial workers get their jobs by coming to a factory looking for work, or by answering a want ad in the newspapers. The Perón government set up a National Employment Service, but it would seem not to be used generally by industrial employers for hiring workers.

Some of the newspapers, especially in Buenos Aires, have gone in heavily for classified advertisements. *La Prensa* is particularly famous for this and *La Nación* is next. Although most classified ads have to do with property, and although most Argentine manual workers in all likelihood do not read *La Prensa,* undoubtedly many white collar workers and skilled manual workers get their employment this way. One of the reasons the Perón government was unhappy about *La Prensa*'s opposition was that many Peronistas read that newspaper because of its want-ad coverage.

There are some trades in which unions have hiring halls and workers seek employment there. Generally, these are found in industries in which trade unionism has the longest traditions. The union hiring hall is particularly prevalent in the hotel and restaurant industry, though in some instances employers refuse to hire through these union halls.

The author visited the hiring hall of the Unión Gastronomica de la Republica Argentina (waiters' union) in Tucumán. There are many workers in the city who have regular jobs as waiters but who give up one day's work a month for those who do not have permanent positions. There are quite a few workers with no permanent jobs who are thus able to receive work nearly every day.

In some other cases, collective agreements reached during the Perón period provided for a modified kind of closed shop and hiring through the union. For instance, the agreement between the trolleycar and bus drivers' union, Unión Tranviarios Automotor, and the Transport Corporation of Buenos Aires, provided "the corporation and the union will share equally any vacant jobs, that is the Unión Tranviarios Automotor may propose people for 50 per cent of these. The firm will inform the Unión Tranviarios Automotor in all cases of the number of vacancies to be filled, and the names of those whom it proposes to fill them. Therewith the Unión Tranviarios Automotor will send the list of those whom it wishes to designate."[1]

An interesting example of the difficulties which sometimes face new industrial firms, particularly in the interior, in the recruiting of skilled and clerical help is the Kaiser automobile plant in Córdoba. Much of this company's engineering and administrative personnel was recruited in Buenos

Aires. For other workers, the company placed advertisements in newspapers throughout the country, and they recruited a considerable number of their employees, particularly skilled workers, from as far away as Buenos Aires, Mendoza, Tucumán, and Rosario, though the larger part of the office workers and manual labor force came from the Córdoba region.

Some firms give tests to job applicants. One of the biggest Buenos Aires department stores, Harrod's, gives its job applicants psychological tests.

Training

There is undoubtedly a shortage of skilled workers in Argentina. Most such employees are trained on the job. However, a number of companies have special training programs for their employees.

For instance, the SIAM di Tella plant in Avalleneda has an apprenticeship school with about one hundred students. These are youngsters who enter the school between the ages of fourteen and sixteen. The course runs for three years and is supervised by the government's Comisión Nacional de Aprendizaje.

The Perón government, as part of its program to encourage industrialization, established a government program for training skilled workers for industry. This was under the control of the Comisión Nacional de Aprendizaje y Enseñanza Profesional, and was patterned on the SENAI program of Brazil, though administered by the government and not by the employers.

All this is paid for by a 1 per cent tax on the wage bill of every industrial employer. The Comisión Nacional de Aprendzaje y Enseñanza Profesional in charge of the program is controlled by the Ministry of Education, though it operates with considerable autonomy. The Comisión was originally set up by Perón as part of the Secretaría del Trabajo when he was Secretary of Labor, but was later transferred to the Ministry of Education.

The schools of the Comisión are adapted to their locations. If an area is principally a textile region, the school will emphasize textile training. In some places the Comisión has established schools to encourage the growth of an industry. For instance, if an employer says that he would be willing to set up a factory if there were sufficient trained labor, the Comisión will set up a school to train the necessary workers. Those administering the system feel that it is better to do this than to try to attract labor from the interior to the already established industries in Buenos Aires. The Comisión has even set up schools in distant Patagonia.

The work of the Comisión, though praiseworthy, is not sufficient to assure a steady supply of trained workers for industry.

The Ministry of Education also maintains other industrial schools as a regular part of the public school system. These much antedate Perón, having been established before World War I. They offer a seven-year secondary school course and the classes are conducted during the day. Many poor families cannot afford to have their sons and daughters go to school until they are nineteen, and this fact explained the establishment of the special training system of the Comisión. The courses in the regular industrial schools are more theoretical and give the student more general education than do the apprenticeship courses of the Comisión.

Seniority and Promotions

Although it does not appear to have been a general practice, many of the collective agreements of the Perón period included a provision that seniority be one of the factors in determining the promotion of workers. For instance, in the contract between the Transport Corporation of Buenos Aires and the Unión Tranviarios Automotor there is a long section dealing with this. In general it provides that the company shall give preference for promotion to those workers with longest seniority. However, the company shall be entitled to test their capacity to perform the new job, and shall have the right, depending on the category of job, to test from two to three times as many workers (going down the seniority list) as the number of jobs it wishes to fill. Once a worker has been promoted, the company is given a certain trial period to determine whether he is able to do the new work before he is regarded as permanent.

Another contract, that of the glass industry, provided for seniority in promotions as follows:

Art. 8.—The companies will respect the seniority of the workers of each section so that promotions which may occur because of vacancies or new posts to be filled may be on the basis of seniority and the capacity of the worker. In case no one in the section involved can fill the vacancy, preference will be given to other workers employed in the firm, always provided that a worker is available who has the qualities for filling the post.[2]

The collective agreement between the Aerolineas Argentinas airline and the Asociación Argentina de Aeronavegantes provided a very complicated method of determining eligibility for promotion from one category to the next. It sets forth the minimum requirements for promotion in each case.[3]

In addition to provisions for promotion from one position to a higher one, many contracts provided for regular wage increases according to seniority. An example of this is found in the metallurgical industry contract. It provides, in Article 25, that after three years a worker is to receive, for each succeeding year to his twenty-fifth, a bonus of two centavos per hour.[4]

Incentive Pay and Productivity

There seems to be a general feeling among both employers and labor leaders that there was a serious decline in labor productivity during the Perón Era. In some cases this was obvious, as in the case of the railroads where employment almost doubled during the Perón period while service on the roads is universally agreed to have deteriorated.

The Perón government declared the glass industry to be unhealthy and reduced the hours of work to six a day. Of these six hours it is estimated that the workers are busy only about four and a half hours. This has resulted in a sharp decline in productivity per worker.

Various reasons are given for the general decline in labor output. One explanation is the great influx of untrained workers from the countryside. Another widely accepted explanation among both employers and some labor leaders is that Perón's demagoguery convinced the worker that he had a right to more pay for less work.

A third explanation is the fact that after 1948 it became increasingly hard for employers to get new machinery. Of course, the result of this was that the industrialists and agriculturalists had to make do with what they had. This lowered the output per worker as well as per machine.

It is clear that shortly before he was overthrown, Perón became aware of this problem. The second Five-Year Plan laid a good deal of stress on increasing productivity. In more and more speeches Perón himself called upon his followers to work harder and to step up their productivity consonant with increases in wages. In 1952 and again in 1954 Perón established definite limits within which wages were to be allowed to increase.

The importance which Perón placed on the productivity problem was indicated by the Congress of Productivity early in 1955 which met in Buenos Aires with delegates present from the labor movement, employers' organizations, and the government. Perón was the star speaker on this occasion. Although nothing concrete came from this meeting it was an indication of the regime's concern with the problem.

After Perón, employers were generally vehement about the necessity of increasing labor productivity. They insisted on the modification of laws and collective contract provisions which they claimed had a restrictive effect on productivity—particularly provisions forbidding the transfer of workers from one part of a plant to another. The government supported the employers in these demands.

When collective contracts came up for renewal during 1956, employers' representatives insisted that any further wage increases must depend on the workers' output. The unions almost unanimously opposed this position and generally there was a compromise on the issue in the final agreements.

As a matter of fact, incentive pay was nothing new in Argentina. The cement industry, the salt industry, the glass industry, and textiles are some of the branches of manufacturing in which piecework has been more or less general for some time.

Many employers have found that incentive pay does not make the difference in output which they had hoped. We were informed that in the glass industry, for instance, the workers refuse to work to full capacity under the incentive system, using fear of unemployment as the excuse for their attitude.

Certainly, a mere substitution of incentive pay for straight hourly pay or a revision of existing piecework rates is not the answer. Undoubtedly a large part of the problem is a matter of the workers' morale. After the fall of Perón, many if not all workers felt that they had lost their protector, that the governments which succeeded him were enemies, and as a result these workers were skeptical of the emphasis on productivity. They felt that this talk was designed to increase profits without any gains for them, that it was part of a campaign to "get back" at them because of their support of Perón.

Wage Levels

There is little doubt that the Argentine industrial workers are among the best paid of their kind in Latin America. There is also little doubt that during the first half decade of the Perón Era, Argentine workers' real wages increased substantially, if not spectacularly. However, during the last part of the Perón period, the position of the worker slipped considerably, and it continued to deteriorate during the post-Perón years. The situation since approximately 1949 has been brought about by the fact that cost of living increased more rapidly than the workers' wages.

During the 1943–1948 period, Argentina was in a peculiarly fortunate position. It had a market for its agricultural exports limited only by what the nation could produce. As a result the total national income went up substantially. And during the 1943–1948 period, Perón forced the employers to share a fair portion of this gain with their workers. Subsequently, with the decline in Argentina's favorable world economic position, the regime sought to underplay wage increases as much as possible.

First, let us look at what happened to the industrial worker's money wage during most of the Perón period. Table 9 indicates the situation in the metallurgical industry.

Table 9. Wages in metallurgical industry under Perón.
(pesos per hour)

Category of worker	1942	1944	1946	1947	1948	1949	1950	1952	1954
Foreman	0.94	1.04	1.55	2.20	2.75	3.20	4.10	5.20	6.00
Subforeman	0.74	0.82	1.15	1.70	2.12½	2.46	3.50	4.30	5.15
Specialized worker	—	—	—	—	—	—	3.65	4.50	5.30
Qualified worker	0.74	0.82	1.10	1.70	2.12½	2.46	3.50	4.30	5.15
Unskilled worker	0.68	0.76	1.00	1.50	1.87½	2.18	3.25	3.95	4.90
Laborer	0.60	0.70	0.95	1.40	1.75	2.05	3.10	3.80	4.75
Cost-of-living index 100 (1943)						237	297	563	

Three things stand out about these figures. First of all, the increases between 1944 and 1949 were considerably more rapid than in the five succeeding years. Second, the increases for unskilled workers were a good deal more than those for workers with greater skill and responsibility, over the whole period. Third, in the earlier part of the Perón regime the cost of living rose a good deal more slowly than the workers' wages, and the situation was reversed in later years.

Alejandro Magnet, the astute Chilean commentator on the Perón regime, notes the following concerning the cost-of-living figures:

The official statistics do not reveal the exact truth. There are sectors, such as foodstuffs, which have really increased more than is indicated, though drastic policy action, and particularly good harvests, have recently slowed down the increase. Rents, legally fixed for a long time, are calculated at their official level, though this is below their real level. . . .[5]

Dr. Arthur Whittaker cites a United States Department of Commerce study of Argentine real wages during the Perón period. This indicates that by 1949 real wages were 34 per cent above their level in 1943, but that from that year on they began to decline. By 1952 price increases had been so drastic that real wages were 13 per cent below those of 1943. By the end of 1952 the real wages of unskilled workers were reported as "hardly any higher" than in 1943.[6] Of course, the real wage of the skilled worker had fallen behind that of the unskilled and so was probably lower than at the beginning of the Perón Era.

The Argentine urban worker is not faced with as gaping a chasm between his former way of living and his new life in the city as is the Brazilian. He gets his job either from newspaper advertisements or from a direct application to a place of business. The government plays a relatively small role in this process of recruiting.

The rapid growth of Argentine industry and the resulting increase in the number of workers engaged in manufacturing has meant a considerable shortage of skilled labor. Most workers still learn their skills by watching an experienced employee. Some firms train their own specialized employees. A small part of the skilled workforce is trained in government industrial schools, while another segment receives training in the apprenticeship schools first established by the Perón government.

Once on the job, an Argentine worker earns a wage which (both in monetary and real terms) is considerably above that of most other Latin Americans of his class. During Perón's administration, the workers' real wage soared, then declined, and by the middle 1950's was probably not much more than at the beginning of the Perón period. It has fallen drastically since Perón's ouster.

In the past, the Argentine worker was considered one of the most efficient in the hemisphere. However, during and after the Perón Era the productivity of the Argentine manufacturing employee fell considerably for a number of reasons, some of which were Perón's demagoguery, the overstaffing of industries (particularly those controlled by the government) and the resistance of workers in the post-Perón period to a government they felt was hostile and to employers they thought to be vengeful.

Argentine labor–management relations were profoundly influenced by the Perón experience. During this era the dictator attempted to channel as completely as possible the expression of the workers' protest through organs of the state which he controlled, at the same time seizing for the government the lion's share in the process of rule determination and rule enforcement. To do so, he reduced the trade-union movement to little more than an organ of the state, and through legislation and political coercion drastically reduced the role of the employer in creating the "web of rule." Much of the pattern of labor–management relations established by Perón continued to exist even after he had fallen from power.

However, Perón did not change the pattern of labor–management relations in Argentina as profoundly as did Vargas in Brazil. This was partly because he was not in power as long as Vargas. But more important, it was due to the fact that in contrast to Vargas who smashed the existing labor movement and substituted an entirely new pattern of labor–management relations, Perón merely adapted to his own use the going system with the considerable tradition behind it.

Labor–management relations in Argentina are rooted in the collective agreement between the workers' union and the representative of the entrepreneur. In periodical collective contract negotiations, management and the workers determine the broad outlines along which they plan to conduct their relations. Interpretations of the terms of the contract and its application are handled first by a grievance procedure established within the firm and then by the Ministry of Labor.

Perón took over this structure and sought to bend it to his own political advantage. Looking for a group to whom he could appeal for support in his political ambitions, Perón very quickly sought out the labor movement. Within two years of the 1943 Revolution, he had behind him the great majority of organized workers as well as many of the unorganized.

Thereafter, the dictator sought to subordinate those who had supported him. He instituted a system of compulsory registration of unions—and near the end of his regime established a similar regimen for employers' organizations—and sought to centralize all collective bargaining in the Ministry of Labor. Not only did he make it necessary to receive the Ministry of Labor's permission to begin collective contract negotiations, but he had officials of the ministry, and for a long time his wife, keep close check on the progress of the negotiations. He furthermore established the procedure whereby serious grievances came to the Ministry of Labor for settlement rather than being dealt with independently by the organizations representing the workers and the employers.

At the same time, Perón crushed the independence of the trade-union movement. He used the compulsory registration law (Ley de Asociaciones Profesionales) to make it virtually impossible for any unions which were not politically friendly to him to function. His wife, Evita, kept an eagle eye on the affairs of the more important labor organizations, and purged officials who showed any independence of judgment. The result was that by the end of the Perón regime the labor movement, in all its upper and middle echelons, was a complete tool of the government. Nevertheless, a certain leeway for criticism and opposition was left as a safety valve in the lowest echelons.

Perón also sought to subject the employers' organizations to government control. He supplemented the existing organizations of employers by establishing federations to cover the whole of an industry in the country; and subsequently gave his blessings to the establishment of the Confederación General Económica as the superorganization of all employers in industry, commerce, and agriculture. At the same time, he sought to regiment the free professions through the Confederación General de Profesionales, but was overthrown before this job had been completed.

Observers inside and outside Argentina have felt that Perón was seeking to establish a corporate state. His move in making all collective agreements expire on the same day seemed to presage the end of collective bargaining altogether, and the substitution of some kind of government regulation of labor conditions. The establishment of special codes for a number of industries seemed also to be a step in this direction.

However, in spite of his attempts to regiment both management and labor, Perón left behind him a trade-union movement which was a principal force in the political sphere and was better equipped financially and organizationally than perhaps any other such movement in Latin America. He also left the machinery of collective bargaining basically intact. Various moves were made by the post-Perón regimes to modify the system as it had existed in the last years of the Perón administration with the object of strengthening independent collective bargaining between workers and employers.

One of the great question marks in Argentina is whether or not the employers had learned that trade unionism is there to stay, and whether or not they realize that if the workers are not met at leas halfway their grievances are likely to be exploited by Perón or some other demagogic and ambitious political leader. There was considerable indication that many employers wished to "take revenge" upon the workers after the fall of Perón—this in spite of the fact that the manufacturers by and large did very well financially during the Perón administration. However, the majority of employers realized that trade unions were a permanent feature of Argentine labor–management relations and that they would have to develop techniques to deal with them on a basis of equality.

The majority of urban workers continued to feel that Perón had their interests at heart and was sincere in his desire to protect and aid them. Their belief was strengthened by what they feel was the antilabor policy of the provisional government of General Aramburu and the constitutional regime of Arturo Frondizi. There are trade-union leaders and rank-and-file workers even among the Peronists who admit that there was excessive corruption in the unions as well as in the public administration, and that there was undesirable use of violence against the opposition inside and outside the labor movement during the Perón regime. There are many who do not want to see these conditions return, and who do not necessarily want to see Perón himself return to power, but who nonetheless are Peronists and look upon the Peronista movement as the political grouping which speaks for the country's working class.

The trade unions themselves need a new orientation. Although they are likely to remain politically partisan for a long time to come, there is certainly a need for them to become better equipped technically to deal with the problems with which the post-Perón period has presented them. They possess the financial resources necessary to engage technicians who can deal with employers on equal terms. The future of the labor movement depends in part at least on the degree to which they prove able to meet this problem.

By the end of the Perón Era Argentina definitely possessed a mixed agrarian–industrial economy. Although it still depended very heavily on its exports of grains, meat, and other agricultural and grazing products, it possessed strong manufacturing industries which had received considerable help during the Perón period. It had entered the epoch of heavy industry with the construction of the San Nicolás steel plant.

The entrepreneurial class was slowly changing from a group of owner-managers to a more complicated pattern. Most Argentine industries had been established either by small craftsmen or by merchants, but by the 1950's firms were beginning to grow large enough to need outside sources of capital. Argentina is a country with a middle class large enough to provide a considerable group of potential stockholders for the corporations which many manufacturing firms were becoming. Increasingly, too, new industries were being established by already existing firms.

All this was bringing about a subtle change in the nature of the Argentine entrepreneur. He was less and less a self-made man, and more and more a professional manager. Although this had by no means gone as far as in the United States or the countries of Western Europe there would seem to be considerable reason to believe it would be the pattern of the future.

Of course, the future of the labor movement depends to a high degree upon the country's political future. If the attempt made since the fall of Perón to find a road to political democracy succeeds, it seems highly likely that the pattern of labor–management relations based on collective bargaining with some of the projections which we have discussed will prevail. The return of Perón or the rise of someone similar would turn the development of relations between the workers and the employers into entirely different channels. Thus, not only has the labor-management system of the early 1960's been determined largely by political considerations, notably the ambitions and administration of Juan Domingo Perón, but the future of this field seems equally likely to depend upon political developments.

PART THREE—CHILE

CHAPTER XVII

Economic, Political, and Social Background

Chile stretches for 2620 miles down the western coast of South America seeming to cling to the continent. Only in its northernmost part does the country reach as much as one hundred miles in width. It is the smallest of the three countries with a population of 7,121,000 in 1957. The mountains and the sea dominate Chile. Ocean currents cause excessive dryness in the north and almost continuous rain in the south.

Agriculture

Chilean rural economy has been described as "semifeudal." One result of the inequitable distribution of land is that agricultural production is a good deal less than might otherwise be the case. The countryside is slow to accept modern methods. In 1940 the amount of arable land in the country was very small, only 7.5 per cent of the total. It has been estimated that erosion has now attacked about one-fifth of the cultivatable land.[1] Furthermore, vast sections of large landholdings remain entirely idle. Thus, in 1940, only 22.8 per cent of the arable land was cultivated. This agricultural lag has caused serious economic, social, and political problems for the country. The standard of living of the average Chilean agricultural worker is extremely low, and the large landholding system has held the country back educationally. The landholders are not eager to educate the workers for fear they will leave the farms.

Agrarian reform is still just conversation in Chile, and in spite of a series of leftist governments between 1939 and 1952, the gulf between the rural worker and his lord and master is still unbridgeable.

With the election of 1920 which put Arturo Alessandri in the presidency, political power in the nation as a whole passed from the rural landlords to the city. However, Alessandri was only allowed to come into office as the result of a tacit agreement that the landlords be left untouched. This meant that there would be no attempt at agrarian reform, and that the government would not allow the organization of agricultural workers into unions.

Chile's principal agricultural products are wheat, potatoes, oats, barley, corn, grapes, beans, peas, lentils, and rice. There was a time when grains were exported as well as some other agricultural products. In the southernmost part of the country there is a flourishing sheep industry mostly for export in the form of wool, sheepskins, and mutton.[2]

In spite of Chile's 2600-mile coastline, the fishing industry was until recently but little developed. Chile produced in the middle 1940's only about 30,000 tons of fish a year, whereas Norway, the geography of which is often compared with Chile, produced annually 1,000,000 tons of fish and even Portugal produced 150,000 tons about the same time. In the decade after World War II the Chilean fish industry expanded considerably and fish consumption rose proportionately.

Mining

For more than fifty years the principal Chilean exports have been minerals—principally nitrates and copper.

In the late nineteenth century the nitrate industry had a virtual monopoly of the world's production of nitrogen raw materials. Before 1882 nitrates were the only source of nitrogen and it was not until World War I that synthetics seriously competed with the natural product. A very severe crisis in the industry during the 1920's and early 1930's finally led to the establishment of the Corporación de Ventas de Salitre y Yodo, a government monopoly for the sale of nitrates and iodine. The industry was reorganized into three groups:[3]

a. The Guggenheim-controlled companies; the Lautaro Nitrate Co. (Pedro de Valdivia) and the Compañía Salitrera Anglo–Chilena (María Elena).

b. The Compañía Salitrera de Tarapaca y Antofagasta, which was until the early 1950's an English-controlled firm, but was then acquired by Chileans.

c. The so-called independent producers, very small Chilean firms.

The Guggenheim firm, in particular, has started a new refining system in recent years which is said to be much cheaper and which is helping to place

Chilean nitrates in a much better situation to face the competition of the artificial nitrate industry.

In the 1930's nitrates gave way to copper as the principal extractive industry in Chile. Copper had been mined in small quantities in Chile since before the arrival of the Spaniards. About the middle of the nineteenth century, Chile became the world's most important producer of copper. Subsequently, the nation's output declined for some decades.

There are some other mining operations in Chile in addition to nitrates and copper. The country's principal iron-mining enterprise is the United States-owned Bethlehem Chile Iron Mines Company. There is some gold mining which flourished particularly during the Great Depression. At that time there was sizable unemployment in the nitrate and copper industries and the government subsidized a number of these unemployed miners to try their luck at gold mining in the Andacolla region near Coquimbo. At its height, gold mining employed about twenty thousand workers, but by the late 1940's the number had fallen to some six thousand.

Coal mining is another completely Chilean-owned industry. Present production of coal is about 2,250,000 tons a year, a large part of which goes to the railorads. Chilean coal can be used for coking when mixed with higher-grade imported varieties and with this use in mind, the country's new iron and steel industry was established near the coal mines.[4]

Of all the large-scale mining enterprises in Chile, the coal mines present the worst picture insofar as living and working conditions are concerned. Housing conditions are particularly bad. It is in the coal mining areas that the Communists are strongest.

Manufacturing

Manufacturing in Chile goes back almost a century and a half. The first important industrial enterprise in the country, the army workshop, was established in 1811 by the new Republic of Chile, in order to have the material to equip its armies in the fight to maintain its independence from Spain.

In 1850 the first woolen mill was set up in Santiago. The Fabrica Bellavista de Tomé, still one of the country's principal textile plants, was started in 1865 and the El Salto plant in Santiago followed in 1870. The first shoe factory of importance was the Rudloff plant in Valdivia, organized in 1850, it is today one of the nation's outstanding shoe manufacturers. A porcelain factory was organized at Lota by the coal mining company in 1854 and was followed by a glass bottle factory. These manufacturing enterprises of the Lota Company were finally abandoned in the early 1950's.

During the last half century three events particularly stimulated the growth of industry in Chile: the two world wars and the depression of 1929–1933. During the wars it was very difficult for Chile to import the manufactured goods which she required and she was forced to produce them herself. And during the Great Depression Chilean exports fell off to such a degree that the country did not have sufficient foreign exchange to import all the things she needed.[5] This led to the organization of the Corporación de Fomento de la Producción.

The Corporación de Fomento operates by giving loans or grants-in-aid, or by making direct investments in industrial enterprises. Generally, at least in the field of manufacturing, the Corporación has followed the policy of expanding some already existing enterprise rather than forming new companies, although where no industry has existed in a field in which the Corporación has been interested a new firm has been established.[6]

With the help of the Corporación de Fomento the nation's industrial capacity has expanded very rapidly since 1939. In 1944 Fomento established the Empresa Nacional de Electricidad, SA (ENDESA). Through its efforts the country's electric power facilities increased rapidly after World War II, the consumption of electric power increasing 150 per cent between 1946 and 1956.

Another major project of the Corporación de Fomento has been the development of petroleum. For this purpose the Empresa Nacional de Petroleo was established. By 1950 it had brought in seventeen oil-producing wells and six others producing only gas. In the beginning all of the production of these wells was sold to Uruguay.[7]

The Empresa Nacional de Petroleo also established a refinery near Valparaiso which in 1956 was producing about 60 per cent of the country's demand for refined petroleum products on the basis of crude oil from southern Chile and some petroleum imported from Venezuela.

Undoubtedly the most spectacular project of the Corporación de Fomento has been the Huachipato steel plant near Concepción. Once it was under way, Huachipato had little difficulty in finding markets. Not only was there an extensive demand in Chile itself, but the plant also provided most of the steel requirements of Peru and Ecuador, and was selling its products as far away as Japan, Great Britain, and the United States. The Huachipato steel plant spurred the development of other industries.

The role of the Corporación de Fomento has been that of a catalyst. It has provided some of the basic necessities of new manufacturing firms, such as electricity and petroleum, and has served to get many new industries started and to put greater vigor into old ones. There are few manufacturing enterprises in Chile which have not received some aid from the Corporación. At the same time, it has not sought to socialize the economy, and has been willing to turn a job over to private enterprise whenever private entrepreneurs have been in a position to assume it.

Much of Chilean industry is still on a small scale. There are few plants in Chile with more than one thousand workers. Of course, the mining companies employ more workers than this, but among the manufacturing industries the only fields with plants employing more than one thousand workers are textiles, and the steel plant of Huachipato.

Chilean industries tend to be concentrated around a small number of cities with Santiago being by far the outstanding manufacturing center.

In this review of the Chilean economy some mention should be made of the transportation system. There is a prosperous airline network and an inadequate system of roads which is gradually being expanded. There are about six thousand miles of railroads, over one-half of which are state-owned. From the labor point of view, the railroads are of very great importance. The Federación Santiago Watt, composed of locomotive personnel, was one of the first trade-union organizations in the country's history, and the working conditions of the railroaders were for years the best of any group of workers in Chile.

Inflation

A key to the development of the Chilean economy during the last quarter of a century is inflation. Since the middle of the depression there has been almost continuous inflation, brought about to a considerable degree by the government's unbalanced budget. It has also been caused by the failure of agricultural development to keep up with the growth of industry.

We shall later discuss inflation's effect on the workers' wages. Here we are concerned with its effect on the growth of industry. There is no doubt that this situation has produced sizable profits which in turn have been reinvested to a considerable degree in the expansion of industry. Furthermore, much of the government's deficit has been due to its economic development activities. Through deficit spending the government has been able to bid away resources for the purpose of industrialization.

By 1955 inflation had become so extreme that it was having a depressing effect on the economy as a whole. Prices rose about 93 per cent during that year, and near the end of the period were rising so fast that consumers had almost lost track of what the goods they bought should be worth.

Beginning in January 1956 the government of President Carlos Ibañez undertook an anti-inflation program restricting automatic wage increases, reducing the government's budget and number of government employees, and restricting credit. Although this program had some success in slowing down the rate of inflation, it imposed considerable hardship on the Chilean workers, who saw their real wage fall even further than had been the case during the intensified inflation before 1956. The government of President Jorge Alessandri, who came into office late in 1958, also had a price stabilization program. Within a year it had succeeded in slowing down the inflationary spiral, but wage increases remained under rigid control. The net result of the stabilization effort was to bring industrial progress to an almost complete halt. Chile has gone a considerable distance along the road to industrialization. However, progress will always be limited by the size of the country's population. There is little discussion of the possibility of immigration and it is unlikely that this will be an important source of population increase in the near future. The expansion of the market for Chilean manufacturing will thus depend upon the normal surplus of births over deaths, the bringing of the million agricultural workers (who still purchase virtually nothing) into the market, the raising of the living standards of the urban masses, and the development of fields in which the country has a natural advantage.

Democratic Traditions

Chile has a long tradition of democratic government. Since World War I there has been only one four-year period of dictatorship. Since World War II, in spite of a difficult economic situation, the country's democratic regime survived.

During the first hundred years or more of Chile's independence, politics was largely in the hands of the landholding aristocracy and certain commercial groups in the cities. However, within that rather narrow framework it remained democratic. Until 1890, the constitution put emphasis on a strong President, but after a short civil war in 1891 a parliamentary form of regime was established which resulted in a change of cabinets as frequent as that of Third Republic France.

In 1920, in a bitter campaign, Arturo Alessandri was elected the first middle-class President of Chile. However, for four years he was hampered by an antagonistic congress.

In September 1924 the army provoked a crisis in a controversy over raising military pay which resulted in the ousting of Alessandri. However, the succeeding military *junta* lasted only three months, after which Alessandri was brought back. During his few remaining months in power he brought about a number of fundamental changes. A new constitution was written ending the parliamentary regime and separating church and state. Labor and social security laws which had been passed during the September 1924 crisis were put into operation.

A year after his first ouster, President Alessandri was again forced to resign to be succeeded by Colonel Carlos Ibañez. Ibañez's four-year regime (1927–1931) was Chile's one experience with dictatorship in the twentieth century. Ibañez was overthrown in 1931.

In November of that year Juan Esteban Montero was elected President. However, his regime lasted only until June 4, 1932, when it was overthrown by a civilian–military coup which proclaimed a short-lived "Socialist Republic."

Finally, in November 1932 further elections were held bringing back Arturo Alessandri who moved to the right during his second administration.

The 1938 presidential election brought victory for his opposition, the Popular Front, and its candidate, Pedro Aguirre Cerda. From then until 1952 the government was in the hands of leftists.

The Radical-led governments followed a consistent policy of encouraging the economic development and industrialization of Chile. It was the Aguirre Cerda regime which established the Corporación de Fomento de la Producción, the Development Corporation which became the principal organ through which this policy was carried out.

It was during the period of Radical government also that the labor movement experienced its greatest period of growth. At that time the present pattern of labor–management relations was established.

After fourteen years in power, the Radicals were ousted in the election of 1952, to be replaced by General Carlos Ibañez again. But by 1957 Ibañez had lost virtually all the popular following which he had had five years earlier and by the 1958 presidential elections no candidate thought it worth while to proclaim himself an "Ibañista."

This election brought to power Jorge Alessandri, son of the former President and a member of the new industrialist class.

Chilean democracy is as strong as that of any country in Latin America.

It combines a strong presidency and a congress with sufficient power to act as an effective check upon the President. The court system is as independent as any judiciary in Latin America.

One of the peculiar features of Chilean democracy is its multiplicity of parties. In 1956 there were over twenty political parties with representatives in congress. Many of these political parties have over the years sought to use the labor movement for their own advantage. Political party rivalries explain most of the splits which have occurred in the labor movement during the last twenty years. Virtually every trade union in the country is under the control of the one or another of the political parties.

One cannot possibly understand labor–management relations in Chile without taking into account the politicization of the trade-union movement, and for that matter, the general politicization of the Chilean people. The end of one election campaign signals the beginning of the next, and there is never a moment when politics is dormant.

The Dramatis Personae

The Chilean people are perhaps the best integrated in Latin America. Among the early colonists were many Basque families and sometime later came a small group of English-speaking settlers. Later still there was an influx of Germans, who settled principally in the southern part of the Central Valley. All during the nineteenth and twentieth centuries there has been a small stream of Italian immigrants. The most famous Chilean public figure of the twentieth century, Arturo Alessandri, was the grandson of the First Minister of the House of Savoy to Chile. In the northern part of the country there are a few Japanese families and in recent years natives of Eastern Europe have joined the Chilean community.

Although immigration into Chile has been diversified, it has not been rapid enough to result in permanent colonies of strangers. To a remarkable degree the Europeans who have come to Chile since the establishment of the republic have been absorbed into the mass of the Chilean nation, and a basic element in that amalgam was and has remained Indian.

The Araucanian Indian of Chile is famous as the only important group of aborigines who never surrendered to the white man. It was not until the late 1880's that the chiefs of the Araucanian nation made a treaty with the Chilean government by which they voluntarily became part of the Chilean people. The modern Chilean takes pride in this stern independence of his American forebears.

As a result of the slowness of immigration and of the fact that a large proportion of the Spanish immigrants of colonial times were people who worked hard to build a home in the wilderness, the distinction between the working Indian and the idle Spaniard never became quite so clear in Chile as in some neighboring countries. And the process of racial amalgamation proceeded to a degree unknown in most other Latin American nations.

One need only compare Chile to its northern neighbor, Peru, where there is a deep-seated mutual distrust among the Indians, mestizos, and whites, or to its eastern neighbor, Argentina, where second generation Italians and Spaniards are not yet really convinced that they are Argentines, to become aware of the significance of Chile's integration.

Nationalism. The Chilean takes his nationality for granted. In spite of the crazy geography which separates a Chilean in Arica by one thousand miles from one in Santiago, and nearly three thousand from one in Magallanes, but puts no Chilean more than one hundred miles from a foreign country, a Chilean in Arica is much the same person as a Chilean in Santiago or farther south.

National self-esteem and community of interest arise not only from racial and national integration but from a shared pride in the accomplishments of the country. Chileans stress the fact that although they have a land much of which is inhospitable and barren, they have created a nation respected throughout the continent, more advanced economically and politically than most of its neighbors.

This is not to say that there are no social problems. Although it is no longer a reason for shame to have Indian blood in one's veins, it is still true that this is more common among the members of the working class than the middle or upper classes. This does have a considerable cultural and social influence.

Even today, the condition of the average Chilean agricultural worker is pitiable and in many parts the relationship between lord and serf has by no means disappeared. This holdover from colonial days is still felt throughout Chilean life influencing not only the economy of the country but its social relations and politics.

The Worker. The most important characteristic about the Chilean industrial working class is that it is new. Most of its members are first generation factory workers.

This newness leads to a number of results. First of all, the worker is not accustomed to the discipline and sense of responsibility necessary for factory work. Many industrial workers were formerly old-style miners or agricultural laborers, accustomed to a more or less nomadic existence, changing from one mine or rural *fundo* to the other as the spirit moved them, or switching back and forth between agriculture and mining with the seasons. This has resulted in a high labor turnover, long a serious problem in Chilean industry. Although there are few if any statistics on the subject, many industrialists seem to feel that the tendency of the industrial worker to drift from one employer to another has lessened in recent years.

The Chilean industrial worker is essentially docile and easily pushed or led. Although the urban worker does not seem to have the exaggerated respect of the rural laborer for his "betters," his passivity shows in other ways.

Many of the Chilean industrial workers have not been away from the semislavery of the countryside long enough to have developed much ambition or much of an interest in cultural pursuits. There is a vivid contrast between the common North American desire of people of all classes for the betterment of their children and the apparent lack of such a desire on the part of many Chilean workers.

To a certain degree perhaps, this can be traced to the largely Indian origin of the Chilean working class. For long centuries it was the Indian's duty to be the servant and the white man's right to be served. There resulted a fatalism, perhaps reinforced by the Indian's natural inclinations, and a conviction of the impossibility of crossing the vast canyon dividing servant and master. Moreover, the everyday fight for existence is still too hard in most cases for a worker to have much time or ambition left for trying to advance his children. In cases where workers are badly paid, fathers often send their children to work at what the Victorians called a "tender age."

However, as the Chilean industrial worker stays in the city and his economic position changes, his ambitions for his children and for himself are kindled. With new interests and more self-discipline, it seems likely that the characteristic vice of the Chilean worker—drinking to excess—will be modified. This heavy drinking leads to absenteeism which the employers have to fight vigorously since it interferes seriously with the rhythm of industrial production. How serious this problem of excessive drinking can become is shown by the fact that one of the textile plants in the Santiago region had in 1946 an absence rate of about 10 per cent five days a week, but one of 50 per cent on Mondays.

As the Chilean urban working class becomes more mature, it is taking its place alongside the world's best, insofar as efficiency and productivity are concerned.

The general manager of one of the nitrate companies, an American, was of the opinion that the Chilean worker is the best piecework laborer in the world. But he pointed out that the Chileans have a pride which does not allow them to be servile and when they feel they are being insulted or imposed upon they will quit, or fight back.

A great distinction has been drawn traditionally, both in Chilean legislation and in the popular mind, between the manual worker (*obrero*) and the white collar worker (*empleado*). Although there is a certain amount of such distinction in any country, it has been greater in Chile than in the more advanced industrial nations. The growth of trade unionism and labor political parties has gradually reduced the social gulf between the man who works with his hands and the man who works with his brain.

Several observations should be made about the position of the white collar worker in Chile. First of all, a very large number of the members of the white collar class is in the employ of the government. There are not only those directly employed by the ministries, but also those on the many special semi-autonomous "funds" and "boards." There are likewise the *empleados* of the state railroads and other enterprises which the government controls.

The tendency of the white collar worker to live beyond his income is widespread. This is not uncommon among *obreros,* but that it constitutes a major vice with the Chilean *empleados* is shown by the fact that one of the most important elements in labor legislation concerning *empleados* is the establishment of ways and means for them to borrow money.

Origin and Form of Industrial Firms

Most Chilean industrial firms are legally corporations or *sociedades anónimas.* Most firms are controlled by one stockholder or a small inside group of stockholders. In other cases, members of the boards of directors represent some other big firm, such as an insurance company or bank.

Perhaps the origin of the metallurgical industry is reasonably typical of most Chilean manufacturing firms. Most of the metal firms were started by skilled workers who set up independent workshops which grew into small factories and in some cases these have grown into large plants. In many cases these workers were immigrants or sons of immigrants.

Most of the corporations in the metallurgical industry are actually either family firms or controlled by small groups. Two exceptions are the Fábrica de Enlozados SA (FENSA) and the Cia. de Acero del Pacífico, the country's iron and steel firm. In the cases of FENSA the largest stockholder has only 16 per cent of the stock and there are two or three thousand other stockholders.

Foreign Firms

There are also numerous Chilean subsidiaries of foreign firms. The most important are the copper- and nitrate-mining firms. The copper industry is largely in the hands of American companies—two of the three large-scale mines being owned by subsidiaries of Anaconda Copper Company and the third by a Kennicott Copper Company affiliate. Two of the three largest operations in the nitrate field are controlled by the Guggenheim interests. The third, the Cia. Salitrera Antofagasta y Tarapaca was formerly British-owned, but in the early 1950's was acquired by Chilean interests.

One of the most important foreign-owned firms outside the mining field is the American-owned Cia. Chilena de Electricidad which serves the power and light needs of Santiago and Valparaiso. RCA Victor makes radio sets and records in its plant outside Santiago. At one time both Ford Motor Company and General Motors had small assembly plants in Santiago. There are British-owned milling firms, Argentine-owned metallurgical plants, and a small French-controlled sugar company. The Grace Company of the United States owns what is probably the largest textile business in Chile.

In some cases foreign firms have joined with local interests to establish or expand manufacturing industries.

Thus, the General Tire Company cooperated with the government's Corporación de Fomento in setting up the Industria de Neumáticos, SA, in the rubber tire field. The Corning Glass interests joined with an existing private glass firm, Cristalerías de Chile, in a program of modernization of Cristalerías' plant in Santiago in return for which the American firm received part interest in the Chilean enterprise.

However, it is important to note that foreign-owned firms in manufacturing and public utilities are of secondary importance to Chilean-owned firms. The metallurgical industry, for instance, is almost completely Chilean, and except for the Grace interests, the textile industry is nationally owned. Except for the Santiago electric company, most public utilities are now

Chilean-owned and the government is extending its own electricity network to cover everything except the Santiago–Valparaiso region, and in time will probably absorb the American-owned firm there. The railroads were never foreign-owned—except for the international railways in the north which are English.

The Manager

Many of the managers, chiefs of personnel, welfare chiefs, etc. of Chilean industries are foreigners. This managerial group seems to have a vital interest in the construction, expansion, and management of Chilean industry as a life work and a creative endeavor apart from a natural interest in the profits of the enterprise.

The general attitude of managers toward the workers is to regard them as children who need to be guided, helped, and chastised, in varying degrees. The social gulf in Chile between worker and manager is a great deal wider than in the United States. The fact that a large number of managers are foreigners probably helps to form this attitude.

In general it can be said that the majority of employers in Chile have come to accept unionism and are really concerned with the welfare of their workers. This concern has led to a great deal of paternalism. On the other hand, there are some managers who have little or no interest in their employees. Certainly the worst offenders are the agricultural employers. These people, particularly in the northern two-thirds of the Central Valley, are the remnants of the fading *ancien regime*. They still hold their workers and tenants in virtual serfdom and have bitterly fought against encroaching agrarian trade unionism. Many of them still regard housing, decent food, and fair pay for their workers as "Communism."

In some cases the political attitude of the unions has lessened the interest of the employer in the welfare of the workers. This is particularly true where Communist influence is present.

His Training. Since most of the Chilean manufacturing firms "just growed" like Topsy as industrialization progressed, many of those who held managerial positions did not have any special training. In many cases they were former craftsmen whose firms had mushroomed, or members of the family of the founder. In other instances the managerial personnel was likely to be rather heavily loaded with people with engineering training but without any special background in managerial techniques.

By the early 1950's the feeling had become widespread that it was necessary to put more stress on efficient production and on modern management techniques. Many employers felt that one of the causes of the continuing inflation was the inefficiency of the nation's industries.

The creation of the Instituto Chileno de Administración Racional de Empresas (ICARE) was one of the most important evidences of the Chilean employer's growing interest in improving his techniques of business organization and management. This is more fully discussed in Chapter XX. However, there were many individual companies which have also shown this interest. An example of this was the reorganization of the Vestex clothing concern in Santiago in 1953 with the aid of the Servicio Técnico Industrial, set up with the help of Point Four. The reorganization of the plant not only resulted in technical changes but also brought about considerable alteration of the firm's labor relations procedures.

The first step in the labor field was to establish a job evaluation system. When this had been completed, the firm introduced a system of incentive wages wherever possible. At the same time profit-sharing with the workers was initiated. The result of this reorganization was a considerable gain in productivity.

The Vestex company is one of the few which has undertaken a scientific reorganization of its operations. However, the movement is gaining strength.

The Foreign Manager

The American mining companies are still the most important industrial enterprises in Chile. In the past some of these companies have had bad labor records. They used extreme methods, including violence to prevent unionization before 1939. However, after 1939 the government was much more sympathetic toward the native worker than his foreign "imperialist" employer. The companies found that the best way to deal with this was to improve relations with the workers. Moreover, there is no doubt that the change in United States labor relations since the 1930's has also changed the behavior of the American companies' Chilean affiliates.

These companies now generally go beyond what the law demands insofar as wages, housing conditions, education, and medical facilities are concerned. Generally speaking, the author has found American managers sympathetic toward the problems of Chile as a nation, and toward the Chileans with whom they are in daily contact. In days gone by there was apparently an almost insurmountable wall between the Americans and the Chileans in the mining camps, but this has been crumbling during recent years. First of all, the local managers of the mining companies have become acutely aware of the increasing nationalism in Chile. They realize that the Americans who are running the country's largest economic enterprises are going to be viewed with suspicion because of the wealth and power of the organizations which they represent and that it therefore behooves them to do away with as many causes of irritation as possible.

Social Problems. The matter of wage and salary differentials between foreign and native workers will be dealt with later, but there is a social problem which warrants discussion now. Until a few years ago, there were separate clubs in all the mining villages for Americans. There were special schools for the children of American personnel. There were special parts of the community set aside for Americans and other foreigners, and personal contact among the foreigners and even the highest ranking Chileans was kept at a minimum.

With the rise in Chilean nationalism this segregated and privileged position of North American and European officials in the mines came to be resented. In recent years there has been a considerable modification of all this. The first people to break through the barriers were the doctors who must by law be Chileans. Subsequently, other Chilean members of management were also allowed privileges formerly reserved for North Americans and other foreigners.

The same thing has occurred with "American" schools. These institutions have not ceased to exist, but they have been opened to children of all the higher ranking Chilean employees. There is still a distinction, but it is now based upon class rather than race or nationality.

Housing distinctions on a nationality basis have also disappeared. In the principal mining camps the North American management personnel and the higher ranking Chilean employees live together without discrimination in the "upper-class" section of the camp.

As far as everyday social contact is concerned, barriers are beginning to break down. On that level, the difference in language is a great handicap since many of the Americans going to Chile do not know Spanish when they arrive. Another drawback to more intimate social contact for many years was the educational gap between the Americans and the higher ranking Chileans. With the Chileanization of the medical staff, and the increasing number of Chileans in important administrative posts, the educational differences no longer exist.

Basically, the North Americans' way of treating the workers is probably not much different from the paternalistic attitude of the better Chilean employers. However, the position of United States managers is modified by their knowledge of United States standards of living—and United States standards of work.

American companies have come to realize that in order to operate they will have to keep one step ahead of the demands of the unions and the government. Also, being interested in getting the most out of their mines at the cheapest price, the managers have come to realize that the Chilean worker is not a very efficient producer if he is underfed, badly housed, insufficiently clothed, uneducated, with no recreation but sex and wine.

Finally, many of the American managers have lived in Chile the best part of their adult lives and have come to associate themselves with Chile and the Chileans.

All these factors have contributed to the breakdown of social barriers between Chileans and North Americans in the mining camps, and to bring them to the realization that the better the Chilean worker is treated, the better off the mining companies—and their United States managers— are likely to be.

The attitude of the average employer in Chile today is a good deal different from what it was twenty-five or thirty years ago. The growth of social legislation and the necessities of a rapidly industrializing economy have made the employer much more conscious of his duties to the worker as well as to his stockholders. And, in case he should forget the interests of his employees, the unions are there—under generally capable leadership protected by the government—to remind him.

CHAPTER XVIII

Organized Labor

The Chilean labor movement[1] was one of the first organized in Latin America. Chile had been greatly influenced by the European Revolutions of 1848 and by the famous Chilean, Francisco Bilbao who participated in them. He came back to his native country and organized a Utopian Socialist group, the Society of Equals. It took part in an unsuccessful uprising against President Manual Montt in 1851 and as a result Bilbao and some of the other figures in the movement were exiled.

However, the influence of the Society of Equals continued. The young men who had gathered around Bilbao were largely responsible for the growth of the workers' mutual benefit society movement in Chile during the third quarter of the nineteenth century. They also took a leading part in organizing the Radical Party and the Partido Democrático, the nation's first Socialist Party.

The first serious strikes in Chilean history occurred on the trolley cars of Santiago in the late 1880's, and the new Partido Democrático took an active part in these walkouts. During the next decade there grew up a number of workers' "resistance societies," many of which were under Anarcho-Syndicalist influence. These were the first important trade unions in Chile. In the nitrate fields they took the name of *mancomunidades obreras* (workers' brotherhoods).

The first decade of the 1900's was a stormy one for the labor movement. It began with a well-organized and successful walkout of the traction employees of Santiago in 1900, and in the succeeding years there were numerous violent incidents still vividly remembered in Chile. A strike of the workers of the Cia. Sudamericana de Vapores resulted in a serious clash between the nascent labor movement and its employer and government opponents in Valparaiso in 1903. In 1907 a massacre occurred in the port of Iquique when troops killed hundreds of striking nitrate miners.

The nitrate workers' organizations were the most militant part of the labor movement and were strongly influenced by the Anarcho-Syndicalists. Some of them, however, followed the Socialist leader, Luis E. Recabarren. He was a typographer and newspaper editor who moved to northern Chile from Santiago in the early 1900's. He had been leader of the left wing of the Partido Democrático in Santiago and Valparaiso, and in 1907 was the party's candidate for deputy in the nitrate province of Antofagasta. In 1912 he led a split in the Partido Democrático and formed the Partido Socialista Obrero.

The Federación Obrera de Chile

Meanwhile in 1909 the Gran Federación Obrera de Chile had been formed in Santiago among the railroad workers. It was at first a mutual benefit society with very limited objectives, but soon began to expand and to recruit others. Many of the newer recruits were more militant and radical than the original organizers of the Gran Federación and these left-wing elements urged Luis Recabarren to bring the nitrate workers' organizations of the northern part of the country into the Gran Federación. In 1916 these groups did enter the organization with the result that in 1917 the Gran Federación was captured by the left wing, and changed its name to Federación Obrera de Chile (FOCh). Two years later a convention of the FOCh decided to join the newly established Third International and was reorganized on a much more centralized basis.

During World War I the IWW was established, patterned after the organization of the same name in the United States and like it, controlled by Anarcho-Syndicalists. It had most of its influence along the coast where it was successful in organizing the majority of the sailors, longshoremen, and other maritime workers. Other Anarcho-Syndicalists succeeded in organizing unions of printing trades workers, leather workers, and construction workers in Santiago and elsewhere. They did not join the IWW but formed a rival organization, the Federación Obrera Regional de Chile (Regional Labor Federation of Chile, FORCh), copying their name from the FORA of Argentina.

Most of the country's labor organizations supported the presidential candidacy of Arturo Alessandri in 1920. Alessandri was a brilliant lawyer and senator from the northern province of Tarapacá. His enemies labeled him a demagogue, his friends worshipped him. During the campaign of 1920 he promised aid to the workers in their organizing activities and won widespread support among them.

With the election of Alessandri by a very narrow majority, a new era began in Chile. Alessandri was the first middle-class President. His election marked the end of the uncontested rule of the country by the old landholding aristocracy which had dominated the nation since independence and although Alessandri's rule was a stormy one, brought to a violent end by revolution in September 1924, Don Arturo made an undoubted impression on the people of Chile.

Although Alessandri found it very difficult to fulfill his promises to the labor movement, because of opposition in congress, important labor legislation was passed just a few days before he was overthrown by the army in September 1924. During this crisis, a number of fundamental laws, including authorizing government recognition and support of trade unions, were rushed through congress.

Meanwhile, the FOCh had grown during World War I. After the entry of the radically led nitrate workers' unions in 1917, it was firmly under the control of left-wing elements of the Partido Socialista Obrero led by Luis Emilio Recabarren. In 1922 the FOCh became a full-fledged member of the Red International of Labor Unions. At the same time, the Partido Socialista Obrero of Luis Recabarren was converted into the Partido Comunista de Chile and joined the Communist International. It continued to have its chief strength in the nitrate regions of the north, although it was beginning to pick up strength also in the coal mining regions near Concepción.

After the overthrow of Alessandri in September 1924 the labor organizations adopted a wait-and-see policy and the most noteworthy labor event of this period was the suicide of Recabarren in December 1924. At the time of the restoration of Arturo Alessandri to the presidency, January to September 1925, the unions and the Communist Party were very active. Representatives of both groups were included in the commission which drafted the new constitution; the unions carried on a very active organizing campaign, particularly in the northern part of the country; and the FOCh as well as the IWW and FORCh began a struggle against government-recognized unions which was to convulse the labor movement during the next decade.

President Alessandri sought to put into practice a law, passed in September 1924 just before his overthrow, which provided for legal recognition of trade unions. All three existing labor groups opposed the establishment of these organizations and sought to prevent their affiliates from seeking recognition. With reason, they feared the government control which would accompany government recognition.

During the next five years while General Carlos Ibañez dominated the republic, the "free" trade unions which refused government recognition suffered a great deal at the hands of the President–dictator. At the same time there was a great increase in the number of "legal" unions. On the political side, there was a serious split in the ranks of the Communist Party which controlled the majority of the free unions. One faction centered around Senator Manuel Hidalgo who had succeeded Recabarren as the party's chief, and the other followed the leadership of Elías Laferte, the secretary general of the FOCh. Laferte had the support of the Communist International and by the time of the fall of the Ibañez regime in September 1931, his group was lined up with the Stalinists, and the Hidalgo group with the Trotskyistes.

By the time Ibañez fell, the power of the "legal" trade unions had become at least as great as that of the "free" organizations. A National Confederation of Legal Industrial Unions was formed in the last days of the Ibañez government. Soon afterward a National Confederation of Legal Professional Unions was established. Within a couple of years after the overthrow of the dictator these two groups were brought together to form the National Confederation of Legal Unions (Confederación Nacional de Sindicatos Legales).

Meanwhile, the Federación Obrera de Chile was reconstituted after the fall of Ibañez, with Laferte as secretary general. The FOCh had been dormant during the last years of the dictatorship when Laferte and most of its other leaders were in exile. The Anarcho-Syndicalist organizations had also been inactive during the last years of Ibañez, but they revived after his fall, and soon thereafter the IWW and the FORCh merged to establish a new Anarcho-Syndicalist labor group, the General Confederation of Workers (Confederación General de Trabajadores, CGT).

The new CGT had within its ranks many construction workers, shoe workers, maritime workers, and printing trades employees. However, in the succeeding years it was not able to keep abreast of its rivals.

The period just after the fall of Ibañez was a stormy one with revolution succeeding revolution. The most important of these upheavals was on June 4, 1932. A short-lived "Socialist Republic" under the leadership of Airforce Colonel Marmaduque Grove was established with the support of all the non-Communist trade-union elements as well as the Hidalgo Communists. The Grove regime lasted only two weeks, but after its overthrow Colonel Grove became a national hero. There gathered around him a powerful group of labor and Socialist elements which finally fused early in 1933 into the Partido Socialista de Chile.

During the second administration of Arturo Alessandri, from 1932 to 1938, there was general reconstruction of the labor movement. Alessandri had by this time become more conservative and in fact governed during these six years as the spokesman for the "right" in Chilean politics. His struggles with the labor movement, and particularly with the new Socialist Party, were bitter. There were several important strikes during his administration, the most noteworthy being the railroad workers' walkout (1935–1936) which the government tried unsuccessfully to break and which gave impetus to uniting all the country's left-wing parties in the Popular Front.

The railroad workers' walkout was also of considerable importance in hastening the unification of the labor movement. Four political groups fought for control in the unions at this time. The Laferte Communists had revived and were in complete control of the Federación Obrera de Chile, which had its chief strength in the nitrate- and copper-mining area in the northern part of the country and the coal mines near Concepción. The Hidalgo Communists worked within the framework of the legal unions and also had some influence in the unions affiliated to the CGT. The Socialist Party controlled the Confederación Nacional de Sindicatos Legales and was more powerful in the Santiago and Concepción regions than anywhere else.

The Confederación de Trabajadores de Chile

In December 1936 the Confederación de Trabajadores de Chile (CTCh) was founded by a congress composed of delegates from the FOCh, the Confederación de Sindicatos Legales, the CGT, and a number of autonomous unions. The new confederation was headed by a Socialist, with a Communist as assistant general secretary. This reflected the approximate political balance in the organization at that time. The Anarcho-Syndicalists after some hesitation decided not to join the CTCh, but rather to keep alive the CGT.

With the election of Pedro Aguirre Cerda to the presidency as the candidate of the Popular Front late in 1938, a new period began in the history of the labor movement. The Popular Front was composed of the Radical, Socialist, Communist parties, one faction of the Democratico Party, and the CTCh. The government during the administration of Aguirre Cerda was composed of Radicals, Socialists, and Democráticos, and the regime's policies were overwhelmingly prolabor—except with regard to the organization of agricultural workers.

It was only after the election of Aguirre Cerda that the labor movement really came into its own. Previously it had represented only a small percentage of the industrial, transportation, and mining workers of Chile but during the next decade the trade unions took within their ranks virtually all organizable workers. At the time of the CTCh's organization in 1936 it included only 200 unions with perhaps 60,000 workers. Twelve years later there were 1849 legally recognized unions, with 263,676 members.

In addition, there were various labor organizations not recognized under the Labor Code. These included the railroad workers' unions with some 30,000 members, several thousand construction workers, perhaps 5000 municipal workers, and 30,000 employees of the national government. There were other scattered groups of "free" labor organizations among teachers, printing trades workers, shoemakers, maritime workers, and sheepherders, with perhaps 15,000 members. Thus, a decade after Aguirre took office there were 85,000 to 100,000 workers organized in "free" unions and a total of approximately 325,000 organized workers.

Most of the organized workers were in the ranks of the Confederación de Trabajadores de Chile. The CTCh was largely a propaganda and political organization to speak for the labor movement before the parties and the government. It had representatives in various official government bodies dealing with economic and labor matters.

The basic affiliate of the CTCh remained the local union of a particular factory or craft. With a few exceptions—in the mining industry, on the railroads, in the maritime trades, and the metallurgical industry, for instance —there did not exist any very strong national union federations. The CTCh, however, established federations of its affiliates in most of the provinces, which brought together all the unions belonging to the Confederación in their particular localities.

The CTCh as such had relatively little control over either the individual local unions or its own regional affiliates. Such control as it had came largely from the fact that the local unions were dominated by the same political parties which dominated the CTCh, the actual reins thus remaining in the hands of the political parties rather than in those of the Confederación de Trabajadores de Chile.

After 1938 the balance of power within the unions shifted, with the Socialists losing ground and the Communists gaining. This came about for various reasons. First of all, the Communists had the same policy in the Chilean Popular Front as did their comrades in Europe. They were part of the Front so they could take credit for its successes, but they were not part of the government, so they could deny any connection with its failures. Since the Popular Front regime had raised hopes of the workers which it could not possibly fulfill, there was bound to be some disillusionment in the regime—upon which the Communists were able to capitalize.

At the same time, the Socialist Party, which bore a large measure of responsibility for the administration of President Aguirre Cerda, entered the government too early. It was a coalition of heterogeneous groups and the five years between its organization in 1933 and its assumption of government responsibility in 1938 were not sufficient for it to settle internal difficulties and establish a disciplined organization.

The result was that during the 1940's the Socialist Party suffered a series of shattering splits which not only destroyed the party as a major force in the political field, but very seriously weakened it in the trade unions. It is undoubtedly true that Communist elements working inside the Socialist Party were partly responsible for these splits, but there were other reasons for the rift.

Personal differences among the leaders probably made up the number one cause for the disintegration of the Socialist Party. Furthermore, the fact that it was a democratic party tended to weaken the Socialist Party in the face of the Communists, particularly in the labor movement.

This fight between Socialists and Communists was the most significant occurrence in the CTCh from 1936 to 1946. Communist influence within the unions continued to grow and was intensified during the latter part of the war while other political groups within the unions—Radicals, Democráticos, Falangistas—swung over from alliance with the Socialists to support of the Communists. The result was that the position of the Socialists as the majority group in the upper ranks of the CTCh became untenable.

Matters came to a crisis within the CTCh early in 1946 as the result of a series of outlaw strikes which had been occurring throughout Chile since the end of the war. These strikes finally led the government to cancel the legal recognition of the striking Mapocho and Humberstone nitrate workers' unions. This brought two general strikes and an incident in Santiago during which the police fired on demonstrators. In the face of this crisis, Acting President Alfredo Duhalde offered cabinet posts to the Socialists and as a result, Socialist CTCh Secretary General Bernardo Ibañez attempted to call off the second general strike, which resulted in a split in the labor confederation.

During the next few months there was a struggle for control of the unions. The balance of power between the two groups was fairly even, with the Communists generally in control of the mining areas and the Socialists having more influence in the industrial regions. However, the election on September 4, 1946, of Gabriel González Videla to succeed President Juan Antonio Ríos who had died in July, pushed the balance in favor of the Communists.

The two principal groups supporting González Videla for the presidency were his own Radical Party and the Communists. As a result of his triumph, three Communist ministers entered the government for the first time with the inauguration of González in November 1946.

During the next six months the Communists gained control of the great majority of the unions. By May 1947 their faction of the CTCh included two-thirds of the organized workers. The author estimated at that time that the Communist Party itself controlled something more than 50 per cent of the organized workers. The Bernardo Ibañez CTCh was reduced to a mere shadow, and in January 1947 almost passed out of existence.

However, growing opposition to the Communists in the early months of 1947 began to revive the Socialist faction of the labor movement, and with the exit of the Communists from the government in April 1947, the balance definitely began to tip in favor of the Socialist faction.

In August 1947 as a result of a series of Communist-inspired strikes, particularly in the mining areas, designed to demonstrate to President González Videla that if he wouldn't govern with the Communists it would be difficult to govern without them, the chief executive broke with his erstwhile Communist friends. In the months that followed, President González Videla helped break the power of the Communists by deporting many of their leaders to the northern town of Pisagua under special powers given by congress. He finally got congress to declare the Communist Party illegal in the middle of 1948.

As a result of this anti-Communist turn of President González Videla, the Communists lost ground in the unions. The railroad workers' federation withdrew from the Communist CTCh and remained independent. In the mining regions the nitrate workers' unions withdrew from the CTCh while the copper miners' unions generally were captured by the Socialists. The coal mining unions, however, remained under Communist control.

The division of the CTCh continued until 1953 with the largest part of the country's trade unions being outside any central labor organization. In some industries, notably textiles, the number of "company unions"—organizations controlled by the employers—increased considerably. Several of the principal national industrial federations, including the Copper Workers'

Confederation, the maritime workers, and railroaders remained independent during this period.

Central Unica de Trabajadores de Chile

Several of the national industrial unions either joined or indicated their intention of joining the International Confederation of Free Trade Unions and its regional organization, the ORIT, or joined one of the international trade secretariats associated with the ICFTU. Through the good auspices of the international free labor movement, an attempt was launched during 1952 to bring together all these national federations into a new central labor organization. As soon as the Communists heard of this they began to urge the need for "unity" in the labor movement and announced their willingness to merge their CTCh in a new central labor organization. Of course, this was small sacrifice since their CTCh had very few unions associated with it by that time.

For a variety of reasons, the non-Communist national labor federations listened to the overture of the Communists and finally agreed to allow the Communists to bring organizations controlled by them into the new group. The first reason for this attitude on the part of the non-Communist union-ists was the fact that all non-Communist political groups of the left, and the labor organizations controlled by them, had developed over the years a marked inferiority complex vis-à-vis the Communists. The latter had succeeded in convincing them that nothing was really "left" in Chile with which the Communists were not associated, and the shibboleth of the "left" has become as well ingrained in the Chilean political scene as in that of France.

Second, the non-Communist unionists were undoubtedly impressed with the "unity" argument. They were aware of the fact that the Chilean labor movement had been weakened during the recent past by the quarrels among the unions and they hoped that a unified labor movement would result in a resurgence of strength for organized labor as a whole.

Third, was the fact that the Partido Socialista de Chile which dominated the non-Communist CTCh, and was very important in outside unions, had made a sudden political about-face during the presidential election campaign of 1952. From being the most strongly anti-Communist party in the nation, it had suddenly become their closest political associate.

Finally, and perhaps most important, there was widespread fear among unionists of all political affiliations of what the new government of General

Carlos Ibañez, elected in September 1952, might do to the labor movement. He had been a dictator when last in the presidency and there was some indication that there was behind him a military *junta* which was toying with the idea of establishing a "pet" labor movement *à la* Perón. Many unionists who had little sympathy for the Communists felt that the only way for the trade unions to defend themselves against such a maneuver was to put up a united front.

As a result, in January 1953 a national labor congress was held in Santiago out of which was born a new central labor group, the Central Unica de Trabajadores de Chile (CUTCh). This congress, like almost all Chilean labor gatherings, was dominated by political maneuvering of different partisan groups. Slates for election to the executive council of the new group were formed on the basis of party alliances within the congress. The result was that of the twenty-four members of the new executive council, the Communist Party had five avowed representatives. In addition, there were several others who ostensibly belonged to other political groupings but were in fact under the direction of the Communists.

On the question of international affiliation, the Communists were not powerful enough to get the CUTCh to join the World Federation of Trade Unions and its American regional grouping, the CTAL, but they were powerful enough to prevent its joining the ICFTU and the ORIT as had originally been planned. However, during the years that followed, the fact that the CUTCh was not a member of the WFTU and the CTAL did not prevent leading officials of the Chilean group from attending congresses of these international organizations and speaking "in the name of the CUTCh."

The CUTCh was even less centralized than the old CTCh had been. The different unions went more or less their own way regardless of the CUTCh. However, on several occasions the central labor body did initiate general strikes to protest actions of the Ibañez government, and it was a useful sounding board for the various political elements active within its ranks—particularly the Communists.

The most catastrophic general walkout called by the CUTCh occurred in January 1956, as a move to protest the Ibañez government's anti-inflation program which was pending before congress. This program called for wage and credit controls and was strongly opposed by nearly all labor groups. However, when the CUTCh called for a general walkout of indefinite duration to protest the proposed law, the workers apparently felt that their organizations had been used too much for political purposes and the general strike call met with little response from the rank and file of the trade-union movement.

Meanwhile, the Ibañez government had not been friendly toward the existing labor movement and the political groups which dominated it. Although Ibañez in his election campaign had promised to bring about the repeal of the Law for the Defense of Democracy, which not only outlawed the Communist Party, but gave the government considerably increased powers to intervene in the internal affairs of the unions, it became evident soon after his inauguration that he had no real intention of doing so. (This law was finally repealed in spite of General Ibañez's protests shortly before the presidential election of 1958.)

Furthermore, there is no doubt that there were elements in the Ibañez coterie who were disposed toward the idea of a "Peronista" labor movement which would be completely under the control of the Ibañez government. Subsequently, Ibañez, who in all probability had had the support of the Communists in the 1952 election (in spite of their apparent support of Socialist Senator Salvador Allende), became increasingly anti-Communist and hostile to the existing labor movement.

In 1955 the Ibañez government issued a decree empowering the General Directorate of Labor to pass on the qualifications of all candidates for union posts in terms of the Law for the Defense of Democracy (which banned Communists from holding union offices). The administration used this decree (until it was repealed in July 1958) to disqualify not only members of the Communist Party but also members of other parties who had been unfriendly to the Ibañez regime or who had been particularly militant in defense of the workers.

The Anarchist-influenced unions withdrew from the CUTCh early in 1957 and a few months later joined with others to establish the Committee for Trade Union Recuperation, the aim of which was to found a rival to the CUTCh. However, when a congress for this purpose met in October 1958 only a small number of labor groups actually participated. The Confederación Nacional de Trabajadores, which resulted from this congress, affiliated with the ICFTU and the ORIT, but it represented only a small minority of the country's organized workers.

Meanwhile, Catholic elements who were attempting to establish another rival to the CUTCh in the form of the Acción Sindical Chilena were having no more success than the organizers of the CNT. The great majority of the unions controlled by the Christian Democratic Party remained in the

CUTCh. It was not until the early months of 1961 that the Christian Democratic elements finally left the CUTCh.

By the end of 1961 the Chilean labor movement continued to be badly divided politically, although most unions remained nominally affiliated with the CUTCh. The top union leaders had lost their former ability to mobilize the nation's workers in general strikes on economic, social, and political issues. Also, government limitations on wage increases, which had been in existence since early 1956, had considerably reduced the range of action of the lower-echelon union groups.

Although there was widespread disenchantment among the rank and file with the partisan political leadership of the unions, the parties continued to play a major role. A rejuvenation of the labor movement seemed to await the reestablishment of economic conditions which would permit greater leeway for collective bargaining activities, or a significant shift in the country's political atmosphere.

CHAPTER XIX

Government Role in Directing Labor Protest

The Chilean government, like those of Brazil and Argentina, has sought to control and divert the workers' protest and to play an important role in molding and applying the rules of industrial relations. For more than a generation the governments of the republic have been under political pressure from the organized labor movement and at various periods during this span the administration has been in the hands of parties directly dependent on the electoral support of workers of the cities.

There has evolved a complicated body of labor legislation, part of which is designed to control labor organizations and supervise the process of collective bargaining which we shall discuss in a later chapter. Much of Chilean labor legislation is designed to extend protection to the worker, to help him meet serious economic crises with health insurance and social security, and to provide him with better housing.

The structure of labor–management relations in Chile in some ways presents a paradox. Since Chile has been a democratic nation for the last thirty years, during which the present pattern of industrial relations has been molded, the workers' organizations, the employers' groups, and collective bargaining itself have generally been freer than in Vargas' Brazil or the Argentina of Perón. Yet, at the same time, the law very carefully and minutely prescribes not only the forms of organizations for workers and employers, but the conduct of labor–management negotiations.

There is a considerable difference between the letter of the law and the facts of Chilean labor–management relations. This can be shown in a variety of ways. Although only "legal" trade unions are supposed to represent the workers in negotiations with their employers, this has not prevented a considerable number of unions from functioning very effectively without legal recognition. Although strikes are supposedly illegal until a certain process has been gone through and are supposedly completely illegal for significant groups of workers, this has not prevented many illegal walkouts from being effective and successful. Nor did it prevent both the government and the employers from dealing with unions out in "illegal" strikes.

The fact is that the legal provisions governing labor–management relations give the government very extensive power to control both parties in a labor dispute and to direct the solution of the labor dispute itself, but these powers are only used occasionally. Whether they will be so used depends on the political situation of the moment. Arturo Alessandri, when he was President from 1932 to 1938, occasionally used the powers the law gave him. Since the governments in power from 1938 to 1952 were leftists and owed their election largely to the votes of the urban workers, they were hesitant to use the full force of their authority. Usually when the legal powers of the government were used, it was for the purpose of combatting Communist influence in the labor movement, as in Vice-President Alfredo Duhalde's action when he was Acting President in 1946 and in President Gabriel González Videla's vendetta with the Communists after he broke with them in the middle of 1947.

Regardless of whether or not the legal powers of the government are used, it is important to know what they are in general terms. In our discussion of the *sindicatos* we shall discuss the controls available to the government in that field, and the influence of the law on the structure of the labor movement; in discussing the process of collective bargaining we shall indicate the legal procedures called for there. In the present chapter we wish only to indicate the broad scope of the country's labor legislation and the government organization which exists for handling relations between workers and employers.

The Labor Code

All phases of labor relations in Chile are covered by the Labor Code. Chile, in fact, took the lead among the nations of Latin America in the development of this new phase of law. Almost forty years ago it was one of the first countries to adopt thoroughgoing legislation in the field. In the years that have followed, almost all the nations of Latin America have adopted comprehensive labor laws and many have followed in Chile's footsteps by bringing together and classifying these statutes into labor codes.

The Labor Code starts out with provisions concerning the labor contract, dealing with both individual and collective agreements and paying special attention to white collar workers and seamen. Book Two consists of measures concerning "The Protection of the Workers While Working," and includes workmen's compensation, protection of working mothers, and legislation for holidays. This section also has some special legislation for commercial employees and for workers in bakeries.

Book Three of the Labor Code deals with "The Social Organizations," by which is meant trade unions and employers' *sindicatos*. Separate treatment is given "industrial" and "professional" unions and a special section is devoted to the penalties to be inflicted in case of violation of rules concerning the organization and functioning of the unions. The next book discusses "The Tribunals and the General Directorate of Labor," and here is outlined the government's conciliation and arbitration machinery as well as the rules which are legally supposed to be followed in handling labor disputes; and the framework of the General Directorate of Labor is sketched. A fifth book of the Labor Code as published consists of "Laws, Decree-Laws, Decrees with the Force of Law, Administrative Decrees and Decrees which Complement or Modify the Labor Code." [1]

Several aspects of the Labor Code are worthy of special mention. The first of these is its age. Francisco Walker Linares notes that "The Chilean environment was not prepared for the innovations which the new laws suddenly appearing in 1924 represented; the economic and industrial development of the country was slight, the standard of living of the people was exceedingly low, the culture of the working classes was pitiable." [2]

In part, this early development of Chilean social legislation was due to the temper of the times. World War I had had important effects on Chile, stirring up latent feelings of unrest and discontent and culminating in the election of Arturo Alessandri as President in 1920. He was undoubtedly the most important Chilean politician of the first half of the twentieth century, and was also by far the most controversial figure in the political life of the period. [3]

The Chilean Labor Code owes its origins to Don Arturo Alessandri, though there had been others before him who had outlined a broad program of labor legislation. Thus, in 1906 Malaquías Concha introduced into the Chamber of Deputies in the name of the Democratic Party a series of projects for a social security system, workmen's compensation, and the legal recognition of trade unions. [4]

However, it was Don Arturo Alessandri who was the first chief executive to take an interest in these problems and who was largely responsible for the adoption of measures to cope with them. As a candidate for the presidency, he made a speech in which he called for compulsory arbitration in labor disputes and then went on to say, concerning the workers:

We must build for them hygenic, commodious and cheap housing which will protect their health and be sufficiently attractive to keep them away from the saloon and generate among them the sentiments of home and family. It is necessary to see to it that the worker is paid so as to give him and his family not only the physical necessities of life but enough for his moral improvement and for honest recreation. It is necessary to protect him from accidents, sickness and old age. Society cannot afford to abandon to misery and misfortune those who have given their whole lives for its service and progress.[5]

According to Alessandri's own testimony, he was inspired by two motives in drawing up and sending to congress a plan for a labor code. First was the desire to do something to help the workers who at that time were exceedingly badly treated by their employers. Their condition, said Alessandri, was little better than that of beasts—in fact some rural employers treated their blooded stock much better than they treated their workers.

The second factor which interested Alessandri in a labor code was the work of the International Labor Organization (ILO), established by the Treaty of Versailles. During its first three meetings the ILO drew up the outlines of a national labor code and recommended its adoption by member nations. Alessandri felt that it was necessary that Chile pass some legislation to carry out the decisions of these three conferences if the nation were to live up to its obligations as a member of the ILO.

President Alessandri commissioned Professor Moíses Poblete Troncoso to draw up a draft for a labor code to be submitted to congress with instructions that it be based on the main accords of the first three conferences of the International Labor Organization. Poblete Troncoso, who taught law at the University of Chile, completed the proposed legislation in a few months. As presented to President Alessandri, it consisted of 620 articles divided into four books: labor contracts, labor regulations, professional organizations and labor conflicts, and social security. The chief executive sent the proposed code to congress for approval in 1922. However, Alessandri was having difficulties with congress at that time and it was only at the beginning of the Revolution of 1924 that the chief provisions of the code were rushed through parliament as individual statutes, not as a codified body of law.

These first statutes were Law 4053 which regulated the labor contract; Law 4054 which set up a system of obligatory social security for manual workers covering sickness, invalidism, and old age; Law 4055 establishing workmen's compensation on the basis of the doctrine of employer responsibility. Law 4056 established tribunals of conciliation and arbitration; Law 4057 legally recognized trade unions and established procedures for their recognition and surveillance by the government. The last two laws were 4058 and 4059 providing for recognition of cooperatives and for special treatment for white collar workers.[6]

This body of labor legislation came fully into effect during the years following the Revolution of 1924 and particularly during the dictatorial administration of President Carlos Ibañez, 1927 through 1931. Just a few months before his overthrow, General Ibañez promulgated the Labor Code as a unified body of legislation. This remains the basic element of Chilean labor law, although it has been modified frequently since that date.

The second aspect of the Chilean Labor Code worthy of comment is the distinction drawn between the *empleado* and the *obrero* (that is between the white collar worker and the manual worker). This distinction not only is made with regard to the form of trade unions which the two groups may constitute, and the fact that the two kinds of workers may not belong to the same union, but is also maintained in social security and labor protective legislation.

Whatever the original reason for the legal distinction between *obreros* and *empleados* may have been, it has aroused a great deal of controversy and the tendency in recent years has been to reduce the difference. The family allowance system and other advantages which were originally extended only to white collar workers have since World War II been made applicable to manual workers as well. There has been considerable agitation for the removal of the distinctions still existing between the rights of the *obrero* and those of the *empleado*. It is worth while noting that this kind of preference has not usually been granted to white collar workers by labor legislation of other Latin American countries which otherwise have frequently patterned their laws in the labor field quite closely on those of Chile.

Dirección General del Trabajo

Chilean labor legislation provides for a wide field of intervention in labor relations by governmental bodies. Government labor officials not only engage in the conciliation and mediation activities common in most industrial countries, but also exert more or less close supervision over the finances, elections, and other activities of trade unions established under the Labor

Code. Finally, the government is responsible for the enforcement of factory laws and other labor protective legislation.

The top figure in the Chilean government labor services, under the Minister of Labor, is the Director General of Labor who presides over the General Directorate of Labor (Dirección General del Trabajo). The director general is a career man, while the minister is a politician, a member of the President's cabinet and by the very nature of the office a transitory figure. The director general is appointed to his post by the President with the advice and consent of the senate and cannot be removed except with the approval of that body.

Undoubtedly, the actions of the Dirección General del Trabajo are greatly influenced by the political orientation of the President and administration in office at any given time. However, it should be noted that in spite of the importance which politics undoubtedly has in the Dirección General, people of various political groups hold positions of importance in the Dirección General. For instance, in 1947 the director general was a Socialist, the Provincial Labor Inspectior of Santiago, at times acting director general, was a Radical, while the head of the international section of the Dirección General was a Conservative. These people were career men who had spent most of their adult lives in the government labor services.

The Dirección General del Trabajo is divided into five departments: administration, conflicts, inspection, legal, and social organizations. The Administrative Department is presided over by a secretary general who supervises the publications, library and archive services of the Dirección General as well as all personnel problems within the agency. The statistical services of the Dirección General are also under the Administrative Department.[7]

The statistical section of the Dirección General was not set up until 1932. During the early 1940's its chief, Luis Cárcamo, was sent to the United States to work with the United States Bureau of Labor Statistics. The section maintains records on strikes and has one of three cost-of-living indices kept by the Chilean government, the other two being compiled by the Dirección General de Estadística and the Central Mixed Salary Commission. One or more of these indices is usually used as a yardstick in collective bargaining contracts to determine wage adjustment. There are some differences among these three cost-of-living indices since they are calculated on somewhat different bases.

One of the chief handicaps of all Chilean government statistical services is lack of funds. Although in 1955 the Dirección General de Estadistia received private funds to make a thorough revision of their cost-of-living index for Santiago, they had been unable by the end of 1956 to obtain any further funds for bringing the statistical services up to date. Throughout the rest of the country, there had been little alteration for several decades of the products in the family budget used in drawing up the cost-of-living material.

The Department of Inspection of the Dirección General del Trabajo is composed of sections dealing with maritime labor; with the labor of women and children; with hygiene and industrial security; and with general labor inspection. The Department of Inspection has jurisdiction over the provincial labor inspectors.

One of the more interesting parts of the Department of Inspection is the women and children section. It was organized in 1932 by Señora M. T. de Armstrong and by 1947 had about twenty-five women labor inspectors under its supervision. This section keeps track of working women and children and tries to enforce the law with respect to their employment. It keeps statistics on women and children in industry and in spite of a limited staff does a fairly good job. One of its activities is to urge women to take a more active part in union activities for it has found that men generally oppose the idea of women being officers in unions and that women are not very aggressive on their own behalf.

The Legal Department of the Dirección General del Trabajo is composed of a legal advisory section, international labor section, law and regulation revision section, and the judicial archives.

Finally, there is the Department of Social Organizations which has a social organization development and control section, a control section for conciliation boards and wage commissions, and a national placement service.

Employees of all branches of the Dirección General must enter on the bottom rung of the administrative ladder. Once employed, one advances by seniority and merit, there being a qualifying board which rates each employee from time to time as being outstanding, efficient, better than average, conditional, or unsatisfactory.

On the local level the work of the Dirección General is carried out by provincial labor inspectors located in the capital of each province, and rated in varying degrees of importance—from first to fourth. Under these provincial officials are departmental and local inspectors.

Of course, the form of organization and operation of the provincial inspectorates differs from province to province, depending on the nature of the economic life of the political subdivision involved. By far the most important provincial inspectorate is that of Santiago where the largest number of Chilean industries are located. The city of Santiago is divided into four zones, each under the charge of a senior-grade inspector, and the outlying parts of the province are covered by other inspectors. The work of this provincial inspectorate includes a variety of activities.

A sizable part of the personnel is constantly engaged in checking the enforcement of factory legislation and other protective labor laws. The inspector inquires into a wide range of problems—whether workers have various kinds of identification and work books, whether there are minors employed and if so, how many and in what capacity; how many hours the workers labor, whether or not machinery is properly protected, whether workers in certain dangerous industries have had physical examinations required by law. He notes the deductions for social insurance funds and reviews the individual contracts which the workers sign when employed. The inspector pays special attention to conditions for women workers.

The labor inspector consults the employer. He does not generally talk to the workers but can demand all kinds of documentary evidence to back up what the employer says. The inspector can also call for the services of doctors and engineers to investigate circumstances which seem suspicious and require the attention of experts. In case an employer is not living up to the law, the inspector so informs the official in charge in the provincial inspectorate who will then lodge a complaint with the labor tribunal (Juzgado del Trabajo). The complaint will specify the amount of fine the inspector thinks the errant employer should pay and in some cases will recommend that the employer be jailed.

The Santiago Provincial Labor Inspectorate has a section where complaints and grievances are received. Sometimes the provincial inspector himself intervenes in the more important cases of protests lodged against an employer.

Another section of the provincial inspectorate deals with the formation and functioning of unions and other organizations established under the Labor Code. Inspectors must be present at the founding meeting of a union to assure that the gathering is legal. They are also present at union elections and are responsible for deciding whether or not a union election has been held legally. Representatives of the provincial inspectorate must also attend all union meetings where revisions of union statutes are proposed or adopted.

This same section of the provincial inspector's office keeps track of the financial situation of the unions within its jurisdiction, studying proposed budgets submitted each year by local unions as well as annual reports on how they have actually spent their money. The provincial inspector may warn unions that certain expenditures are borderline cases or absolutely illegal. The inspector pays particular attention to money which unions receive as a result of profit-sharing, and sits on the boards which decide how this money is to be spent. If necessary, the provincial inspector may draw up a complaint against union leaders misusing funds of their organizations, and ask the Juzgado del Trabajo to fine or imprison offending unionists.

Each provincial labor inspectorate maintains a control division which gathers and tabulates the results of the activities of the inspectorate personnel. In the Santiago Labor Inspectorate the second-in-command has charge of personnel problems in the organization and assigns inspectors to do various jobs.

The Labor Courts

There are two other government labor agencies which are of very great importance: the conciliation and arbitration boards (Juntas de Conciliación y Arbitraje) and the labor tribunals. The first of these agencies provides government mediation and conciliation for labor disputes and will be discussed more fully in Chapter XXI.

The labor tribunals are composed of professional judges, and concern themselves solely with violations of labor law. They deal with labor disputes only insofar as the law has been breached. There are two steps in the labor court hierarchy: the Juzgados del Trabajo and the Alzadas or Cortes del Trabajo, which are courts of appeal.

There is supposed to be a Juzgado del Trabajo in each department (equivalent to a county in the United States) of Chile, but such is not always the case. In smaller departments where there is no labor court, its duties are carried out either by magistrates who correspond to county court judges in the United States, or if there are no such officials, by the governor of the department.

The Juzgados del Trabajo deal with cases concerning "all contentious questions concerning the application of the dispositions of this text and of the stipulations of labor contracts," according to the Código del Trabajo. The courts also have jurisdiction over cases involving failure to comply with the manual workers' social security system. However, cases involving the social security funds can only be carried to the labor courts on appeal from a decision by the governing board of the social security fund.[8]

Labor justice in Chile is simple and lacking in formality. The judge first tries to conciliate the parties and help them reach an understanding. If that is not possible he hears witnesses and the arguments of both sides often rendering a decision in the same sitting. Ordinarily both sides are represented by lawyers. In some cases, however, only the parties themselves appear. There are six labor courts in Santiago and others are distributed throughout the country. The work of these judges is apportioned to them by the Cortes del Trabajo. Promotion of the judges is on the basis of seniority. The Cortes del Trabajo are the courts of appeal. The third step is appeal from a Corte del Trabajo to the Supreme Court of the Republic.

Thus, the Chilean labor court system is a compromise between the Argentine and Brazilian labor judiciary. Unlike the Argentine system, the Chileans have functional representatives on their labor appeal courts; but unlike Brazil, where these representatives have vote as well as voice, the Chilean workers' and employers' nominees are only advisors. As in Argentina, the Chilean labor courts deal only with issues of law, and not—as in the case of Brazil—with collective disputes.

Medical Aid

One of the aspects of industrial relations in which the government's role as rule-maker has been most important has been in the protection of the workers' health. Chile was the first country in Latin America to provide general compulsory health insurance for industrial workers. The medical services established by the government, in spite of all their weaknesses, have undoubtedly been of prime importance in converting the raw agricultural worker into a modern industrial laborer.

In developing an extensive health service, the government has laid down detailed rules for the behavior of both employers and workers and thus has contributed greatly to developing that "web of rule" essential to an industrial society. At the same time the early establishment of health insurance was undoubtedly an attempt by the government to handle some of the labor protests in early mining and industrial enterprises.

Law 4054 of September 1924, one of the original elements of the Labor Code, provided for considerable medical benefits under the administration of the Caja de Seguro Obligatorio. In 1952 the medical section of the *caja* was merged with the government's National Hospital Board and the National Fund for Child Care to form the new Servicio Nacional de Salud.

The Servicio Nacional de Salud maintains first-, second-, and third-class dispensaries. If a worker feels ill while on the job or at home, he goes to the nearest clinic or hospital of the Servicio. Medical services are also available for the worker's dependents. In addition to direct medical aid, a sick married worker receives a subsidy from the Servicio Nacional de Seguro Social (National Social Security Service). The Servicio Nacional de Salud also administers the Law of Preventive Medicine of 1938. This law requires regular surveys of insured workers to seek out those who have chronic diseases such as tuberculosis, rheumatism, venereal diseases, heart and kidney ailments, or occupational diseases such as silicosis.

Where the doctors of the Servicio find incipient cases of these diseases, they are empowered to order a partial or total rest for the worker. If the order is for a partial rest, the worker labors only half the time and during hours prescribed by the doctor. The Servicio pays one-half his wage during this period. If the patient requires total rest the Servicio gives him his full wage.

Working mothers are given special attention under the Servicio Nacional de Salud. They receive medical attention during pregnancy and at the time of birth, and the *caja* pays them a subsidy of 50 per cent of their wage during two weeks before and two weeks after confinement and will pay 10 per cent of the wage for a period of twelve months thereafter. Moreover, the working mother is entitled to medical care for her child until the infant is two years of age.

The Servicio Nacional de Salud is organized on the basis of eighteen regions, four of which are in the province of Santiago. In each of these regions there are various health centers most of which are located in a hospital.

There are some four million people—including workers and their families—out of Chile's more than six million population who are covered by the Servicio. About a half million people in Chile can afford to pay for their own medical treatment and do so. Almost all the remaining million and a half—composed of small farmers, small businessmen, white collar workers, public employees, members of the armed forces—have some kind of medical service of their own in the country's social security system. Some of those thus covered go to private doctors' offices rather than use the free services because they feel that treatment in these private offices is more considerate.

There are serious criticisms which can be made of the Servicio Nactional de Salud. Workers and employers both complain, for instance, about the long time spent waiting to be attended. There is little doubt that in some areas the doctors of the Servicio are overworked.

In the second place, the Servicio Nacional de Salud has considerable financial difficulties. It is supposed to receive some three and a half billion pesos annually from the Servicio Nacional de Seguro Social which collects this from the workers and employers. The government is supposed to pay about four and a half billion pesos out of the general treasury. However, the government had not by the middle of 1956 paid a single peso of this to the Servicio since its establishment, and owed ten billion pesos.

The Servicio also has other sources of income which bring its total budget up to almost thirty billion pesos. These include government budget items which formerly went to the hospital board and the National Fund for Child Care. These moneys are generally paid by the government, though usually they are late. The Servicio also has the revenue from one of the country's biggest lotteries, the Polla de Beneficencia, agricultural properties and other minor sources of income.

Of the nearly thirty billion pesos in the budget of the Servicio about seventeen or more are used to pay wages and salaries. There are admittedly too much bureaucracy and red tape in the Servicio. Politics also played a nefarious role in its first years: most of the officials of the Medical Department of the old Caja de Seguro Obligatorio were leftists and were opposed to the Ibáñez administration which put the Servicio Nacional de Salud into operation, and conflicts between these and the administration lessened the efficiency of the Servicio. However, by 1956 the control of the Servicio was in the hands of Ibáñistas.

Financial difficulties have very much hampered the operation of the Servicio. Upon occasion the Servicio has been on the point of suspending the operation of hospitals because it did not have money to buy food for the patients; the pay of employees of the Servicio has several times been in arrears; the Servicio has not been able to expand its hospitals. By the middle of 1956, however, it was said to be on the road to greater financial stability.

Government Housing

The efforts of private enterprise have never been sufficient to cope with the great lack of decent low-income housing in Chile. Therefore, workers' housing was one of the first fields of social legislation in which the Chilean government took an interest. However, it was not until 1936 that the Caja de la Habitación Popular was established and was given the main burden of government housing efforts in behalf of the underprivileged.[9]

The Caja de Habitación Popular was allotted various sources of income, including an annual state appropriation, loans from the funds of the Caja de Seguro Obligatorio, the proceeds of a government bond issue, loans from the National Savings Fund, income from investments and 25 per cent of the return from taxes on incomes from real estate. However, in spite of all these resources, the *caja* continued to be poorly financed until Law 7600 of October 20, 1943, provided a number of additional sources of income. The most important provision of Law 7600 was that requiring employers with profits of more than fifty thousand pesos to pay 5 per cent of their net profit to the Caja de Habitación Popular if they did not themselves spend that amount on housing for their employees.

Houses of the *caja* were built both for rent and sale to the workers. In the case of houses built for sale, an occupant first rented the building for two years, after which he might apply to buy the house. A *caja* social worker then visited the prospective purchaser to find out how he kept up the house, as well as the family's financial condition and probity. If the report was favorable, a contract was signed for a thirty to thirty-five year period of amortization and the family received title to the house.

In 1953 the Caja de Habitación Popular was reorganized and rechristened the Corporación de la Vivienda. The principal income for the corporation comes from the general appropriations from the government treasury which in 1955 amounted to two billion pesos. By that time, the 5 per cent profits tax on employers amounted to only a small part of corporation's income.

In its first three years of existence, the Corporación de la Vivienda was reported to have constructed about fifteen thousand houses throughout Chile. In 1956 it had under construction or in the planning phase another ten thousand homes.

The Corporación was experimenting in 1956 with a special program, operating in the housing project known as Población German Riesco in Santiago. In this program the Corporación was providing the materials and technical direction needed while the workers provided the labor for their own houses. Six hundred homes were being built under this system which was receiving cooperation from Point Four.

In the government housing developments, renters' committees are usually formed, and are recognized by the housing authorities for the purpose of discussion of problems of the projects. However, the housing authorities have been somewhat cautious about giving too much recognition to these committees because they often fall into the hands of politicians and the housing authorities do not want to get embroiled in the political feuds of its tenants.

The Social Security System

One of the most important aspects of government intervention in the labor–management field is that of social security. In the beginning, Chilean social security consisted largely of health insurance, but in time other benefits were added. In 1952 the health insurance aspects of the social security system were separated and placed under the Servicio Nacional de Salud. However, the various social security "funds" continued to play an important role in determining the conditions of life and labor of the Chilean working class.

Chile was the second country in Latin America—after Uruguay—to establish social security on a wide basis. However, the country still has no over-all social security system. In the early days of the Popular Front government in 1939, the Socialist deputy, Natalio Berman, presented a bill to congress which would have provided for a complete social security system.[10] However, this bill was never enacted into law.

A somewhat haphazard collection of social security "funds" covering most workers has arisen over a period of more than three decades. There are more than thirty *cajas* or funds, covering different workers. These funds vary greatly in the kinds of benefits they offer members.

The industrial and agricultural workers are covered by the Servicio Nacional de Seguro Social. Other *cajas* of considerable strength are the Caja de Empleados Particulares, covering privately employed white collar workers; the Caja de Empleados Públicos, treating with government employees, journalists, and lawyers; the Caja de Previsión de los Carabineros (national police); the Caja de Previsión de los Empleados y Obreros de la Empresa de los Ferrocarriles del Estado (state railroad workers). In addition to these, only the funds of the merchant marine, white collar workers of the nitrate industry, municipal laborers of Santiago, and municipal employees cover more than one thousand people. Some funds are almost ludicrously small having less than one hundred members.[11]

Between 1924 and 1952 the manual workers and agricultural laborers were covered by the Caja de Seguro Obligatorio, which had been established by Law 4054 of 1924. However, in 1952 the whole social security system of these groups of workers was reorganized. The Medical Department of the

Caja de Seguro Obligatorio was made part of the Servicio Nacional de Salud, and the remaining parts of the Caja de Seguro Obligatorio were reconstituted as the Servicio Nacional de Seguro Social.

The Servicio Nacional de Seguro Social since 1952 has collected the social security deductions from workers and employers, and administers pensions for aged workers, widows, and orphans. In 1953 it also added to its work the collection and dispensing of family allowances and dismissal payments.

Under the new legislation it was possible for firms with their own agreements to this effect to continue paying family allowances and dismissal payments if their system had been in operation before the law was enacted, and if their benefits were larger than those offered by the Servicio Nacional de Seguro Social. Firms maintaining such separate systems do not have to pay the part of social security taxes designed to cover family allowance and dismissal payments.

The funds of the Servicio which are designed to cover medical benefits are passed to the Servicio Nacional de la Salud. The remainder is supposed to be invested in large housing projects which in 1956 were in the drawing-board stage.

The retirement benefits which the workers receive from the Servicio Nacional de Seguro Social are proportional to length of service and average wage received during the five years previous to retirement. They are considerably larger than those previously paid by the old Caja de Seguro Obligatorio.

The Servicio Nacional de Seguro Social has some difficulty in collecting the appropriate taxes for its benefits. Since many workers do not like laws which take money out of their current income, there are many instances in which the workers and the employers agree to have the employer report a wage payment which is less than the real one. This works against the worker when it comes time for him to receive his retirement benefits. Many employers, particularly in rural areas, evade social security taxes by reporting fewer workers in their employ than they really have.

The Servicio Nacional de Seguro Social is run by an administrative council, and a director general who takes the place of the old executive vice-president of the Caja de Seguro Obligatorio. The council consists of three workers' representatives, three employers' representatives, and four representatives of congress, plus the Minister of Health and Social Security. The Servicio is under the general supervision of the Ministry of Health and Social Security.

Second in importance among the social security institutions is the Caja de Previsión de Empleados Particulares. This covers white collar workers in private employment, and although it performs many of the same functions as the Servicio Nacional de Salud and Servicio Nacional de Seguro Social, it offers some additional services. Its Retirement Fund which allows workers upon reaching fifty, or having been out of the profession for two years, to withdraw their money in a lump sum is supplemented by an unemployment insurance fund paying 75 per cent of the minimum white collar workers' salary for a period of six months.

The white collar workers' *caja*, like the Servicio Nacional de Seguro Social, provides monthly family allowances for the workers belonging to it. A special fund in the *caja* receives from each employer an amount equal to 19.33 per cent of his white collar workers' salaries and from each worker 2 per cent of his salary. The employer deducts from his contribution the amount he is paying his *empleados* in family allowances.

Every member must have life insurance with the *caja* for at least twenty thousand pesos.

One of the principal functions of the *caja* is to lend money. There are two kinds of loans: those for emergencies and those for the purchase of homes. In the former, the loan can amount to as much as 50 per cent of the funds the *empleado* has contributed. Such loans are paid back by payroll deductions over a forty-eight week period. The *caja* used to lend money for the purchase of homes already constructed, but now funds are extended only for the construction of new houses since the primary purpose of the *caja's* program is to help combat the housing shortage.

The control of the Caja de Previsión de Empleados Particulares is in the hands of a council consisting of six representatives of *empleados* and members of both houses of congress. This council takes a very active part in the administration of the *caja* and looks into all phases of its activities. The *empleados'* organizations also participate actively, presenting grievances and keeping their members informed of what the *caja* is doing. The actual day-to-day administration is in the hands of an executive vice-president.

The third important social security fund is the Caja de Empleados Públicos y Periodistas, covering national government employees, journalists, and lawyers. Some of its officials claim that it is the best of the country's social security systems. The *caja* was organized in 1925. Previous to its establishment, public employees were entitled to a retirement pension payable out of general government funds, while other phases of their social security were covered by a number of private funds some of them dating as far back as 1855. A proposal for a more extensive coverage of the economic risks of public employees was first presented in congress in 1921 but such a project did not actually become law until the period of Arturo Alessandri's return to the presidency in 1925. In July of that year, Don Arturo established the *caja* by presidential decree.[12]

Those covered by the *caja* receive a pension after thirty years of service, a pension for their wives and children in case of death, life insurance worth a year and a half's salary, and a funeral fund. In addition to these services, the *caja* lends money to its members in three different forms: mortgage loans, loans for repair of property, and emergency loans. The government or employer pays 4 per cent of its payroll to the *caja,* the worker 10 per cent of his salary.

The funds which the Caja de Empleados Públicos y Periodistas does not invest in loans to its members are invested in urban and rural properties. The agricultural holdings of the *caja* are under the management of a group administering all government-owned agrarian holdings. The urban properties are generally apartment houses. Formerly the *caja* bought up sites already constructed but in 1946 it launched a program of its own to build apartment houses which it rents to public employees and other members of the *caja*. This scheme helps to solve the housing problem and gives the *caja* good, paying properties in the bargain.

The Caja de Empleados Públicos y Periodistas is controlled by a council of eighteen members representing the public employees, the journalists, the lawyers, and both houses of congress. This council meets twice a week and takes a very active part in the administration of the *caja.*

The last of the first-rank social security funds covers the railroad workers. After six months of employment a worker has full rights in the social security system. He pays 5 per cent of his wages and the state railroads contribute an amount equivalent to 5 per cent of its wage bill. This *caja* has an insurance company and owns stock in private companies.

The Caja de Previsión de los Empleados y Obreros de la Empresa de los Ferrocarriles del Estado keeps a separate account for each member. When a worker leaves the employ of the state railroads he can request payment of his full account—both his and the employer's contribution—unless he has been dismissed for misconduct, in which case he can only withdraw his own 5 per cent contributions. In case of a death in his family or a transfer from one part of the country to another, a worker can get a loan. A worker is eligible normally for a loan after every four 5 per cent payments to the *caja.*

The *caja* also has charitable functions. It provides education for orphans of railroad workers. It provides free medical service and free drugs. This aid is extended to the worker's family upon an additional payment of one-half of 1 per cent of his salary.

This railroad *caja* is administered by a council of eleven people, including the Minister of Public Works, who acts as president, a representative of the railroad companies, usually an official of the state railroads; and eight members of the unions, three white collar workers and five manual workers. The executive vice-president of the *caja* is named by the President of the Republic.

In spite of the fact that the railroad workers are very proud of their *caja* and think of it as the best in the country, Dr. Julio Bustos Acevedo notes that there is not medical service adequate for the families of the workers and says that "in general the system in this industry is confused, inadequate and expensive." [13]

Of less importance are the other *cajas*. Together they make up a complicated but inadequate social security system. One Chilean commentator notes that, "It is very curious that in spite of the excessive number of existing *cajas,* there is always at any given moment, another being projected." This same writer suggests that all be consolidated, saying in this connection:

> To say this is easy, to do it is much more difficult. It is a serious matter to try to formulate a basic system adequate to the necessities of all the working population and the possibilities of the national economy. It is even more difficult to carry out such a scheme after twenty years of social legislation which have created rights, legitimate expectations and strong interests which are resolved to defend themselves with all means available.[14]

There is little doubt that the system is very expensive, adds a good deal to industry's costs of production, and thus adds to inflationary pressure. It has been criticized for providing for too early retirement. A case in point is the railroad workers' fund which permits a railroader to retire after only ten years' work. Equally serious is the overlapping in retirement programs of different funds.

One of the most controversial aspects of the Chilean social security system concerns its effect on the medical profession. Dr. Figueroa Castro, employed as a physician by one of the larger manufacturing establishments, blamed the *cajas* for holding back the medical profession in Chile. He said that almost every doctor is now an employee of one or the other of the funds, that they all tend to work only their prescribed number of hours a day, get paid bad salaries, and become bureaucratized. Finally, the doctors are overworked, said Dr. Figueroa, since each one has to have three or four jobs in order to have a really decent income.

An attempt was made to overcome some of these difficulties with the passage of the Ley de Médicos Funcionarios in 1951 but some of the flaws still remained.

By 1956 virtually all doctors in Chile were employed either with the Servicio Nacional de Salud or with one of the other social security groups. Their payment was established by the Ley de Médicos Funcionarios. It provided that for each two hours' service with the public institutions, the doctor would get the daily pay of a "grade 13" public employee. A doctor could not work for more than six hours—in which case he would get three times the day's pay of a "grade 13" public employee. A top figure was set for how much a doctor could earn.

Most doctors have their private practices in addition to social security work. If for special reasons they cannot have a private practice they are either given permission to work eight hours a day in the Servicio Nacional de Salud or are given 20 per cent extra as compensation. Doctors in mining centers are always given this permission.

There is a need for a better distribution of doctors throughout the country. The Colegio Médico calculates that one doctor to fourteen hundred patients is a decent average for Chile. At the present time there is one doctor to eighteen hundred patients, but the physicians are very badly distributed. There should be from six hundred to a thousand more doctors in the country. The Colegio Médico is trying to get the universities to increase the number of medical students—if they could turn out sixty more than they do now per year, they could abolish the deficit in ten years or more.

The Chilean social security system differs from those of Brazil and Argentina in one fundamental aspect. Both Chilean social security and housing legislation permit employers to obtain exemption from taxes for these purposes if they provide the services themselves. In the case of medical aid, dismissal pay, family allowances as well as housing, the employer is free to provide these things himself if the provisions he makes for them meet the specifications set up by the government. In that case he does not need to contribute to government funds for the purpose. Many employers take advantage of these provisions of the law since the employer in Chile does not differ fundamentally from his counterpart in other countries in his distrust of government.

This provision of the Chilean law is perhaps a reflection of the democratic nature of Chilean society. Although the government has been interested in exercising control over labor conflicts and in meeting labor grievances so that they will not cause political crises, there has been little attempt upon the part of the government to centralize in the hands of the state all expression of the worker's grievances or to set up the state as the principal molder of the "web of rule" of industrial relations.

No matter what the drawbacks of the Chilean system of social insurance funds may be, it is undoubtedly true that Chile was a pioneer among the Latin American countries in the field of social security and that the existing system has rendered a great service to the working people. It has been a big factor in preventing the industrialization of Chile from being accompanied by the extreme exploitation of labor, distress and disease which were part of the process in the countries first influenced by the Industrial Revolution.

CHAPTER XX

Workers' and Employers' Organizations

Chilean labor legislation set the precedent in Latin America in providing legal recognition for trade unions. In doing so the Labor Code gave the government power to determine the structure of the labor movement and to exercise considerable power over the internal affairs of the legally recognized trade unions. As a result, there are two kinds of unions in Chile: those with *personería jurídica* or legal recognition, and the so-called "free" unions which operate without benefit of government recognition and support and which, according to a strict interpretation of the law, cannot participate in collective bargaining or other normal activities of trade unions, but do so nonetheless.

At least two-thirds of the unions functioning in Chile are "legal" unions. The principal exceptions are the workers on the state railroads, national and municipal government employees, and certain unions under Anarcho-Syndicalist influence in the building, printing, and shoemaking trades. In actual fact these "free" unions are just as active as the "legal" organizations and in practice they have many of the rights of recognized unions.

The Labor Code provides that everyone over eighteen years of age is eligible for membership in a *sindicato* or labor union. Workers in the same trade or profession or in similar or allied trades or professions, or workers in the same enterprise can band themselves together to form unions. Exceptions are made in the case of municipal and government employees (including railroad workers) as well as members of the armed forces and the national police.

Alfredo Gaete Berrios, writing in 1943, stated that unions are "completely independent insofar as their internal affairs are concerned,"[1] though Francisco Walker Linares is nearer the truth when he comments that "Chilean legislation . . . greatly restricts the principle of trade-union liberty, submitting the unions to excessive surveillance by the state."[2] The conduct of union affairs is severely circumscribed by the Labor Code and subsequent regulations—which admittedly are not always enforced but which nevertheless give the government great leeway to intervene in the internal affairs of the unions if it so desires.

The right of organization into *sindicatos* is not confined to manual workers. White collar workers, professional workers, and even employers can form organizations recognized by the state under the Labor Code.[3] In practice there are few *sindicatos* made up of employers.

"Industrial" and "Professional" Unions

Two kinds of unions are provided for in Chilean labor legislation—the *sindicato industrial* or industrial union, and the *sindicato profesional* or craft union. The first of these is in a preferred position since it enjoys certain rights, such as profit-sharing, which are not extended to the craft or professional unions.

The *sindicato industrial*[4] can be composed of workers in "any mine, nitrate establishment, workshop or other industrial or commercial enterprise" with more than twenty-five workers and it must bear the name of the enterprise in which it operates. At least 55 per cent of the workers in the enterprise must join the union for it to obtain legal recognition, but once this has been obtained membership is compulsory for all workers in the establishment.[5] Employers are obliged to allow the posting of notices of meetings and reports on the financial condition of the union on bulletin boards inside the plant.[6]

The employer must check off the dues of each worker of a plant which has a legalized industrial union. He is only obliged to deduct the regular dues provided for in the statutes of the union and does not have to discount any special assessments.[7] In practice, however, if relations between the employer and the union are friendly, the employer will often agree to deduct whatever assessments are authorized by general assemblies of the union. Dues and a record of them are turned over by the employer to the president and treasurer of the union with the employer keeping a record of the amount paid.

If one employer has various establishments in different cities or towns, the workers may form industrial unions in each plant, but if there are several plants of the same employer in the same town all must be in one industrial union unless special permission is obtained from the Directorate General of Labor. This permission may be given on grounds of the diversity of the work done by those employed in the different establishments.

Industrial unions are empowered to sign collective contracts with their employers, to represent the workers in exercising the rights granted under collective contracts, and to represent the workers in collective conflicts before government conciliation and arbitration boards. They are authorized to receive a share of the profits of the enterprise under certain conditions. They are also permitted to organize mutual benefit activities and to establish industrial and professional schools and popular libraries. They can organize consumers' and producers' cooperatives, although the latter can only be set up when they are making something different from the product made by the plant in which the union members are employed. In general, industrial unions can carry on any cultural, cooperative, or social activities authorized by the membership and provided for in the statutes of the individual union.

A *sindicato profesional*[8] may be formed by "persons who practice the same trades, industries or work for the exclusive purpose of study, development and legitimate defense of their members.[9] Manual workers, white collar workers, employers, and members of liberal professions are all eligible to form *sindicatos profesionales* and there is no incompatibility to concurrent membership in both an industrial and a craft union except in the copper mines.[10]

In practice, craft unions are established principally by white collar workers, by skilled workers who for one reason or another want to form an organization separate from that of the mass of workers, and by groups of manual workers who labor in plants with less than the twenty-five workers needed for the establishment of an industrial union. Thus, employees of bakeries, small shoe shops, and similar establishments often form *sindicatos profesionales* because there are not enough of them employed in any one establishment to set up an industrial union.

Craft unions are also found in the building trades, where painters, carpenters, masons, and so on are organized in separate unions. Some of these organizations do not have *personería jurídica*. The printing trades are generally organized on the basis of *sindicatos industriales,* each of which covers a single firm. Many unions in this field also lack *personería jurídica,* and the Anarcho-Syndicalist tradition still persists.

Although many white collar workers are today organized into *sindicatos profesionales,* this is not all the representation and protection which the law establishes for them. The Labor Code provides for the election of a *delegado* or delegate in any establishment having more than five white collar workers, whose duty it is to represent these employees in relations with the employer and government labor officials. The delegate has the same right to his job as do the directors of the unions: he cannot be dismissed while he is serving as a delegate or within six months thereafter. The delegate is elected to serve for one year and can be reelected.

The existence of the *delegado* can, of course, cause difficulties. It establishes two centers of influence among the white collar workers if they are organized in a union—the *delegado* and the union directors. In many cases, as in the newspaper *El Sur* of Concepción, the *delegado* has often been a director of the union. However, it is conceivable that the *delegado* could be played off against the union leadership by the employer and it is not unlikely that such cases do occur.

Although dual membership in an industrial and a craft union is possible, in such a case the claims of the industrial union will usually be paramount. For instance, a number of craft unions were formed in the 1940's in the mining and nitrate camps in the northern part of the country, among the mechanics and other skilled workers who had special interests to protect and who were often of a different political inclination from the majority of their fellow workers. No difficulty was put in the way of the formation of these unions. However, they were largely ineffective because the employers refused to deal with them except on an informal basis, maintaining that these same workers were included in the contract negotiated with the industrial union, and that they should present their case through that union in the process of negotiating annual contracts.

The Copper Workers' Statute of 1956 provided for the abolition of all *sindicatos profesionales* in the nation's copper mines. In the case of Chuquicamata, the effect was to reduce the seven unions which existed before the passage of the statute to two, a *sindicato industrial* for the manual workers and a *sindicato profesional* for the white collar workers.[11]

The *sindicato profesional* has to have a minimum membership of twenty-five people and, like the industrial union, has a five-man directorate elected annually. All workers who cease to be employed in the trade for more than six months lose their memberships in the union. Both Chileans and foreigners can belong to the union, but the latter cannot serve as directors until two years' residence in the country.

The craft unions can negotiate and sign collective contracts, represent members in conflicts with employers and engage in mutual benefit and cultural activities, but they have no right to profit-sharing as do the industrial unions. Article 414 of the Labor Code provides that parts of the code relative to the industrial unions apply also to craft organizations unless it is incompatible with the nature of the union.[12]

Obtaining Legal Recognition. A union is legally constituted when it receives *personería jurídica* or legal personality. Thereafter it has the right to acquire property and to contract civil obligations and be represented in the courts. It can only be dissolved by the will of its members or the decree of the power which gave it legal recognition. Legally, an unrecognized union may not represent workers in collective bargaining although, in fact, unrecognized unions do deal with employers. What is true is that only recognized unions can appear before government conciliation boards.

To obtain recognition, the provisional executive of a new union must send an application to the Directorate General of Labor through the local labor inspector, stating the address of the union and asking approval of its statutes and the granting of legal recognition. In the case of industrial unions this application must be signed by the members of the provisional executive of the union, but in the case of the professional union it must also have the signatures of twenty members.[13]

This application must be accompanied by the minutes of the meeting founding the union, the minutes of the meeting approving the statutes, and the minutes of the meeting authorizing the application for legal recognition, all of which can be included in a single document. In addition, the union must submit the text of its proposed statutes in triplicate, the names of the members of the provisional executive with their trade, their numbers in the national identification system, and their addresses. Finally, there must be a complete list of the names of those making up the new union, and a copy of the letter to the employer notifying him of the union's existence. In the case of a professional union this last requirement is changed to copies of the local newspaper in which the organization of the union has been advertised for three consecutive days.

When the local inspector of labor receives these documents, he transmits them within forty-eight hours to the Director General of Labor and at the same time asks the National Office of Identification (plain clothes police) for any information it may have on the members of the provisional directorate.

The social organizations section of the Directorate General of Labor closely scrutinizes the application and from time to time one is disallowed. For instance, in the case of professional unions, often there will not be the legal number of workers required to form the union which they desire to organize. Or, a union which is to be called a Sindicato Profesional de

Mecánicos will perhaps have in its ranks a number of individuals who are not mechanics at all, but who are brought in to fill up the legal number. Other reasons for rejection of application include errors in the organization of the union—an insufficient number of people present at the first meeting, or other formalities not complied with. Often there is something wrong with the union's statutes.

The members of the provisional executive committees are investigated very thoroughly. The police ascertain whether the individuals have criminal records. Occasionally a case will occur in which one of the directors has once been indicted for a crime but was never convicted, whereupon the worker involved must prove that he was cleared, either by a statement of the judge in the case or some other concrete evidence.

Between 1955 and 1958 the provisional directors were also investigated for their membership in the Communist Party. Such membership alleged by the Dirrección General de Investigaciones (the secret police) was sufficient to ban a worker from membership in the union's executive committee. However, the problem of Communist Party membership ceased to be relevant with the repeal of the statute outlawing the party in July 1958.

Once these details have been carefully checked by the social organizations section, the Directorate General of Labor returns the application, with its suggestions, to the local labor inspector who informs the union of necessary changes. When these have been made, the application is returned to the inspector who again forwards it to the Directorate General. If the application is in order, the Ministry of Labor then issues a decree declaring the union constituted, and sends all the papers to the Ministry of Justice. It is the Minister of Justice who, in the name of the President of the Republic, issues the decree giving legal personality to the union.[14]

The Ministry of Justice maintains a register of legal personality where records on all unions are kept, including the name of each organization, the number of the decree giving legal recognition, and in case such an event occurs, the number of the decree dissolving the union. In addition, the labor inspectors have a register of all the unions within their jurisdiction, which has the name, address, date of organization of each union, and notes also the date of its recognition by the Ministry of Labor, its legal recognition by the Ministry of Justice, and the dues, initiation fees, and death duties provided in the union statutes. The local inspectorates of labor also try to keep an up-to-date record of the number of members in each union, the names of directors, the collective contracts each has signed, and the financial status of each organization. Union officers must communicate monthly with the inspector of labor concerning any changes.[15]

Government Control of Union Elections. The law provides that the leadership of each union shall be in the hands of five directors who must be at least twenty-five years of age and Chilean citizens, or foreigners who meet rather rigid tests. In addition, labor union directors must be able to read and write. A person is not eligible for membership on a union's governing body if he has ever been convicted of a crime or is currently under indictment for one. He must have an identification card issued by the National Office of Identification, and in the case of an officer of an industrial union, must have been employed at least a year in the plant. Finally a prospective union official must have either served his term of military service or have been legally exempted. Professor Gaete Berrios thinks that this last provision is wrong since one's service in the armed forces has little to do with one's capacity for running a union.[16]

All lists of candidates for union office (who must be nominated in an open meeting) are sent to the employer and to the local labor inspector. The inspector passes the names on to the Directorate General of Labor, which asks the Dirección General de Investigaciónes for information on the nominees. The names of all those on the lists must be cleared before union elections can be held.

This preelection checkup for possible Communist Party membership was introduced in 1955 by a ministerial decree, signed by Minister of the Interior Koch and Minister of Labor Yanez. The decree was based on the Law for the Permanent Defense of Democracy and altered the previous situation under which no preelection checkup on political affiliation was necessary, but in which the government had the power to oust any union officials found to be Communists.[17] This decree automatically expired when the Law for the Permanent Defense of Democracy was repealed in the middle of 1958.

All elections have to be presided over by an inspector of labor who has the power to settle any controversy and who must be notified by the union at least forty-eight hours before the poll. Elections must take place annually, and usually occur during the month of May. In case an election cannot be held within the twelve-month period, the old directorate remains in office on a provisional basis.[18]

The Directorate General of Labor has final authority on the validity of union elections. The names of all newly elected union officials must be sent to the social organizations section of the directorate for checking as in the case of provisional officers of new unions. Occasionally, some elected union official is declared ineligible, and it is necessary to hold a supplementary election to fill his position. The newly elected directors choose from among themselves the president, secretary, and treasurer.[19]

Once elected, union directors have *fuero sindical* or trade-union immunity. They cannot be dismissed by their employer during their period in office and for six months thereafter, except with the permission of the local labor judge. This also applies to all candidates for director during the period just before the election and it applies to members of provisional directorates during the organization of a union. In case of a reduction of staff or the elimination of the section of the enterprise in which the union official works, the union director must be transferred to another part of the plant at the same pay he was receiving before the transfer. This trade-union immunity applies only to officials of individual professional and industrial unions enjoying legal recognition and does not extend to officers or federations and confederations of workers, even though these may be legally recognized.[20]

The law does not provide for full-time paid union officials. Union officers are supposed to work full time in the plant whose workers they represent. Only on exceptional occasions, as when they are called to Santiago or some other place by the authorities of the Ministry of Labor or some other government agency, can the union pay them. They are not supposed to receive more than their daily wage plus costs, and such payments by a union must be authorized in its budget.[21]

An exception to this general rule was created by the Copper Workers' Statute issued early in 1955. According to this statute, elected officials of the confederation are required to work on their company jobs one month out of three. The other two months they can spend on confederation business. Local leaders of the constituent unions of the confederation are required to work a good deal more steadily than this.

The general restriction which the Labor Code places on paid union officials is a great handicap to the development of a democratic trade-union movement in Chile. Most trade-union officials must work eight hours a day in their factories or workshops and can only devote their attention to trade-union matters in leisure hours. This makes difficult the development of a well trained corps of trade-union leaders in Chile.

The major exception to this general rule of no full-time trade-union leaders is the Communists. The Communist Party is supplied with ample funds making it possible for the party to maintain a large corps of party members who do nothing but party business. Many of these are engaged in trade-union activities. This large body of full-time Communist officials is one of the explanations of the continuing influence of the Communist Party in the trade-union movement in spite of the fact that their rank-and-file support is quite limited and has been for more than a decade.

Of course, the highest authority within the union rests in the meeting of the members. Such meetings are usually called *asembleas generales* or general assemblies, and are held at least once a month. Usually, one meeting will be held for all members of the organization, but in cases where the workers are on different shifts, as among the trolley car men of Santiago, it may be necessary to have separate meetings for the day and night workers.

Both craft and industrial unions can be dissolved, either by the agreement of their members at a general assembly called for the purpose, or by government decree. The President of the Republic is authorized to dissolve a union when it violates the Labor Code or the regulations issued under the code, when the membership of the union falls below the legal minimum, or when the organization has ceased to function for a year or more.

All organizations which declare strikes or walkouts without first going through proper conciliation procedure are considered "contrary to the spirit and the letter of the law," and are subject to dissolution by the government. This regulation is not very often enforced, although in January 1946 two nitrate workers' unions in the north had their legal recognition withdrawn as a result of wildcat strikes. After his break with the Communists in 1947 President Videla used this same weapon against some unions controlled by the Communist Party.

A government decree dissolving a union must name a liquidator to handle the final disposition of union funds, as provided for in the union's statutes. In the case of voluntary dissolution, the union must agree by an absolute majority and an inspector of labor must be present at the dissolution meeting. This final meeting must also appoint a liquidator to handle the last of the union's funds. The money remaining in the treasury can only be used for a limited number of things and cannot be divided among the members of the organization.

Control of Union Funds. Legally recognized unions are allowed to own property in their own right. This property is defined by the Labor Code as consisting of dues or other assessments made by the general assembly of a union, voluntary gifts by union members, employers, or third parties; a union's portion of profit-sharing; income from union property; fines levied on members; and furniture, inventories, and bank accounts held by a union. In case of any change in dues or other permanent charges of a union on its members, the local inspector of labor is supposed to be notified immediately.

The funds of the unions must be deposited in the local branch of the National Savings Bank (Caja Nacional de Ahorros), and the union is not permitted to keep more than five hundred pesos on hand. Any checks drawn by the union must have the signature of the president and the treasurer, and any expenditure of more than two thousand pesos must be authorized by the local labor inspector.[22]

In order to open an account in the National Savings Bank a union must present the bank's local office with a copy of the decree granting legal personality, and a copy of the union's statutes, both of which must be vouched for by the local labor inspector. The union must also present a statement by the labor inspector giving the names of the officers of the union and those officers' signatures. Thereafter it is the duty of the labor inspector to notify the local office of the bank every time there is a change in the directorate of the union.[23]

The property of the union is the responsibility of the union's directors and the treasurer is charged with keeping the books showing income and outgo of the union's funds.[24] When the directorate changes each year, there must be a general accounting by a certified public accountant approved of by the Directorate General of Labor which, after approval by the general assembly of the union, must be sent to the Directorate General of Labor through the local labor inspector and must be accompanied by a statement of the local branch of the National Savings Bank as to the union's current balance. The books of the union are always to be held open to investigation by the local labor inspector.[25]

The unions are only authorized to spend their money on certain things. They are flatly forbidden to set up strike funds and other measures of "resistance" although some unions build them up illegally. Unions are also forbidden to use any of their funds for loans to members or for the payment of personal expenses of any member, or for the establishment of bars or gambling games.

The unions are allowed to use their money for the acquisition of property, and the establishment of schools and professional training for the children of members although educational expenses can only be incurred with the approval of the Directorate General of Labor. Unions can also spend money on the creation and maintenance of libraries and other cultural activities, including the granting of prizes for cultural achievements. They can use their funds for the organization and maintenance of mutual benefit projects, cooperatives, and low-price stores.

Investments in cooperatives can be made only if at least 50 per cent of the capital is held by members of the union and if the losses of the cooperatives are less than 25 per cent of the capital. The books of the cooperatives run by unions must be kept entirely separate from those of the union itself. The local labor inspector can control the prices charged by the cooperative.

Union funds can be spent for sports activities, medical, dental, and maternity aid, and subsidies for sick members as well as payments to hospitals and rest homes attended by members. Workers' vacations and scholastic colonies can be paid for by the unions. Expenditures such as lump-sum payments in case of unemployment of a member, death benefits and the building of mausoleums for members and their families are also authorized by the Labor Code.

Medical services offered by a union must be complementary to those provided by the social security system, and money so invested must be used according to rules established by the social security officials. Benefits cannot be greater than those provided under social security regulations.

The unions can spend their money for *fiestas*. Administrative costs are also authorized and it is possible for the unions to put aside some money for an emergency fund, although this may not include more than 5 per cent of the year's total expenditures. A reserve fund is also provided.

Finally, some money can be authorized for trade-union solidarity, including payments to other labor organizations and confederations. Such expenditures must be approved by two-thirds of the members of the union and cannot amount to more than 25 per cent of the total regular dues.

In December of each year the directors of both industrial and craft unions must present to the general assemblies a proposed budget based on the regular sources of income of the union. Once this budget has been agreed upon by the members, it must be turned over to the local labor inspector who has to approve or modify it within ten days. If the budget amounts to more than thirty thousand pesos, it must be sent to the Directorate General of Labor for approval. The income of the union must be classified to show the amount left over from the previous year, the ordinary income, extraordinary income, and miscellaneous income.

Most unions' budgets actually reach the Directorate General of Labor where they are scrutinized by the social organizations section of that body.

The section uses its influence to get the unions to reduce the amount of money they appropriate for *fiestas* and celebrations of the union anniversary, and increase the funds allotted to educational and other cultural activities. Budgets for unemployment funds are given particularly close scrutiny, and a minimum accounting standard is demanded for the whole budget.

At the end of the year each union must turn into the social organizations section a complete record of expenditure. If this differs too widely from the budget proposed at the beginning of the year the section brings the matter to the union leaders' attention and if the discrepancy is too flagrant, presses charges in the criminal courts. If a union wants to change its budget during the year, it is supposed to apply for permission to the Directorate General of Labor.

In 1946 the Minister of Labor ordered a special checkup on the use of union funds and as a result criminal proceedings were started against a number of union leaders who were accused of misappropriating some eight million pesos. However, usually the Directorate General doesn't have the staff to make a thorough checkup on the funds of all unions whose budgets pass under its scrutiny. Some of the *sindicatos* handle millions of pesos a year and in order to check on them effectively it would be necessary to have an accountant working full time. However, there are less than a dozen accountants in the Santiago office of the Directorate General inspecting union books, and it can handle the records of about fifty unions a day.

Profit-Sharing. Industrial unions have one source of income not available to craft organizations—a share of the profits of the employer. In 1948, profit-sharing netted Chilean unions over thirty million pesos compared with nineteen million collected in dues.[26] Chile was one of the first countries of Latin America to provide by law for profit-sharing. Subsequently a number of other countries have also passed such legislation or embodied the principle in their constitutions. No other country provides for participation by the unions in profit-sharing, however.[27]

In order to qualify for profit-sharing, a union must be legally recognized and have been in existence for at least one year. The law lays down exact details for determining the amount to which the workers and their unions are entitled. The "liquid profit" the employer has made is determined from his annual report to the Director General of Income Taxes. From this amount is deducted 8 per cent for interest on the employer's capital and 2 per cent for unforeseen necessities. The rest is subject to profit-sharing.

The Director General of Income Taxes informs the local inspector of labor of the amount involved and the inspector notifies the employer.

Within thirty days after notification, the employer must pay the workers and the union the amount to which they are entitled. Payment is mandatory in all companies with more than twenty-five workers. The employer is permitted to choose between paying 10 per cent of his "liquid profit" or 6 per cent of the wages bill during the previous year.[28] If the latter method of payment is used, the 6 per cent of the wages of the workers must take into account overtime, family allowances, and any special sums paid out to the workers during the preceding calendar year.

One-half of the profit participation is payable directly to the workers in two equal parts: one prorated in accordance with the size of the daily wage of each worker, the other apportioned on the basis of the workers' attendance records. All workers who were on the job 70 per cent of the time covered, are eligible. In the case of workers in companies exempted from the obligatory one day of rest a week, calculation is made on the basis of 70 per cent of the days worked by the company.

Payments to individual employees must be previously approved by the local inspector of labor, and the records of payment of profit participation must include the name of each worker, his daily wage, the number of days he has worked, the proportion of payment made in lieu of days worked, and the amount prorated according to the daily wage.[29]

Only half of the profit participation fund is paid to the workers directly. The other half goes to the industrial union. There are restrictions on what this money can be spent for, and a budget for its expenditure must be drawn up by a so-called Orienting Commission (Comisión Orientadora) consisting of the president of the union, the manager of the company or his representative, and the local labor inspector who presides at all sessions of the commission.[30]

Attendance at the meetings of the commission is mandatory for the president of the union and the company manager and they can designate deputies only in case they have a reason approved by the local labor inspector. In case agreement cannot be reached by the commission, final decision is made by the Director General of Labor. Once accord has been reached as to how the union's share of the profit is to be spent, the agreement is put into writing. Only then can the money be transferred to the union.

Once the commission's work has been approved, expenditures agreed to by that group can only be changed by the unanimous agreement of its members after approval by the general assembly of the union. If changes amount to more than 50 per cent of the total amount, the Director General of Labor must give his approval. The Comisión Orientadora can keep its eye on the way in which the money is spent and it or any of its members may denounce any alleged misspending to the local labor inspector or labor judge.[31] The profit-sharing money the unions receive is usually spent on social services, cooperatives, or cultural activities. Frequently it is used for constructing or improving union headquarters.

Mutual Benefit Activities. The activities of the unions are varied. They of course include collective bargaining but they also encompass a great deal of mutual benefit work. The latter includes payments to sick workers and to the families of deceased union members. In many cases there is regular provision in the statutes of unions for payments to sick members and in other instances such sums are raised either by a collection at a union meeting or by a resolution of the general assembly of the union to impose a special assessment. This is comparatively easily done when the employer is willing to check off such an assessment from the wages of the worker, although in other cases it involves a good deal of work for the union officials to raise the money.

Some unions engage in cultural activities. The Braden Copper Company union in Rancagua in 1947 had one of the best libraries in the province. The same union was running a night school with two hours of classes a day, and offered courses in Spanish, English, arithmetic, accounting, and typing.

One of the most extensive union programs of educational activities in Chile is that of the sugar workers' union of Penco. This group maintains a complete primary school for the first six grades. The company donates the building, the state provides some of the teachers but the union pays the rest and also supplies student necessities, such as books. This same union also has a school to teach women members and wives of members various crafts, such as dressmaking. As a result of this instruction, many of the women made clothes for themselves and clothes to sell. There is also a fund for aiding the children of members to go to secondary schools and even to take advanced study.

Company Unions

Company unions, in the sense of organizations subject to employer control, are not entirely unknown in Chile. Before the Pedro Aguirre Cerda government in 1938 and the subsequent expansion of trade unionism, there was a considerable number of such organizations. For some years after that, there were few. However, with the wide-open division in the labor movement in the middle 1940's, the number of company unions again increased considerably, particularly in the textile industry.

The most notorious company union in Chile is probably that in the Yarur textile plant in Santiago. That union was founded in 1939 and at the beginning was Communist-controlled. However, before very many months were out, the Communists lost control and an administration very friendly to the company came into office. The former leaders of the union were dismissed after their *fuero* had expired, and the company has kept a firm hand on the union with short interruptions, down to the present time.

The union during most of this period has had its headquarters in the plant itself; it has seldom presented a list of demands to the employer; it has usually cooperated in keeping "agitators" out. Relations between the company and the union have generally been very cordial. It has held its general assemblies in a big room in the factory, its books have been kept in an unlocked drawer in one of the company offices.

Of course, this lack of militancy on the part of the union has been encouraged by the company. It has been the company's rule that the workers were to bring any complaints straight to the director of social service of the company rather than to the union. The company is said to have an efficient spy system to ferret out "agitators." Also, the company has not permitted the union to have anything to say about hiring or firing, or any other question concerning the management of the enterprise. It has been the avowed purpose of Yarur to keep the union as weak as possible. This policy has been reinforced by extensive social welfare programs including a sizable housing project.

Local trade unions in Chile, then, are for the most part organized under the Labor Code which provides a great deal of leeway for government interference in the internal affairs of the labor organizations. As a matter of fact, the actual amount of interference is generally a great deal less than provided for in the law.

Many of the unions are fairly wealthy organizations, due to compulsory unionization, the checkoff system, and sharing by the unions in company profits. However, due to provisions of the Labor Code which militate against full-time union officials, limit the unions' expenditures, and limit the possibilities of developing strong national labor unions, the labor movement is weaker than it might otherwise be. The unions, although they are principally engaged in collective bargaining with the employers, engage in a good deal of mutual benefit and social service work for their members.

Federations and Confederations

The Labor Code is rather sketchy in its reference to trade-union groups above the *sindicato* level: federations and confederations of workers. The former, indeed, are not mentioned, though there is discussion at various points of *confederaciones* and *uniónes sindicales,* the latter being, perhaps, the equivalent of a federation. The federations and confederations play an important part in Chilean labor relations although most of them are "free," that is, do not enjoy legal recognition. (It should be explained that some of the labor federations use the word "confederation" in their titles.)

The most important legally recognized federation is the Confederación de Trabajadores del Cobre. Established late in the 1940's when the copper workers withdrew from the Communist-controlled Federación Minera, the confederation was officially recognized by the government by the Copper Workers' Statute, decreed by President Carlos Ibañez early in 1956 as a result of the passage of a law for the reorganization of the copper mining industry the year before.

According to the provisions of this statute, the Copper Workers' Confederation was granted legal recognition and the employers were obliged to bargain with it as the representative of the copper workers. The union leaders of both the individual affiliates and the confederation were given the right to spend a considerable portion of their working days conducting union business.[32]

Another important industrial federation is the Confederación Marítima de Chile (COMACH), with its headquarters in the port city of Valparaiso. This organization includes virtually all the port and maritime workers of the nation and in the middle of 1956 claimed some forty thousand members. The only important unions in the field which are not affiliated are the two industrial *sindicatos* of the Chilean Line and the Compañia Interoceanica. The Confederación Marítima includes virtually all dockers, coastal sailors, whalers (both on the ships and in the factories processing the whales), and some fishermen. Some of the affiliates, made up of employees of government-owned shipping services are not "legal" but are nonetheless strong and effective.

The COMACH, as the maritime group is usually known from its Spanish initials, was established in the late 1940's after a considerable period of dissension and schism within its predecessor, the Federación Marítima de Chile. It is generally recognized by the government as the representative of the maritime workers and as such is given representation on the licensing board which passes periodically on the qualifications of seamen, as well as on the social security fund for the industry.

In the railroad field, the "free" Federación Industrial Ferroviaria de Chile (FIFCH) plays a very prominent role. The federation was founded in 1938 but its component parts are much older. There are three organizations making up the Federation: the Federación Santiago Watt (engineers, firemen, waterers), the Unión de Obreros Ferroviarios (nonoperating manual workers), and the Asociación de Empleados Ferroviarios (white collar workers).

Each of these three affiliates of the FIFCH has a congress every two years and the federation itself has one every three years. The author attended the Fourth Congress of the Federación Industrial Ferroviaria in January 1947. The meeting dealt with all phases of railroad activities. Perhaps the most interesting committee was the grievances commission to which were submitted more than one hundred petitions for improvement of working conditions. The commission worked to consolidate these petitions into a single memorandum which after the closing of the congress was submitted to the management of the state railways. Individual delegates to the congress also presented personal grievances of their local comrades to the directors of the state railways.

This congress of the FIFCH was dominated by politics. The majority in this case was a coalition of the Socialists and Radicals, while the Communists were the minority group. By 1956 the FIFCH was controlled by the Partido Socialista Popular, though there were Radical Party and Communist minorities, as well as a growing group of Independent workers.

Although the railroad workers are for the most part government employees and therefore have no right to form "legal" *sindicatos,* either on a local or national level, the government gives *de facto* recognition to the workers on the state railroads. The federation is the workers' agency for presenting grievances and is closely integrated in the extensive social security establishment on the railroads. Lack of legal "recognition" does not prevent the "free" organizations of the railroad workers from being as effective as any recognized groups and more effective than most.

The principal Chilean trade-union federations in 1961 were those listed below. The membership figures of those for which reasonably reliable data are available are indicated.[33]

Federación Industrial Ferroviaria (railroad workers)	25,000 members
Confederación Marítima de Chile (maritime workers)	40,000 members
Federación Telefónica (telephone)	—

Federación Electro-Gas (gas and electric workers)　　　　　　—
Federación de Trabajadores Farmacéuticos (pharmaceuti-
cal employees)　　　　　　　　　　　　　　　　30,000 members
Federación Nacional Industrial de la Construcción (con-
struction workers)　　　　　　　　　　　　　　—
Confederación de Trabajadores del Cobre (copper workers)　25,000 members
Federación Minera (coal, iron, and nitrate miners)　　　30,000 members
Asociación Nacional de Empleados Fiscales (government
employees)　　　　　　　　　　　　　　　　50,000 members
Federación del Cuero (shoe and leather workers)　　　　4000 members
Printing trades workers (three organizations)　　　　　—
Federación de Panificadores (bakers)　　　　　　　15,000 members
Federación de Trabajadores de Hoteles (hotel workers)　50,000 members
Unión de Profesores (teachers)　　　　　　　　　　—
Confederación de Beneficencia (hospital workers)　　　—
Federación de Molineros (millers)　　　　　　　　10,000 members
Federación Metalúrgica (metal workers)　　　　　　—
Federación de Bancarios (bank clerks)　　　　　　　—
Confederación de Empleados Particulares
(white collar workers)　　　　　　　　　　　　60,000 members
Textile Workers (three organizations)　　　　　　　—
Unión de Obreros Municapales (municipal workers)　　—
Asociación de Empleados Municipales (municipal white
collar employees)　　　　　　　　　　　　　　—
Federación Sindical Cristiana de la Tierra (agricultural
workers)　　　　　　　　　　　　　　　　　5000 members

Most textile workers' unions are outside any of the existing federations. Many are company unions in the United States sense.

Federations. In almost all cases, the federations have hard going financially. One of the salient features of Chilean trade unionism is the difficulty in collecting dues. This is not just characteristic of the trade unions, but of most mass organizations in the country. Even the political parties, strongly partisan as they are, find difficulty in making their members pay dues regularly.

The railroad workers', copper miners', and maritime workers' federations were perhaps the only groups in 1961 which did not have difficulty with their finances. The state railroads deduct federation dues by checkoff if the local unions ask for this procedure. And although all unions are not dues-paying members of the federation, the majority are.

The Copper Workers' Confederation was given the right to the checkoff by the Copper Workers' Statute. In the case of the Maritime Workers' Confederation, most local unions contribute regularly to the national organization.

Due to their financial difficulties, most federations do not have their own headquarters. Some have space in the offices of one of their more powerful affiliates as in the case of the Hotel Workers' Federation. The Federación Minera and the national government employees union, the ANEF, have their headquarters in the seat of the central labor group, the CUTCh.

Financial difficulties restrict many activities of the federations. Although the copper, railroad, and maritime federations as well as the Communist-controlled Federación Minera and Construction Workers' Federation are exceptions, quite a few federations do not have more than one paid official and some do not have any. In some industries it is dangerous to be an official of a trade-union federation. In 1947 officials of the mining and wood industries told the author that blacklists in their industries included the names of the officials of the federation. In the textile industry one or two employers said that they would not knowingly employ any federation leaders.

Generally speaking, the federations tend to coordinate the activities of their member unions. They frequently intervene to strengthen the hands of their affiliates in negotiating with the employers and they often raise money for unions engaging in strikes or other costly activities. In some cases they carry on organizing activities.

Some federations help to train new officials of member unions. A green office holder can come to the federation and learn how to do the paper work necessary to submit a list of demands to the employer or how to carry on some other activity. Also, the leaders of the federation affiliates are often brought together to see how things are being done in other unions and compare notes.

Confederations. Bringing together the federations and the unfederated individual unions have been the confederations or central labor organizations. The Código del Trabajo provides for these organizations but no government has so far seen fit to recognize any of them. Therefore the confederations have been "free" organizations.

However, as the late President Juan Antonio Rios pointed out, the labor confederations have been recognized unofficially by succeeding governments, which during the late 1930's and early 1940's appointed representatives of the CTCh to the executive council of the Chilean Development Corporation, to the highest price control body, and to various other semi-autonomous government bodies.[34]

The principal central labor organization since 1952 has been the Central Unica de Trabajadores de Chile, the CUTCh. It, like previous confederations, is largely a political organization. It has served as a means of propaganda for the affiliated organizations and to bring pressure on public officials and parliament.

The executive council of the CUTCh is nicely divided among the various political groups which have influence among the affiliated unions. In 1956 there were representatives of the Communist Party, the Partido Socialista de Chile, Partido Socialista Popular, Radical Party, Anarchists (who withdrew backing in 1957), and the Social Catholic Falangista Party. Votes within the executive of the CUTCh were almost always on party lines.

Two smaller confederations also existed in 1960. One of these, the Confederación Nacional de Trabajadores (CNT), was affiliated with the International Confederation of Free Trade Unions and its American regional grouping, the ORIT. In 1959 it claimed some seventy-five thousand members, principally grouped in local unions scattered throughout the country. The only national federation belonging to the CNT was the Unión General de Trabajadores de Construcción, one of several national groups in the building trades.

The second small confederation is Acción Sindical Chilena, a Catholic group. It had by 1959 organized ten small national unions, but remained a relatively minor force in the Chilean labor movement. Its principal strength was among the agricultural workers.

Union Leadership

The quality of working-class leadership is high. The capability and honesty of most of the union leaders is revealed by the fact that though many Chilean union officials handle large sums of money during a year, there is generally little defalcation and few serious mistakes are made.

The class of professional union leader such as is common in the United States is as yet only in its infancy in Chile. An outside observer is struck by the very rapid turnover in trade-union leadership. This same turnover is found in the industrial federations, and even more so in the local unions.

Even in cases where a man is reelected to an official position in a union, this will not necessarily mean that he is working full time for the union. Indeed, one of the outstanding facts about the trade-union situation in Chile is that most union leaders only work as such part time. Of course, there are exceptions. Union officials ostensibly working in the company often spend much of their time on union business, presenting grievances or doing some other union job, although still being carried on the employer's payroll. Under Chilean labor legislation a local union leader cannot hold office unless he is employed in the company whose workers are covered by his union.

The lack of a full-time union leadership—except in the case of a few non-Communist and Communist federation and confederation officials whose income comes from sources outside the union movement—is one of the principal handicaps of the trade-union movement. Since employers in Chile have become increasingly concerned with problems of efficiency and productivity, it is becoming more and more necessary for the trade unions to develop a full-time leadership with time to acquire the skills necessary for dealing with the new problems raised by the increasingly complicated nature of collective bargaining.

The unions have the financial resources necessary to develop such leaders. However, to do this, three fundamental changes will be necessary in the Labor Code. First, the law that officials of a local union must be full-time workers in the plant or office of the employer whose workers they represent will have to be amended. It might be well for the law to provide for the reemployment of a union official as such, but he should certainly be freed of the necessity of doing eight hours' work in shop or office before engaging in union activity.

The second change is a liberalization of the government's financial control over the unions. At the present time, a union is forbidden to pay a salary to any of its officials. Furthermore, the unions, if they are to be effective in dealing with productivity, inflation, and the like, must be in the position to make use of the services of experts who are not necessarily elected union officials. The unions will increasingly need the services of industrial engineers, economists, and other technicians, but it is highly improbable that the Directorate General of Labor would under the present circumstances allow a union to spend its funds on the employment of such individuals.

The third necessary change in the Labor Code is one which would give greater emphasis and encouragement to the development of national unions (the "federations" which we have discussed previously). Much of the technical work of collecting statistics, training people who can negotiate concerning piece rates and incentive pay and the like, should be done at the national union level.

At the present time, with the exception of the Confederation of Copper Workers which is covered by a special law, the Labor Code is vague about the national unions. Many local union officials are not sure whether it is permissible for them to use part of their organizations' funds to pay dues to a national organization. The federations are generally poor and weak. This situation puts a premium on the politicalization of the federations, and particularly on Communist influence in them, since it is principally those organizations which can get the services of full-time officials paid by some group outside the labor movement which can be most effective.

Political Nature of Unions. Labor leaders in Chile are still deeply influenced by the idea of the "class struggle." There are not many of the *genus lider laboriensis* in Chile who would be classified as "labor statesmen." This is due largely to the exceedingly political atmosphere which surrounds Chilean trade unionism. The parties are constantly seeking to get control of the unions, and very frequently a leading trade unionist will also be a figure of importance in a political party. Representatives of labor sit in important government bodies, either in an elective or appointive capacity, and they have a good deal to say about government policy; but they usually speak more as members of the particular party to which they belong than as trade-union representatives.

As a result of this situation, Socialist, Communist, Christian Democratic, or Radical labor leaders, as politicians must continue to talk and think in terms of the diametrically opposed interest of the working and employing classes, which is the stock in trade of their respective parties. Failure to do so will get a trade-union leader in difficulties with his political group upon whose support he depends. This situation is intensified by the traditional division of Chilean political opinion into "left" and "right"—and labor leaders must at all costs be on the "left." It is only when the current political line of his party veers toward "national unity" that the labor leader can let down his guard, so to speak.

During the 1950's there was increasing disillusionment of the rank-and-file workers, and the lower ranking trade-union leadership in the political parties which had traditionally been active in the labor movement. Concomitant with this was a growing feeling of the necessity for a less partisan leadership of the trade unions themselves. It seems likely that a liberalization of the Labor Code in the directions which we have already indicated, and the increasingly technical nature of trade-union leadership which would develop, would lead away from the excessively partisan political leadership of the unions. As union leaders became more concerned with the technical details of working out collective agreements, and dealing in a practical way with such problems as increasing productivity and getting a fair share for the workers in return, there would be less time and less concern for active partisan political activities.

Of course, one contributing factor to the partisan political nature of labor leadership has been the fact that many Chilean employers have also had a "class-struggle" outlook. Until recently there were probably few Chilean employers willing to give the union the information concerning their operation which would be necessary for really technical collective negotiations. However, during the 1950's, with the establishment of ICARE and the growing concern of many Chilean employers with the problem of efficiency and productivity, there has been a marked change in the attitude of the employers and an increasing concern on their part for the problems of human relations and improving communications and understanding with their workers, organized and unorganized.

Employers' Organizations

The Chilean entrepreneurial class is well organized although for the most part its organizations exist outside the Labor Code. The law, of course, provides for *sindicatos* of employers as well as for workers, but in manufacturing industries there were only four such groups existent in 1947, and very few if any were established subsequently. The employers have not been willing to submit their activities to the kind of supervision and direction by the state that is entailed in the case of *sindicatos* recognized under the Codigo del Trabajo.

The highest organization of the entrepreneurial class in Chile is the Confederación de la Producción y del Comercio. Under it are four subsidiary groups, covering different aspects of the economy: the Sociedad Nacional de Agricultura (National Agricultural Society), and the Sociedad Nacional de Minería (National Mining Association), the Sociedad de Fomento Fabril (Manufacturers' Association), and the Cámara Central de Comercio de Chile (Chilean Central Chamber of Commerce).

These organizations, all of which date from the nineteenth century, are not principally concerned with labor relations and deal with this phase of their members' interests only tangentially. They are principally concerned with providing technical facilities for their members and with lobbying on their behalf. Membership in these organizations is entirely voluntary and there has been no attempt, such as those made in Brazil under Vargas and in Argentina under Perón, to use them as the basis for the organization of a corporate state.

The Sociedad de Fomento Fabril takes rather more interest in labor matters than do the other three. Its members are divided into subsidiary organizations, established along industrial lines, and a few of these are *sindicatos* legally organized under the Labor Code. The legal section of the Sociedad de Fomento Fabril not infrequently advises its members in labor disputes, and the Sociedad occasionally holds conferences to discuss industrial relations problems. In 1956 the Sociedad de Fomento Fabril established a research- and statistics-gathering agency to give special attention to problems in the labor–management field. It received the advice of a representative of the National Industrial Conference Board in the establishment of this agency.

There are various organizations affiliated with the Sociedad de Fomento Fabril which are particularly concerned with labor–management relations. Perhaps the outstanding group of this kind is in the metallurgical industry, the Asociación de la Industria Metalúrgica (ASIMET).

ASIMET has a man on its staff who consults with the firms belonging to the organization in the process of their negotiations with their unions. He tries insofar as possible to coordinate the attitudes and activities of the members of the organizations, vis-à-vis their workers, and to standardize conditions in the industry as much as possible.

ASIMET has also established a Caja de Compensación to handle the problem of payment of family allowances in the industry. The law permits the establishment by groups of employers of such organizations to handle family allowances which would otherwise be paid by the Servicio de Seguro Social. Through this *caja* the employers in the metal industry contribute the same amount that they would turn over to the government and the workers pay nothing—whereas without the *caja* they would pay 2 per cent of their wage—and the workers get the same service as they would receive from the government. The officials of ASIMET maintain that the *caja* operates more efficiently than does the Servicio de Seguro Social and this will make it possible in time to pay the workers additional benefits such as subsidies for sending their children to school. The *caja* was established in September 1955.

ASIMET also has a program for training social workers in the industry which is designed not only to make them more efficient but also to raise their prestige. The organization gives courses in its headquarters in industrial social work and arranges week-long seminars for the social workers.

The organization had plans in 1956 for developing a housing project for the industry in the vicinity of Santiago. The law provides that employers must pay 5 per cent of their profits to the Corporación de la Vivienda, but if they have housing of their own they are excused from paying this tax. Although many of the larger employers in the metallurgical industry have some housing facilities of their own, none has sufficient housing accommodations for all its workers.

Another important employers' group is the Federación de Industriales de Pan (Master Bakers' Federation), which has affiliates throughout the country. The most important unit of this federation is the Unión de Industriales de Pan, covering the Santiago area and representing virtually all the bakeries in the city and province. It is the organization which negotiates and signs each year a collective agreement with the Bakery Workers' Federation.[35]

Some important employer groups are outside the Confederación de la Producción y del Comercio. One of the most important of these is the Sindicato de Constructores y Contratistas of Santiago which includes most of the builders and contractors of the capital. It was founded in 1935 and was the first organization of its kind in the field. The *sindicato* performs various services for its members such as helping them secure scarce materials and representing them on various official bodies. It also has certain mutual benefit activities, making payments to the heirs of a member upon his death.

The *sindicato* maintains a blacklist of "undesirable" workers and at the organization's meetings, opinions are voiced about various workers who have been "causing trouble." However, the *sindicato* does not enter into any collective bargaining agreements as a unit, with any of the building trades workers unions. Such negotiation is conducted by individual construction firms.

The Sindicato de Constructores y Contratistas is organized under the Código del Trabajo—one of the few groups so established. Another is the Sindicato Nacional Vitivinícola, made up of wine prodcuers, which was set up at the end of 1931 by a group which included the future President of Chile, Pedro Aguirre Cerda, one of the first chiefs of this *sindicato*. This employers' organization has a social insurance system for its members.[36]

The organization whose principal purpose is the handling of labor relations in the maritime industry is the Cámara Marítima y Portuaria which with its local affiliates carries on nearly all the negotiations with the maritime unions. This group, organized outside the Labor Code, was established in 1942 and has within its ranks the shippers in almost every port in Chile except in Magallanes and Chiloé in the extreme south where the local chamber of commerce represents the shippers. The activities of the *cámara* are discussed at considerable length in Chapter XXI.

Instituto Chileno de Administración Racional de Empresas

Until the early 1950's there was no management organization, properly speaking, in Chile. However, in 1953 the Instituto Chileno de Administración Racional de Empresas, or ICARE as it is familiarly known to the Chilean managerial class, was established. It received enthusiastic support from most of the nation's principal firms. The purpose of ICARE was to improve management procedures in all aspects. The Chilean managerial class had become aware of the need for increasing the efficiency of the country's industries and ICARE set out to provide expert instruction and advice to Chilean managers on how this might be accomplished. One of the most important fields in which ICARE is interested is that of labor and human relations in industry.

ICARE has received a great deal of cooperation from the Servicio de Cooperación Técnica Industrial, financed by Point Four funds from the United States. The first project which the Servicio carried out was to conduct several pilot studies in leading firms in Santiago. Experts of the Servicio went into a leading metallurgical firm and the city's principal clothing plant. They studied the methods of organization, production, and human relations and then suggested changes. These pilot studies were very successful. They were intended as practical demonstrations of the methods which the Servicio is trying to introduce.

The Servicio also brought several people from the United States to study the situation in Chilean industry and to talk to the industrialists on management problems. In 1956 ICARE and the Servicio cooperated in organizing what they called Operación Jefe. This was a month-long conference of selected managerial personnel held in 1956 in Viña del Mar. ICARE provided the local arrangements and some local personnel for the staff of the conference while the Servicio brought down several experts from the United States, including Dr. Earl Planty and Dr. William Newman of the Marketing Department of Columbia University. Newman had had considerable experience running similar conferences for Columbia at its Arden House conference quarters. Similar sessions were held annually thereafter.

The American experts associated with the Servicio have felt that the problems of Chilean management are approximately in the same state as those of United States industry in the early 1920's. They have realized that advocacy of time-study methods and other new management techniques might result in exploitation and hence arouse strong trade-union opposition which would seriously hamper the efforts of ICARE and the Servicio to raise the productivity of Chilean industry and they have been anxious to avoid this. They have felt that these problems should be approached slowly and, insofar as possible, with the cooperation of organized labor.

The activities of ICARE and the Servicio indicate a new concern on the part of Chilean management for raising the efficiency of the country's industry. It represents the opening of a new chapter in Chilean industrialization as well as in labor–management relations.

CHAPTER XXI

Collective Bargaining and the Collective Agreement

Collective contracts are provided for in the Código del Trabajo and it goes into some detail concerning them. However, the kind of contracts provided for in the Código are seldom entered into by workers and employers. In their place most unions and unionized employers draw up what are known as *convenios* rather than *contratos*.[1] These documents are also sometimes called *Actas de Avenimiento* or Minutes of Settlement. They generally deal only with wages and monetary fringe benefits.

The Labor Code lays down rather detailed provisions concerning how negotiations for a collective agreement are to be carried on and neither a strike nor a walkout is legal until these provisions have been followed. The code applies to all enterprises with ten or more workers or even to those with less than ten "when the conflict affects various establishments in the same industry or in similar or connected industries in the same locality.[2] The same provisions apply to disputes arising from day-to-day grievances as to discussions of prospective labor contracts.

A collective conflict originates when a meeting of at least two-thirds of the workers in an establishment decide to submit to the employer a list of demands, known as a *pliego de peticiones*.

Minutes of this meeting must be sent to the local Junta de Conciliación (conciliation board), and to the employer along with the list of demands. The legality of such a meeting is decided by the Junta de Conciliación. Conflicts can occur either in a part or all of an establishment, and the list of demands must state the group of workers involved.

The Labor Code provides that a delegation of five workers wait upon the employer with the list of demands and that no delegate can be less than twenty-five years of age or have been employed less than one year in the plant. In the case of an industrial union the delegation shall consist of the five directors or if it is impossible for them to attend, other workers designated by the meeting which draws up the list of demands. In the case of white collar workers the delegation must include the personnel delegate or the directorate of the union to which the workers belong, or other workers designated by the meeting. Where there are only five workers or less employed, all of them make up the delegation. No outsider can be on this delegation.

The employer or his representative must receive the delegation of workers within twenty-four hours of their request to wait upon him, and if he cannot immediately settle the matter at issue, he must not delay his reply for more than five days. In any case, from the moment the *pliego de peticiones* is presented no worker can be dismissed without previous permission of a labor judge who can only grant such permission in case of robbery or attack on the property of the employer, the completion of the work for which the worker was hired, immoral behavior, or abandonment of work.

The employer's reply to the *pliego de peticiones* must be in writing and a copy of it must be sent to the local Junta de Conciliación, along with a list of workers employed, their wages during the last normal pay period, and a copy of the company's last financial statement.

If an agreement is reached in direct negotiations between the employer and his workers, this accord must be embodied in a document which bears the date, the duration of the accord, the terms of the agreement, and the signatures of the union and employer representatives. One copy of this document remains with the workers, another with the employer, while the Junta de Conciliación is supposed to receive a third within twenty-four hours after the signing.

The Junta de Conciliación

If agreement cannot be reached between the employer and his workers within five days, the matter passes partly out of their hands and into those of the local conciliation board because as the Labor Code says "Conciliation will be obligatory." There is a Junta de Conciliación in each of the departments into which the country is divided. In towns where there is a large number of plants in one industry, a special conciliation board may be set up for that industry.

Each Junta de Conciliación is composed of seven members, three of whom represent the workers, three the employers, and one an impartial government chairman. Two of the workers' representatives must come from the *obrero* group, while one must be an *empleado*. (The *junta* deals with the problems of both *obreros'* and *empleados'* unions.) The *junta* functions in the capital of the department over which it has jurisdiction and is presided over by the local labor inspector with highest rank.

The members of the *junta* are chosen by lot from lists submitted annually to the governor of the department by the *sindicatos* and employers' organizations in the department. When there are no groups of employers set up as *sindicatos* under the Labor Code, any employers' organization with legal personality can submit names for the consideration of the governor. In case only one list is presented by either the unions or the employers' groups, the people named on that list automatically become members of the *junta*. If no such lists are submitted, the governor of the department is empowered to select the necessary members.

In order to be a member of a Junta de Conciliación, one must be a Chilean, at least twenty-five years old, able to read and write, have lived for at least six months in the department in which the *junta* functions, and never have been convicted of a crime. Anyone currently under indictment is ineligible. Those who are chosen as members of the *junta* cannot be excused from functioning "except for a legitimate reason certified by the governor." As long as they remain on the *junta* and for six months thereafter working class members of that body cannot be fired from their regular jobs except with the consent of the labor judge.

Most members of these Juntas de Conciliación take their responsibility very seriously. One of the workers' delegates on the Santiago provincial *junta* in the 1946–1947 period, made it his business to find in advance what cases were to appear before the *junta* at its next meeting and then to interview people involved—particularly trade-union people—so as to become aware of as many of the facts in the case as possible. Of course, all this work was done after his own laboring hours since he was employed full time as a shoemaker and was also a union official. Interestingly enough, this member of the *junta* belonged to an ostensibly Anarcho-Syndicalist union organization, the Federación Nacional de Cuero, which did not, however, prevent him from participating in the deliberations of this government institution.

The Labor Code specifies that a *junta* must have all its members present at a meeting but goes on to say that if the meeting cannot be held because of the absence of a member, a second meeting can be called and this will be held if at least two members and the president are present. Upon the third meeting call, the *junta* can function with anyone who attends. The president always has to be present, and if he is alone at this third call to the meeting he can sit in the name of the *junta*. As a matter of fact, it seems that in many instances, these provisions of the law are not strictly enforced and meetings are held with whoever appears.

The meetings of the *junta* are supposed to take place after work. According to the law, the *junta* must meet whenever called by its president and whenever there is a strike or lockout in the department.

Within forty-eight hours of the outbreak of a collective conflict the Junta de Conciliación must be notified and must call together both sides. The *junta* is supposed to confer separately with the parties and then try to bring them together on an agreement within two weeks. This means that the parties have to appear before the *junta* three different times. The first time, if no agreement can be reached, the *junta* orders them to come back one week later, and if the second meeting still cannot resolve the problem, they are called before the *junta* for the following week.

If the conciliation process is still not successful, the *junta* draws up in a private session what it considers to be a fair solution to the problem, and presents this to both parties. They have either to reject it or to accept it; they may not modify it. If it is rejected, it is then the duty of the president of the *junta* to suggest that the parties agree to arbitration. Whereas conciliation is obligatory, arbitration is not. Both employers and workers are very hesitant to submit anything to arbitration.

The meetings of the conciliation boards are very informal, the employers' and workers' representatives are not usually versed in law, and the emphasis is laid on common sense and reasoning rather than on legalism.

The importance of the labor inspector who serves as president in the proceedings of the *junta* is obvious. It is he who attempts to bring together not only the ideas of the other members of the board but those of the parties who appear before the *junta*.

It is notable that the *junta* makes its own decisions as it goes along. When, for instance, the legal advisor of the *junta* thinks one way and the members of that body another, it is the *junta* which has the final word. A friendly attitude of the members of the *junta* toward one another makes it possible to reach unanimous decisions on most issues.

It is only after this conciliation procedure has been tried that a strike or a lockout becomes legal. The Labor Code provides that after the last meeting of the Junta de Conciliación the union has twenty days in which to declare a strike. A walkout must be called by a meeting of at least two-thirds of the members of the union in which an absolute majority of those present support the strike vote. These moves must be attested to by a delegate from the Junta de Conciliación—who is chosen by the *junta* upon the request of the union involved—before the strike is legal.

As a matter of fact many of the strikes which occur in Chile are illegal. Late in 1945 President Juan Antonio Rios, in summing up the strikes which had occurred during the three years of his administration, noted that there had been 103 legal walkouts and 242 others which had been outside the law. However, he noted at the same time that only 9.2 per cent of all collective conflicts actually reached the strike stage.[3]

Once a legal strike has been called, the Labor Code provides for the formation of a strike committee of five chosen from members of the union who fulfill the requirements for election to the union directive committee.

As to the conduct of the strike, the law includes provisions against "crimes against the freedom to work," designating a sentence of sixty days in jail for offenders. These crimes include any menace against a worker by an employer or employer's association or by a *sindicato* or federation, suspension of work without fulfilling the legal requirements for a strike, and any act which destroys materials, instruments, or products or diminishes their value.[4] These provisions are rarely enforced.

Industry-Wide Negotiations

It can be seen that the conciliation procedures provided by the Labor Code lay stress on negotiations between individual employers and their respective unions. Although the possibility of industry-wide collective agreements is not eliminated, this writer has been able to discover no industry-wide agreements in Chile. However, the state railroads do have industry-wide collective bargaining, without a written contract.

Perhaps the nearest thing to a nation-wide, industry-wide contract exists in the maritime industry. The employers' Cámara Marítima y Portuaria has charge of labor relations with all stevedores and other port workers in Chile. It has local delegations in almost all the country's ports—except in Magallanes and Chiloé in the far south where the local chambers of commerce perform the functions of the Cámara Marítima y Portuaria. When a delegation of the *cámara* is formed, all the local shippers who join agree to sign over to it the right to fix the conditions under which the workers will labor and to do the collective bargaining. For instance, in Valparaiso the *cámara* has contracts with unions of stevedores, launch operators, launch watchmen, and office and clerical workers.

Demands are presented by the unions to the respective local *cámaras* from thirty to sixty days before the old contract expires. When possible these demands are settled on the local level in discussion between the union directors and the local delegation of the *cámara*. In these negotiations it was for many years a nation-wide rule of the *cámara* to grant wage rises only to the point that the government cost-of-living figures indicated cost of living had risen since the last contract.

When a list of demands is presented by a local union, a copy is immediately sent by the local delegation of the *cámara* to the national headquarters of the organization in Valparaiso along with the local chamber's suggestions for a counterproposal. The national office informs the local group if that counterproposal conforms to the general policy of the national organization. If so, it is presented and bargaining begins.

When difficulties arise in these local negotiations, the manager of the national *cámara* flies to the locality and sits in on the conference, or he summons the local chamber heads and the union directors to Valparaiso. Whenever possible, he does the latter, since it is felt that the psychological advantage is then with the employer since the workers' representatives are away from home base.

If no settlement can be reached, the general manager of the *cámara* presents the case to the Minister of Labor or even to the President of the Republic. The *cámara* tries to avoid such action, however, since its leaders have the impression that arbitrators more often make settlements on a political than on an economic basis.

An interesting sidelight on this collective bargaining procedure in the maritime industry is the refusal of the *cámara* to recognize the workers' Confederación Marítima de Chile on the grounds that it is largely a political organization and has little to do with the welfare of the workers. For several years the *cámara* manager refused to allow officials of the COMACH's predecessor, the Federación Marítima, inside his office—in the capacity of federation officials—although in some cases when a local union sent a delegation to discuss its list of demands, it designated a federation official as one of its own delegates. In this case, the employers had no alternative but to accept the man, but merely as a representative of the local union and not of the federation.

Regional Negotiations

There are various industries, particularly in the Santiago area, where negotiations are handled on a regional scale. However, the agreements, in accordance with the provisions of the Labor Code, are always signed by individual unions and individual employers. One somewhat peculiar example of this situation is the baking industry. All the bakeries in Santiago are organized. The city is divided into six districts with one union in each district and these are identified merely by number. However, only one of these, Sindicato 3, is a legal union, organized under the Labor Code. All the rest are "free" organizations—a result of the long Anarcho-Syndicalist tradition among the bakers.

When *pliego de peticiones* time rolls around, the personnel of each of the bakeries in the city presents to its respective employer a list of demands which has been drawn up previously in meetings of the Bakery Workers' Federation, to which all the unions are affiliated. One of the proposals in each *pliego* is that the workers deputize the directors of Sindicato 3 to speak for them in the Junta de Conciliación. Negotiations then begin between the Bakery Workers' Federation and the organization of the employing bakers of the province, the Unión de Fabricantes de Pan, and when the agreement is reached it is signed by Sindicato 3, which has legal recognition and is thus empowered to sign such a document, and by the Unión de Fabricantes. Usually in this industry, agreements are reached in direct negotiations with the employers. This system of negotiation has been in use for several decades.

A different approach is used by the plasterers' union of Santiago, an Anarcho-Syndicalist-controlled "free" union. It has a standard contract which it attempts to force on all the employers of the province. Its technique is to try to get its members placed on all possible jobs. Soon after the commencement of work on a building project, the plasterers on that project present the employer a list of demands—which will bring that employer up to the standard set by the union for the whole region. If the employer agrees, those become the working conditions on that project and if the employer does not agree, the workers go out on strike. The union is seldom without a strike somewhere in the city. In some of the other building trades, where legal unions exist, the regular Junta de Conciliación procedure is used.

Collective Agreements

Whether they be negotiated on an individual company basis or on a regional or national basis, there are collective agreements covering most of the country's unionized workers. The average labor agreement in Chile differs markedly from a similar document in the United States. (The Appendix illustrates a typical Chilean collective agreement.)

The content of these collective agreements has changed somewhat over the years. In the 1946–1947 period many contracts were providing for the payment of family allowances and the payment of seven days' pay for six days' work. However, these measures were subsequently enacted into law, so that they no longer needed to be discussed in labor–management negotiations.

Perhaps a typical example of a Chilean collective bargaining agreement is the *Acta de Avenimiento* between the management of the Cervecerías Unidas brewery in Concepción and its workers' union. The document was signed in the presence of the regional labor inspector by the administrator of the factory for the management and the five directors of the union on its behalf.

The first article of the agreement regulates the procedure under which the company will give dismissal pay to the workers on the basis of their years of service with the company. It is noted that this agreement has the approval of the government's social security service, which would pay this indemnity, though at a lower rate, if it were not provided for in a collective agreement.

The second item of the agreement discusses wages. It provides the maximum increase permitted under the law for the Stabilization of Prices, Wages and Salaries of January 20, 1956, that is, a boost of 46.5 per cent. The third article provides that the workers on the brewery's swing shift will receive 45 per cent more than the base wage.

The fourth article provides that the company will pay 1050 pesos a month to the workers as a housing allowance if the company does not provide them with homes. In the case of the workers who receive company housing, who have been receiving 600 pesos allowance, they will get an additional 5 per cent.

The fifth article provides for the continuance of a number of concessions which the union had previously received from the company from a Christmas bonus down to such details as thirty-six half bottles of beer for New Year's.

In the case of some enterprises, such as the telephone and electric light companies, in which there is often direct intervention by a cabinet minister or perhaps even by the President himself, the accord is likely to be a good deal longer than this agreement between the Cervecerías Unidas and its workers.

Chile, as one of the most democratic countries of Latin America, has developed the mechanism of collective bargaining to a greater extent than have some of its neighbors and it can be said that the great majority of labor disputes in the country are settled through the machinery provided by the Labor Code. For instance, in 1956 it was estimated that 95 per cent of all disputes in the metallurgical industry of Chile were settled peacefully through the Junta de Conciliación procedure.

However, a certain number of disputes cannot be adequately handled by the Juntas de Conciliación. This is especially true in the mining industry which is of particular importance because of the key role of nitrate and copper exports in the nation's foreign trade. Frequently disputes in the mining industry come to the Minister of Labor and occasionally even to the President.

The degree to which labor disputes must be settled outside legally established channels depends a great deal upon the political situation at a given time. During the first months of the administration of President Gabriel González Videla from 1946 through 1947, for instance, when there was particularly widespread political agitation in the labor movement a good part of the time of the Minister of Labor and the President was taken up with settling labor disputes. After González Videla's break with the Communists, labor disputes again tended to be settled more generally in the process of the legally provided procedures, and in the 1950's only in rare instances did labor–management disputes reach the ministerial level.

Although the crises which arise from time to time and which call for the intervention of high government officials are spectacular and sometimes of great importance, they are only one side of the picture. The disputes which are settled peacefully through the legal mechanism do not get the public attention which the others receive, but they are of great significance in labor relations in Chile. It can be said that the machinery for negotiating collective agreements works reasonably well, perhaps as well as is possible in view of the exceedingly political nature of the trade unions and the political considerations which go into the solution of any important labor dispute in that country.

The Grievance Procedure

Grievance machinery in Chilean industry is generally rudimentary. The question is seldom if ever discussed in *pliegos de peticiones* or in collective agreements, and the Labor Code in spite of being quite complete in its treatment of labor problems makes no specific mention of grievance machinery. From the context one gathers that day-to-day grievances as well as annual bouts over collective bargaining contracts are to be settled by the conciliation machinery established by the code if they become serious, but the matter rests there insofar as the law is concerned.

In fact, grievances are generally handled through direct negotiations between the employer and representatives of the union. However, particularly in the mining areas, grievances sometimes lead to appeals to the national government authorities, or even to strikes, when the procedure for settling them breaks down.

There are comparatively few industries in which there are regularly scheduled meetings between the workers and the employer. Two plants we visited in the Santiago area have a regular system of grievance procedure: the Manufacturera de Papeles y Cartones (paper-making plant) in Puente Alto and the SIAM di Tella (metal products company) in the industrial rim of the capital. Each of these companies holds regular weekly meetings of the plant manager with the five directors of the union during which problems are discussed and ironed out if possbile. This regular meeting does not completely exclude the possibility of emergency meetings, but such sessions are not frequent.

Generally the problems arising in a plant are not presented and discussed in an organized manner. Some employers accept grievances only at certain hours, but most are willing to discuss problems whenever they arise.

The number of times union leaders confer with management depends very much on the general relationship between the workers and the employers, and on the political situation within the union. Some employers complained that their union directors spent most of their time looking for things about which to complain, while others reported that the directors came in very seldom.

Most industries are small enough so that many of the grievances will go to the top management, either after several lower steps or in the case of the smallest firm, as the first step.

In the maritime industry the grievance procedure is rather different from that among land workers. When a problem cannot be straightened out right away on ships belonging to either of the two principal shipping companies (the Cia. Chilena de Navegación Interoceanica and the Cia. Sudamericana de Vapores), the crew list their complaints in a grievance book. When the voyage is over, the union leaders go aboard and examine this book to see what problems have arisen between the officers and men and then take them up with the company. On some occasions the crew will write to the union headquarters in Valparaiso and the union directors will deal immediately with the employers concerning the problem raised. Generally grievances concern differences in the interpretation of the collective agreement on the part of the captain and the crew members.

Shop Stewards. The system of shop stewards or *delegados* is quite common in Chilean industry and mining. In a business of some size there are usually delegates in various sections of the factory or mine. These stewards do not have any legal protection nor are they recognized in any way in the Labor Code, unless they happen to be directors of the union. For this reason, it is often the practice for the stewards rather than taking up the matter with the foreman themselves, to report to the members of the directorate of the union so that the latter can take up the grievances with the employer. Furthermore, many employers refuse flatly to deal with anyone in connection with grievances except the duly elected directors of the union.

However, some employers give recognition to this system of shop stewards though there is no provision for it in the law. This is the case in the country's largest textile plant at Chiguayante, a few miles outside of Concepción.

Others find it more convenient not to recognize the system in any way. For instance, in one of the big copper mines, the *delegados* are generally recognized throughout the ore reduction plant, but the management in the mine itself came to the conclusion that it was better to deal with as few workers' representatives as possible. They found that when there were recognized delegates in all sections of the mine these people often would stir up trouble in order to demonstrate their own importance within the union. The company therefore refused to recognize anyone except the five union directors. Thereafter, though the system of *delegados* continued to exist, the stewards merely served to bring grievances to the attention of the five union directors.

The degree of recognition of shop stewards differs from factory to factory. It can be said, we believe, that where the delegates exist they are usually recognized unofficially by the management. In one case, we came across an indication of the importance such recognition sometimes may have. During negotiations on a new contract with the union, the employer's representative in a big textile plant was fairly certain that the union directors were not telling the truth to the members about what was going on. So he demanded that a meeting of *delegados* be called. The stewards met and the employer's representative spoke to them, told them his side of the story with regard to negotiations and won them over to his point of view.

Usually employer recognition of *delegados* is confined to recognizing the fact that when the steward presents a problem to the foreman, it behooves the latter to take heed of what is being said.

Where the shop-steward system exists, the second step in handling grievances is for the *delegado* to present his problem to the five directors of the union. The directors, of course, are legally protected against discharge while in office and for six months thereafter, so they can face up to the boss with much more assurance than the average worker or steward.

If the factory is a very large one, the union directors deal first with the head of the shop or section in which the aggrieved worker labors. This is the case, for instance, in the Braden Company's foundry in Rancagua. In that case, many of the supervisors encourage the workers to bring their problems to them personally.

Frequently, however, the union directors have to take up matters directly with the management of the plant or mining enterprise. One employer told us that he would only allow one union director to come at a time—that he did not see why they needed more than one. Sometimes the workers themselves decide that only one or two of the directors shall take up the point.

In other cases, the political complexion of a union directorate will determine whether or not all the directors will bring cases in a body before the management. For example, in one large metal-working plant in the provinces, the manager admitted that the one minority member didn't usually get much of a hearing when he came with grievances, though the manager was very attentive to what the four majority members had to say. In the case of one mining enterprise on the other hand, where there was also a minority of one, that one union director assured us that his political partisans in the union usually brought their grievances to him and that he was generally successful in getting them straightened out. Sometimes it was reported that an employer frankly favored one group or the other in a union directorate, where the groups were more or less evenly balanced.

Problems in the Grievance Procedure. Practices differ with regard to who among the management personnel handles labor relations on the plant level. There is a widespread tendency to have the day-to-day relations with the workers handled by either a chief of welfare or chief of personnel. Whatever his title, this official will frequently deal not only with problems of collective bargaining but with every phase of relations with the workers. Of the employers who answered this question on a questionnaire we sent to most Chilean industrial employers, seventy-one replied that they had such directors, while sixty-four answered in the negative. Every employer in the mining and ceramics industries who answered the question had one or the other.

There are some welfare directors who do not wish to handle grievances and other collective bargaining matters, feeling that it should be a staff rather than a line function. In any case, if matters cannot be settled by the welfare or personnel director, they are referred to the manager of the local factory or plant.

In cases where the central office of the company is situated in Santiago or some other central location away from the actual enterprise, this central office is usually the next court of appeal. This is particularly true in the mines because in the capital the union is able to get the ear of the government. In the case of the mines, problems are often dealt with by the Minister of Labor or even the Minister of the Interior, since the government is very anxious that production not cease in the mines and hence is willing to intervene.

Sometimes special grievance problems arise. For instance, companies which have foreign employees in supervisory positions encounter much difficulty. Frequently, the foreigners do not know the Spanish language as thoroughly as they might, and confusion results from lack of understanding on both sides. Furthermore, Europeans and North Americans are unacquainted with the habits and customs of the Chilean workers and often misinterpret customary behavior. It is perhaps inevitable that there should be a certain amount of antagonism on the part of the Chilean workers against foreign bosses.

Many foreign-owned firms have put Chileans in charge of labor relations in recent years and have found that these people handle the workers and their problems better than their foreign predecessors. It is found that the number of cases in which a Chilean supervisor has come to personnel offices to straighten out problems which he does not understand or cannot cope with are few, while this was a common occurrence when most of the supervisors were foreigners.

Some grievances arising in Chilean industry are certainly of less importance in some of the more advanced industrial countries. The excessively political nature of the Chilean trade unions and the very great political consciousness of many of the workers sometimes leads to complicated problems. For instance, a supervisor in one of the copper mines noted that he was frequently faced with the situation in which workers of one political color came protesting that conditions were impossible because everyone on their shift belonged to the opposite political side. He then had to try to transfer the protesting workers to a more politically congenial shift. In fact, when the division in this mine was sharp between Socialists and Communists, the administrator in question tried to arrange for all the Socialists to be on one shift, all the Communists to be on the other, for he found that that way he got much better results from both groups.

The Chilean workers probably come to their employers with personal problems more frequently than is the case in the more advanced industrial countries, because the tradition of paternalism still lingers. This tendency to look upon the boss as a combination Simon Legree, Santa Claus, and father confessor continues even though the workers move to the cities or the mining camps.

Government Intervention. If grievances cannot be settled at the top management level, one or the other of the ministries is called in to deal with the situation if it concerns an industry of considerable importance. The following examples occurred during December 1946 and the early months of 1947: The Minister of Transportation and Communications intervened to settle a walkout of workers in the San Bernardo railroad workshops over the transfer of a worker there to another city.[5] There was intervention by the Minister of Health and the Minister of the Interior in a walkout in the hospitals of Santiago.[6] A conflict of the Braden Copper Company with its workers was immediately handled by the Minister of Labor.[7] The Superintendent of Banks was called in to mediate a dispute between A. Edwards and Cia. Bank in Valparaiso and its employees.[8]

The final court of appeal is the President of the Republic, and a good part of his time is sometimes devoted to solving labor disputes which would elsewhere be resolved through ordinary grievance procedure. During the first months of the administration of President Gabriel González Videla in late 1946 and early 1947, he was called upon to arrange settlements in a great variety of disputes of this nature.

Lack of Regular Arbitration. In Chile there are few if any instances of the North American custom of using an outside arbitrator as the last step in the regular grievance procedure. There are probably several reasons for this. First of all, the "class-struggle" attitudes of the trade-union leaders and many employers make this a difficult solution for the problem. The unionists conceive of themselves as being in perpetual and inevitable conflict with their employers and would be in danger of being regarded as "yellow" unionists if they were to accept such an arrangement.

In the second place, there is probably a lack of qualified people to function as impartial arbitrators. Most professional people who might serve in this capacity are active in politics. Government functionaries are equally influenced by political considerations and would probably make decisions with a weather eye out for what their superiors in the Ministry of Labor would say, in the light of current government policy.

Generally speaking, then, grievance procedure in Chile is still on an informal and *ad hoc* basis and is seldom if ever set forth in collective agreements. The intricate arrangement of grievance procedure found in American collective contracts is completely lacking in Chile. Along broad lines, however, it is possible to sketch the usual grievance machinery—starting with shop stewards and foremen (though shop stewards are by no means universal and have no standing in the law), progressing to negotiations between factory management and the union directors. The third step is usually appeal by the union directors—often in company with federation officials—to the central office of the company, if it is separate from the factory or mine itself. Fourth appeal is to some government official, quite often a cabinet minister, and finally if no solution is reached and the case is an important one, the matter may be thrown into the lap of the President of the Republic. The lack of formal grievance machinery and the necessity for the chief executive and his ministers to spend so much of their time in settling labor problems are two of the distinctive features of labor relations in Chile, and are perhaps not unrelated.

CHAPTER XXII

Employer Efforts to Limit Workers' Protest

A characteristic feature of Chilean labor–management relations is extensive employer paternalism. The employer extends aid to the worker which would seem unusual to a North American.

There are undoubtedly three reasons for this. In the first place, the employers have sought to divert the workers' protest. They have also on frequent occasions sought to avoid the interference of the state in what they considered their own affairs by anticipating government rules and regulations —in terms of medical service, housing, and other matters—and establishing services for the workers under their own control.

Finally, the employers have realized the tremendous problem of adapting the agrarian semi-serf to the ways of modern industrial life. The agricultural worker who had little acquaintance with money and who had depended upon his employer for virtually everything was ill-equipped to provide these things for himself out of his wages. Hence, employers have undertaken such varied activities as education, housing, medical aid, and social service work, in an attempt to adapt the rural worker to his new life in the city and at the factory bench.

The third reason for employer paternalism is the fact that many new industrial firms had no alternative. Building new industries in an under-developed country, they found that if they did not supply housing, schooling, medical aid, even retail stores, no one else would.

Hence, there has grown up a system of widespread paternalism. Workers are paid much of their real income in the form of wage supplements, some of them in cash, but many of them in kind. The worker, for his part, does not resent these wage supplements as untoward interference in his private affairs because he was used to them in the rural areas from which he came.

Wage Supplements

In some mining and industrial enterprises, supplements to wages are almost more important to the worker than his basic income. This is particularly true in the mining camps where the whole community is the creation of the mining company and nearly all necessities and comforts are provided by it. Wage supplements may be of a monetary nature—either additions to basic pay, overtime, or reductions in prices—or they may take the form of medical aid, education, and other facilities provided by the employers.

In the mining camps one of the most important forms of wage supplement is the company store. Although in the United States we regard such enterprises as a means of "exploiting" the workers, this is certainly not so in the majority of Chilean mining camps. In fact, in some it is a source of considerable loss to the company.

The company stores were generally established in the early 1930's when the peso was varying in value from day to day. They were an attempt to stabilize the wages of the workers and reduce their suffering from monetary fluctuations. The headaches of the management of the mines have come from the fact that they have been unable to raise the prices of many essential articles in these stores since the depression.

By the middle 1950's the copper- and nitrate-mining companies were anxious to get rid of their subsidized company-store system and raise prices. The unions, too, were willing to abolish the system, but it has been difficult for them to come to terms with the management.

In the case of the nitrate mines of Pedro de Valdivia and María Elena, the management decreed the abolition of the subsidized store system in the middle of 1956 without waiting for an agreement with the nitrate workers' unions. The result was a strike which closed the nitrate *oficinas* for more than two months. However, the copper mining companies have not been willing to risk such a protracted walkout and the subsidized company-stores system remains intact.

The company-stores system was not completely bad from the point of view of the companies. Copper mine officials admitted that as a result of the fact that the workers can obtain all the food they need for a small fraction of their wages, health conditions have greatly improved in the mining camps. The workers are a great deal stronger than they were a generation ago and therefore are better employees.

In the coal-mining regions the companies have had trouble with their stores. At one time they not only had their own retail establishments, but paid their workers in script good only at those stores. With the rise of unionization in the coal-mining regions, this system had to be abandoned. (Payment in script was of course illegal in any case.) The unions organized a boycott against the company store of the Schwager mines and the company finally turned the whole business over to a concessionaire with the result that the workers began to purchase there again. Sometime later the company once again tried taking over the stores, but the union again boycotted them. Thereafter, the company returned the stores to a concessionaire. By 1956 there was also a consumer's cooperative functioning at the Schwager mine.

Some manufacturing enterprises also have company stores. For instance, the sugar refinery in Penco had a store in 1947 which sold everything at prices that merely covered purchasing and merchandising costs. The company owned a farm which provided the milk and other dairy products sold in the stores. Company stores are operated by some of the larger textile plants, such as the Fábrica Italo Americana de Paños in Tomé, not far from Concepción. In this particular case the company sells only essentials such as flour, oils, coffee. The company pays the salaries of the employees who manage the store and goods are sold at cost.

The Cia. de Acero del Pacífico, the Huachipato steel plant, sought to avoid all paternalistic devices. Instead of establishing a company store, it encouraged the workers to establish consumers' cooperatives. The company does not intervene in the management of the cooperative, though it does advance the organization enough money to hire a capable manager chosen by the workers themselves. In 1956, only a year old, it was already in a position to give a consumers' dividend.

The largest employer-aided cooperative is that of the railroad workers. The cooperative is given free rent, light, and heat by the state railroads, and through large-scale buying has been able to pass on extensive savings to the railroaders. However, in recent years the railroad workers' cooperative is reported to have suffered considerably from corruption.

The company restaurant, a monetary wage supplement very common in the United States for various reasons is not so widely found in Chile. First of all, lunch time in Chile is generally two hours, giving the workers a chance to have even a short siesta. Most workers live near enough to their place of work to be able to go home. Second, a company restaurant is almost always a fertile source of grievances and many employers do not want to undertake to establish one.

Two companies in Santiago which maintain restaurants are the National

City Bank and the Vestex clothing firm. The bank has a cafeteria and the workers pay a token amount each month for the lunch so that it will not be something given free. The Vestex company has a dining room where there are facilities for heating food. However, the workers bring their own lunches.

Chilean employers are called on to a much greater degree than are their American or European counterparts to extend loans to their employees. A large number of Chilean workers live beyond their incomes and find it necessary to borrow.

The exact reasons why the Chilean worker should be so prone to borrow money are not immediately obvious. However, it seems likely that one cause is the low wage levels. Furthermore, many workers are inexperienced in handling money. Their tendency to live beyond their income once they come to the city is part of the problem of becoming acclimated to urban, industrial living.

Chilean banks have not yet established the policy of making small, unsecured personal loans. In any case, the interest rate would be a considerable handicap to most workers. As a result, it is the employer's task to meet emergencies of his workers by lending them the necessary funds.

An example of the loan policies of a Chilean company is that of the Cia. Chilena de Tabacos which grants loans for emergencies or for the purchase of furniture and other household necessities. However, the company carefully considers the loans, and the borrowers must clearly show their need. Moreover, loans never exceed ten days' pay.

Two other kinds of direct monetary supplements which were becoming widespread in collective agreements in the 1940's and which were finally written into law in 1948 were family allowances and payment of "seven days' pay for six days' work." The former became increasingly popular in Chile after its adoption during and after World War II in Great Britain, Canada, and other highly industrialized nations. The latter represents part of the attempt of the manual workers of Chile to narrow the difference in law and fact between themselves and the white collar employees. Its objective was to make the "wage" more nearly like the "salary" of the office worker.

The government's family allowance scheme provided that employers could enter into agreements with their workers' unions to provide the allowances directly, instead of through the country's social security system, if their family allowance payments were greater than those paid by the government. The law also provided that groups of employers could establish "compensation funds" to handle family allowance payments if they desired to do so.

One of the most important "compensation funds" established under the law was that of the Asociación de la Industria Metalúrgica.

Paid vacations are another form of wage supplement. Article 98 of the Labor Code provides that:

> Workers who have worked two hundred eighty-eight days during the year in an enterprise will have an annual vacation of fifteen days with full pay during that period. This vacation will be seven days for those who have worked more than two hundred twenty days and less than two hundred and eighty-eight days. . . .

Some companies go further than the legal requirement in the form of bonuses, vacations, etc.

Retirement and Dismissal

A number of companies have retirement systems for their workers. For instance, the Cia. Chilena de Teléfonos has such a plan and about thirty employees were retired in 1954 and 1955. One woman who retired was receiving thirty-two thousand pesos a month compared with thirty-eight thousand pesos she had been receiving before retirement.

The Schwager coal company, which in the 1940's had had the policy of giving old workers sinecures instead of pensioning them off, had by 1956 adopted a retirement system for deserving workers. These pensions were somewhat less than the worker's former salary and the decision as to whether a worker was to receive a pension remained entirely with the company.

The most extensive retirement system in Chile is that of the railroads. Workers can retire after fifteen years' service or after ten years' service if they are over forty-five. This very early retirement is justified by railway labor leaders on the grounds that the life expectancy of a worker of forty-five is less than a dozen years. A worker's retirement pay is based upon his length of service—with thirty years as the base. Hence, if a worker retires after ten years his retirement pay is only ten-thirtieths of his regular wage. However, those with twenty-five years' service in the night traffic department receive full pay because their job is considered more rigorous than the average. In addition to regular retirement, a railway employee can retire for reasons of health if the medical service says that further work will imperil him or imperil the railroad.

Workers who are dismissed are entitled under a law of the early 1950's to a payment depending on their length of service with the firm. The law provides that employers must pay a certain amount into a government fund for this purpose, unless they make arrangements with their workers' union to bear this cost themselves. The worker must legally receive two weeks' pay for every year of service with the firm.

Many firms continue to pay the *desahucio*—dismissal pay—themselves and generally they pay more than provided for in the law. For instance, the Gas Company of Santiago pays thirty days' pay for each year of service. The Chilean Match Company had paid dismissal allowances before they were required by law and when the law was passed, raised the amount from fifteen to thirty days' pay for each year of service. The country's principal paper company also pays dismissal allowances directly and pays more than the law demands. So does the principal petroleum distributing firm in Chile.

Some companies found it more practical to give up their own dismissal pay plans and pay money into the government's fund for the purpose. Thus, the Chilean Telephone Company, which had a system of giving twenty-five days' pay for each year of service—a system which sometimes costs as much as a million pesos—decided in 1955 to abandon its agreement with the union for this purpose and to contribute instead to the Servicio de Seguro Social fund for dismissal pay.

Employer-Sponsored Programs

Numerous employers make special agreements with the Servicio Nacional de Salud by which they agree to perform the services which are generally the duty of the Servicio. Many of these private clinics run by the more important private employers are much better than those operated by the Servicio where red tape has a tendency to create difficulties.

The mining companies undoubtedly have the most extensive medical services provided by employers in Chile. For instance, the Chuquicamata mine provides complete medical care for the workers and their families. The company employs one of the best corps of physicians in all Chile.

Many industrial employers also provide a great deal more in the way of medical aid than is demanded by social legislation. For instance, the Cia. Acero del Pacífico (Huachipato) has doctors on the job who take care of workers who get sick or have an accident while at work. Any other illness of the worker or his family is taken care of by the Servicio Nacional de Salud.

The Vestex clothing company has a doctor on duty two hours a day and a *practicante* all day. The company figures that they save at least as much as the doctor's salary in workers' time.

The Santiago Gas Company has a medical service right near the gas works. The managers of the company feel that the workers and families are much better treated by the company's doctors than they would be by those of the Servicio Nacional de Salud.

In 1956 the metal employers' Asociación de la Industria Metalúrgica (ASIMET) was studying the possibility of setting up a Hospital Metalúrgico. In doing so, ASIMET would take advantage of a provision in Chilean legislation which permits a group of employers to set up their own health facilities and thus not have to pay the social security tax for health purposes.

All the country's principal mining enterprises and some industrial employers provide educational opportunities for their workers. Although Chile's educational system is one of the best in Latin America and has been used as a model by a number of other countries in the region, the country is still plagued with a high illiteracy rate. The public educational system in the big cities is fairly good and most urban children go to public school. The situation in the rural areas and smaller towns is not as good even though there has been an extension of rural schools particularly since the days of Pedro Aguirre Cerda's Popular Front regime (1939–1942). As in most other countries, Chilean schools tend to be overcrowded and the teachers poorly paid.

Various employers report an increasing interest in education on the part of the workers. In their opinion it was caused partly by the times, and partly by the fact that many jobs now have stricter requirements. Also, a worker must read and write in order to vote and the political parties making an appeal for the workers' votes urge them to get at least that much education. Finally, the trend toward higher education levels can be credited in part to the fact that employers are raising the employment age, thus forcing young people to stay in school longer.

The mining companies and some industrial employers give educational aid to the workers and their children. The mining companies generally build the schools and subsidize the teachers' pay. Industrial employers who interest themselves in this problem frequently make scholarships available for education beyond the primary level.

Most of the large mining and manufacturing companies employ social workers. In some instances the social workers are quite frankly only serving the employers; in others they act as go-betweens for the workers and the employers; and in still others they are entirely at the service of the workers.

When the first industrial social workers started their jobs they encountered difficulties with both employers and workers.

Difficulties with the workers were more serious since the unions opposed the social workers fearing that they were employed to break the unions. The fact that they asked intimate questions in connection with their duties reinforced this feeling that the *visitadora social* was the employer snooping in the private lives of the workers. Furthermore, it was felt that the *visitadora* was trying to find out the workers' political views, which information would be used by the employer to fire "undesirable" workers. However, as Alfredo Bowen says:

> Experience soon demonstrated to the workers their mistake in the light of the point of view which the *visitadoras sociales* held, and they reacted giving the *visitadoras* their confidence, using and recommending their services and even cooperating in their work.

The problems with which the social worker in industry has to cope are complex. They make regular visits to the homes of the workers so that they are familiar with their troubles. Often the *visitadora* deals with the constitution of the family. Sometimes the administration of the family allowance is in their hands. In many cases social workers select the families who are to occupy employers' housing projects, attempting to exclude immoral individuals, and seeking to allocate houses on the basis of need.

Some social workers have also been entrusted with loans to workers. They investigate the need for loans, try to discourage workers from living on borrowed money, and urge husbands to give their wives sufficient household money instead of drinking up the week's pay.

The *visitadora social* usually works closely with the company doctor or the doctor of the Servicio Nacional de Salud, giving him information on the background of the family and sending the workers to the policlinics and hospitals when necessary. Sometimes the social workers do special work with the wives and daughters of the workers, organizing classes in reading, writing, and sewing, and advising them in connection with child raising and domestic economy. The *visitadoras* often check on the children's attendance at school and work with teachers to combat juvenile delinquency by organizing sports and other activities, in some instances establishing kindergartens.[1]

Since the social workers in Chilean industry play such an exceedingly vital role in maintaining the morale of the workers and aiding them in the transition from the semifeudal agrarian society to the higher standard of living and increased discipline of modern industrial life, their background and outlook is extremely important. Most of the industrial social workers encountered were young women of considerable intelligence and human sympathy who had received creditable training.

The housing problem has become an increasingly serious phase of labor relations in Chile. In the mines, which are a long way from the older cities and towns, it is necessary to start from the beginning and build housing accommodations even before work is started. The problem is not quite so pressing for the employer in a large city or town since the addition of one factory will generally not have much effect on housing conditions there. However, in both urban and mining areas the general housing situation is closely tied up with the whole problem of efficiency. Bad housing conditions lead to bad health conditions and low moral standards which further reduce an already low output per worker. On the other hand, if he lives in a decent home and apparently has a stake in society, the worker is more likely to work hard and earn more.

The mining companies have had a particularly pressing job to accomplish in the field of housing. For instance, there are eight thousand workers employed at the great Chuquicamata copper mine, the world's largest, which means that the company has had to build a city for twenty-five to thirty thousand people.

In most of the mining companies the houses of the white collar workers are considerably better than those of the manual workers, while those of the higher officials of the company, both Chilean and foreign, are a great deal better. At the Braden Copper Company's mine at Sewell there are four classes of facilities. Class A houses are one-family buildings occupied by the Americans on contract there. Class B homes are for high Chilean officials of the company and are also one-family affairs, virtually the same as those used by the Americans.

Class C are apartment houses occupied by white collar workers. The apartments consist of four rooms and are on a par with what one would expect in a good apartment house in the United States.

Class D houses at Sewell—four- or five-story apartment buildings with doors opening outside—are for lower grade white collar workers and manual workers. These, in contrast to the other three classes, are not rented to the occupants but are given to the workers without charge.

A number of manufacturing employers have also done a great deal in the field of housing. Many of them carried out extensive projects even before the passage of Law 7600 on October 28, 1943, which provided that each employer must contribute part of his profits to the Caja de Habitación

Popular (Popular Housing Fund), except those who constructed workers' houses to the value of 5 per cent of their profits.[2]

This law gave considerable stimulus to employers' home-building activities, since most businessmen prefer to carry out housing programs themselves rather than to throw the money down what they conceive to be the government's bottomless well. A number of Santiago employers have pooled their efforts to build a large-scale workers' housing project just outside the capital on the road to Puente Alto.

Among the best industrial employers' housing projects are those of the paper-making plant in Puente Alto, the sugar refinery in Penco, the tobacco company in Valparaiso, the Yarur textile plant in Santiago, and the Chiquayante textile plant a few miles from Concepción.

The industrial employers are faced with many of the same problems as the mines. They, too, have to teach the people how to live in the houses which are provided for them. The living standards of the average Chilean rural worker are distressingly low and more than likely he has but rudimentary sanitary facilities. When a worker moves into a well constructed building with toilets, running water, and good floors, he does not immediately change his living habits.

Thus, the average Chilean urban wage worker does not receive his full income in his pay envelope. A large part is in the form of wage supplements. This situation is undoubtedly a direct result of the rapidity of Chilean industrialization and the great gap which exists between the rural areas from which the industrial or mining worker comes and his new environment. Although the tendency in recent years has been away from paternalism, these wage supplements play a much bigger role in the life of the Chilean worker than they do in that of his Argentine counterpart, or in that of a comparable worker in the United States.

As the worker became accustomed to trade unionism he did not seek to throw off the paternalism of the employer. His unions were too largely concerned with pushing up the worker's monetary wage in the face of continuing inflation to seek to substitute cash payments for the surer payments in kind which he received. Rather, the unions tended to regard these evidences of employer paternalism as *conquistas* (conquests) of the union, and sought to extend and amplify them rather than suppress them.

The impetus for lessening paternalism has come from the employers rather than from the workers. This change of attitude is particularly noticeable in the copper mines. Also, many industrial employers such as the steel firm, Cia. de Acero del Pacífico, have been anxious to deemphasize paternalistic practices and have the worker rely on a decent wage for his support rather than upon a multiplicity of employer-managed services. The directors of the steel company have felt that their job was to produce steel not to run a complicated set of social institutions. This point of view was encountered among other smaller manufacturers.

The growing maturity of the Chilean working class is likely to make for less paternalism in the future. The major handicap to this development is inflation. Undoubtedly so long as inflation continues paternalism will remain a major factor in Chilean labor relations.

CHAPTER XXIII

Recruitment, Commitment, and Working Conditions

The average Chilean worker does not live as well as his Argentine brother, or probably as badly as his Brazilian counterpart. A traveler from Buenos Aires to Santiago is struck immediately by the relative poverty of the Chilean capital. Santiago has a certain dinginess about it which is not completely retrieved by its beautiful setting.

It is hard to say with any certainty whether the Chilean urban worker is any better off materially than he was a quarter of a century ago. He is represented in greater number, and those who have come in from the countryside are undoubtedly a great deal better off in the city.

There is no doubt that the city worker, particularly the manual worker, is poor. In his struggle to raise his level of living he has had a bitter battle against inflation. Every annual wage increase has been soon eaten up by a new round of price increases. In spite of his apparently hopeless battle with inflation, it is argued that by and large the level of living of the worker of Santiago, Concepción, and other cities is higher now than it was a generation ago. It is pointed out that clothing standards have improved; that few city workers go barefoot anymore; that the diet of the worker is more varied than it was twenty-five years ago.

It is certainly true that in some ways many workers have improved their lot—in housing for instance, although whether the construction of houses for workers has any more than kept up with the influx of the workers to the cities is not so certain. The fact is that most Chilean urban workers are still miserably poor and will probably remain so for quite a time to come.

The white collar workers are somewhat better off. They generally have higher incomes, they have better educations, and they have greater opportunities for going into debt. Indeed, the ability to borrow is one of the greatest advantages which white collar workers have over manual laborers in Chile. And it is a very widely used privilege.

There has certainly been an improvement in working conditions during the last quarter of a century. For one thing, the great number of new factories built on modern lines has created much healthier and more comfortable places to work. Vigilance on the part of the government agencies charged with factory inspection as well as the growth of the trade-union movement have also contributed greatly to this improvement.

As in Argentina and Brazil, the average Chilean worker finds employment by soliciting a job. White collar workers and some skilled workers may find openings through advertisements in newspapers though this is not as widespread as in Argentina.

In some of the big new plants it is necessary for the employer to search out the workers he wants. Thus, when the Cia. de Acero del Pacífico was being set up, the Development Corporation which was in charge of the operation recruited workers from railroad workshops and other metallurgical enterprises for special training. Some of these were sent to the United States, others were trained locally. The unskilled workers were largely drawn from the neighborhood of Concepción near which the new plant was located.

Once a worker has requested employment the prospective employer may or may not put him through some kind of test. Testing is more likely in the case of skilled workers.

In some instances the employer will look into the background of prospective employees. This is true in the Yarur textile plant in Santiago, for instance, where the management does not wish to employ any worker who has been previously employed in a textile plant or who has been active in union affairs. In some trades there are blacklists containing the names of particularly active trade unionists.

The Training of Workers

As in Argentina and Brazil, most skilled workers learn their skills from practicing them. The author has encountered comparatively few training courses in factories in Chile. Workers who claim to have skills are given a chance to prove it. Those who want to acquire skills do so by working alongside an experienced worker who has probably learned his trade in the same manner.

An important factor in the improved ability and better training of the Chilean laborer is the increasing adaptation of the urban working class to industry. Increasing numbers of young workers are entering industry who have grown up in the cities and are themselves sons of industrial workers. These young people are literate and are much better equipped than their fathers to deal with problems of technical skill, factory discipline, and the general routine of industrial life. They are able to learn in a few weeks things which it had taken their fathers—who had come in off a farm—a whole lifetime to learn well.

A growing number of workers are obtaining formal training in a school. One of the most important institutions offering technical education is the Universidad Técnica Santamaria, outside of Valparaiso. This school was founded in 1932 as the result of a bequest by one of Chile's leading millionaires, Federico Santamaria.

The Universidad Técnica Santamaria has about five hundred students in its regular daytime courses. About one-fifth of these live in dormitories on the university grounds. The institution trains skilled workers, foremen, and engineers. Its graduates have little difficulty in obtaining jobs; employers from all over Chile send representatives to the school to solicit the graduates of all levels of training.

The Universidad Técnica del Estado, a government institution, gives somewhat the same kind of training. This university was established in 1952 by bringing together a number of preexisting institutions. Most of the students in the Universidad Técnica del Estado are drawn from the forty-two government industrial schools throughout Chile. In these schools the students learn the rudiments of mechanical, electrical, woodworking, and other trades and in the university they receive additional specialized training in their chosen field of interest. Most of the students in the university leave with the grade of *técnico,* which is something more than a foreman but less than an engineer. A few students go on to the university's engineering school. Like the Universidad Técnica Santamaria, the state school gives its students background in cultural as well as technical materials. A considerable number of the students of the state institution receive training in the Instituto Normal Técnico which prepares them to be teachers in the national industrial schools and similar vocational institutions. The Universidad Técnica del Estado is run by a board of trustees which contains representatives of the Development Corporation, the mining interests, the Manufacturers' Association, the mutual benefit societies, and the trade unions.

Wages and Salaries

Once on the job, the Chilean worker finds that his wage is determined by law, collective agreements, and his own skill. In fact, the cause of most disputes between employers and workers in Chile is wages. The problem has been particularly pressing because of the catapulting cost of living in the years since World War II. Chilean employers frequently complain that their workers' unions are willing to sacrifice virtually every other possible gain if they can win an increase in wages.

The Chilean Labor Code goes into some detail with regard to the regulation of wages. First of all, it provides that all wages must be paid in legal money, that payment in kind or script is not to be considered legal. Interpretative decisions have held that payment in food is also illegal. Equality of payment for women when they do the same work as men is stipulated in the code.

Wages must be paid periodically at stipulated times. Salaries must be paid at least once a month, and the recipient is entitled to an advance on the amount due him of not more than 25 per cent payable after the fifteenth day of the month. Daily wages can be paid by the week, fortnight, or month while workers by the hour must be remunerated at least once every fifteen days. Labor undertaken on contract must be paid for at the end of the week: the full amount if the work has been completed in that period, and otherwise payment proportional to the work accomplished during the week. Finally, seasonal casual labor must be paid at the completion of the season, though the workers are entitled to receive an advance on their wages every two weeks, not to exceed 50 per cent of the value due.[1]

These provisions of the law make it possible for wage payments to become pretty complicated sometimes. For instance, in the Lota coal mines, although the workers can draw on their pay twice a week, and most of them do so once a week, there is a general clearing of accounts only on the fifth day of each month. At that time any extra payments such as bonuses for steady attendance at work, are computed and the monthly wage is completed.

The salary or wage of the worker cannot be garnished or embargoed. There is only one exception to this. If a worker is responsible for the support of someone and does not fulfill his responsibilities, a judge can require that a part of his wages (not in excess of 50 per cent) be paid to this dependent. In cases of husbands legally adjudged "vicious," the wife can collect her husband's wages. The same procedure holds in the case of a minor adjudged "vicious," whose mother thereupon receives the right to collect his wages.

The Código del Trabajo forbids employers from taking deductions from workers' wages "for rent of homes, light, water or medicine, use of tools or other reasons," or for fines not provided for in the Internal Regulations of the enterprise. On the other hand, the law provides that "the employer will deduct from the wage contributions for social security, dues for the unions and cooperatives."

The prohibitions on deductions from workers' wages lead to numerous controversies. For example, there is endless discussion as to just what "dues for the unions" consist of. Some employers will include dues which the unions themselves pay to federations or confederations to which they may belong, though most will not. Other employers will deduct various other assessments made by the unions. The deduction of death duties is fairly general on the part of the Chilean employers, while levies by general assemblies of the unions to aid some sick member are less frequently deducted. Some few are willing to deduct anything the union wishes.

The White Collar Worker. An important difference exists between the wage problems of the manual and white collar workers in Chile. The preferential position of the white collar workers was probably due to the weaker bargaining position of that group at the time the Labor Code was enacted, and the desire of those writing the legislation to strengthen the hand of this relatively unorganized group. The Chilean white collar worker was protected until early 1956 by minimum wage legislation, although there was no adequate minimum wage for manual workers. Although the nation is a signatory of the ILO convention providing for minimum wages (May 30, 1928) and ratified by the convention in 1933, it has never set up a country-wide system of minimum wages. There is provision in certain instances for establishing wage councils with representation of employers and workers as well as of the government, which can establish minimum wages in a certain industry and area. However, the number of these councils which actually have been set up is very small.

In spite of the rapidly increasing cost of living during the past few years, there have been few if any collective agreements which tied wages to the cost of living. This was largely due to the fact that agreements are renegotiated each year. Until the 1956 anti-inflation program went into effect, annual collective agreements usually provided for bringing the wage level up to the increase in the cost of living during the previous year.

Between the passage of the white collar workers' minimum wage law in

1937 and the 1956 price stabilization measures, minimum salaries for white collar workers were redetermined each year, so as to take into consideration changes in the cost of living and provide an income "indispensable to cover the imperious necessities of life of the white collar worker—such as food, clothing, social security." Virtually all those classified as white collar workers were supposed to receive this *sueldo vital,* the exceptions being workers of less than eighteen years of age whose salary could be as much as 30 per cent less than the minimum, workers between eighteen and twenty-one whose salary could be reduced to not less than 75 per cent of the *sueldo vital,* and workers of over sixty-five whose ability to work has been seriously impaired. Exception was also made in the case of apprentices but no one could be classified as an apprentice for more than six months. Also, salaries of workers who labor less than twenty-four hours a week could be reduced in proportion to the reduction in their working hours, but only after approval by the Mixed Salary Commission (Comisión Mixta de Sueldos). Finally, teachers in private schools and workers in hospitals and other charitable institutions were not subject to the minimum salary law.

The *sueldo vital* was calculated each year by a Comisión Mixta de Sueldos in each province. The mixed commissions were composed of two members and two substitutes representing the white collar workers, two members and two substitutes representing the employers, and a government-named chairman. In practice the decision of the government representative was usually final. Although the Supreme Court ruled that each person's vote can be counted separately, the custom was for the employers' and employees' representatives each to vote *en bloc.*

The employees' representatives on the Comisión Mixta de Sueldos were elected by the white collar workers' unions in the province covered by the Comisión, one vote being cast for each hundred members of a union. The representatives of the employers were chosen by the Cámara de Producción y Comercio or other responsible employers' groups. These mixed commissions were autonomous organizations, but in administration and the appointment of their personnel they were under the Ministry of Labor.

This system was altered by the measures taken in January 1956 and thereafter to restrain the country's riotous inflation. Salary increases were only allowed up to a maximum of 50 per cent of the previous year's rise in prices.

The legal minimum salaries of most white collar workers in Chile are supplemented by an annual bonus which Dr. Walker Linares maintains is really participation in their employers' profits. Companies must proportion

20 per cent of their net profits to pay a bonus not to exceed 25 per cent of the annual salary of the white collar workers. This sum is prorated, 50 per cent according to the amount earned by the worker 50 per cent according to his length of service with his employer. Employers are allowed to deduct from their net profits 8 per cent for interest on their capital and 2 per cent on the capital investment put aside as a contingencies fund. Thus, a company making only 10 per cent profit on its investment would not legally have to pay this white collar workers' bonus.[2]

Inflation. For a generation the Chilean urban manual and white collar workers have been fighting a running battle against the rising cost of living. The process of continuous price increases started in the 1930's and had already come to constitute an important problem by the end of World War II. However, after the war the inflationary spiral was intensified.

The increases in prices continued during the 1950's. A study of Chilean economic development published by the University of Chile's Institute of Economics in 1956 had the following to say about these increases:

For the purposes of comparison, the cost of living between 1939 and 1950 increased in Chile less than six times; but between that latter year and the beginning of 1956 it increased six times more, so that the increase compared with prewar was 35 times over.[3]

The workers' wages were not able to keep up with this steep increase in the cost of living. This is indicated in Table 10 which shows the increase in both the money wage and the real wage during the same period. At best the urban worker's real wage did no more than keep up with the increase in the cost of living during the decade after World War II.[4]

Table 10. Changes in money wages and real wages in Chile.
(1927–1929 = 100)

Year	Money wages	Real wages
1946	768.9	154.2
1947	960.1	144.2
1948	1173.5	149.3
1949	1389.0	148.8
1950	1672.5	155.6
1951	2071.5	157.6
1952	2746.1	171.0
1953	3308.8	164.0
1954	4501.1	129.9
1955 (December)	9164.4	115.6

The unsuccessful struggle of the urban worker to keep his wage ahead of the increased cost of living had effects which were not limited to the field of labor–management relations. It was one of the principal causes of the growing disenchantment of the urban working class with the parties of the left which had been governing the country since December 1938, and does much to explain the almost constant political turmoil which has marked Chile's political life since the Second World War. It gives some indication why the urban voter in the 1952 and 1958 elections supported the candidates who seemed most willing and able to do something about inflation.

The inflationary spiral has constituted an ever present problem in the field of labor–management relations. The constantly increasing level of prices is the principal explanation for the apparently single-minded concentration of most Chilean trade-union leaders on the problem of wage increases and augmentation of monetary fringe benefits which would give the worker more take-home pay.

The full impact of the Chilean inflation on the worker perhaps cannot be fully comprehended if one does not bear in mind that it has coincided with a large increase in the urban labor force. This has meant that it has taken place at a time when large numbers of workers were for the first time attempting to get accustomed to living on a regular wage payment instead of the meager but certain supplements offered by the rural employer. The inflation has also coincided with the first awakening of the worker's realization of the greater social and economic fluidity of the urban areas as compared with the country. Hence, just at the moment the new urban worker first achieves an ambition to improve his status or that of his children, he is faced with an apparently hopeless attempt to keep the rise in his money wages equal to the increase in the cost of living.

Inflationary pressures are also probably a partial explanation for the average trade-union leader's willingness to accept employer paternalism in such forms as housing, subsidized stores, improved medical service. Because these things have promised to provide the union members with an increased real wage, the union leader has chosen to regard them as *conquistas* rather than as a means to keep the workers quiet and undermine the position of the unions.

The "Gold Roll." There is one salary problem which has caused a good deal of discontent among certain classes of Chilean white collar workers. This is the custom of the American-owned mining companies and other concerns to pay their U.S. employees in dollars instead of in Chilean pesos. In a period in which the black market value of the dollar in terms of Chilean money was anywhere from 50 per cent to 100 per cent greater than the legal rate, this was a matter of some importance.

In recent years there has been a tendency to include a certain number of the top ranking Chilean employees in the mining camps in the "gold roll," paid in dollars. This practice was initiated to counteract the resentment among Chilean employees who were doing more or less the same kind of work as the Americans and yet were paid a great deal less for it because of the depressed value of the peso.

This question of payment of North American employees of the mining enterprises in dollars is all part of a larger problem, that of the payment of higher wages and salaries to foreigners, particularly Americans. This difference in payment is very much resented by many Chileans—not only those who are on the same general social level as the North Americans, but by the manual workers who regard this as one more example of "Yankee imperialism."

As in most things, there are two sides to this question. First of all, foreign technical help is still necessary to run the mines. Furthermore, some North American management representatives claim that the Chileans are not being trained as rapidly for these higher posts because until recently they have not been willing to go to the isolated mining camps and do the hard manual labor required of beginning engineers.

If the need for North American and other foreign technical personnel is admitted, the problem then arises as to their recompense. A North American engineer who comes down to Chile, five thousand miles away from home to live in isolation among people strange to him, speaking a language which he probably does not understand, is going to be well paid.

On the other hand, housing, food, and social status of such American personnel is usually a good deal better than would be achieved in the United States until late in their careers. They have considerable vacation periods and can go home—at the expense of their employers—once every three years. Moreover, many of the higher Chilean personnel are in a position not dissimilar to that of their American associates in that they too are living a long distance from the country's principal urban centers, in a desolate part of the country.

But, on the whole it is probably fair to say that some added pay inducement is necessary to bring skilled American technical personnel to the Chilean mining camps, and that there is some justification for the pay differentials between North Americans and Chileans. However, this question will remain for some time to come a matter of discussion—often very heated—in the field of Chilean labor relations.

Hours

The normal laboring period for the Chilean worker as specified in the Labor Code is a forty-eight hour week spread over not more than six days. The code also specifies, in the case of *obreros* that the day of rest shall be Sunday and that those workers are not to be required to work on public holidays, including May Day.[5]

This prescription of the Labor Code is generally followed in Chile. There are in the law itself some exceptions to the general forty-eight hour week in trades where continuous operation is necessary, and in other cases where for one reason or another a shorter work-week is deemed desirable.[6] Some employers have also found it preferable to limit the working days to five, instead of six, and to spread the forty-eight hours over these five days. These exceptions are relatively few, however, and generally in manufacturing the forty-eight hour, six-day week is standard.

The portal-to-portal issue which at one time caused so much controversy in mines in the United States has not been unknown in Chile. At the Potrerillos copper mine the problem was settled to the worker's advantage. His eight hours commence when he gets his ticket upon entering the mine and end when he returns this ticket at the end of the day—also at the mouth of the mine. Thus, he walks to work on the company's time and also walks out at the company's expense. Sometimes it takes as long as twenty minutes for a man to get to work from the mine entrance.

Article 130 of the Labor Code requires that the work day of white collar workers be divided into two equal halves, with at least two hours in between for lunch—probably a holdover from the traditional *siesta* period. The workers like to go home for lunch and if they live some distance from the factory need considerable time to get there.

As the result of this provision for a two-hour lunch period, the work day of the Chilean white collar worker is a good deal longer than that in the United States. Of course, the Chileans have the Latin habit of eating their evening meal quite late, judged by North American standards, so that the fact that the worker does not get home until seven o'clock does not interfere with routine.

The code does not strictly forbid work over the forty-eight or fifty-six hour limit but designates any labor performed beyond those limits as "extraordinary" and requires that overtime at the rate of time and a half be paid. Such overtime payment is usually enforced in the larger enterprises and the mines, but is not always rigidly adhered to by smaller enterprises.

Some special requirements govern overtime—there is supposed to be a written contract between the employer and the worker which specifies working hours, or if there is no such contract, overtime is to be figured from the employer's record of attendance. In any case, the workers cannot have more than two hours overtime per day when the regular work week is forty-eight hours, or forty minutes a day in the case of a fifty-six hour week.

In some exceptional cases, more than time and a half is paid for overtime. A spectacular instance of this concerned the launch operators in the port of Talcahuano in 1947. The men were working two to a launch at a given amount per ton, divided between them. Overtime beyond eight hours during the five working days of the week was paid for at four times the amount per ton per man. On Saturdays and Sundays the same 400 per cent overtime held except for the hour from midnight to one A.M. on Saturday through Sunday when they were paid at the rate of 800 per cent overtime.

Chilean labor legislation restricting working hours has helped to avoid the horrors which accompanied the earlier introduction of industrialism in other countries. Anyone who has read Frederick Engels' *Condition of the English Working Class in 1844* will remember the stories of women and little children working sixteen and eighteen hours a day in the early textile mills and virtually living and dying in those damp, dark holes.

Although many people tend to treat Latin American social legislation lightly, claiming that it is on the books merely to assuage the pride of the nations of those countries and is rarely enforced, this stricture certainly does not apply to the Chilean legislation concerning hours of labor which is generally enforced and has definitely eased the lot of the industrial worker.

Working Conditions

Of equal importance along with wages and hours of work are working conditions and these, too, are regulated by law in Chile. Article 91 of the Labor Code is very explicit, stating that: "No enterprise may initiate, renew or paralyze its activities or effect important changes without first having given notice according to the formalities provided for in the regulations, to the corresponding inspector of labor." [7]

Each employer must draw up and submit to the Dirección General del

Trabajo for approval two so-called Internal Regulations, one dealing with manual workers, the other with white collar workers. In the case of the manual workers, this Internal Regulation must include the following items:

1. The hours at which work begins and ends, and the hours of each shift, if the work is done in that way.

2. The rest periods.

3. The wage scale.

4. The minimum wage in case there is one fixed for the particular industry.

5. The place, day and hour of wage payment.

6. The obligations and prohibitions to which the workers are subject.

7. The fines applicable for violations of the Regulation.

8. Rules concerning order, hygiene and security.

9. Designation of persons to whom grievances or requests for better conditions are to be submitted.

10. Any special rules concerning particular parts of the plant with regard to the age and sex of the workers.

11. The means of fulfillment of the laws concerning social security, obligatory military service, identification card, and in the case of minors, the fulfillment of school attendance obligation.

The Internal Regulation covering white collar workers differs slightly from this and must include provisions concerning the way in which the *empleados* are to apply for their annual vacations and the procedures for electing the legal delegate of the *empleados*.[8]

Copies of the regulations must be clearly posted and each worker must receive a booklet containing these regulations. In case he desires to change them, the employer must not only get the approval of the Dirrección General del Trabajo, but must bring the changes to the attention of his workers two weeks before they go into effect.[9]

Although the law with regard to the Internal Regulations is almost universally obeyed, it should be noted that the regulations themselves are apparently not given too much thought either by the employers or the workers. They are usually very old, and are apparently seldom brought up to date.

Comparatively little attention is actually given to "working conditions" in Chilean collective agreements, although they are frequently taken up in grievance sessions. Wages are the over-all consideration in collective agreements from the point of view of the workers, hours are of somewhat less importance, and it would seem that working conditions are of least interest.

Workmen's Compensation. The prevention and compensation of accidents is a subject well covered by Chilean labor legislation. Articles 254 to 306 of the Labor Code deal with this problem and there are in addition various supplementary decrees and regulations. Chilean legislation clearly establishes the principle of employer responsibility for accidents incurred by the workers while on the job and requires the employers to pay medical costs as well as monetary compensation.

The employer is held to be responsible when an accident occurs "because of or in connection with work" and when the accident causes the incapacity for work or the death of the worker involved. There are two exceptions which it is up to the employer to prove. The first is that the accident was caused by an "Act of God outside of and without relation to the work," the second that the injury was intentionally self-inflicted. There is no provision for freeing the employer from responsibility if he can prove that an accident was caused by the negligence of the worker himself.

"All industries or employments whatsoever their nature, which employ white collar workers, manual workers or apprentices" give rise to the employer's responsibility for accidents. These include even national government and municipal employment, except in instances where the workers involved are covered by special legislation as in the case of the railroad workers. Agriculture is covered by workmen's compensation legislation. The only exceptions to this general coverage are jobs which are transitory by their very nature and jobs which employ no more than three people, and it is up to the employer to prove these exceptions.

In compensation for temporary disability, the worker is entitled to 75 per cent of his daily wage during incapacity. Compensation for partial permanent incapacity is figured on the basis of a given percentage of the base amount, which is two years' wage or salary. Article 45 of the regulations provides a list of injuries with their percentage of this base. In case of loss of some part not provided for in Article 45, the employer and worker are to agree in conjunction with the local inspector of labor and the decision reached must be reviewed by the local labor judge.[10]

In case of permanent disability, the worker will be paid a pension of 60 per cent of his annual wage, subject to Article 256, which specifies minimum and maximum payments. This pension will be paid monthly. It dates from the day on which the worker is injured, and all provisional payments must be discounted. If the totally incapacitated worker needs the constant attention of another person, he can apply to the labor judge to order payment of supplementary aid, not to exceed 20 per cent of his base pension.

In case of the death of the worker, Article 391 specifies the monthly payments of pensions or incomes, which are due from the day of death. Lump-sum payments can be arranged with the approval of the local inspector of labor.

Claims for workmen's compensation are protected by a privileged creditor status, being first-class debts of the employer, according to Article 302 of the Codigo del Trabajo. In the case of pensions for the death or permanent incapacity of the worker, the employer must guarantee payment by offering a mortgage equivalent to the amount of the debt to the Caja de Accidentes del Trabajo (Labor Accidents Fund). An alternative is for an employer to take out a policy with an insurance company whose statutes have been approved by the President of the Republic and whose paid capital is at least one million pesos, 50 per cent of which is Chilean.

The employer is obligated to submit a report of an accident immediately to the local labor judge. The latter will, if necessary, investigate the situation to see if the facts are as stated by the employer. The victim or anyone witnessing the accident may also report it. The judge then calls the parties together and tries to get them to agree on terms of compensation which he embodies in a legal decision. If it is impossible to reach such agreement the judge gives his decision on the case within three days.

The problem of industrial accidents is the responsibility of the Caja de Accidentes del Trabajo. This organization, which was set up by Decree 1267 of August 24, 1942, took over the duties which had formerly been in the hands of the accidents section of the Caja Nacional de Ahorros. It is administered by a council of which the Minister of Health is the titular head, made up of the Vice-President as chief executive officer of the caja, four members of the Chamber of Deputies, two doctors—one named by the Santiago Regional Medical Society and one by the National Medical Society, and one representative each of the employers and workers covered by the caja. The last two are appointed by the President of the Republic.

Between 70 and 75 per cent of the workers of Chile are insured with the Caja de Accidentes del Trabajo. It is not mandatory for the employer to insure with the caja; he can insure with a private insurance company and there is a certain rivalry between the private companies and the caja. The caja maintains hospitals in the principal industrial centers of the country.

The safety section of the *caja* works with employers and workers in trying to teach them the need for safety. They estimate that they have reduced accidents between 10 and 15 per cent in those plants in which they have been able to work. However, the inspectors of the safety section still run into a good deal of resistance among both workers and employers who don't understand the importance of the safety work.

The safety section has fourteen inspectors for all of Chile. When they visit a plant, a mine, or a large farm they make suggestions as to changes which should be made. Frequently these suggestions are adopted. The Servicio Nacional de Salud also does some of the same work.

The safety section has an educational program bringing engineers, employers, foremen, and workers of the Santiago area into the headquarters of the *caja* for training in safety. The growing interest of Chilean employers in improving the efficiency and productivity of their enterprises has resulted in concern for safety problems. Indicative of this was the fact that the Asociación de Industriales Metalúrgicos, one of the country's most powerful employers' groups, had agreed in the middle of 1956 to cooperate with the Caja de Accidentes in conducting a series of lectures on safety problems for the metal trades factories in the Santiago area.

Wages, hours, and working conditions in Chilean industrial and mining enterprises are thus regulated by both the government and union—employer negotiation. The technical competence of the Chilean worker has been improving, due both to experience and more adequate training. With the increasing interest of employers' groups in stepping up productivity and lowering costs, there is greater awareness on the part of employers of the need for improvement in both human relations in their enterprises and in the general working conditions in their plants.

Chile was the first of our three countries to provide for legal recognition and registration of labor organizations. Its labor code was the first of the hemisphere, and labor–management relations have grown up within its framework. However, it is characteristic of labor–management relations in Chile that the law is a good deal more strict on paper than in fact.

The development of labor–management relations in Chile cannot be understood unless one takes into account the country's economic development during the past quarter of a century and its long tradition of political democracy. Starting with the Great Depression, Chile began a rapid process of industrialization which reached a high point in the late 1940's with the establishment of the government-owned Pacific Steel Company near Concepción. Although Chile's economic progress has received considerable assistance from foreign sources, particularly the Export-Import Bank and the International Bank for Reconstruction and Development, it has been largely self-financed with a great deal of the investment being done directly or indirectly by the government. Much of this government financing has been brought about through loans from the Central Bank. This contributed heavily to the inflationary spiral which was so noticeable after the middle 1930's and was particularly rapid after the end of World War II.

The country's political democracy and the existence of a sizable number of political parties has led to great rivalry among the various parties for influence over and control of the labor movement. This political dissension in the trade unions has frequently directly influenced the relations of the workers' organizations with the employers, and has also led to political strikes and the frequent division of the labor movement into rival central labor bodies. It has also frequently resulted in the isolation of individual unions from the general body of the labor movement and sometimes to their conversion into employer-dominated company unions.

At the same time, the political importance of the unions has contributed considerably to the development of the country's social and labor legislation. Politicians of many parties have courted favor with the organized workers by passing new labor legislation or by extending social security.

Thus, the state has sought frequently to direct the workers' protest. At the same time, the politicians in control of the government have also tried to keep this protest within bounds by establishing controls over the organization and the function of the trade-union movement. They have not only established laws which provide for state supervision of union finances, elections, and even the jurisdiction and form of organization of the unions, but they have likewise established tripartite conciliation boards as a procedure for settling labor disputes. At the same time, however, the government has forced employers to deal with recognized unions and has provided the unions with considerable financial resources.

On paper these restrictions have generally been more severe than they have been in fact. However, in recent years the limitation on payment to full-time labor officials and the general limitations on the expenditure of union funds have hindered the unions' ability to deal adequately with an increasingly complicated economic situation, and to meet on even terms with employers who are newly concerned with productivity and efficiency.

There is need for a revision of the Chilean Labor Code to permit the employment by the unions of paid officials and technicians to help them in negotiations with the employers.

Such changes in the Labor Code would lead to further development of the collective bargaining procedure. It would probably lead to more complex collective agreements than those now current, which are concerned almost exclusively with wages and closely related issues.

The employers as well as the state have tried to direct the workers' protest while transforming the backward agricultural workers into modern industrial laborers. The system of paternalism is much more widespread than in either Argentina or Brazil.

In recent years there has been a trend among employers away from paternalistic practices and an increasing desire to get the worker to stand more on his own feet. However, this is new and will continue to meet resistance from the unions which have come to regard employer subsidies to the workers' standard of living as *conquistas*.

The drift away from paternalism is perhaps part of the growing interest of Chilean employers in greater productivity and lower costs, and their desire to establish labor relations similar to those of more highly developed industrial nations. Faced with an inflationary spiral which was threatening to get out of hand and seriously undermine the markets for their products, Chilean industrial employers have become increasingly interested in combatting this trend by keeping costs down themselves and getting more for their wage peso. The most obvious indication of this interest has been the creation of the Instituto Chileno de la Administración Racional de Empresas (ICARE), which is seeking in a variety of fields to encourage the rationalization of Chilean enterprises.

Note should be taken of the importance of Chilean labor–management relations in the great mining enterprises, particularly those of copper and nitrates which provide the majority of the country's foreign exchange. These firms employ the largest groups of workers of any enterprises in the nation; stability of labor relations in the mines is basic to the economic health of the country, and the situation in the mines in many ways mirrors the general situation insofar as labor–management relations are concerned Not only have the mines gone further than anyone else in paternalism, but they have been among the first employers to move away from this. Political trends among the miners are soon reflected among other groups of workers throughout the country. In recent years the Copper Statute has perhaps heralded changes in the general structure of labor organization and relations with the employers throughout Chile.

Finally, it is hard to see how either the government's extensive role in economic development or the pace of Chilean economic growth has greatly influenced the differences which one finds in labor–management relations in Chile and in the other two countries which we have studied. These differences are to be found rather in the political climate which has prevailed during most of recent Chilean history, and in the legal structure which the Labor Code imposed on labor–management relations in the nation.

CHAPTER XXIV

Inflation, Labor, and Economic Development in Argentina, Brazil, and Chile

As we have noted elsewhere all three countries have been faced with a serious problem of inflation since economic development got seriously under way in the 1930's. The rise in prices has varied in intensity from time to time. It was for a considerable period much more serious in Brazil and Chile than in Argentina, though since the late 1940's it has been as severe in Argentina. Inflation has tended generally to be more rapid in these three nations than in the highly industrialized countries, and in particular, has been more severe than in the United States.

Inflation has a serious impact upon both labor–management relations and economic development. It has engendendered widespread discontent among the urban workers in all three countries, because the workers have been forced constantly to seek new wage increases as the result of rises in the cost of living. It has tended to center the emphasis of collective bargaining and similar processes on the problem of wages. It has contributed to the considerable degree of employer paternalism existing in Brazil and Chile.

The effect of inflation on the economic development of Argentina, Brazil, and Chile has been widely debated. Generally speaking, observers feel that inflation was detrimental to development. The author disagrees. Although it has been detrimental to certain groups in the economy, inflation has been the means for providing more investment capital to those who are willing to use it than they would otherwise obtain. Although theoretically there might be other ways to accumulate capital which would be economically more efficient and socially more just, the political and social realities of the three countries have made it impossible to apply these methods sufficiently to provide the amount of capital needed. Inflation, therefore, has been virtually inevitable, if Argentina, Brazil, and Chile were to achieve economic development with the speed public opinion widely demands.

Table 11[1] indicates the increases in prices which have occurred in the three countries in recent years. For purposes of comparison, it might be noted that United States consumer prices increased 16.7 per cent between 1948 and 1957 or an annual rate of increase of 1.9 per cent.

Table 11. Cost-of-living increases in Argentina, Brazil, and Chile.
(1948 = 100)

Year	Argentina (B.A.)	Brazil (Rio)	Chile
1946	77.9	89.6	63.4
1947	88.4	90.7	84.7
1948	100.0	100.0	100.0
1949	130.0	108.3	118.8
1950	164.6	114.2	136.8
1951	224.9	123.5	167.2
1952	325.3	146.0	215.6
1953	318.4	169.8	314.7

Price increases continued in all three countries during the rest of the 1950's. They slowed appreciably in Chile as a result of the Ibañez and Alessandri governments' price stabilization programs beginning in 1956; and somewhat in Argentina after 1958, but the tempo of price rises became greater in Brazil.

Fundamental Cause of Inflation

The fundamental problem which gives rise to inflation in Argentina, Brazil, and Chile is that of finding a way to meet the needs for goods and services engendered by the drive for economic development. The stepping up of economic growth creates a large new demand for goods and services which tends to outrun the supply of these same goods and services. João Paulo de Almeida Magalhães has described this situation in general terms as it occurred in Brazil:

. . . Obliged to undertake industrialization, it was forced to create all of the capital necessary for its economic growth. Furthermore, modifications in the structure of international trade were making impossible the entry of liquid capital in sufficient quantity to help effectively in development. Our material progress depended, therefore . . . on the same conditions of austerity which accompanied the same process in France and England. We saw then a similar transition in the problem which interests us. Until 1930 the propensity to consume was high . . . let us suppose that it was approximately 90 per cent of the National Income. Investments, on the other hand, were also high because Brazil was undergoing development. We had, then, an "inflationary gap" of 10 per cent. However, this gap did not become apparent at that time, because internal savings (10 per cent) were supplemented by returns from new land and by foreign investment. If each of these elements contributed 5 per cent, we had the 10 per cent necessary to eliminate the "inflationary gap" and permit development without inflation. . . . After 1930, however, the subsidy from arable reserves and foreign capital disappeared. The potential "gap" of 10 per cent became effective, and we had, therefore, the inflationary process which today confronts the country.[2]

Dr. P. E. Ellsworth has described the role which the increased demand for investment funds arising from the economic development program played in Chile in generating the inflationary spiral (which still continues) in the period from 1939 to 1942:

It may be seen . . . that while the Central Bank has been the heaviest lender to development institutes, the other banks have joined in this financing activity. Moreover, it is noteworthy that commercial banks and the National Savings Bank expanded their loans to the government and its agencies much more rapidly than ordinary business loans, while the Central Bank has favored the two about equally.

This development contains elements of danger. In the first place, the expansion of this class of loans, especially those to development institutes, enlists the political support of important groups in the community, on the one hand by providing aid to considerable numbers of small miners, farmers and employers, on the other hand by partially embodying the deep-seated desire of influential Chileans for the economic development of their country. Merging as it does with the broad plans of the Corporación de Fomento, this lending program achieves a status and degree of influential support greater than ordinary. In the second place, since it involves the use of Central Bank funds, which can become part of the reserves of other banks, the inflationary danger of this type of financing is especially great.[3]

Another way of analyzing the basic cause of inflation in Argentina, Brazil, and Chile is to look at the problem of the relationship of savings and investment in these countries. Before industrialization began on an intensified scale, all three countries had a relatively low level of domestic savings. Investment was largely for mining or agricultural industries producing goods for sale in the highly industrialized countries, and for transportation and public utility industries serving them. Most of the savings to offset this investment came from abroad.

The beginning of industrialization, in contrast, led to a demand for large amounts of machinery, power plants, transport facilities, and other capital equipment for industries largely serving the domestic economy.

There was not sufficient an increase in voluntary domestic savings with which to offset this demand for investment goods. The nations' propensity to save remained low and the propensity to consume most of any increase in income remained high. If there were to be greatly increased investment so that development could proceed at the rate generally demanded by public opinion and government policy, extraordinary means had to be found to generate sufficient savings. It was necessary to limit the increase in expenditure on consumption goods as the total productivity of the economy rose so that increased output could be ploughed back into capital accumulation.

Composition of Demand

The increased demand which has arisen in Argentina, Brazil, and Chile as a result of industrialization has come from various sources. In the first place, the general poverty of the populace, especially in Brazil and Chile, assures that most people will spend on consumers' goods virtually all of any increase in income which they may receive.

Furthermore, the process of industrialization has brought in workers who enter the urban economy at the lowest money income level and will have to spend it all.

Added to this high tendency to consume is the demand for capital equipment. The faster the tempo of industrialization, the larger is the need for machinery, as well as for raw materials and fuel. Furthermore, the construction industry expands, in order to build the factories, housing, and roads necessary for the industrializing economy.

Industrialization also increases the demand for social services. There is also the need to divert income to training skilled personnel who can man these social services—as well as industry itself—and to pay this personnel once it has been made available.

This demand for social services is worthy of special mention. Argentina, Brazil, and Chile differ in this respect from Great Britain and many other countries which preceded them in the process of industrialization. As we have seen, there exist in these three nations not only trade-union movements, but strong political pressures for enactment of extensive labor and social security legislation. As a result, many social services which were postponed until industrialization had progressed further in Great Britain have coincided with the early stages of industrialization in these South American nations.

Finally, all three countries have experienced a kind of increased demand which has nothing to do with economic development and industrialization, but which constitutes an important drain on available savings. This is military expenditure. Argentine, Brazil, and Chile have all found it expedient to provide their army, navy, and air force with more and more expensive armaments and munitions. Pressure from politically powerful military men and competition among the South American nations have both contributed to this situation. Considerable pressure on the available supply of goods and services would be relieved if the countries would reduce their unproductive expenditures on armaments and armed forces.

In 1957, Argentina spent 5179 million pesos, 25.8 per cent of its total budget on military expenditures; Brazil, 34,048 million crubeiros, 29.2 per cent of its toal budget; Chile, 55,400 million pesos, 23.6 per cent.

All these factors which contribute to increased demand in Argentina, Brazil, and Chile also considerably increase the propensity to import in these countries. Some of the income going to the growing number of industrial workers becomes a demand for goods from abroad, since none of the three countries is completely self-sufficient in manufactured consumers' goods, and Brazil and Chile still import grains and other foodstuffs. The growth of manufacturing results in an increase in the demand not only for machinery, but also for raw materials, and even for highly skilled foreign personnel. The social services also demand foreign medical supplies and other imported products. Finally, most of the warships, airplanes, and much of the armed forces' materiel as well come from abroad.

Possible Sources of Savings

Theoretically, there are several sources from which savings can be engendered to offset the increased demand arising from industrialization. To some degree these sources have been available in Argentina, Brazil, and Chile, though we shall see that they are insufficient to meet the actual needs of those countries.

The first, and perhaps most obvious, is increased personal savings by individuals. However, the general poverty of the people of Argentina, Brazil, and Chile is the most serious limitation of all on personal savings.

In the second place, important groups in the economy with higher than average incomes who theoretically should be able to save, have only a small propensity to do so. Dr. Simon Kuznets, writing on "Economic Growth and Income Inequality" in the *American Economic Review* in March 1955, has noted this phenomenon as being general in the underdeveloped countries:

> Even disregarding the implications for the lower-income groups, we may find that in at least some of these countries today the consumption propensities of upper-income groups are far higher and savings propensities far lower than were those of the more puritanical upper-income groups of the presently developed countries. Because they may have proved favorable in the past, it is dangerous to argue that completely free markets, lack of penalties implicit in progressive taxation, and the like are indispensable for the economic growth of the now underdeveloped countries. Under present conditions the results may be quite the opposite . . . withdrawal of accumulated assets to relatively "safe" channels, either by flight abroad or into real estate; and the inability of governments to serve as basic agents in the kind of capital formation that is indispensable to economic growth.

This lack of the saving instinct is notably true of many agricultural landlords in Brazil and Chile. They tend to spend virtually all their income, leaving very little for investment even in their own *fazendas* and *fundos*. Those who do save are often misdirected, and are particularly drawn into urban real estate speculation. The Abbink Report commented on this situation in Brazil:

> . . . The concentration of the Brazilian investment potential in the construction of office buildings and of apartment houses for the relatively small groups of wealthy and moderately well-to-do people—types of investment which contribute less to a balanced economic development than do many other types of investment—has been adjudged by all observers as one of the most serious of the economic distortions experienced during the war.
>
> Many things contributed to this situation. In the first place, the general rise in prices, supported by monetary inflation, was alone enough to create a rapid increase in the value of real estate. But this increase in value was augmented by the constantly increasing use of steel-reinforced concrete construction, allowing more intensive utilization of urban land, and by the growth of the buildings. A speculative boom ensued, which rent control was powerless to stop. The capital of private persons used to construct or purchase modern apartment and office buildings, as well as smaller structures, was supplemented by the mass application of collective savings (funds of social security institutes, savings banks, etc.) and of commercial bank credit in the financing directly or indirectly of real estate.[4]

Furthermore, there are sociological factors intensifying the tendency to misdirect investment into land and urban buildings. The wealthy landlord in Brazil or Chile, who constitutes those countries' old aristocracy, has traditionally received his position of social prestige exactly because he

was an owner of large amounts of land. He still tends to think of investment in manufacturing or mining as "dirtying his hands," and as socially
beneath him. Insofar as he is inclined to do anything with his income
except spend it on conspicuous consumption, he is only willing to put his
funds in something with which he is acquainted and which he feels is
consonant with the maintenance of his social status, that is in rural or urban
land.

Another cause of the misdirection of savings in Argentina, Brazil, and
Chile has been that the means of mobilizing savings is badly organized
in all three countries. We have noted the limited range of activity of the
stock exchange as well as the fact that the majority of the industrial enterprises are still closely held corporations in which corporate stock is not
widely offered to the public.

Finally, it should be noted that there is no long tradition of saving in
these three countries. The degree of "small saving" which characterizes
the economies of most of the highly industrialized nations is lacking in
Argentina, Brazil, and Chile.

Taxation. Another possibility for mobilizing savings might be government taxation of those groups which have a "saving income" and diversion of
these savings into investment. However, this too presents serious problems.

One of the groups which might most logically be more heavily taxed
are the agricultural landowners of Brazil and Chile. At the moment, they
pay virtually no direct taxes and so pay a very small share of the total
tax bill. However, these groups have until now been sufficiently powerful
politically to prevent the governments from imposing on them their appropriate tax load. Even their small taxes are more often than not evaded.
Nonetheless, this situation is changing, with the growing relative power
of the urban areas and it seems likely that in the near future, a larger
share of the tax burden in Brazil and Chile will be borne by the argricultural
landowners. Taxes might also be designed to force them to invest more
heavily in the more vital segments of the economy.

The case of the Argentine landowners is different from that in Brazil
and Chile. During the Perón Era they were subjected to a type of price
discrimination equivalent to very heavy taxation. The government's Instituto Argentino de Producción e Intercambio bought most staple products
grown by Argentine agriculture and sold them in domestic and foreign
markets paying the agriculturalists prices far below those in the world
market. Indeed, Perón went so far in "taxing" the Argentine landlord
class that his policy did serious damage to the country's agricultural output.

In any case, the Argentine landowner has tended in the past to save a considerable part of his income and to invest it rather heavily in the improvement of his land, equipment, and cattle.

The effects on inflation which would arise from heavier taxation of some other groups with a "saving income" in Argentina, Brazil, and Chile are debatable. If, for example, heavier income taxes were laid on the industrialist class in the three countries, the net result might be to discourage saving by the single group which is presently most inclined to put its savings into industrialization. Certainly any increased taxation of this group should be so designed as to encourage rather than discourage further savings and investment by the owners of industry.

Theoretically, it might also be possible to force saving among the lower income groups by indirect taxation. Indeed, most of the tax burden of the governments of the three countries is at the present time borne by these groups. However, there are practical political limits to increasing indirect taxation, as the governments of Chile and Brazil have found out at various times when they have attempted this, only to provoke riots and other protests. These governments might be excused for choosing less obvious methods than indirect taxation for making the lower income groups increase their savings.

Foreign Sources. There are two possible ways of acquiring some of the necessary savings for economic development from abroad: increasing exports and foreign investments. Both of these have their limitations, however.

Sale of their principal mineral and agricultural products abroad have certainly played an important role in financing economic development in the recent past in all three countries. In Chile, copper sales provided in the years 1950 through 1953 between 43.9 per cent and 57.3 per cent of the country's total export income each year.[5] Between 1950 and 1954 the copper mining industry's taxes amounted to from 26 per cent to 37.5 per cent of the total amount of taxes collected by the Chilean government.

Foreign exchange turned over to the government by the copper companies was used to subsidize imports, making it possible to provide importers of goods deemed "necessary" with foreign exchange at cheaper rates than the official one. Although consumers' goods imports were given a larger subsidy by the government than capital equipment, capital goods were the single most important item benefiting by the subsidy, amounting to from 33.5 per cent to 38.9 per cent of all subsidized imports between 1950 and 1953.

Argentina in the middle 1940's presented an extraordinary example of the way in which increased returns from foreign sale of local primary products could be used to finance capital accumulation. In an article on "The Argentine Situation and the New Economic Policy" in the January 1956 issue of the Economic Commission for Latin America's *Boletín Económico de America Latina,* the anonymous author comments on this situation:

> . . . Capitalization—which must in large part be realized with imported goods—depends on the capacity to import. . . .
> Industry received an extraordinary impulse in the postwar period. During the years of the conflict the decline of imports constituted a stimulus to industrial production, thus alleviating the scarcity resulting from the restrictions and emphasizing an experience which could be used later under the stimulus of decided protection and extensive importation of capital goods. . . .
> . . . Industrial development received . . . a decided impulse from the government and in the first years after the war enjoyed external circumstances which were exceptionally favorable. . . . Industry . . . could accumulate capital thanks to the extensive imports of those years. . . .

Brazil has also depended very heavily on the foreign exchange received for its major crop, coffee, to finance that part of its industrial equipment which has had to be imported from abroad. Available foreign exchange has been channeled through the Banco do Brasil and has been made available in considerable quantities to manufacturers for importation of capital equipment.

Although foreign exchange earnings will remain an important part of the savings made available for capital accumulation, they constitute an erratic and unreliable resource, and in any case are inadequate for the rapid development which these countries seek to achieve. Furthermore, they are not likely to be subject to any rapid or sizable increase in the near future, at least in the cases of Brazil and Chile.

The difficulty with attempting to increase exports as a means of providing a margin of savings which might be used for investment is that Argentina, Brazil, and Chile have relatively little ability to influence the sale of their own exports. Raúl Prebisch, the Argentine economist who is Director of the Economic Commission for Latin America of the United Nations, has summed up the general situation of the Latin American countries in this regard:

> If we confine ourselves to the Latin American countries, it is a well known fact that their industrial imports depend decisively upon their exports of primary products. But the reverse is not true. . . . If Latin America increases in an autonomous way its purchases from the "center," the "center" will not for that reason purchase a larger quantity of Latin American primary product exports. The quantity of these (which can be sold) is controlled by factors so

powerful that the effect of variations in Latin American demand are insignificant. In consequence, any autonomous increase in Latin American imports not provoked by a previous increase in exports will only tend to create a disequilibrium in the balance of payments.[6]

The effect of this situation in creating instability in the economies of Argentina, Brazil, and Chile—and therefore making increase in exports at best an unreliable source for capital for investment—is graphically demonstrated by the situation Brazil faced when coffee prices and demand dropped in 1957. Hansen's *Latin American Letter* of September 28, 1957, comments thus on this problem:

> On a drop of 1.3 million bags in exports in the second quarter of 1957, as against the same period of 1956, Brazil saw its net reserves of gold and exchange drop by some 30 per cent and its net reserve position reduced by June 30 to *less than eight weeks* [italics Hansen's] minimum essential import requirements for economic stability.
>
> The forecast of export volume for Brazil for the year beginning October 1, 1957 would involve a 12 months' loss of about $150 million as compared with coffee-export receipts for the calendar year 1956. The price decline would involve at least another $100 million on the current expectations and could run more. . . .

The possibility of significantly increasing the exports of these three countries during the proximate future is slight. Argentina probably presents the best opportunity of the three. Reequipment of Argentina agriculture, the improvement of productive methods and possible shifting from wheat to other products for which there is a greater effective world demand might considerably raise that country's export income within a relatively short time.

Foreign Investment. Another way of getting the savings necessary for investment in Argentina, Brazil, and Chile is to acquire them from abroad through the mechanism of foreign investment in these countries' economic expansion. This has been very important in the past, as we have indicated elsewhere in this book. The Argentine railroads, packing houses, and public utilities were largely constructed with the aid of foreign funds; Brazil's railroads, mining enterprises, and public utilities were built through the same means; Chile's mines, some of her railways, and many of her public utilities were also built with foreign funds.

However, the investments which we have cited generally were either for the purpose of providing some product which was much needed in the already industrialized countries, or for service industries to help get these products to market. Today, the three countries need to accumulate capital for industries serving their own markets, not those of the United States and Western Europe. The investments these countries need today will not so quickly or so obviously "pay for themselves" in terms of foreign exchange as did investments which would almost immediately mean an increase in these nations' earnings in the industrialized countries.

Although in our opinion it would be to the advantage of the three countries to rely more heavily on savings accumulated in other countries to offset their need for capital goods, there are at least two reasons why foreign investment is not likely to provide more than a relatively small proportion of their requirements. These reasons are: (1) the lack of sufficient foreign investment and (2) the hesitancy of Argentine, Brazil, and Chile to allow foreign investment in certain very important parts of their economies.

Again, to cite Raúl Prebisch, Table 12 presents his estimates of investments from the United States in all of Latin America in the early 1950's:

Table 12. United States' investments in Latin America.
(in millions of dollars)

Year	Total of public and private investment	Repatriation and amortization	Interest and dividends	Total	Net investment
1950	265	87	554	641	376
1951	671	82	685	767	96
1952	797	93	637	730	−67
1953	714	96	648	744	30
Total	2,446	358	2,254	2,882	436
Yearly average	611.5	89.5	631	720.5	109

He goes on to note that about 30 per cent of the investments by private firms was in mining and petroleum. Prebisch also notes that part of the funds going from Latin America to the United States was covered by the increase in Latin American exports. He concludes that foreign investment during this period was "notoriously insufficient."

There is no reason to think that this situation will change drastically in the near future. The expansion of the United States economy will undoubtedly continue to use most of the private savings available in that country leaving relatively small amounts for foreign investment in Latin America or anywhere else. Although some of the European nations and

Japan may be able to supplement to some degree the savings from the United States made available to Argentina, Brazil, and Chile, these increments will be of a relatively limited nature.

Furthermore, the governmental and international public lending institutions now available are severely handicapped in making up for the lack of sufficient private funds. Not only do they have to meet the needs of all the world's underdeveloped countries as well as some needs in the economically more advanced ones as well, but their funds are in any case not sufficient to provide the kind of aid which is needed by Argentina, Brazil, Chile, and all the other countries seeking their help.

In addition to the limitation of available foreign savings now existing, there is a further difficulty with foreign funds as an aid to capital accumulation within the three countries themselves. None of them is willing any longer to have most of the investment needed in public utilities and communications done by foreign firms. Brazil is not willing to have foreigners develop her oil reserves. All have at one time or another placed certain restrictions on the repatriation of capital and the remittance of dividends on other kinds of foreign investments, because of their shortages of foreign exchange.

In the light of all these facts, it does not seem likely that foreign savings will contribute in a major degree to the further progress of the three countries' industrialization—and they have done so only to a limited degree in the past. Hence, Argentina, Brazil, and Chile have been and will be in the near future forced to rely largely on their own limited resources.

Forced Savings

One of the aforementioned means of providing the savings necessary for the investment needed for industrialization, or all of them combined, would be preferable to forced savings in terms of the welfare of the people of Argentina, Brazil, and Chile. However, the conditions surrounding their economic development make these sources insufficient for the rapid growth which these countries seek. Therefore, these nations have resorted in the past and will in all likelihood resort again in the future to forced savings as an important means of putting necessary funds into the hands of those who would invest it in economic development.

Ever since the beginning of industrialization on a large scale, Brazil and Chile have financed a considerable amount of their economies' growth through forced savings. In the case of Argentina, the period of most rapid development in industry was during the middle 1940's, when due to the very great demand for and very high prices of Argentine export products, this forced savings was channeled through IAPI, the government firm which monopolized the purchase and sale of these exports. After 1949, growth slowed down, and much of the development that did take place was due to direct state investment or state aid to private industrialists, the income for which may be said to have come in part at least from forced savings of agriculture.

The importance of forced savings in the economic development of Brazil and Chile has been attested to by various observers. In the former case, we have already noted that the Brazilian economist João Paulo de Almeida Magalhães has estimated that his country's total demand for goods and services tends to run approximately 10 per cent ahead of its normal supply of these goods and services, and that it is therefore necessary to force a reduction of this amount on consumption, if the desired rate of development is to be maintained. The United Nations Economic Mission to Chile from 1949 through 1950 estimated that for 1950 "our conclusion is . . . that it will be necessary to fill a gap of about 2000 million pesos by means of obligatory savings." This represented about 2 per cent of the total national income, and about one-fourth of the total investment needs of the year. However, in addition to this, the commission noted that the state would collect another 2000 million pesos in forced savings through the social security funds.[7]

The facts which we have discussed in previous sections of this chapter indicate that the need for forced savings is likely to continue in Brazil and Chile for some time into the future. It is likely that they will continue for a considerable period to rely on inflation and social security funds, the two principal sources of forced savings, for much of the savings which are necessary for capital accumulation. Argentina, likewise, will probably have to rely for part of its investment capital on forced internal savings, since the extraordinarily advantageous foreign trade situation she enjoyed in the late 1940's (which then provided her the necessary savings) is not likely to be repeated in the near future.

Social Security Funds. One of the two principal sources of forced savings in all three countries consists of the funds of their social security institutions. As we have noted in the respective chapters dealing with these institutions in the three countries, the social security systems receive from urban employers and their workers amounts equivalent to as much as 20 per cent of the total wage bill. These contributions are compulsory for both parties. In Chile in

1950 the contributions of employers and workers amounted to only a little less than 2 per cent of the total national income. In the other countries they also amount to an appreciable source of funds. The governments of Brazil and Chile are also supposed to contribute to the social security systems, but as we have noted elsewhere in this volume, they frequently do not do so.

Some of the funds gathered by the social security institutions of the three countries are directly invested by the social security systems themselves in developing the nations' social capital—particularly medical facilities, and to a less degree, housing. Surplus funds of the social security systems of all three countries are used to buy government bonds, thus providing the government with funds for investment and other purposes. In addition, the Brazilian institutes have by law been forced to invest in the Volta Redonda steel plant and other government development projects. The same has been true of the Chilean social security *cajas,* which have had to invest in the Huachipato steel plant and other parts of the government's development program.

Inflation. The mechanism by which inflation brings about forced saving, and in doing so stimulates economic development, in Argentina, Brazil, and Chile, and similar countries is easily described. The government, by consistently maintaining an unbalanced budget, an appreciable part of which it invests in economic development projects, pours more into the national income stream than it takes out of it in taxes. At the same time, the banking system adds to the total available income by a liberal credit policy. These processes are reflected in a rapid increase in the circulating medium.

The result of government deficits and extensive banking credit is to push prices up. As prices rise, wages go up less slowly. This results in a larger profit for the owners of industry. Since we have noted elsewhere in this volume that most manufacturing industries of all three countries have grown principally from the ploughing back of profits, this inflation and the resulting increase in profits aid the process of industrialization.

In all three nations, there has been a great deal of talk about the calamity of inflation and foreign observers have almost unanimously held that inflation was an evil. Henry Spiegel has commented on the public attitudes on this subject of politicians in Brazil, a comment which would apply as well to their confrères in Argentina and Chile.

To raise the question whether governmental ideology favors inflation as a means of forcing saving is to inquire whether the government openly favors sin. There are few Brazilian statesmen in responsible positions who have not, time and again, and in the strongest terms, professed profound aversion to inflation and promised to prevent or relieve it. Inflation has progressed notwithstanding these protestations. . . .[8]

The principal arguments offered by those who maintain that inflation is more detrimental than helpful to development are the following:

(1) Inflation leads to a distortion of the investment process, encouraging potential investors to put their funds in real property which will rise in money value as prices rise.

(2) Inflation leads to general economic instability and hence encourages many potential investors to send their funds abroad—in other words, inflation stimulates a flight of capital.

(3) Inflation, by holding down the purchasing power of the urban masses, limits the markets for industrial goods.

(4) Inflation reduces the incomes of fixed-income earners, who are generally savers. It thus cuts down a potential source of investment funds.

(5) Inflation is accompanied by a depreciation of the national currency in terms of the dollar and other "hard" currencies, and thus makes necessary imports of capital equipment more expensive in terms of the local money.

We should like to comment briefly on each of these arguments.

(1) It is certainly true that recent years have seen an extensive tendency in all three of these countries to invest in urban real estate—particularly in office buildings and upper-class housing. However, one may question whether those who are investing in this type of project would in any case be inclined to put their funds in manufacturing. Rural landowners, for instance, who are looking for a place in the urban areas to invest surplus funds would most naturally turn to real estate. As we have indicated, there are prejudices among rural landowning groups in Brazil and Chile, at least against investment in industry.

The tendency of many banks and insurance companies to invest in this same urban real estate property is in part at least the result of tradition, and could be met, in part at least, by changes in banking laws. There are signs in Brazil that rent control, particularly in office buildings, is making the kind of urban real estate speculation less profitable than it once was.

Furthermore, at least some of the investment in urban real estate is by no means a loss to economic development. Some of such investment, particularly in Chile and Argentina, has gone to build housing for white collar and manual workers. With the rapid growth of the cities concurrent with industrialization, housing is high on the list of capital needs. It might even be argued that the upper-class apartment buildings are not a dead loss to economic development since frequently they result in other buildings vacated by those occupying the new apartments becoming available for lower-income groups. However, there is little doubt that social security funds could be better used, if they were invested (particularly in Brazil) more widely in low-cost housing for members of the social security institutes, and less on speculative construction of office buildings and upper-class housing.

(2) There is certainly some truth to this. However, it would seem likely that political instability is a much more important cause for the flight of capital than is inflation. In any case, it does not seem likely to us that (with the possible exception of Brazil) the industrialists are involved to any considerable degree in this capital flight.

(3) Viewed strictly from the point of view of the rapidity of economic development, the holding down of the purchasing power of the masses is not at this moment a disadvantage, but rather an advantage. The problem of these countries is not, as in the already industrialized nations, to find sufficient aggregate demand. Rather, it is to get the supply to meet the demand already existing. That is the essence of the problem of economic development. In any case, the process of industrialization, accompanied as it is by urbanization, is creating its own demand, and will probably continue to do so for some time to come. By attracting to the cities people who have been making virtually a subsistence income in agriculture, and giving them a sizable money income for the first time, industrialization is bringing more and more people into the market for its own products.

(4) Fixed income receivers are as yet a relatively small and unimportant element in the economies of these three countries. Most government bonds are not in the hands of the general public, and other sources of fixed income are few. Perhaps the most numerous element in the fixed income group consists of social security pensioners, who are not, in any case, likely to be savers.

(5) This is undoubtedly true, and constitutes perhaps the most serious economic criticism of inflation as a means of achieving economic development in Argentina, Brazil, and Chile. However, even it may be compensated for in part by the fact that inflation limits the demand for consumers' goods—both foreign and domestic—and perhaps thus makes a larger share of foreign exchange resources available for capital goods than might otherwise be the case.

The net result of the use of inflation as a means of capital accumulation is to redistribute income in an upward direction. Insofar as this means that greater income (greater profits) is placed in the hands of the industrialists, it follows that they have more resources available for expanding their plants and equipment. Since there is relatively little investment in manufacturing from outside the ranks of the industrialists themselves, this logically leads to more investment than would be possible if they had smaller profits.

Of course, the other side of this picture is that the real wage of the workers in industry is kept lower than it would be without inflation. Table 13[9] indicates that in recent decades there has been relatively little net rise in the real wage of the industrial worker in any of the three countries.

Table 13. Real wage of workers in Argentina, Brazil, and Chile.
(1948 = 100)

Year	Argentina	Brazil	Chile
1946	70.0	92.2	91.5
1947	78.8	100.2	92.6
1948	100.0	100.0	100.0
1949	95.8	106.1	101.1
1950	92.8	107.8	102.7
1951	81.0	108.4	93.4
1952	74.9	103.0	100.0
1953	76.5	99.8	98.3

What the stability of the industrial worker's real wage over a considerable period of time means is that he has been able to benefit only in small degree from the increase in his own productivity which has arisen from his transfer from agriculture to industry. There is no doubt that the increase of his productivity resulting from this transfer has been very substantial, especially in Brazil and Chile, where most of agriculture is still highly inefficient, and where many workers are less than fully employed in it. Although the difference between the productivity of the rural worker and the industrial worker in Argentina is undoubtedly less than in the other two nations, it is still substantial. However, there too, except for the short period from 1943 to 1949, when the extraordinarily large amounts of foreign exchange earned by the country permitted an increase in both the profits of ownership and the wages of the workers, the industrial worker has received only a relatively small part of the increase in his own productivity.

Although we feel that inflation has generally tended to aid the process of economic development in Argentina, Brazil, and Chile, there is one exception to this. By the middle 1950's the inflationary spiral in Chile was rapidly getting out of hand. Prices were going up so fast that inflation was threatening the whole process of economic growth. In 1955 the cost-of-living index rose almost 100 per cent. Hardly a day passed without noticeable rises in the price of virtually all consumers' goods, as well as in raw materials and other producers' goods.

Although Chilean industrialists had become accustomed to the steady upward march of prices, the increases during 1955 became so rapid that they made reasonable calculation of costs increasingly difficult. As a result, many industrialists were reported as hesitating to make investment decisions. Since wages tended generally to lag behind prices, the rapid price increases seriously threatened to restrict the market for the products of Chilean industry. Although we have indicated that normally the question of demand is not a serious one in any of these countries, it was becoming so, late in 1955, and there was fear that the situation would get worse in this regard.

The industrialists had been demanding that action be taken for some time before the Ibañez government put into effect a program designed to slow down the tempo of inflation early in 1956. We have discussed this program at more length elsewhere in this volume.

Several conclusions follow from what we have discussed in the foregoing pages of this chapter. First of all, inflation is obviously not the most beneficial method of raising funds for capital accumulation and economic development, from a social point of view. Second, it has contributed toward such accumulation insofar as it has been a means of providing the government with those resources which it has dedicated to investment, and to the degree that it has redistributed income in the direction of the industrialists, who are in all three countries the principal investors in manufacturing.

In the third place, it is clear that some of the generally accepted arguments against inflation in an underdeveloped country do not apply, for one reason or another, to Argentina, Brazil, and Chile.

However, there are definite dangers in the use of inflation in these countries as a means for capital accumulation. On the one hand, these dangers are political and social, since inflation stirs up wide unrest among the workers. On the other hand, inflation may become so extreme as to endanger the whole process of economic development, as it threatened to do in Chile in 1955 through 1956.

Finally, less reliance would have to be placed on inflation as a source of investment funds, if these countries were willing and able to take some or all of the following measures: (1) Reduce drastically their military expenditures and divert some of these funds into economic development; (2) Establish more modern tax systems, which would adequately tax the upper-income groups, particularly those which make little or no contribution to economic development; (3) Increase their exports and divert the added income into development; (4) Provide a larger role for foreign investment.

CHAPTER XXV

Politics—the Question and the Answer

Argentina, Brazil, and Chile are all going through the growing pains of economic development and industrialization. Each nation has in its own way evolved a system of handling the inevitable conflicts between management and labor and has developed rule-making and rule-enforcing procedures for its evolving industrial economies.

There are important differences in the way labor's protest is expressed and in the way the "web of rule" is forged in the three countries. The legal structure of labor–management relations varies significantly; the degree of state control over both the expression of protest and the rule-making procedure differs in the three countries; the form and nature of the labor movement has important differences; and the role of employers in diverting labor protest and in structuring the labor force varies significantly.

What accounts for these differences? To answer this question we must take into account the similarities and differences in the economic development pattern and labor movement history in the three countries as they have been brought out in the preceding chapters.

A Background Comparison

Brazil is well endowed with the raw materials necessary for an industrial economy. She has virtually every important mineral resource except coal, and is blessed with potential or actual sources of agricultural raw materials.

Argentina also has a wide range of agricultural resources from those of her tropical north to her subarctic southland in Patagonia and Tierra del Fuego. She is less richly endowed with minerals than with agricultural resources, though in all likelihood many of the country's minerals remain undiscovered.

Chile is world-famous as a mining country, possessing copper, nitrates, coal, gold, and a host of other metals. She is enriched by agricultural resources in her Central Valley, though as yet she has not been able to develop sources of tropical agricultural raw materials and foodstuffs.

All three countries have relatively small populations in relation to the size of their territories and the size of their potential economic resources. Brazil has by far the largest population of the three, and the second largest in America, which gives her a potential market large enough to maintain one of the world's major industrial economies.

Argentina ranks second in terms of population, and also has enough people to give her a sizable internal market. Chile has the smallest population of all, a limiting factor to future economic development.

In all three countries the effective market is considerably smaller than the total population since large sections of the rural population are still virtually out of the market. In the case of Brazil, perhaps only a third of her sixty-five million people are effective consumers; in Chile a million of her six million people buy practically nothing, and many others purchase comparatively little. Argentina has the largest percentage of her population in the market as effective consumers and the market was considerably expanded during the Perón regime from 1943 to 1955.

There is little in the picture of the natural resources of Argentina, Brazil, and Chile to explain the differences in their patterns of labor–management relations. None of the three is in the position of having to substitute human labor for scarce or unavailable natural resources, as might be the case in China or India, for instance.

The tempo of development has until recent years been remarkably similar in the three countries. In all three instances, the first great impetus toward industrialization came during the First World War when the countries were cut off from their customary sources of supply for manufactured goods. The depression, by cutting down drastically on the foreign currency necessary to purchase manufactured goods, provided protection for native industry in all three countries. It also convinced large sections of public opinion of the necessity of encouraging the growth of manufacturing. The Second World War had much the same effect as the First World War, and reinforced general public opinion in favor of industrialization.

All three countries began industrialization first in the field of textiles and other consumers' goods, and textiles still remain quantitatively the most important manufactured product in all three nations. Food processing, light metallurgy, and the refining of minerals were other fields which developed during the first phase of industrialization.

World War II ushered in the era of heavy industry in both Brazil and Chile, whereas Argentina did not begin to establish its first iron and steel plant until a decade after the war. However, in all three cases, heavy industry remains a relatively small part of the industrial economy.

Since World War II the tempo of economic development has been more rapid in Brazil than in the other two countries. However, during this period labor-management relations have weakened, not strengthened, the strait jacket of state control established in the immediately prior period. The greater extent of state intervention in the processes of industrial relations in Brazil than in Argentina and Chile, therefore, cannot be explained in terms of this more rapid tempo of economic development which has transpired in recent years.

The three countries present important differences in the degree to which the state has intervened in the process of economic development. State participation has been greatest in Chile where the government's Development Corporation played a predominant role in the process for a period of fifteen years after its establishment in 1939. The least state intervention in economic development has come in Brazil, where the government has largely confined itself to trying to overcome bottlenecks in power, transportation, and other fields and to launching the first major heavy industry enterprise, the Cia. Nacional Siderúrgica. Argentina stands somewhere between Brazil and Chile in terms of state participation in economic development. During the Perón period the government played an important role through its Industrial Bank and through launching a number of projects such as a steel plant, an auto plant, an agricultural machinery factory, and an airplane motor enterprise.

A priori, one would suspect that in the country in which the state was most directly interested in the economic development process, it would be most inclined to keep a close rein on labor–management relations. In the case of Argentina, Brazil, and Chile, however, the exact opposite is the case. Industrial relations are freer of government restraint in Chile, the country in which the state is most deeply involved in economic development, and most restricted is Brazil, where economic development, particularly since World War II, has been most completely in the hands of private entrepreneurs.

There are important differences among the three countries in the role of foreign investors in economic development. The American-owned mining companies loom much larger on the economic horizon of Chile than do any foreign-owned firms in either Argentina or Brazil. In these two countries the production of the principal export products has been largely in the hands of native entrepreneurs.

In manufacturing, too, the role of foreign firms is greater in Chile than in the other two nations, being of key importance in textiles, metal products, and other fields. Finally, the participation of international lending agencies —the Eximbank and International Bank for Reconstruction and Development—has been proportionately greater in Chile than in Argentina and Brazil.

It is not clear how this greater influence of foreign capital in the economic development of Chile explains in any way the difference between the labor relations pattern there and in the other countries. Perhaps one might argue that the importance of foreign-owned enterprises in larger number has given a greater nationalist impulse to trade unionism in that country, and helps explain the greater freedom which the Chilean labor movement enjoyed over a long period of years. However, this argument is only of relative validity, and is certainly not a major cause of the differences among the three countries.

There is a striking similarity in the origins of the industrial entrepreneurial group in the three countries. Most industrialists in Argentina, Brazil, and Chile have come out of the artisan class. It has been the owners of small workshops who have built these into small factories, and have continued to pour the proceeds of the business back into its enlargement.

A secondary source of the industrial owner class in all three countries has been the old merchant group. Traders who sold goods began to make them for themselves and in time came to be more industrialists than merchants. In contrast, very little capital or personnel for the formation of industrial firms has come out of agriculture in any of the three countries. In fact, the old agricultural landlord class is inclined to look down socially on the upstart industrialists, even though the latter may be considerably richer than the old aristocracy.

It has only been in recent years that there has developed what can properly be called an industrial entrepreneurial and managerial class. It is still true in all three nations that the owners and the top managers of any given enterprise are likely to be the same individual or group of individuals. Although most manufacturing enterprises in all three countries have the corporate form of organization, there are very few which have a controlling share of their stock in the hands of the general public. Government bonds and securities rather than private stock issues are still the principal items traded in the stock exchanges of all three nations, although in Argentina there is probably wider stock ownership than in the other two countries.

As a result of the origins and nature of the majority of the industrial firms in the three countries, their owners are usually self-made men. They have not had time for the formal training characteristic of their class in the United States. As a result, it is not surprising that the managerial techniques employed by the entrepreneurial classes in these countries have been picked up in the process of directing the industries. Scientific management is still in its infancy in all three countries.

In view of the similar origins of the industrial entrepreneurs in Argentina, Brazil, and Chile, there is little here to explain the differences which have developed in their methods of handling relations with their workers.

Nor can one find in the early history of the trade-union movements in the three countries an answer to our question. The early development pattern of the workers' organizations was strikingly similar.

During the first period of the history of labor in all three countries, the trade-union movement existed principally among craftsmen rather than factory workers. There was a marked tendency toward Anarchist influence among the unions and toward a highly decentralized form of organization.

A second stage, when factory workers began to play a much more significant role, brought a shift from Anarchist to Socialist or Communist influence. At the same time, it also involved a leaning toward the organization of national unions of a given industry or trade, instead of loose federations of local labor groups. This period in all three countries began during World War I. In Chile the labor movement became largely Communist-dominated for more than a decade and since then has been mostly Socialist and Communist. In Argentina the majority of unions became Socialist in the 1920's and remained so until the rise of Perón. In Brazil the 1920's saw a bitter struggle between Communists and Anarchists, ending in a Communist victory.

This chain of development would seem to indicate that small craftsmen whose market is largely local and who still aspire to becoming master craftsmen are prone to the extreme individualism of the Anarchists. However, factory workers who are producing for the whole nation and who are subjected to a much more impersonal kind of discipline are more favorably disposed to political groups which emphasize the use of the state as a counterbalance to the employers, while at the same time they feel a greater need to put up a united front to all the employers within their particular trade or industry.

There is a common tendency among the unions of all three countries to come under the control of a political party. This would seem to be a characteristic of organized labor in virtually all underdeveloped nations—indeed, it was typical of the labor movement of the United States in the decades immediately following the Civil War.

There have undoubtedly been a variety of reasons for this partisanship on the part of the Argentine, Brazilian, and Chilean unions. Certainly in the early years of the labor movement in all three countries the only political groups which displayed any sympathy at all for the trade-union movement were the Socialists, Anarchists, and Communists, and it was therefore not surprising that most union members would look with sympathy on these three groups. In Argentina and Brazil there was the added factor that the large groups of Spanish and Italian immigrants were already disciples of the Socialist or Anarchist philosophies.

A bit later on, it was Vargas in Brazil and Perón in Argentina who were the first government leaders who actively aided the unions. It was not surprising that these two presidents were able to gain a wide following among the trade unionists.

In Chile the trade unions have for many years felt the need to have friends in congress and local governments. The workers, therefore, have been generally sympathetic to Socialist, Communist, and other parties which seemed to have an attitude favorable to the labor movement. They also generally supported the leftist governments in power from 1939 to 1952.

There is little doubt that the trade unions have both gained and lost as a result of being dominated by politicians. They have gained in terms of labor and social legislation and in given moments of crisis in labor–management relations when governments have sided with the workers. They have lost in Argentina and Brazil in terms of the independence of their trade unions from the government and in terms of the politicians' belief that pure demagoguery is the easiest way to win the ears and votes of the workers. In Chile the excessive politicization of the unions has led to constant dissension, the use of the unions for political purposes resulting not infrequently in disastrous defeats for the labor movement as a whole.

Thus, since the labor movements of all three countries have had a similar early history there would still seem to be an inexplicable difference in the labor relations of the three countries. In all three countries, the workers have not participated as much as they would like to have done in the increased productivity resulting from industrialization. However, in this regard there is an important—if temporary—difference in the situation.

During the first years of the Perón regime the workers of Argentina undoubtedly experienced the kind of increase in their real wages which the workers of Brazil and Chile have never enjoyed. This came about not only as a result of the demagoguery of Perón, but because of the peculiar circumstances in which Argentina then found herself. Being one of the world's largest producers of grains and meat, which were in critically short supply, she was able to sell these products at very high prices. Part of the return from these sales was passed on to the workers.

However, after the recuperation of European agriculture, Argentina's special position disappeared. The Argentine workers have since then been in much the same situation as those of Brazil and Chile, and have been able to share relatively little in increased returns from industrial productivity.

The reactions of the workers have undoubtedly been more violent in Chile than in the other two countries. That country has a much longer record of strikes, including general walkouts, than either of the other two. The workers' reactions have been least in Brazil, and the Brazilian workers are undoubtedly more placid and submissive than those of the other two countries. This would lead one to expect that government controls over labor relations would be greatest in Chile and least in Brazil. As we know, exactly the opposite is true.

Although some of the factors which we have discussed may give limited and partial answers to the question of why the patterns of industrial relations differ so much in Argentina, Brazil, and Chile, they are by no means separately or taken together an adequate answer. That lies in a completely different direction.

The fundamental factor in determining the different roles of the state, the trade unions, and the employers in expressing or diverting the workers' protest and in forging and applying the rules of industrial relations in the three countries has been the different political experience through which these nations have passed. It was the dictatorships of Getulio Vargas in Brazil and Juan Domingo Perón in Argentina which determined the basic nature of contemporary labor–management relations in those two countries. It was the policies of the administrations of Arturo Alessandri, Carlos Ibañez, Pedro Aguirre Cerda and their successors in Chile which have established the underlying pattern of labor relations in that country.

Thus, we have seen that it was Vargas who established the framework of the corporative *Estado Novo,* which brought into the hands of the government not only the supervision of the workers' and employers' organization, but the actual conduct of labor–management relations through the labor court system. It was the *Estado Novo,* the structure of which is still largely in existence, which substituted appeals to government tribunals for collective bargaining, which was just beginning to develop. Fifteen years of democratic government and a great deal of agitation and discussion of "free trade unionism" have not been sufficient to change the basic pattern set up by the Vargas dictatorship.

Likewise, it was the dictatorship of Juan Domingo Perón in Argentina which converted the collective contract, used before on a limited scale, into the pattern for labor–management relations in Argentina. It was the Perón regime which highly centralized not only the organization of the trade unions, but also the conduct of collective negotiation and put the control of both in the hands of the state. It was Perón, too, who established most of the labor legislation which now characterizes the labor–management field in Argentina, and established a judicial system to enforce this legislation. Finally, it was the Perón regime which converted the trade-union movement from a minor factor in the country's life into a major economic and political force.

Vargas and Perón thus sought to concentrate in the hands of the state all channels of labor protest and seize for the state the lion's share in the establishment and enforcement of the rules of industrial relations. They did so for political, not economic, reasons. Both were trying to establish totalitarian dictatorships and they could not allow the all important field of industrial relations to escape the purview of their absolutist regimes.

Furthermore, both dictators sought to base the popular support of their governments on the urban workers. For this reason it was essential that the workers have the feeling that the dictators were their only defenders. Hence, it was necessary to destroy the workers' reliance on their organizations for their defense. It was also essential to take out of the employers' hands as much of the rule-making and rule-enforcing process as possible.

On the other hand, Chile's long history of democratic government and its multiple party system is clearly reflected in the nature of that country's trade unions and their relations with the employers. It was the Alessandri administration in the early 1920's which, responding to demands of its working-class supporters, first put extensive labor legislation on the Chilean law books. It was the prolabor administrations of President Pedro Aguirre Cerda and his successors, dependent on labor votes for their election, which after 1939 were largely responsible for the growth of the trade unions into the major economic and political force which they constitute in contemporary Chile.

It is Chilean democracy, too, which explains the fact that that country's government never has tried to absorb the expression of workers' grievances and has not set itself up as the supreme arbiter of rules and regulations governing labor relations. Its democratic form of government explains why the actual controls over both labor and management are never as strict as the law would seem to indicate they should be. It explains why collective bargaining has remained the keystone of relations between workers and employers in Chile.

Thus, political factors rather than economic ones have determined the differences in the legal structure of labor relations in the three countries. It has been political considerations, too, which have determined the different degrees of state control over the expression of labor protests and the structuring of the labor force in the three nations. The form and nature of the contemporary labor movements in Argentina, Brazil, and Chile have also been determined by politics rather than economics.

The political history of the three countries has also largely determined the different role which the employers play in diverting labor protests and developing the web of rule in industry. In Chile the employers have been free to practice paternalism, and have been encouraged by legal provisions which exclude employers from paying certain social security and housing taxes if they provide the same services for their workers. In Argentina, on the other hand, at a point in the early 1940's when the fast-growing urban labor force was largely recruited from semiliterate countryfolk, and the employers might have been expected to develop more paternalistic programs than had been their wont, the Perón regime made this impossible. Perón, wanting all the credit, discouraged the employers from measures of their own.

In the case of Brazil, the paternalistic activities of the employers have also been determined largely by political considerations. After the end of the *Estado Novo,* the employers were faced with a rapid rise in Communist influence, and the establishment of the SESI and SESCI were largely motivated by this fact.

Finally, the development of labor legislation and social security in all three countries has been more dependent on political considerations than on economic ones. There was no economic justification, for instance, for such a measure as the Brazilian tenure law which forbids the dismissal of a worker after he has been employed for ten years, and which is economically damaging to both employers and workers.

The same political motivations are obvious in the social security systems of the three countries. In a quite irresponsible way successive governments in Brazil and Chile, and to a less degree in Argentina, have continued to enact law after law providing for benefits to be paid to workers who are sick, injured, and aged, and to their heirs.

The various governments have passed this legislation with little regard for the country's ability to pay for it. The demagogic nature of much of this legislation is shown by the fact that once these laws have been enacted there has been notoriously little attention paid in Brazil and only a little more in Argentina and Chile to collecting the amounts supposedly due to the social security institutions.

What is the future of labor–management relations in Argentina, Brazil, and Chile? Of course, this question will depend upon the political future. If any of these nations falls under the control of a dictator it will be impossible to predict the future of labor relations or any other phase of the life of that country. However, basing one's supposition on the hope that the three nations will continue on a democratic path there are certain generalizations concerning future industrial relations which can be made.

First of all, it seems likely that collective bargaining will continue to be the predominant pattern in Chile; to become once again the typical method of expressing the workers' protests and determining the rules of industrial relations in Argentina; and to become of increasing importance in Brazil. Although the state will continue to have a key position in these matters, its importance seems likely to decline in Argentina if democratic government and economic stability are firmly established there. If the trends in post-*Estado Novo* Brazil continue, it also seems likely that the role of the state will continue to decline as collective bargaining becomes more important. In Chile, although the government interfered more in labor affairs under Presidents Carlos Ibañez (1952 to 1958) and Jorge Alessandri (1958–60) than it had done in previous years, this interference has been motivated principally by the immediate need to slow down inflation.

Second, the profound change in attitudes of employers toward labor relations and the general problem of the organization of their industries, which we have noted, is likely to continue.

If these three countries are any indication, it would seem that in the first stages of economic development there is relatively little concern with such problems as the lowering of costs, the efficiency of management, and the extensive formal training of labor. There are undoubtedly a number of reasons for this early attitude on the part of industrial employers. For one thing, they themselves are feeling their way and have their hands full with the establishment and functioning of their firms, without paying attention to problems of scientific management.

In addition, new industrial firms in such countries as these enjoy a high degree of monopoly. They are protected from foreign competition by tariffs, exchange controls, or conditions such as war and depression, which occur in other nations and over which they have little or no control. Furthermore, there is likely in the early period of industrialization to be only one or a relatively small number of firms in any line of manufacturing, so that every firm in the field can sell its products almost without regard to costs.

However, in recent years the employers of all three countries have become increasingly concerned with costs and efficiency. This is partly due to the continuing inflation in Brazil and Chile and the beginning of an inflationary spiral in Argentina. It is due also to the broadening of the scope of industrialization and the development of greater competition among local firms. In part, too, it is due to the fact that businessmen in these countries have had increasingly greater contact with their counterparts in other countries, particularly in the United States. Not only are there branch plants of United States and European firms in these three countries, but the businessmen of Argentina, Brazil, and Chile have been visiting North America and Europe in increasing numbers. Furthermore, they are reading more and more periodicals in their field published in the more advanced industrial countries which preach the doctrines of lower costs and better human relations in industry.

All these factors have stimulated an increasing concern for the reduction of costs, the increasing efficiency of management, and the improved training of workers. The most outstanding indication of this growing interest is the establishment of the Instituto Chileno de Administración Racional de Empresas in Chile, but there are also evidences of the same concern in the other two nations. With the awakened interest of the businessmen of the three countries in the problems of developing managerial talent and putting it to the best use, and for getting greater output per worker, it is likely that a good deal more will be done in this direction in the proximate future than has been done in the past.

This increased interest of the employers in problems of labor efficiency will necessitate certain changes both in the labor law and in the trade-union organizations of the three countries. We have noted that the trade unions of Argentina are in a particularly advantageous position for dealing with these problems. Possessed of considerable amounts of money, a full-time trade-union leadership, and strong national unions, the Argentine labor movement is in a position to adopt a more technical and economic approach to their problems than they have in the past. The Argentine unions can well afford to use the services of industrial engineers, economists, and other technicians who will make it possible for them to discuss problems of labor productivity and increasing output on equal terms.

The Chilean unions, too, need this kind of approach. However, as we have indicated, the Chilean labor movement is faced with certain inconveniences in the Labor Code in the form of prohibitions against full-time labor leaders, restrictions on what the unions can use their funds for, and lack of strong national unions, which are likely to make the development more difficult.

The Brazilian unions seem for the moment least likely of any of the three labor groups to enter this phase of development. For the moment, their chief problem is acquiring more independence from the state, so that they can really engage in collective bargaining.

Industrialization has been part of and given great stimulus to a process of social revolution in Argentina, Brazil, and Chile. The evolution of a pattern of labor–management relations in each of the countries is part of the process of developing a new institutional framework to take the place of the traditional one destroyed by economic change, nationalism, and social revolt. Although there are certain common characteristics in the pattern of industrial relations in the three nations, each has been molded principally by the political experiences which the individual country has undergone in the process of being transformed from an extractive, landlord-dominated culture into a twentieth-century mixed society.

This process of social revolution has reached a critical stage in all three countries. Economic growth slowed down in both Argentina and Chile in the late 1950's, while both countries were faced with the threat of runaway inflation. In Brazil, although economic development continued under President Kubitschek from 1955 to 1961, the inflationary spiral threatened to get completely out of control.

Anti-inflation measures taken by the Ibañez and Alessandri governments in Chile and all the Frondizi regime in Argentina, under prodding of the International Monetary Fund and the United States goverment, slowed down price increase and stabilized the international value of the Chilean and Argentine currencies. However, they brought economic depression, falling national income, and a decline in real wages, thus intensifying social unrest.

The democratic future of all three nations, as well as the pattern of their labor relations, depended by 1962 on their ability to renew energetically the process of economic growth. Failure to do so seemed almost certain to bring a serious social and political crisis. Although the program of hemispheric cooperation for political development, launched in the Alliance for Progress, offered some hope that Argentina, Brazil, and Chile could once again achieve a rapid tempo of growth, which would result in at least some increase in workers' living standards, the outcome was by no means certain. The widespread feeling of frustration and even desparation among the workers of the three countries might well find expression in one or more of these nations seeking to resolve their dilemma along the lines already made popular in the hemisphere by Fidel Castro.

APPENDIX

Chilean Collective Bargaining Agreement

MINUTES OF AGREEMENT

In Concepción on February 13, 1956, in the Office of the Administrator of the Concepción Brewery of United Breweries, and in the presence of the Provincial Labor Inspector, there met Don Rene Novoa Carabantes, Administrator of the Brewery in representation of the Firm, and the Directors of the *Sindicato Industrial,* consisting of its President, Don Temistocles Burgo, its Secretary, Don Luis Soto, its Treasurer, Don Hector Ayala, and Directors, Messrs. Bernardo Hermosilla and Gilberto Susperreguy, who were duly authorized to conclude a total and definitive agreement to end the collective conflict commenced by the list of demands dated December 29, 1955, in the following terms:

1. INDEMNITY FOR YEARS OF SERVICE.—After informing and getting permission from the Servicio de Seguro Social, the Company will continue paying directly to its workers dismissal pay on the following basis: For 1953 and previous years, calculations will be on the basis of complete years of service worked in the Industry, at the rate of twenty-five days' wage per year's service at the 1953 rate. For 1954 and 1955 payment will be twenty-five days' basic wage at the 1955 rate. For the period after January 1, 1956, the Company will pay an indemnity for years of service equivalent to 8.33 per cent of the base wage gained from that day forward.

This indemnity for years of service will be paid only when the termination of the worker's contract comes about because the worker is dismissed by the Company or dies while his contract is still in force. It will not be paid when the worker's contract is ended because of reasons set forth in sections 6, 7, 8, 9, 10, and 11 of Article 9 of the Codigo del Trabajo.

The Company will also pay this indemnity in case of voluntary withdrawal, with the limitation that it will not be paid to more than two such workers, and must be in conformity with the Regulations which govern this matter.

2. WAGES.—Wages will be increased in conformity with the Law for the Stabilization of Prices, Salaries, and Wages, No. 12,006 which has been in effect since its promulgation and publication in the *Diario Oficial* on January 20, 1956 . . . and which says that privately employed workers in Industry and Commerce will have increases in their basic wages equivalent to 50 per cent of the rise in the cost of living determined by the Central Bank and the National Statistical Service, which is to say, according to official statistics, 46.5 per cent.

Therefore the base wages which applied in the Concepción Brewery of the United Breweries on December 31, 1955, will be increased by 46.5 per cent.

3. BONUS FOR SHIFT C.—The early morning shift (Shift C) will receive a bonus of 45 per cent of their base pay, with the exception of porters and watchmen.

4. RENT ALLOWANCE.—The Company will pay monthly to its workers who do not occupy houses belonging to the Company a monthly allowance of 1050 pesos.

The workers who occupy houses belonging to the Company and who now receive a rent allowance of five hundred pesos will receive an increase in this allowance of 5 per cent and the rent which they now pay for these houses will be increased 5 per cent.

5. MAINTENANCE OF BENEFITS.—The following benefits will be maintained:

(a) Christmas Bonus.—Twenty days of the base wage to workers with more than six months' service in the Industry.

(b) Vacation Bonus.—When the workers take their legal vacation they will receive a special allowance of 4800 pesos each. This will not form part of the base wage.

(c) Clothing.—The grant of work clothing already established in accordance with the Hygiene and Industrial Security Regulation will be maintained.

(d) Birth Allowance.—The birth allowance will be 3200 pesos, for each child of legitimate birth, and accredited as such by the Social Worker of the Factory.

(e) Death Benefits.—The Company will grant death benefits of 8000 pesos to the family of workers who die, to be paid by the Administration.

(f) Beer and Soft Drink Ration.—The Company will give the workers thirty-six half bottles of beer and thirty-six bottles of soft drinks on the National Holiday and thirty-six half bottles of beer on New Year's.

(g) Christmas Fiesta.—The children of the workers will continue to be given toys and candies in accordance with the regulations now in force.

(h) Leave for Union Leaders.—Union officials will continue to receive authorization to attend up to two meetings a year of their Federation, for a maximum of three days apiece.

(i) Family Death.—The agreement not to suspend payment of seven days' wages per week if the cause of missing work is death of a member of the immediate family is maintained, and permission for such payment must be applied for to the Administration.

It is emphasized that aside from the benefits herein stated, there are no other benefits in effect, and the Company will not grant, and the workers have no right to any other which is not provided for in the Law.

OVERTIME WORK.—Since this is a seasonal industry, the workers agree to work up to two hours a day extra, when the Administration requests it in the departments of the Brewery and where there is the necessary personnel.

RETROACTIVE EFFECT.—In view of the willingness of the *Sindicato*

Industrial to reach a direct agreement with the Company, the wages provided in this agreement will be considered as in effect since January 1, 1956.

DURATION OF CONTRACT.—The present agreement will remain in effect until January 31, 1957.

It is emphasized that this contract was negotiated directly and that so long as it is in effect the Sindicato Industrial will not be able to present any demands, either economic or social, in conformity with provisions of Decree 939 of November 30, 1944.

The present Minutes of Agreement will be drawn up in SEVEN copies, one remaining in the power of the *Sindicato*, two with the Administrator of the Brewery, and the rest to be given to the Labor Inspector.

Notes

CHAPTER I. INDUSTRIALIZATION AND ITS IMPACT

1. United Nations, *Statistical Review, 1957* (New York, 1958).
2. United Nations, *Monthly Bulletin of Statistics* (January 1958).
3. Clark Kerr, John Dunlop, Frederick Harbison, and Charles Myers, "The Labour Problem in Economic Development," *International Labor Review* (March 1955).
4. There is considerable objection in some quarters to foreign investment, both private and public. But these objections are based on nationalistic considerations and not on Capitalist vs. Socialist controversy.
5. Clark Kerr, Abraham Siegel, "The Structuring of the Labour Force in Industrial Society: New Dimensions and New Questions," *Industrial and Labor Relations Review* (January 1955).
6. Harold Davis (ed.), *Organized Labor in Politics* (New York, 1958), chap. VI.
7. Alfredo Palacios, *El Nuevo Derecho* (Buenos Aires, 1935), p. 83.
8. Alfredo Gaete Berrios, *Derecho del Trabajo* (Santiago, 1943), p. 17.
9. Alfredo Gaete Berrios, *Origines, Fundamento, Desarrollo y Porvenir del Derecho del Trabajo—Sindicalización Campesina* (Santiago, 1944), pp. 6–7.
10. Francisco Walker Linares, *Panorama del Derecho Social Chileno* (Santiago, 1947), pp. 10–12, 25, 30–31; Palacios, *El nuevo Derecho*, pp. 55–61.
11. A North American observer might note somewhat similar developments in the United States as a result of the establishment of machinery for recognition of unions under the Wagner Act.

CHAPTER II. ECONOMIC AND POLITICAL BACKGROUND

1. United Nations, *Demographic Yearbook—1957* (New York, 1957).
2. Reynold Carlson's "The Bases of Brazil's Economy" in T. Lynn Smith and Alexander Marchant (eds.), *Brazil: Portrait of Half a Continent* (New York, 1951), pp. 228–229.
3. United Nations, *Economic Survey of Latin America, 1949* (New York, 1951), pp. 236–237.
4. George Wythe, *Industry in Latin America* (New York, 1946), pp. 137, 139.
5. Carlson, "The Bases," p. 230.
6. State Department, *Report of Joint Brazilian-United States Technical Commission* (Washington, 1949), p. 67.
7. Wythe, *Industry in Latin America*, pp. 41–42, 49–50.

Chapter III. The Dramatis Personae

1. Fernando de Arevedo, *A Culture Brasileira* (São Paulo, 1944), p. 33.
2. *Statesman's Yearbook 1957* (London, 1957).
3. *Boletim Mensual da Federacão das Industrias do Distrito Federal* (January 1956).
4. Article by George Wythe in Simon Kuznets, Wilbert E. Moore, and Joseph J. Spengler (eds.), *Economic Growth: Brazil, India, and Japan* (Durham, 1955), p. 57.

Chapter IV. Labor–Management Relations

1. Robert J. Alexander, "Brazilian 'Tenentismo,'" *Hispanic American Historical Review* (May 1956).
2. "Quadro de Actividades e Profissões a Que se Refere O Artigo 577 da Consolidacão das Leis do Trabalho," Annex to *Consolidacão das Leis do Trabalho* (São Paulo, 1956), 2nd edition.

Chapter V. Government Control over Class Organizations

1. By 1960, the Communists had only one daily newspaper, that of São Paulo. They had been forced to suspend all others for financial or other reasons.
2. *Consolidacão des Leis do Trabalho* (São Paulo, 1956), Decree-Law 7038 of November 10, 1944, p. 409; Portaria No. 11 of February 11, 1954, p. 774ff.

Chapter VI. Government Direction of the Workers' Protest

1. *Consolidacão das Leis do Trabalho* (São Paulo, 1956), Title VII, Chap. II.
2. Seccão do Estatistica, *Poder Judiciario—Justiça do Trabalho—Producão Verificada nos Diversos Orgaõs, Seccão de Estatistica, 1955* (Rio de Janeiro, 1955).
3. Seccão de Estatistica, *Justiça do Trabalho: Tribunais Regionais do Trabalho—Resumo dos Principais Trabalhos Judiciarios do Hno de 1955* (Rio de Janeiro, 1956).
4. Accordo entre a Compania Telephonica Brasileira e o Sindicato dos Trabalhadores em Empreses Telefonicas do Estado de São Paulo, Rio de Janeiro (March 12, 1956).
5. Estatutos do Servico Social de Industria do Papel Papelão e Cortica do Estado de São Paulo (mimeographed copy in author's possession).
6. *Poder Judiciario.*
7. Instituto de Previdencia e Aposentaduria dos Servidores do Estado, *Decreto-Lei 2865 de Dezembro de 1940* (Rio de Janeiro, 1955).
8. State Department, *Report of Joint Brazilian–United States Technical Commission* (Washington, 1949), p. 102.

Chapter VIII. Recruitment and Commitment of the Workers

1. International Labor Organization, *Vocational Training in Latin America* (Geneva, 1951), p. 145.

Chapter IX. Working and Living Conditions of the Workers

1. *Brazilian Bulletin,* New York (February 13, 1950).
2. João Paulo de Almeida Magalhães, *Condicães Economicas de Desenvolvimento* (Rio de Janeiro, 1955).

3. Conselho Nacional de Estatistica, *Anuario Estatistico* (Rio de Janeiro, 1954, 1955, and 1956).
4. *Consolidacão das Leis do Trabalho* (São Paulo, 1956), Articles 372–401.

CHAPTER X. ECONOMIC, POLITICAL, AND SOCIAL BACKGROUND

1. United Nations, *Demographic Yearbook—1957.*
2. A. H. Tandy, *Argentina: Economic and Commercial Conditions in the Argentine Republic* (London, 1956), pp. 9, 11.
3. George Wythe, *Industry in Latin America* (New York, 1946), p. 87.
4. Quoted in *La Vanguardia,* Buenos Aires (August 28, 1958).
5. Domingo F. Sarmiento, *Facundo* (Buenos Aires, 1952), pp. 18, 23.
6. United Nations, "Per Capita National Product of Fifty-Five Countries, 1952–1954," *Statistical Papers, Series E/4* (New York, 1957).
7. Food and Agricultural Organization, *World Fiber Review 1949* (New York, 1949).

CHAPTER XI. LABOR–MANAGEMENT RELATIONS BEFORE PERON

1. The Argentine labor movement is one of those of Latin America which has been best described by historians. A number of unions have published histories of their own organizations, the best of which is Juan B. Chitti's and Francisco Agnelli's *La Fraternidad—Fundacion, Desarrollo y Obra* (Buenos Aires, 1945). Of a more general nature is Martin S. Casaretto's *Historia del Movimiento Obrero Argentino* (Buenos Aires, 1945). A Perónista history, which discusses both the evolution of various central labor organizations and the history of all national unions existing when it was written, is Juan C. Juarez' *Los Trabajadores en Funcion Social* (Buenos Aires, 1947).
2. For a discussion of this, see José Figuerola, *La Colaboración Social en Hispano America* (Buenos Aires, 1943).

CHAPTER XII. GOVERNMENT DIRECTION OF LABOR PROTEST UNDER PERÓN

1. For interesting, though not completely reliable, evidence of the Argentine army's relations with Germany before 1943, see Silvano Santander's *Técnica de Una Traición* (Montevideo, 1953).
2. Adelaida Logrippo, *Las Fuerzas Economicas Argentinas* (Rosario, 1954), pp. 271–274, 285–291.

CHAPTER XIII. RISE AND DECLINE OF COLLECTIVE BARGAINING

1. Robert J. Alexander, *The Perón Era* (New York, 1951), pp. 144–145.
2. Cámara Gremial de Fabricantes de Vidrio, *Convenios Celebrados con los Sindicatos de Obreros y Empleados, a Regir desde el l de Marzo de 1954* (Buenos Aires, 1954).
3. Jeronimo Remornio, *La Nueva Legislación Social Argentina* (Buenos Aires, 1953), p. 224.

CHAPTER XIV. LEGISLATIVE ATTEMPTS TO FORESTALL WORKERS' GRIEVANCES

1. See Russell Fitzgibbon's *Constitutions of Latin America* (Chicago, 1948).
2. Jeronimo Remorino, *La Nueva Legislación Social Argentina* (Buenos Aires, 1953), pp. 52–57, 59, 60–61.

3. *Leyes del Trabajo Actualizadas* (Buenos Aires, 1956).
4. Robert J. Alexander, *The Perón Era* (New York, 1951), pp. 168–169.
5. Remorino, *La Nueva Legislación Social Argentina,* pp. 89–91, 96–97, 106, 119–124, 171–222.

Chapter XV. Effect of "Revolución Libertadora"

1. *Leyes del Trabajo Actualizadas* (Buenos Aires, 1956).
2. *La Vanguardia,* Buenos Aires (September 12, 1957).
3. *La Prensa,* Buenos Aires (May 24, 1956).
4. *La Vanguardia* (June 8, 1958).
5. *New York Times,* New York (May 14, 1958).
6. *Noticiario Obrero Interamericano,* Mexico (June 1958).
7. *La Vanguardia* (June 15, 1958).
8. *Inter-American Labor Bulletin,* Washington (November 1958).
9. *New York Times* (August 9, 1958).

Chapter XVI. Recruitment and Commitment of Workers

1. CTCBA, *Reglamento de Trabajo y Escalafón para el Personal de la Corporación de Transportes de la Ciudad de Buenos Aires (En Liquidación) (Buenos Aires).*
2. Cámara Gremial de Fabricantes de Vidrio, *Convenios Celebrados.*
3. Asociación Argentina de Aeronavegantes, *Convención Colectiva de Trabajo y Escalafon Profesional entre l Ministerio de Transportes de la Nación y la Asociación Argentina de Aeronavegantes para el Personal Navegante* (Buenos Aires, 1954).
4. Cámara Argentina de Industrias Metalúrgicas, *Convenio Colectivo No. 97 Actualizado para Empleados y Obreros de la Industria Metalúrgica* (Buenos Aires, 1954).
5. Alejandro Magnet, *Nuestros Vecinos Justicialistas* (Santiago, 1953), p. 134.
6. Arthur P. Whitaker, *The United States and Argentina* (Cambridge, 1954), p. 205.

Chapter XVII. Economic, Political, and Social Background

1. Humberto Aguirre Doolan, "Perspectivas Económicas," *Panorama Económico,* Santiago (March 1947).
2. P. T. Ellsworth, "Chile," *Economic Problems of Latin America* (New York, 1944), p. 307.
3. José Joaquin Prieto, *La Industria Salitrera—Su Historia, Legislación y Desarrollo para el Futuro* (Santiago, 1945), p. 21.
4. Carlos Sanchez Hurtado, *Evolución Historica de la Industria Sidcrúrgica Chilena e Ibero Americana* (Santiago, 1952), pp. 161–162.
5. Dirección General de Informaciónes y Cultura, *Anuario DIC 1946* (Santiago, 1946), pp. 526–528.
6. Oscar Gajardo Villarroel, *Corporación de Fomento de la Producció—Realizaciones y Propositos* (Santiago, 1946), pp. 11–18.
7. Harold A. Sutphen, "A Banker's Report in Chile," *United Nations World* (May 1950).

Chapter XVIII. Organized Labor

1. Some of the standard sources on the history of Chilean labor relations are Moises Poblete Troncoso's *La Organización Sindical en Chile y Otros Estudios Sociales* (Santiago, 1926), *El Movimento Obrero Latino Americano* (Mexico, 1946), by the

same author; Tulio Lagos' *Bosquejo Historico del Movimiento Obrero en Chile* (Santiago, 1947). There are also extended references in Francisco Walker Linares' *Panorama del Derecho Social Chileno* (Santiago, 1947), and Alfredo Gaete Berrios' *Derecho del Trabajo* (Santiago, 1943).

CHAPTER XIX. GOVERNMENT ROLE IN DIRECTING LABOR PROTEST

1. Alberto A. Ruiz de Gamboa, Juan Diaz Sales, and Carlos G. A. Ruiz de Gamboa, *Legislación Social—Codigo del Trabajo (1946-1956)* (Santiago, 1946-1956). Hereinafter referred to as *Codigo del Trabajo*.
2. Franciso Walker Linares, *Panorama del Derecho Social Chileno* (Santiago, 1947), pp. 11-12.
3. See Ricardo Donoso, *Alessandri: Agitator y Demoledor* (Mexico, 1952).
4. Hector de Petris Giesen, *Historia del Partido Democratico—Posición Dentro de la Evolución Political Nacional* (Santiago, 1942), p. 42.
5. Arturo Alessandri, *El Presidente Alessandri su Gobierno* (Santiago, 1926), p. 19.
6. Walker Linares, *Panorama*, pp. 56-57.
7. *Codigo del Trabajo*, Articles 559, 560, 564, 568-570.
8. Alfredo Gaete Berrios, *Derecho del Trabajo* (Santiago, 1943), pp. 193-197, 428.
9. Luis P. Lungo Escalena, *El Problema de la Vivienda* (Chile, 1946), pp. 72-76, 102-103.
10. Natalio Berman, *S.S.S.—Seguro de Solidaridad Social* (Santiago, 1939).
11. Director General de Estadistica, *Veinte Años de Legislación Social* (Santiago, 1946), p. 224.
12. *Caja Nacional de Empleados Publicos y Periodistas: 15 de Julio de 1925—15 de Julio de 1945* (Santiago, 1945), pp. 11-12.
13. Julio Bustos Acevedo, *Reforma de las Leyes 4054 y 4055* (Santiago, 1946), p. 11.
14. Marcos Flores Alvarez, "El Problema de la Unificación de la Previsión Social," *Previsión Social*, 138 (April-May-June 1946).

CHAPTER XX. WORKERS' AND EMPLOYERS' ORGANIZATIONS

1. Alfredo Gaete Berrios, *Derecho del Trabajo* (Santiago, 1943), p. 395.
2. Francisco Walker Linares, *Panorama del Derecho Social Chileno* (Santiago, 1947), p. 125.
3. *Codigo del Trabajo*, Vol. III, Articles 363.
4. The *sindicato industrial* is really more a company union than an industrial union in the United States sense. However, because of the connotation of subservience to the employer which is attached to "company union" in North American parlance, we have preferred to use "industrial union" as a translation for *sindicato industrial*.
5. Gaete Berrios, *Derecho del Trabajo*, p. 402.
6. *Codigo*, Regulatory Decree 734 of November 14, 1944, Vol. III, Article 8.
7. Gaete Berrios, *Derecho del Trabajo*, pp. 402, 404.
8. The translation "craft union" is frequently used in these pages for *sindicato profesional* because though there are some differences between Chilean concept and that current in the United States, this is about as close as one can get in direct translation and will impart to the North American reader a general picture of the nature of *sindicatos profesionales*.
9. *Codigo*, Article 407.
10. Gaete Berrios, *Derecho del Trabajo*, p. 408.

11. *Codigo,* Regulatory Decree 734, Articles 109–116.
12. Gaete Berrios, *Derecho del Trabajo,* pp. 408–411.
13. *Codigo,* Article 379; Regulatory Decree 734, Article 13.
14. Gaete Berrios, *Derecho del Trabajo,* p. 347.
15. *Codigo,* Regulatory Decree 734, Article 64.
16. Gaete Berrios, *Derecho del Trabajo,* p. 399.
17. *Codigo,* Decree 4161, January 14, 1956, Vol. VII, pp. 484–487.
18. Gaete Berrios, *Derecho del Trabajo,* p. 399.
19. *Codigo,* Article 388.
20. Gaete Berrios, *Derecho del Trabajo,* p. 397.
21. *Codigo,* Regulatory Decree 734, Articles 6, 34, 56–59.
22. Gaete Berrios, *Derecho del Trabajo,* p. 405.
23. *Codigo,* Regulatory Decree 734, Article 74.
24. Gaete Berrios, *Derecho del Trabajo,* p. 406.
25. *Codigo,* Regulatory Decree 734, Articles 68, 70–83, 87.
26. Moises Poblete Troncoso, *El Derecho del Trabajo y La Seguridad en Chile* (Santiago, 1949).
27. Moises Poblete Troncoso, *El Standard de Vida de las Poblaciones de America* (Chile, 1942), p. 138.
28. Gaete Berrios, *Derecho del Trabajo,* pp. 405–408.
29. *Codigo,* Regulatory Decree 734, Articles 97–104.
30. Gaete Berrios, *Derecho del Trabajo,* p. 408.
31. *Codigo,* Regulatory Decree 734, Articles 109–116.
32. Estatuto del los Trabajadores del Cobre de la Gran Mineria (mimeographed copy in the possession of the author.)
33. These figures are gathered from interviews of the author with Chilean trade-union leaders.
34. Juan Antonio Rios, *Una Politica Sindical—Discurso Pronunciado el dia l de Mayo, Fiesta del Trabajo* (Santiago, 1944), p. 10.
35. General Directorate of Labor, *Revista del Trabajo,* Santiago (April 1946).
36. Anonymous, "El Trabajo de Chile," *La Nación* (Santiago, 1945).

CHAPTER XXI. COLLECTIVE BARGAINING AND THE COLLECTIVE AGREEMENT

1. Franciso Walker Linares, *Panorama del Derecho Social Chileno* (Santiago, 1947), p. 69.
2. *Codigo del Trabajo,* Articles 510, 511–512, 513–515, 517, 518–520, 521–522, 525–529; Regulatory Decree 839, Articles 9–10, 18, 23–27, 106.
3. General Directorate of Labor, *Revista del Trabajo, Santiago* (January 1946).
4. *Codigo,* Articles 548–562.
5. *La Opinión, Santiago* (December 29, 1946).
6. *El Mercurio,* Santiago (January 30, 1947).
7. *El Siglo,* Santiago (February 1, 1947).
8. *El Mercurio, Santiago* (April 12, 1947).

CHAPTER XXII. EMPLOYER EFFORT TO LIMIT WORKERS' PROTEST

1. Speech by Alfredo Bowen, Professor of Sociology in Elvira Matte de Cruchaga School of Social Work, before the First Pan American Social Service Congress, Santiago, 1945.
2. *Codigo del Trabajo,* Law 7600 of October 28, 1943, Vol. III, p. 531.

CHAPTER XXIII. RECRUITMENT, COMMITMENT, AND WORKING CONDITIONS

1. Alfredo Gaete Berrios, *Derecho del Trabajo* (Santiago, 1943), pp. 162–163, 164–168.
2. Francisco Walker Linares, *Panorama del Derecho Social Chileno* (Santiago, 1947), pp. 92–93.
3. Instituto de Economía de la Universidad de Chile, *Desarrollo Económico de Chile* (Santiago, 1956), p. 19.
4. *Estadística Chilena, Santiago,* (December 1955).
5. Gaete Berrios, *Derecho del Trabajo*, p. 158.
6. *Codigo del Trabajo,* Articles 24–33; Gaete Berrios, *Derecho del Trabajo,* pp. 156, 246–251.
7. *Codigo,* Articles 91, 93.
8. Gaete Berrios, *Derecho del Trabajo,* pp. 242–243.
9. *Codigo,* Articles 94, 266–268, Dictamen 478 of *Inspección General del Trabajo,* April 27, 1939, Vol. II, p. 296; Law 8198, September 14, 1945, Vol. III, p. 443.
10. Gaete Berrios, *Derecho del Trabajo,* pp. 359–361, 362–363, 368–370.

CHAPTER XXIV. INFLATION, LABOR, AND ECONOMIC DEVELOPMENT
IN ARGENTINA, BRAZIL, AND CHILE

1. This table is made up from figures taken from the United Nations' *Economic Survey of Latin America, 1953* (New York, 1953), pp. 74, 80, 84.
2. João Almeidade Magalhães, *Condicães Económicas do Desenvolvimento* (Rio de Janeiro, 1955), pp. 111–112.
3. P. T. Ellsworth, *Chile: An Economy in Transition* (New York, 1945), pp. 112–114.
4. State Department, *Report of Joint Brazilian–United States Technical Commission* (Washington, 1949), p. 7.
5. Anonymous "Algunos Aspectos de la Aceleración del Proceso Inflacionario en Chile," *Boletin Económico de America Latina,* 45–46 (January 1956).
6. United Nations, *La Cooperación Internacional en la Politica de Desarrollo Latino-Americana* (New York, 1954), pp. 18, 74.
7. United Nations, *Report of the United Nations Economic Mission to Chile 1949–1950* (New York, 1951), p. 31.
8. Henry William Spiegel, "Brazil: The State and Economic Growth," in Simon Kuznets, Wilbert E. Moore, and Joseph J. Spengler (eds.), *Economic Growth: Brazil, India, Japan* (Durham, 1955), p. 416.
9. This table is made up from figures from United Nations' *Economic Survey of Latin America 1953* (New York, 1953), pp. 74, 80, 84.
10. United Nations, *La Cooperación Internacional,* p. 18.

Index

401

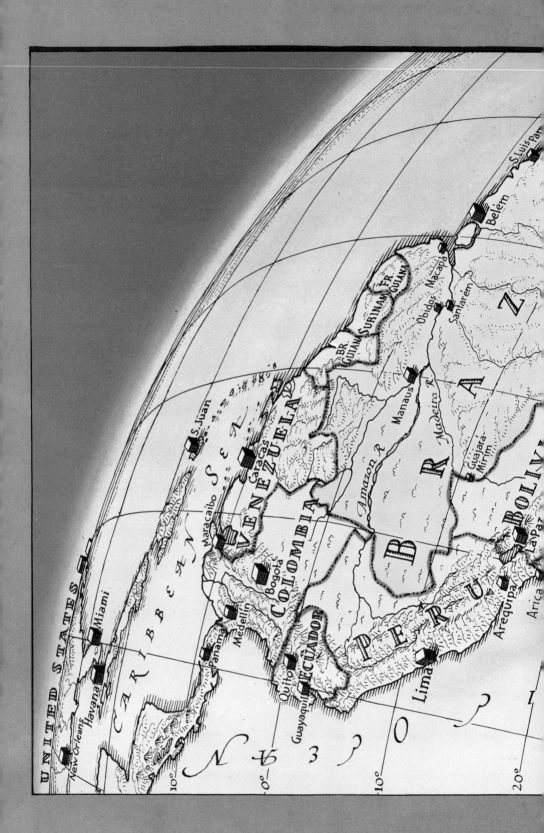